Politik, Wirtschaft und Gesellschaft im Spannungsverhältnis der Regionen Südosteuropa und Mittlerer Osten

Mit dieser Reihe erfolgt ein interdisziplinärer und grundlegender Austausch. Ziel ist es, die im In- und Ausland gewonnenen, und in wissenschaftlichen Beiträgen zusammengefassten Forschungsergebnisse der Wissenschaft und Praxis zur Diskussion zu stellen. Qualitative Diskurse aus den Bereichen der Politik-, Rechts-, Wirtschafts-, sowie Kulturwissenschaften, aber auch der Soziologie, Psychologie, Pädagogik und Geschichte sollen ihren Raum finden. Insbesondere ist das herausarbeiten der Verbindungslinien zwischen den einzelnen wissenschaftlichen Disziplinen erwünscht.

In der Reihe werden Theorie- und auch Praxisbezüge hergestellt, damit die entsprechenden Länder- sowie Wirtschaftsanalysen als auch Kulturuntersuchungen besser vermittelt werden. Bedeutsam ist es daher nicht nur deutschen Wissenschaftler*innen, sondern insbesondere auch Wissenschaftler*innen aus den Regionen Südosteuropa und Mittlerer Osten eine Austausch- und Diskussionsmöglichkeit zu bieten. Die Reihe ist offen sowohl für Monographien, Sammel- und Tagungsbände als auch für herausragende Qualifikationsarbeiten (Dissertationen, Habilitationen).

Der Türkeiforschung kommt inhaltlich dabei eine besondere Bedeutung zu, da der türkische Einfluss auf die Regionen Südosteuropa und Mittlerer Osten als ehemaliges Osmanisches Reich messbar ist. Inwiefern die türkische Außenpolitik sowie Kulturkooperationen erfolgreich oder nicht erfolgreich sind gilt es fortlaufend zu untersuchen, ebenso, der Frage nachzugehen, inwieweit die Türkei als geopolitisch wichtigster Kooperationspartner und Vermittler zwischen den Kulturen einzustufen ist. Grundsätzlich wird im Deutschen zwischen dem Nahen Osten, dem Mittleren Osten und dem Fernen Osten unterschieden. Im Englischen Middle East sowie in zahlreichen nahöstlichen Sprachen wird die Region als Mittlerer Osten bezeichnet, insbesondere auf Arabisch الشرق الأوسط asch-scharq al-awsat, Hebräisch המזרח התיכון haMizrach haTichon, Türkisch Orta Doğu, Kurdisch rojhilata navîn und Persisch خاورمیانه. Die G8-Definition von Middle East bezieht das gesamte Nordafrika (Mittelmeeranrainerstaaten) mit ein.

Die Reihen-Herausgeber legen das kulturgeographische Verständnis der Region zugrunde um insbesondere eine westlich-ethnozentrisch geprägte Sichtweise aufzubrechen. Die Namenszuweisung stammt aus der römischen Antike, die den „Orient" als eine von vier definierten Weltgegenden ausmachte und zwar als „Osten", in dem die Sonne aufgeht (lat.: sol oriens). Demgegenüber stand der „Okzident", der Westen, in dem die Sonne untergeht (lat.: sol occidens). Der Begriff des Nahen Ostens ist ein überaltertes und west-ethnozentrisches Konzept ohne formalen inhaltlichen Bezug. Die Begrifflichkeit stellt keinerlei Relevanz für die kulturelle und ethnische Identität dar, sondern fungiert vielfach (sowohl im alltäglichen als auch wissenschaftlichen Sprachgebrauch) weiterhin als Stereotyp über Menschen und Kulturen. Die Region des Mittleren Ostens umfasst somit in der Reihe den Raum Nordafrika bis zum Südrand der Sahara, von Mauretanien im Westen bis zum Sudan im Osten, und außerdem in Asien das gesamte Gebiet von der Arabischen Halbinsel im Süden und von Kleinasien im Norden über das Iranische Hochland bis einschließlich Pakistan.

Südosteuropa ist ein ebenso kontroverser Begriff und steht in einem ambivalenten Verhältnis zu Europa. Zeitgeschichtlich betrachtet teilt die Region ihre Geschichte mit dem Rest des Kontinents. Gleichzeitig jedoch fungiert Südosteuropa seit Jahrhunderten als Projektionsfläche für das Fremde. Die Reihe beabsichtigt die beiden Räume Südosteuropa und Mittlerer Osten näher zu beleuchten damit diese Fremdheit abgebaut und zukünftig neue Brücken aufgebaut werden können.

Hayk Gabrielyan

Turkey's Water Policy as Part of the Political Strategy

The Evolution of Turkey's Water Policy

Springer VS

Hayk Gabrielyan
Yerevan, Armenia

ISSN 2730-7107 ISSN 2730-7115 (electronic)
Politik, Wirtschaft und Gesellschaft im Spannungsverhältnis der Regionen Südosteuropa und Mittlerer Osten
ISBN 978-3-658-44069-5 ISBN 978-3-658-44070-1 (eBook)
https://doi.org/10.1007/978-3-658-44070-1

This Springer VS imprint is published by the registered company Springer Fachmedien Wiesbaden GmbH, part of Springer Nature.
The registered company address is: Abraham-Lincoln-Str. 46, 65189 Wiesbaden, Germany

Paper in this product is recyclable.

Foreword

"Integrating Water Policy as a Fundamental Element in Turkey's Foreign Relations"

Water, a valuable resource, is facing a growing scarcity exacerbated by factors such as population growth, industrialization, and urbanization, resulting in a substantial global increase in water consumption. While the world's population has tripled, water consumption has multiplied sixfold during the same timeframe. Climate change further adds pressure to water resources, and the demand for water is projected to continue its upward trajectory over the next twenty-five years.

Contrary to popular belief, Turkey does not boast abundant freshwater resources and is not the most water-rich country in its region. Positioned in a semi-arid region, Turkey has only approximately one-fifth of the per capita water availability compared to regions rich in water, such as North America and Western Europe. Countries with over 10,000 cubic meters of water per capita per year are considered water-rich, surpassing Turkey's 1,350 cubic meters per capita. It is anticipated that by 2030, this quantity will further decrease to 1,000 cubic meters per capita per year with an expected population of 100 million.

Turkey's water resources often do not align with current and future needs, with certain regions having ample but unusable freshwater while more populated and industrialized areas experience water scarcity. In the dry and semi-arid regions of Turkey, where precipitation typically occurs for only four or five months per year, projects aimed at developing water resources have become imperative for sustainable socioeconomic development.

In recent decades, Turkey has made significant strides in utilizing water resources for domestic purposes, irrigation, flood protection, and power generation. Constructed dams and reservoirs have allowed Turkey to store water from brief rainy periods and use it for various purposes throughout the year. Turkey has implemented an integrated program for managing natural water resources in watershed areas.

Turkey's energy consumption is on the rise due to rapid urbanization and industrialization. It is noteworthy that per capita energy consumption in Turkey is only one-sixth of the EU average, and an increase in energy consumption correlates with an enhancement in the quality of life for Turkish citizens. As a non-producer of oil or natural gas, Turkey aims to meet the growing energy demand through diverse approaches, including an increased focus on domestic energy sources, particularly hydroelectric power.

Turkey assumes a significant role in Europe, functioning as a regional powerhouse, a key trading partner, a prospective member of the European Union, and a collaborator in migration management. The rise of Recep Tayyip Erdoğan and the shift toward a more Islamic-oriented autocracy signal a noteworthy evolution in Turkey's regional foreign policy, reflecting a heightened assertiveness. Serving as a bridge between the East and the West, Turkey presents a substantial challenge in the arena of foreign policy.

Departing from its previous reactive stance, the country, especially under the AKP and Foreign Minister Ahmet Davutoğlu, actively engages in shaping and influencing external developments. The introduction of the Neo-Ottomanism concept, anchored in historical legacies, illustrates Turkey's efforts to bolster its influence in the region. Despite the perceived Neo-Ottomanism connotation, various studies explore diverse foreign policy instruments such as the Zero-Problems Policy, support for pro-Turkish entities in neighboring countries, and resolute opposition to Turkey's adversaries.

In this context, the dissertation delves into the strategic use of water policy as a pivotal aspect of foreign policy, requiring fresh research to consolidate existing insights and contribute innovative perspectives. The author's study not only addresses a research gap but also introduces novel viewpoints in this domain.

Focusing on the major river systems of Eastern Anatolia—the Euphrates, Tigris, and the Orontes Basin—the study also examines transnational rivers like the Kura, Aras, and Çoruh, originating in the Anatolian Highlands and flowing into neighboring countries. This raises interest in their relevance to water policy within the context of foreign relations. The dissertation poses explicit guiding questions, exploring the initiation and motivations behind water policy in the Euphrates-Tigris Basin, the reactions of neighboring countries, and the impact of this policy on strengthening the Kurdish PKK. These questions serve as the framework for the extensive study.

Additionally, the author asserts two theses: firstly, that Turkey's assertive water policy, reducing water flow to neighboring countries, garnered increased support for the PKK from former Syrian leader Hafez al-Assad; and secondly, the author aims to illustrate Turkey's strategic leverage in utilizing water policy against eastern countries, Syria, Iraq, partially Iran, and the PKK in Kurdistan. Through its water policy and the vulnerability of water-receiving nations like Syria and Iraq, Turkey effectively advanced its foreign policy objectives. The author convincingly argues that water played a central role as a resource in shaping Turkish foreign policy in its favor.

In the ever-evolving landscape of global challenges, few issues are as pressing and complex as the management and geopolitics of water resources. The United Nations World Water Report serves as a crucial annual assessment, offering insights into the state of our world's water, its challenges, and the collaborative efforts required for sustainable solutions. Compiled by UNESCO and its World Water Assessment Programme for UN-Water, this report stands as a testament to the collective commitment of over 30 UN organizations working in tandem with UNESCO.

The 2023 World Water Report paints a stark picture, revealing that two to three billion people face water scarcity for at least one month each year. Over the past four decades, global water consumption has increased by approximately one percent annually, a trend expected to persist until 2050. Factors such as population growth, socio-economic development, and shifting behavior patterns contribute to this rise. Moreover, water quality concerns loom large, with inadequate wastewater treatment posing challenges in many Global South countries, while agricultural practices contribute to groundwater contamination in the Global North. Sovereign states recognize the strategic importance of securing access to groundwater, adding a geopolitical dimension to water resource management.

The historical context of water agreements, exemplified by the 1946 accord between Turkey and Iraq regulating water flow, reveals the intricate interplay of geography, power, and resource management. In the geopolitical theater of Turkey, Syria, and Iraq, Turkey's upper riparian position in the Euphrates-Tigris Basin affords it a dominant role. This dominance is further solidified through initiatives like the Southeastern Anatolia Project (GAP), initiated in the early 1980s.

In this context, the author's study emerges as a beacon of scholarly excellence. Spanning more than 400 pages, the dissertation navigates ten meticulously crafted chapters, each contributing to a nuanced understanding of Turkey's water policy within the broader geopolitical framework. The author's writing reflects a commendable mastery of language, with clarity and readability as its hallmarks. The dissertation's structure seamlessly blends analysis and argumentation, guiding the reader through the gradual development of the problem statement and the establishment of theoretical insights.

An extensive literature review showcases the author's analytical depth, demonstrating his ability to engage with complex issues without sacrificing clarity. The accessible introduction to Turkey's water policy, skillfully integrated into the broader context of the country's foreign policy strategy, is particularly noteworthy. In conclusion, the author makes an indelible mark on the field. Addressing geographical and technical nuances within a political science framework, he illuminates regional political connections, contributing significantly to scholarly research.

The water policy of Turkey is an essential component of the country's political strategy, aiming to efficiently utilize and manage its water resources. This policy not only impacts sectors such as agriculture, energy production, environmental preservation, and regional collaboration but also forms a fundamental pillar for broader governance.

In the agricultural context, Turkish water policy concentrates on optimizing the utilization of rivers and water sources for irrigation purposes. Dams and irrigation systems are implemented to improve agricultural productivity. It is crucial to note, however, that these measures may affect the water supply in transboundary river basins, potentially leading to tensions with neighboring countries. Another noteworthy aspect involves the utilization of water for energy generation, particularly through an increased focus on hydroelectric power plants. This emphasis contributes not only to the diversification of energy sources but also plays a vital role in meeting Turkey's escalating energy demands.

The Turkish water policy also advocates for the safeguarding of water resources against environmental impacts, encompassing pollution and overuse. The rising importance of environmental regulations and sustainable practices is emphasized to ensure the enduring preservation of these indispensable resources. In terms of regional cooperation, Turkey actively participates in various transboundary water issues, particularly those related to rivers flowing through multiple countries. This collaboration not only presents diplomatic challenges but also necessitates international cooperation to guarantee the sustainable utilization of shared water resources.

Overall, the Turkish water policy constitutes a dynamic and intricate subject that encompasses various political, economic, and social dimensions. Its objective is to achieve a balanced and sustainable use of the country's water resources, effectively addressing the challenges that lie ahead.

Wolfgang Gieler

Contents

Introduction

1

1.1 Dissertation Description

Water is the source of life. In many religions it is portrayed as something sacred—a gift from God. Water is required for almost all a society's activities, such as the very visible ones of washing and cooking, but also in less visible areas such as food production. While in certain areas access to clean water is plentiful, in many parts of the world this is not the case. It is therefore no surprise that increasing attention is being given to the importance of the world's water resources and aquatic systems.

Water is essential for human security and one of the engines of sustainable socio-economic development. It is an essential element for the eradication of poverty and hunger. Water is a precious resource which is gradually getting scarcer. Population growth, industrialization, urbanization and rising affluence in the 20th century resulted in a substantial increase in water consumption. While the world's population grew three times, water use increased six times during the same period. The demand on water resources will continue to increase during the next twenty-five years. The problem is further aggravated by the uneven water distribution on earth *(Rep. of Turkey Ministry of Foreign Affairs, Turkey's Policy on Water Issues)*.

Earth is often called the "Blue Planet", because of its abundance of liquid water. Water covers 70% of our planet, and it is easy to think that it will always be plentiful. However, freshwater—the stuff we drink, bathe in, irrigate our farm fields with is incredibly rare. But only 3% of water on the surface is fresh; the remaining 97% resides in the ocean. Of freshwater, 68,7% resides in glaciers, 30,1% underground, and less than 1% (0.9%) is located in lakes (87%), rivers

H. Gabrielyan, *Turkey's Water Policy as Part of the Political Strategy*, Politik, Wirtschaft und Gesellschaft im Spannungsverhältnis der Regionen Südosteuropa und Mittlerer Osten, https://doi.org/10.1007/978-3-658-44070-1_1

(2%), and swamps (11%). Looked at another way, only one percent of the water on the Earth's surface is usable by humans, and 99% of the usable quantity is situated underground (*Bice and Bralower*).

As a result, some 1.1 billion people worldwide lack access to water, and a total of 2.7 billion find water scarce for at least one month of the year. Inadequate sanitation is also a problem for 2.4 billion people, they are exposed to diseases, such as cholera and typhoid fever, and other water-borne illnesses. Two million people, mostly children, die each year from diarrheal diseases alone. Many of the water systems that keep ecosystems thriving and feed a growing human population have become stressed. Rivers, lakes and aquifers are drying up or becoming too polluted to use. Climate change is altering patterns of weather and water around the world, causing shortages and droughts in some areas and floods in others. At the current consumption rate, this situation will only get worse. By 2025, two-thirds of the world's population may face water shortages. And ecosystems around the world will suffer even more. In the last 50 years, the human population has more than doubled. This rapid growth with its accompanying economic development and industrialization has transformed water ecosystems around the world and resulted in a massive loss of biodiversity. Today, 41% of the world's population lives in river basins that are under water stress. Concern about water availability grows as freshwater use continues at unsustainable levels. Furthermore, these new faces also need food, shelter, and clothing, thus resulting in additional pressure on freshwater through the production of commodities and energy *(WWF—World Wildlife Fund, Threats, Water Scarcity).*

Thus, the life of people, animals and plants depends on the availability of water. In the 21st century, water is turning into the most strategic resource, and the struggle for water will intensify in the near future, taking into account that the world population continue to grow, and the water demand follows population growth. Unlike oil there is no alternative to water. In this sense, the water themes are quite interesting to us. As for Turkey, which is Armenia's immediate neighbor, there are also water problems here.

Contrary to the general perception, Turkey is not a country rich in freshwater resources. Water rich countries are those which have 10.000 cubic meters of water per capita yearly. This is well above the 1.500 cubic meters per capita in Turkey. Another point is that Turkey's water is not always in the right place at the right time to meet present and anticipated needs. Certain regions of Turkey such as the Black Sea region have ample but unusable freshwater, while some of the more heavily populated and industrialized regions such as the Marmara and the Aegean regions lack sufficient fresh water (*Rep. of Turkey Ministry of Foreign Affairs, Turkey's Policy on Water Issues*).

Many people, including in Armenia, have a misconception that Turkey is very rich in water resources, but it seems so only in comparison with the water-stressed countries of the Middle East. Actually, as mentioned above, Turkey is not such a country. We are interested in Turkey's hydro policy as the main rivers of the region (Euphrates, Tigris, Kur, Araks and Chorukh) originate from the eastern part of Turkey and flow to neighboring countries: Syria, Iraq, Georgia, Armenia, Azerbaijan, Iran. We have chosen for the dissertation the largest rivers of Western Asia, the Euphrates and Tigris, as well as the Orontes river flowing from Syria to Turkey, because the developments related to the latter are interrelated to the Euphrates. The topic became more interesting to us when we managed to see the Euphrates and Tigris in person in Turkey and make a river cruise on them.

In this work we analyze the interests and actions of not only states but also non-state actors such as Kurds. We find this topic is actually as water crisis is worsening in the world. This will especially be felt in the Middle East, whose population is increasingly growing more and more. It means that in the near future, water wars can arise in the Middle East. Turkey's economy and population are growing too and it will make the situation more complicated. Recent regional developments have revealed new water players and have compounded the situation. In our opinion, this topic will be useful for understanding water crisis in the near future in the Middle East region.

In this work we investigate water issues in Turkey, as well as in Syria and in Iraq. Building on the basic assumption that water has played and will play an important role in the Turkey-Syria-Iraq triangle and in Turkey's Kurdish policy, the overall aim is to identify factors that led to the evolution of Turkey's hydro policy.

The aims of work are to emphasize:

- the internal and external factors that impact/determine Turkey's hydro policy,
- the targets and their modifications of Turkey's hydro policy in the 20th and 21st centuries,
- the impact and the interdependence of Turkey's hydro policy on its domestic and foreign policies,
- hydropolitical interdependence between Turkey and neighboring countries,
- sensitivity and vulnerability of neighboring countries and the Kurds on Turkey's hydro policy,
- challenges and opportunities of Turkey's hydro policy

The focus of the analysis is on Turkey's water conflicts with neighboring south-eastern countries and their influence on Turkey's domestic political sphere and especially the Kurdish question. In the dissertation, emphasis is placed on the factors of interdependence of Turkey's water projects and the Kurdish question. The time constraints of this dissertation refer to the second half of the 20th century and the beginning of the 21st century. It gives an opportunity to compare the historical significant events of those centuries with each other. The space constraints of this dissertation relate to the territories of Turkey, Syria, Iraq, Iran and especially their Kurdish regions. I limit my research to those areas. Our work's time frames are divided into four parts, which are designed to show the evolution of Turkey's water policy:

- The Ottoman era (until 1923), where we talk about the importance of water in the Ottoman Empire.
- 1923–1975, when Turkey began to emphasize the importance of water resources management and to take its first steps in water sphere, constructing first dam on Euphrates.
- 1975–2000, when Turkey started to realize the Southeastern Anatolia Project, building many dams in the Euphrates-Tigris basin.
- 21st Century, when Turkey started build new dams not only in the Euphrates but also in the Tigris basin, which created new problems with neighboring countries as well as with the Kurds.

Our work consists of theoretical and empiric parts. Empiric part includes six chapters.

- **The first chapter** is about the rise of hydropolicy and about hydropolitical interdependence. I describe hydro policy as a part of foreign policy, as well as present details of international water law and Turkey's transboundary water policy direction. First of all, we felt it necessary to show what hydropolitics and transboundary water management are, to emphasize the importance of technical interaction, to show the types of hydro-hegemons, the importance of role of river basin organizations in the cooperation of river basin countries, the nature and chronology of transboundary water conflicts, comparison of various water conventions, their strengths and weaknesses. At the end of this chapter, Turkey's official version of its own country's transboundary water policy and our approach to Turkey's hydro policy are presented.
- **The second chapter** shows the importance of water in the Ottoman Empire, describes the first steps taken in the water sector of the modern Republic of Turkey. It presents the historical-geographic (physical) characteristics of the Tigris–Euphrates basin, as well as Orontes basin, important information

about these rivers, which helps to correctly understand the sources of water disagreements and conflicts between Turkey, Syria Iraq and Iran. At the end of this chapter, we describe the construction of the first large reservoir (Keban Dam) by Turkey in the Euphrates basin, emphasizing that after that Turkey begins to have water problems with the downstream countries (Syria and Iraq).

- **The third chapter** refers to the general information of Southeastern Anatolia Project (GAP)—the hydro projects of the Tigris–Euphrates basin, as well as Orontes basin in Turkey, Syria and Iraq. The case of the Orontes River is quite interesting and important, because here Turkey is not an upstream country (is a downstream country), as in the case of the Euphrates and Tigris. The major reservoirs that the three riparian countries built in the basins of these rivers are described. At the end of the third chapter, we talk about the Peace Water Pipeline project, through which Turkey could be able to supply water to the countries of the Arabian Peninsula.
- **The fourth chapter** is about water conflicts and cooperation between Turkey, Syria and Iraq in the 20th century. Water conflicts refer to the Euphrates and Orontes basins: the Tigris basin is missing because in the 20th century Turkey did not implement large water projects in the Tigris basin. Besides, the Tigris does not enter Syria. Water conflicts between the three riparian countries pertained to both water quantity and water quality. The quantity of water seems to be paramount, but if the upstream country degrades the water quality of the river and makes it unusable, it will not matter how much water it releases to the downstream country.
- **The fifth chapter** is about water projects' impact on the Kurds of Turkey (PKK). At the beginning of this chapter, the violation of the rights of Kurds in Turkey and the birth of the PKK, then the Kurdish migration and the impact of the GAP project on it are presented. Then we describe beginning and characteristics of the armed struggle of the PKK in Turkey, the connection of Turkey's water policy with it, as well as the crucial role of Hafez Assad in the processes of the PKK's survival and further strengthening. It is emphasized that without the active support of Hafez Assad, the PKK would have never been able to achieve such results as are known. At the end of chapter 5, a financial comparison is made between the financial benefits of Turkey's major water projects in the Euphrates basin and the financial losses incurred in Turkey's armed struggle against the PKK. It is taken into account that the construction of major reservoirs on the Euphrates by Turkey played an important role for Hafez Assad to support the PKK and to cause serious damage to Turkey through it, make it more lenient towards him.

- **The sixth chapter** refers to GAP implementation in the 21st century. This chapter presents the attitude of the AKP (JDP) to the implementation of the GAP, that in the 21st century Turkey is already emphasizing the construction of major reservoirs in the Tigris basin (as it did the same in the Euphrates basin in the 20th century). Then the attempts of cooperation and rapprochement between Turkey, Syria and Iraq in the water sector in the 2000s are presented. We emphasize that with the strengthening of Turkey in the 21st century and the weakening of Iraq and Syria at the same time, Turkey gets greater opportunities to use water as leverage against these countries to extract various concessions from them. At the end of the sixth chapter, it is shown how Turkey uses water as a weapon against its Kurds, as well as against the Kurds of Iraq and Syria.

1.2 Research Question and Sub Questions

Coming to the research question and sub questions of the topic, we are interested in how does Turkey's hydro policy impact/determine it's foreign (neighboring countries) and domestic (Kurds) policies and vice versa? And simultaneously the sub questions are the followings:

- When and why Turkey started implementing major water projects in the Euphrates-Tigris basin?
- How Turkey's hydro policy in the Euphrates-Tigris basin harms neighbors and what is the reaction of neighboring countries (Syria, Iraq, as well as Iran)?
- How has Turkey's hydro policy promoted the formation and strengthening of the PKK?
- How much Turkey can be called a unique country in the world in terms of hydropolicy?

1.3 Literature Review and the Contribution of My to This Literature

The list of literature consists of books, articles, reports of international organizations and Turkish state structures, Internet sources. English, Turkish, Russian, Armenian, Persian sources were used, which made it possible to look at Turkey's water policy from the perspective of different countries and international organizations.

Most of the scientists describe the water problems between Turkey, Syria and Iraq, trying to act as an arbiter between them, to justify one side or the other, to remain neutral, etc. However, the problem is complicated by the fact that Turkey, Syria and Iraq spread conflicting information, often do not provide data on the flow of rivers, etc., which makes it difficult to interpret many problems from the side. Perhaps everything in this field has been researched, and that's why it didn't seem attractive to us. Our main point is presented in the last two chapters (about it in the next point). We have not come across that other scholars have raised such questions.

In my dissertation, I highlight two important/new ideas:

1) Describing with 7 points that without the support of Syrian President Hafez Assad, the PKK would not have been able to survive, let alone grow stronger, we emphasize that financially, Turkey has actually suffered significantly from implementing large water projects in the Euphrates basin, if we consider instead, he received an armed struggle of the PKK in return, in which his expenses are incomparably more. We have not come across such a financial comparison among other authors. We argue that Hafez Assad thus managed to cause much greater damage to Turkey through the PKK (which is not limited to the financial sector), in exchange for the reduction of the flow of the Euphrates.
2) We try to show that in the 21st century, Turkey is a unique water country, as it is able to use water as a lever on the one hand against the neighboring countries of Syria, Iraq and, to some extent, Iran, and on the other hand, against the Kurds of Turkey, as well as the Kurds of Syria and Iraq. In other words, Turkey's water policy has 6 targets at once in the Euphrates-Tigris basin alone. By playing the water card, Turkey is able to extract various concessions from the neighboring countries, as well as to cause some damage to the Kurds. Based on all this, we believe that Turkey is a unique country in terms of water policy, that no other country in the world is able to use water in such a multi-purpose way on (inside the country) and external (abroad) 'fronts'. In fact, Turkey has achieved all that due to its historical and geographical features.

1.4 Methodology

Various research methods were used in the dissertation. The first is the quantitative method, according to which a large number of data, facts and tables were presented. In the framework of the dissertation, although we did not personally conduct interviews with local residents, focus groups and so on, it can be said that our work indirectly also includes typical elements of qualitative research, taking into account that the used internet sources included such interviews. And finally, the descriptive, analytical and predictive research methods were used to answer the "what", "why" and "what's next" questions related to various issues.

1.5 Research Findings

In this context, we have two central findings, one of which relates to the 20th century, and the second to the 21st century.

1) Asserting that without the great support of Hafez Assad, the PKK would not have been able to achieve serious success in its activities in Turkey, we emphasize that in reality, Hafez Assad has managed to cause hundreds of billions and even trillions of dollars in damage to Turkey, which is tens of times higher than the financial benefits received by Turkey from building large dams on the Euphrates.

We naturally do not argue that the large reservoirs built by Turkey in the Euphrates basin were the only reason for the creation of the PKK and Hafez Assad's support for that organization. But we also argue that Turkey's water projects were the main reason why Assad gave shelter to the PKK leaders, saved it from being crushed after the Turkish military coup in 1980, and then began to strengthen it by various means and target Turkey.

Moreover, Hafez Assad managed to harm Turkey through the PKK not only in military and financial terms. On November 8, 2012, Turkish Foreign Minister Ahmet Davutoglu stated in Brussels that the Balkans were undergoing changes in the 1990s, while Turkey prioritized its security due to the terrorist threat (PKK), which delayed reforms in Turkey and resulted in Turkey missing the EU train.

2) We argue that Turkey's hydro policy has experienced a certain evolution over time, and in the 21st century, Turkey's potential to use water leverage against neighboring countries and the Kurds has become more prominent. In our opinion, this potential was smaller in the last quarter of the 20th century compared to the first quarter of the 21st century. This is explained by the fact that in the previous century, Turkey with its potential was not much superior to Hafez Assad's Syria and Saddam Hussein's Iraq (even in terms of the number of tanks/army power, the latters perhaps had an advantage over Turkey).

Meanwhile, in the 21st century, especially in its second and third decades, the situation is completely different. Turkey has become quite powerful, turned into a regional superpower with global ambitions. At the same time, Iraq and Syria experienced a major setback, losing their positions in the region. This gives Turkey the opportunity to use the water lever quite effectively both against Syria and Iraq and against the Kurds of Syria and Iraq.

In the 21st century, the implementation of major water projects in the Tigris basin further strengthened the potential of Turkey to use water as leverage, and Syria and Iraq are essentially simply condemned to ask Turkey for water, making various concessions in return. These concessions may refer to Syria's recognition of Turkey's territorial integrity, Iraq's permission to make a military invasion of Turkey on its territory, which the Turkish president needs before the elections to raise his rating, earn additional votes among nationalists and win the elections (the implementation of water projects can also serve to try to raise the profile of the authorities among the Kurdish electorate).

In addition, during the Syrian conflict, Turkey widely used the Euphrates in its various military operations against the Syrian Kurds (with its hydro projects in the Euphrates basin, Turkey also creates problems between Syria and Iraq). By building major reservoirs in the Tigris river basin, Turkey simultaneously creates problems in the relations between Iraq and Syria, Iraq and Iran, between the Iraqi central authorities and the Kurdish autonomy of Northern Iraq.

In the 21st century, Turkey began to build "security dams" on the border with Iraq (on its own territory) in order to submerge the exit and entry routes of PKK militants (Turkey also uses reservoirs to flood many unwanted historical and cultural monuments and areas). In our opinion, the construction of long canals by Turkey in the Kurdish region can serve the same purpose (block the movement of PKK militants). Turkey is also using a new 'water tactic' against the Kurds on its territory, building reservoirs in an attempt to turn the war-torn Tunjeli (Dersim) province into an island, thus also preventing Kurdish militants from entering. In fact, Turkey has started to widely use its "water weapon" against the PKK.

All of this reminds us of Turkey's "2.5 water war" strategy against Syria and Iraq, as well as the PKK (in the 1990s, the former Turkish ambassador to the US, Sükrü Elekdag, put forward the 2.5 war strategy, according to which Turkey should be ready simultaneously waging 2.5 wars: for instance, against Greece in the northwest, and against Syria in the southeast, as well as against the PKK inside the country). Based on all this, we dare to assert that Turkey is an extremely unique country in the water sector in the world, which is able to simultaneously use water leverage in so many purposes and does this in various ways: against the authorities of neighboring countries, against the Kurdish territories of those neighboring countries, and against the residents of its own Kurdish regions.

It can be said that my findings met my expectations. From the beginning, we noted that Turkey's hydro policy towards neighboring countries and Kurds had a certain evolution in the 21st century. As a result, Turkey was able to use the versatile water lever against the neighboring countries, as well as the Kurds of those countries and its own Kurds. In this context Turkey can be considered unique country in the whole world.

We have seen that hydro policy is interconnected with both foreign and domestic political aspects of Turkey. In the field of foreign policy, hydro policy has brought both benefits and harm. Among the benefits, we can mention the fact that Turkey thus gained serious leverage over neighboring countries, and always used when necessary. As for the damages, it is primarily about the fact that Turkey got a powerful PKK as a result. Once again, we emphasize that Syria did not establish the PKK, but first saved it from crushing, then strengthened it and started using it as a lever against Turkey.

In this sense, we can argue that Turkey's water policy predetermined the foreign policy, led to the fact that Turkey first of all had problems with the neighboring, downstream countries. And the more these problems grew, the more heated the military conflicts against the PKK inside Turkey were. In our opinion, Turkey's problems with neighboring countries will become more and more serious in the future, because if in the 20th century, Turkey first of all wanted to get cheap electricity, then in the 21st century, a great place is reserved for food security, that's why Turkey began to build irrigation canals.

Domestically, Turkey's hydro policy was successful for emptying the Kurdish region, demographic engineering, depriving PKK militants of seeking local supporters, flooding its roads, etc. However, on the other hand, the Kurds believe that the major hydroelectric dams built in their regions will one day remain theirs (in case of gaining independence).

1.6 Conclusions

This research shows how multifaceted the use of water can be, and what kind of issues can be solved by using the water factor in domestic and foreign political spheres. The research also shows that the reservoir may have not only 4 functions as stated on the DSI website, but many more and in particular political, military, security functions. I believe that my findings will contribute to the fact that more attention will be paid to the use of the water factor against ethnic-religious minorities by the authorities in different countries and more studies will be done on the given topic (the domestic political aspect of the water factor).

Theoretical Framework 2

2.1 What is Realism?

According to Joshua Goldstein (professor of international relations), there is no single theory that can explain the wide range of international interactions, both conflictual and cooperative. He further posits that there is a theoretical framework that has traditionally held a central position in the study of international relations. Goldstein called this approach 'Realism'. Realism is a school of thought that explains international relations in terms of power. The exercise of power by states toward each other is sometimes called 'realpolitik' or 'power politics'. From the realists' perspective, the international system is anarchical. It is anarchical because relations among states take place in the absence of a world government. Thus, international relations are best understood by focusing on the distribution of power among states.

Goldstein has averred that realism developed in reaction to a liberal tradition that realists called 'idealism'. Idealism emphasizes international law, morality, and international organization, rather than power alone as the key influences on international events. Idealists think that human nature is good and see the international system as one based on a community of states that have the potential to work together to overcome mutual problems.

Power is central to the realist's explanation of international relations and the uneven distribution of power means that the arena of international relations is a form of 'power politics'. Realists believe that struggles between states to secure their frequently conflicting national interests are the main action on the world stage. Since realists also believe that power determines which country prevails, they hold that politics is aimed at increasing power, keeping power, or

H. Gabrielyan, *Turkey's Water Policy as Part of the Political Strategy*, Politik, Wirtschaft und Gesellschaft im Spannungsverhältnis der Regionen Südosteuropa und Mittlerer Osten, https://doi.org/10.1007/978-3-658-44070-1_2

demonstrating power. However, since power is not easily quantifiable and there is no consensus among states about how it should be distributed, it thus turns international relations into a realm of necessity and continuity over time.

Realists generally took state's pursuits of power as their point of departure. The pursuit of power brings to the fore the centrality of military strength within that power and the conflict which this will engender in a world of multiple sovereignty. While not denying entirely a role for morality, law and diplomacy, realist laid greatest stress on armed might as an instrument of maintaining peace. They placed high premium on the use of the balance of power as a central mechanism for regulating conflict. Through this mechanism, the undue strength of one state would be compensated for by increased strength or expanded alliances on the part of others.

The rational use of power is a core assumption of realism. It states that a state should neither waste power on peripheral goals nor pursue goals that it did not have the power to achieve. This frequently makes realists reluctant warriors. That is to say that actual, and not the potential power of the state should be tailored in such a fashion as to allow the state achieve its goals or aspirations in the international system at the shortest possible time and at the minimum of cost. This was what Richelieu referred to as "raison d'etre" in politics. Failure to carry-out-this balancing act will generally result in a state's inability to achieve its stated objective in the international system *(Falode 2009: 35–47).*

In contrast to liberals, realists are pessimists when it comes to international politics. Realists agree that creating a peaceful world would be desirable, but they see no easy way to escape the harsh world of security competition and war. Creating a peaceful world is surely an attractive idea, but it is not a practical one. "Realism," as Carr notes, "tends to emphasize the irresistible strength of existing forces and the inevitable character of existing tendencies, and to insist that the highest wisdom lies in accepting, and adapting oneself to these forces and these tendencies."

This gloomy view of international relations is based on three core beliefs. First, realists, like liberals, treat states as the principal actors in world politics. Realists focus mainly on great powers, however, because these states dominate and shape international politics and they also cause the deadliest wars. Second, realists believe that the behavior of great powers is influenced mainly by their external environment, not by their internal characteristics. The structure of the international system, which all states must deal with, largely shapes their foreign policies. Realists tend not to draw sharp distinctions between "good" and "bad" states, because all great powers act according to the same logic regardless of their culture, political system, or who runs the government. It is therefore difficult to discriminate among states, save for differences in relative power. In essence, great powers are like billiard balls that vary only in size.

Third, realists hold that calculations about power dominate states' thinking, and that states compete for power among themselves. That competition sometimes necessitates going to war, which is considered an acceptable instrument of statecraft. To quote Carl von Clausewitz, the nineteenth-century military strategist, war is a continuation of politics by other means. Finally, a zero-sum quality characterizes that competition, sometimes making it intense and unforgiving. States may cooperate with each other on occasion, but at root they have conflicting interests *(Mershaimer 2001: 43–44).*

Although much of the literature in international politics concentrates on states as the fundamental units in the international system, in recent years some writers have argued that other entities have acquired sufficient power to be regarded as important actors. These include multinational corporations, intergovernmental organizations, and international nongovernmental organizations. Once an international system structured by states is in place, it makes sense to examine the power and roles of these other entities, all of which operate within a context of constraints established and operated by states (Lentner 2000). Furthermore, the power of most of these non-state entities is linked closely with states. For example, multinational firms are headquartered and do most of their trade within a home state, and they operate by grants of access and within legal systems of host states. International organizations are the creations and instruments of states. Many nongovernmental organizations operate not only by grants of operational authority of states but often are subsidized by and act as arms of states *(Haugaard & Lentner 2006: 100).*

Realism is the foundational school of thought about international politics around which all others are oriented. It follows that any foreign policy analyst who wishes to make use of International Relations theory must understand realism. To apply realism to foreign policy analysis, one has to bridge the gap that divides highly general, 'top down' theory from the 'inside-out' analysis of specific cases. Realism itself embodies this tension, reflecting the desire to be both realistic (that is, grounded in actual foreign policy practice) and theoretical (that is, aspiring to general, timeless knowledge). Realists seek to distill the accumulated wisdom of generations of foreign policy practitioners into general theories of international relations. Realism's basic conceptual foundations derived from the close observation of lived politics. But in seeking to construct and apply a reality-based theory, realists constantly face the challenge of cycling between the nuanced subtleties of real foreign policy situations and the razor-sharp assumptions and deductions of theory.

Realism is a school of thought based on three core assumptions about how the world works:

- Groupism. Humans face one another mainly as members of groups. To survive at anything above a subsistence level, people need the cohesion provided by group solidarity, yet that very same in group cohesion generates the potential for conflict with other groups. Today the most important human groups are nation-states and the most important source of in-group cohesion is nationalism. For convenience, I shall use the term 'states' henceforth. But it is important to stress that realism makes no assumption about the nature of the polity. It may apply to any social setting where groups interact.
- Egoism. Self-interest ultimately drives political behaviour. Although certain conditions can facilitate altruistic behaviour, egoism is rooted in human nature. When push comes to shove and ultimate trade-offs between collective and self-interest must be confronted, egoism tends to trump altruism. As the classic realist adage has it, 'Inhumanity is just humanity under pressure.'
- Power-centrism. Power is the fundamental feature of politics. Once past the hunter-gatherer stage, human affairs are always marked by great inequalities of power in both senses of that term: social influence or control (some groups and individuals always have an outsized influence on politics) and resources (some groups and individuals are always disproportionately endowed with the material wherewithal to get what they want). Key to politics in any area is the interaction between social and material power, an interaction that unfolds in the shadow of the potential use of material power to coerce. As Kenneth Waltz (1979: 186) put it, 'The web of social and political life is spun out of inclinations and incentives, deterrent threats and punishments. Eliminate the latter two, and the ordering of society depends entirely on the former—a utopian thought impractical this side of Eden.'

If one believes the world generally works by these rules, then many important consequences follow for how one thinks about international politics: that the main groups with which people identify be they tribes, city-states, empires, or nation-states—will exert a major influence on human affairs; that the group's collective interest, however defined, will be central to its politics; that necessity as the group interest defines it will trump any putatively universal morality and ethics; and thus that humankind is unlikely ever to wholly transcend power politics through the progressive power of reason.

This way of thinking about international relations leads immediately to an identifiably realist approach to foreign policy: an orientation toward the most powerful (that is, most resource rich and influential) groups at any given time (today this means major powers like the United States or China); a scepticism toward professed aims of foreign policy other than the state interest; a tendency to question the ability of any state's foreign policy to transcend power politics; and a penchant for looking beyond rhetoric to the power realities that realists expect nearly always underlie policy. These precepts represent a simple realist checklist for foreign policy analysis: look for where the power is, what the group interests are, and to the role power relationships play in reconciling clashing interests.

Certain types of thinkers tend to share similar bets about how the world works. Critics like to say that the kind of person most likely to accept the core realist assumptions is a congenital pessimist and cynic. Realists counter that these assumptions are simply realistic—based on the dispassionate observation of human affairs the way they are, as opposed to the way we might wish them to be. There is a degree of truth to both views, and they add up to produce a unity of realist thought stretching from Thucydides to Machiavelli, Weber, Carr, Morgenthau, and Waltz. Even though the thinkers indelibly associated with realism are a highly diverse lot, and even though their ideas often contradict each other, the threads of those three core assumptions tie them all together into a coherent intellectual school. Reading any of the writings of any of these thinkers concerning the foreign policies of their day, one immediately discerns the unmistakably realist approach to foreign policy.

To be sure, realism is more than academic theory. It is also a tradition of statecraft that tends to reflect these same basic assumptions. But the focus here is on the use of scholarly theory to inform the analysis of foreign policy. For that purpose, it is important to be clear about how scholars transform the basic assumptions about the world into theories. And that demands clarity about what we mean by the word 'theory'. Confusingly, scholars use 'theory' to refer to three distinct things: realism itself (a large and complex school of thought); sub-schools within realism such as neorealism (smaller but still complex schools of thought fitting within the realist tradition); and specific realist theories like the balance of power, the security dilemma, or the offense-defense balance (all propositions about patterns of relations among states or pressures facing a particular state) *(Smith, Hadfield, and Dunne 2016: 32–33).*

2.2 The Development of Political Realism

There have been many thinkers over the centuries who have emphasized international anarchy, reliance on self-help, the utility of military force, and the importance of balance-of-power calculations. Thucydides, Machiavelli, and Thomas Hobbes are frequently cited as intellectual ancestors of realism. Likewise, various thinkers have emphasized international economic interdependence, international law and institutions, international communication, and societal norms. The mercantilists, who dominated international thought in the seventeenth and eighteenth centuries, viewed both wealth and power zero-sum terms. That is, one country's gain was another's loss. In their emphasis on preparation for war and relative gains, the mercantilists can be viewed as foreshadowing some of the concerns of later realists *(Baldwin 1993: 11).*

Realism has strong historical antecedents. It was first noticed over 2000 years ago in the writings of ancient Chinese strategists such as Sun Tzu. Sun Tzu advised the rulers of states how to survive in an era when war had become a systemic instrument of power for the first time. He showed rulers how to use power to advance their interests and ensure their survival.

At roughly the same time, in Greece, Thucydides wrote an account of the Peloponnesian War (431—415 B.C.) focusing on relative power among the Greek City states. He wrote that "the strong do what they have the power to do and the weak accept what they have to accepts". Much later in Renaissance Italy in about 1500, Niccolo Machiavelli admonished Italian princes to concentrate on expedient actions to stay in power and to pay attention to war above all else.

Many realists would trace their intellectual heritage to such political philosophers as Thomas Hobbes (1588—1679). He believed that humans have an urge to dominate, an animus dominandi, a natural, animal-like instinct to gain power as an end in itself. He also discussed the free-for-all that exists when government is absent and people seek their own self-interest. He called it 'the state of war' in contrast to the rule of law. Hobbes favored a strong monarchy to prevent this condition. In the nineteenth century, the German military strategist Karl Von Clausewitz said that war is a continuation of politics by other means. Realists see in these historical figures evidence that the importance of power politics is timeless and cross-cultural *(Falode 2009: 35–47).*

In the twentieth century Woodrow Wilson joined the idea that free trade promotes peace with the idea of a universal international organization to promote the same goal. According to Felix Gilbert, "intellectually, a straight line leads from the enlightenment to Wilson's 1 concept. His ideas about a 'new diplomacy' were definitely depen-dent on and influenced by the ideas which the eighteenth century, had developed on this subject" (Gilbert 1951:37).

During the period between the two world wars, international relations began to emerge as an academic field, especially in the United States. William T. R. Fox describes this period as characterized by the assumption of an underlying harmony of international interests coupled with a belief that improved understanding and international institutions could rid the world of the scourge of war (Fox 1949). He points to the "failing of events in the 1930s to accord with the expectations generated by the academic study of international relations in the 1920s" (Fox 1949:67). The invasion of Manchuria, the signing of the Molotov-Ribbentrop agreement, and the fail of League of Nations sanctions against Italy disillusioned international relations scholars and planted the seeds from which modern realism grew.

After World War II realism emerged as the dominant paradigm among international relations scholars. Although a debate between realism and idealism occurred in the 1945—55 period, among politic scientists "authentic self-proclaimed idealists were hard to find" (Fox 1989:239; see also Wolfers 1949; Herz 1950; Morgenthau 1952; Wright 1952; Cook and Moos 1953; and Schilling 1956) *(Baldwin 1993: 12).*

Realism became the dominant, if not sole, approach to the study of international relations after the Second World War. Scholars like Hans Morgenthau, Kenneth Waltz, E. H. Carr, Henry Kissinger etc. argued that international politics is governed by objective, universal laws based on national interest defined as power. While not denying entirely a role for morality, law and diplomacy, they laid greatest stress on armed might as an instrument of maintaining peace.

In a parallel development, a group of realists on the European side of the Atlantic developed what came to be known as the 'English School'. Scholars like Charles Manning, Martin Wight, Hedley Bull and Fred Northedge emphasized the degree to which the international system was 'anarchical', that is, without a central ruler. They saw it as a society, which is to say as a group of states that interacted according to certain conventions. These included diplomacy, international law, war etc.

In spite of the fact that since the end of the Second World War, realism has become the dominant approach to the academic study of international relations, its dominance began to be challenged in the 1960s. From the early 1960s onwards, behaviouralism constituted an alternative to orthodox international relations at both the methodological and conceptual levels. This new scientific school of international relations sought to get away from the traditionalists use of history and orthodox political terms such as 'state' to a new study of what could be observed i.e. 'behaviour' meaning international processes and interactions. Prominent scholars in this field include Karl Deutsch, James Rosenau and Morton Kaplan.

The challenges to realism of behaviouralism in the 1960s eroded the former's monopoly on the subject and produced a more diverse and competitive discipline. This in turn encouraged a variety of other approaches to emerge in the 1970s. One of these new approaches was 'neo-realism'; which was meant to reaffirm the dominant role of realism in international relations. It sought to re-establish the primacy of states, and politico-military concerns.

The central tenets of neo-realism were most clearly laid out in two major works of the late 1970s—Hedley Bull's 'The Anarchical Society' and Kenneth Waltz's 'Theory of International Relations'. They stressed the primacy of states in the international system, and the subordinate power and role of 'non-state' actors. Waltz further emphasized the importance of analyzing the structure of inter-state relations.

Since the 1980s a number of new schools of thought within the realist school have flowered, giving birth to many new branches and sub-branches of realist thought. Against this backdrop of this debate within the realist school, comparison and analysis of its different branches have moved to the fore front of research in international relations.

Realism further splintered in the 1990s to accommodate other theories with bewildering nomenclatures. Among these is 'Defensive Realism'. Others are 'Offensive Realism' which is the particular favourite of Mearsheimer, and of recent, there is Stephen Brooks', 'Post Classical Realism' and 'Neo-Classical Realism' of Gideon Rose. All these are branches of the same tree with their unique interpretation and re-interpretation of realism.

Jack Synder in his Myths of Empire differentiated between aggressive and defensive realism. This became the dividing line between the two distinct branches of thought that eventually emerged: Offensive and Defensive Realism. At the center of the distinction between offensive and defensive realism are different assumptions with respect to whether states maximize security or power, that is to say, whether power is a means or an end.

Some scholars contend that the primary goals that states seek to achieve are survival or security. For these scholars, power is a tool for achieving a goal, and not a goal in itself. Those holding this view can be classified as defensive realists. Such include Kenneth Waltz, Randall Schweller, Robert Jervis and Glaser Charles.

Those scholars that fall within the camp of offensive realism assume that states seek power as both a means and an end. They argued that states maximize their power and tend toward aggressive policies. John Mearsheimer is a quintessential example. He asserts that states seek opportunities to weaken potential adversaries as a means of enhancing security and hence to regard security as being scarce within the system.

As Glen Snyder points out, there are now, in the field of contemporary international relations two types of structural realisms, three types of offensive realism and numerous brands of defensive realism. Michael Doyle has also identified four types of realism (i) Thucydides' Complex Realism, (ii) Machiavelli's Fundamentalist Realism, (iii) Hobbes' Structural Realism and (iv) Rousseau's Constitutional Realism. John Mearsheimer has also attempt to distinguish between three different branches of realism: Human Nature Realism, Offensive Realism and Defensive Realism. If one then tries to extrapolate for example, Morgenthau's strand of realism will be classical (human nature) realism, Kenneth Waltz's defensive (structural) realism; Stephen Brooks, neo-realism and post—classical realism, and Gideon Rose's neo-classical realism. These different arrays of realism undoubtedly create confusion and unnecessary obfuscation of realism's core *(Falode 2009: 35–47)*.

Debate involves a disagreement over the sources and motivations that drive the quest for power in international relations. Mearsheimer (2002: 19–22) classifies realist thought into three categories representing different understandings of motivations for seeking power: human nature, defensive, and offensive. Morgenthau (1973), for example, argues that human beings by nature seek to dominate others and that states, as human institutions, endlessly quest for power. In contrast, Waltz (1979) argues that states may at a minimum wish to survive but their ambitions may go so far as to seek preponderance. At the same time, he thinks that major powers largely aim to maintain their positions in the international system. Thus, there can be satisfied or status quo powers. Mearsheimer labels these writers respectively as human nature and defensive realists. His position is one of offensive realism in which he argues that the structure induces states to gain power in order to survive and the striving remains endless and states are never satisfied *(Mearsheimer 2001: 42–46)*.

Offensive realism assumes that the international system strongly shapes the behavior of states. Waltz, for example, challenges Morgenthau's claim that multipolar systems are more stable than bipolar systems. Multipolar systems are more war-prone than are bipolar systems and these multipolar systems that contain especially powerful states—potential hegemons—are the most dangerous systems of all. From there, it is easy to determine whether the system is hegemonic (directed by a single great power), bipolar (controlled by two great powers), or multipolar (dominated by three or more great powers).

The prospects for buck-passing are largely a function of the particular architecture of the system. What matters most is the distribution of power among the major states, and geography. Power is usually distributed among great powers in three ways. Bipolar systems are dominated by two great powers of roughly equal military might. Unbalanced multipolar systems contain three or more great powers, one of which is a potential hegemon. Balanced multipolar systems have no aspiring hegemon; instead, power is divided rather evenly among the great powers, or at least between the two most powerful states in the system. No buck-passing takes place among the great powers in bipolarity because there is no third party to catch the buck. A threatened great power has little choice but to balance against its rival great power. It is also not possible to form balancing coalitions with other great powers in a world with just two great powers. Instead, the threatened power has to rely mainly on its own resources, and maybe alliances with smaller states, to contain the aggressor. Because neither buck-passing nor great-power balancing coalitions are feasible in bipolarity, we should expect balancing in this kind of system to be prompt and efficient *(Ibid: 43–44, 284–285, 353).*

But in modern international society there has been a persistent distinction between great powers and small. Great powers have not been vulnerable to violent attack by small powers to the same extent that small powers have been vulnerable to attack by great ones. Once again it is only the spread of nuclear weapons to small states, and the possibility of a world of many nuclear powers, that raises the question whether in international relations, also, a situation may come about in which 'the weakest has strength enough to kill the strongest'. Great powers contribute to international order by maintaining local systems of hegemony within which order is imposed from above, and by collaborating to manage the global balance of power and, from time to time, to impose their joint will on others.

Great powers contribute to international order in two main ways: by managing their relations with one another; and by exploiting their preponderance in such a way as to impart a degree of central direction to the affairs of international society as a whole. More particularly, great powers manage their relations with one another in the interests of international order by (i) preserving the general balance of power, (ii) seeking to avoid or control crises in their relations with one another, and (iii) seeking to limit or contain wars among one another. They exploit their preponderance in relation to the rest of international society by (iv) unilaterally exploiting their local preponderance, (v) agreeing to respect one another's spheres of influence, and (vi) joint action, as is implied by the idea of a great power concert or condominium.

This, of course, is not a description of what great powers actually do. It is rather a statement of the roles they can, and sometimes do, I play that sustain international order. In fact great powers, like small powers, frequently behave in such a way as to promote disorder rather than order; they seek to upset the general balance, rather than to preserve it, to foment crises rather than to control them, to win wars rather than to limit them, and so on *(Bul 1995: 48, 200–201).*

The powers in a bipolar world promptly respond to unsettling events. In the multipolar world dangers are diffused, responsibilities unclear, and definitions of vital interests easily obscured. Where a number of states are in balance, the skillful foreign policy of a forward power is designed to gain an advantage over one state without antagonizing others and frightening them into united action. In a multipolar world, states often pool their resources in order to serve their interests. Roughly equal parties engaged in cooperative endeavors must look for a common denominator of their policies. They risk finding the lowest one and easily end up in the worst of all possible worlds. In a bipolar world, alliance leaders make their strategies mainly according to their own calculations of interests. Strategies can be designed more to cope with the main adversary and less to satisfy one's allies. Alliance leaders are free to follow their own line, which may of course reflect their bad as well as their good judgment, their imaginary as well as their realistic fears, their ignoble as well as their worthy ends. Alliance leaders are not free of constraints. The major constraints, however, arise from the main adversary and not from one's own associates. In a multipolar world, who is a danger to whom is often unclear; the incentive to regard all disequilibrating changes with concern and respond to them with whatever effort may be required is consequently weakened. In a bipolar world changes may affect each of the two powers differently, and this means all the more that few changes in the world at large or within each other's national realm are likely to be thought irrelevant *(Waltz 1979: 170–171).*

Power has always been an elusive concept for statesmen and analysts of international politics; now it is even more slippery. The traditional view was that military power dominated other forms, and that states with the most military power, controlled world affairs. But the resources that produce power capabilities have become more complex. In the eyes of one astute observer, "the postwar era has witnessed radical transformations in the elements, the uses, and the achievements of power." And Hans Morgenthau, author of the leading realist text on international politics, went so far in his reaction to the events of the early 1970s as to announce an historically unprecedented severing of the functional relationship between political, military, and economic power shown in the possession by militarily weak countries of "monopolistic or quasi-monopolistic control of raw materials essential to the operation of advanced economies." Power can be thought of as the ability of an actor to get others to do something they otherwise would not do (and at an acceptable cost to the actor). Power can be conceived in terms of control over outcomes. In either case, measurement is not simple. We can look at the initial power resources that give an actor a potential ability; or we can look at that actor's actual influence over patterns of outcomes *(Keohane & Nye 2012: 10–16).*

Hans Morgenthau emphasizes 8 components "power of a nation" or of "national power". According to him, two groups of elements have to be distinguished; those which are relatively stable, and those which are subject to constant change.

1) **Geography**—The most stable factor upon which the power of a nation depends is obviously geography. Geographical situation has been important element in the political and military considerations of different countries (USA, Great Britain, Italy, Soviet Union/Russia).
2) **Natural Resources**—Another relatively stable factor which exerts an important influence upon the power of a nation with respect to other nations is natural resources. Natural resources are important for industrial production and, more particularly, for the waging of war.
3) **Industrial Capacity**—Another factor for the power of a nation is industrial capacity. Actually, a country will not become a great power so long as it is lacking in other factors without which no nation can attain in modern times the status of a great power. Of these factors industrial capacity is one of the most important.
4) **Military preparedness—**What gives the factors of geography, natural resources, and industrial capacity their actual importance for the power of a nation is military preparedness. Military preparedness requires a military establishment capable of supporting the foreign policies pursued. Such ability derives from a number of factors of which the most significant are technological innovations, and the quantity and quality of the armed forces.
5) **Population**—When we turn from material factors and those compounded of material and human elements to the purely human factors which determine the power of a nation, we have to distinguish quantitative and qualitative components. While among the latter we count national character, national morale, and the quality of diplomacy, the former needs to be discussed in terms of size of population. It is still true that no country can remain or become a first-rate power which does not belong to the more populous nations of the earth. On the other side, it would, of course, not be correct to say that the larger the population of a country, the greater the power of that country.

6) **National Character—**Of the three human factors of a qualitative nature vhich have a bearing on national power, national character and national morale stand out both for their elusiveness from the point of view of rational prognosis and for their permanent and often decisive influence upon the weight which a nation is able to put into the scales of international politics. Certain qualities of intellect and character occur more frequently and are more highly valued in one nation than in another.
7) **National Morale**—More elusive and less stable, but no less important than all the other factors in its bearing upon national power, is what we propose to call national morale. National morale is the degree of determination with which a nation supports the foreign policies of its government in peace or war.
8) **The quality of diplomacy**—Of all the factors which make for the power of a nation, the most important, and of the more unstable, is the quality of diplomacy. Diplomacy, one might say, is the brains of national power, as national morale is its soul *(Morgenthau 1948: 80–108).*

The concept of power has traditionally played a central and crucial role in the analysis of International Relations and World Politics. It has been seen as the key factor, variable, driving force or 'currency' in relations among states. Indeed, this role has been seen by many observers since Thucydides as the defining attribute of the international system itself. This interpretation of the role of power is said to derive from the understanding that no seriously effective level of organized, authoritative or legitimate governmental or socio-political structure exists above the level of the state that does not itself emanate from and, in the last analysis, remain responsible to autonomous, sovereign states—i.e., that there is no genuinely supranational power structure or political process in world politics. Therefore in order to explain what happens in world politics—as distinct from politics within states—it is necessary to privilege (a) power-seeking actions of states (taken as structurally coherent 'unit actors' in and of themselves: Waltz 1979) and of 'state actors' (actors acting through or on behalf of states) and (b) structured, ongoing relations of power between and among states, over the claims of other potential causal variables. This interpretation is usually labelled the 'realist'—or, in a revised version that has become widespread in academic International Relations since the 1970s, 'neorealist'—paradigm, derived originally from the thought of such political theorists as Machiavelli and Hobbes and central to the nineteenth century German concept of Realpolitik *(Clegg & Haugaard 2009: 383).*

Since Hans Morgenthau and Kenneth Waltz are chosen as representatives of classical realism and neorealism on basis of their reputation as the most influential thinkers in their respective branch of realism, we will focus more on their positions.

2.3 Hans Morgenthau—the Six Principles of Political Realism

Hans J. Morgenthau is deservedly recognized as the founder of post-World War II realist theory in international relations (he is also considered one of the "founding fathers" of the realist school in the twentieth century). This school of thought holds that nation-states are the main actors in international relations and that the main concern of the field is the study of power. Morgenthau emphasized the importance of "the national interest", and in "Politics Among Nations" he wrote that "the main signpost that helps political realism to find its way through the landscape of international politics is the concept of interest defined in terms of power." Starting with the second edition of "Politics Among Nations", Morgenthau included a section in the opening chapter called "Six Principles of Political Realism".

2.3.1 First Principle—Politics is Governed by Objective Laws Which Have Roots in Human Nature

Political realism believes that politics, like society in general, is governed by objective laws that have their roots in human nature. In order to improve society, it is first necessary to understand the laws by which society lives. The operation of these laws being impervious to our preferences, men will challenge them only at the risk of failure.

Realism, believing as it does in the objectivity of the laws of politics, must also believe in the possibility of developing a rational theory that reflects, however imperfectly and one-sidedly, these objective laws. It believes also, then, in the possibility of distinguishing in politics between truth and opinion-between what is true objectively and rationally, supported by evidence and illuminated by reason, and what is only a subjective judgment, divorced from the facts as they are and informed by prejudice and wishful thinking.

Human nature, in which the laws of politics have their roots, has not changed since the classical philosophies of China, India, and Greece endeavored to discover these laws. Hence, novelty is not necessarily a virtue in political theory, nor is old age a defect. The fact that a theory of politics, if there be such a theory, has never been heard of before tends to create a presumption against, rather than in favor of, its soundness. Conversely, the fact that a theory of politics was developed hundreds or even thousands of years ago—as was the theory of the balance of power—does not create a presumption that it must be outmoded and obsolete. A theory of politics must be subjected to the dual test of reason and experience. To dismiss such a theory because it had it's flowering in centuries past is to present not a rational argument but a modernistic prejudice that takes for granted the superiority of the present over the past. To dispose of the revival of such a theory as a "fashion" or "fad" is tantamount to assuming that in matters political we can have opinions but no truths.

For realism, theory consists in ascertaining facts and giving them meaning through reason. It assumes that the character of a foreign policy can be ascertained only through the examination of the political acts performed and of the foreseeable consequences of these acts. Thus, we can find out what statesmen have actually done, and from the foreseeable consequences of their acts we can surmise what their objectives might have been.

Yet examination of the facts is not enough. To give meaning to the factual raw material of foreign policy, we must approach political reality with a kind of rational outline, a map that suggests to us the possible meanings of foreign policy. In other words, we put ourselves in the position of a statesman who must meet a certain problem of foreign policy under certain circumstances, and we ask ourselves what the rational alternatives are from which a statesman may choose who must meet this problem under these circumstances (presuming always that he acts in a rational manner), and which of these rational alternatives this particular statesman, acting under these circumstances, is likely to choose. It is the testing of this rational hypothesis against the actual facts and their consequences that gives theoretical meaning to the facts of international politics.

2.3.2 Second Principle—National Interest Defined in Terms of National Power

The main signpost that helps political realism to find its way through the landscape of international politics is the concept of interest defined in terms of power.

This concept provides the link between reason trying to understand international politics and the facts to be understood. It sets politics as an autonomous sphere of action and understanding apart from other spheres, such as economics (understood in terms of interest defined as wealth), ethics, aesthetics, or religion. Without such a concept a theory of politics, international or domestic, would be altogether impossible, for without it we could not distinguish between political and nonpolitical facts, nor could we bring at least a measure of systematic order to the political sphere.

We assume that statesmen think and act in terms of interest defined as power, and the evidence of history bears that assumption out. That assumption allows us to retrace and anticipate, as it were, the steps a statesman–past, present, or future–has taken or will take on the political scene. We look over his shoulder when he writes his dispatches; we listen in on his conversation with other statesmen; we read and anticipate his very thoughts. Thinking in terms of interest defined as power, we think as he does, and as disinterested observers we understand his thoughts and actions perhaps better than he, the actor on the political scene, does himself.

The concept of interest defined as power imposes intellectual discipline upon the observer, infuses rational order into the subject matter of politics, and thus makes the theoretical understanding of politics possible. On the side of the actor, it provides for rational discipline in action and creates that astounding continuity in foreign policy which makes American, British, or Russian foreign policy appear as an intelligible, rational continuum, by and large consistent within itself, regardless of the different motives, preferences, and intellectual and moral qualities of successive statesmen. A realist theory of international politics, then, will guard against two popular fallacies: the concern with motives and the concern with ideological preferences.

To search for the clue to foreign policy exclusively in the motives of statesmen is both futile and deceptive. It is futile because motives are the most illusive of psychological data, distorted as they are, frequently beyond recognition, by the interests and emotions of actor and observer alike. Do we really know what our own motives are? And what do we know of the motives of others?

Yet even if we had access to the real motives of statesmen, that knowledge would help us little in understanding foreign policies, and might well lead us astray. It is true that the knowledge of the statesman's motives may give us one among many clues as to what the direction of his foreign policy might be. It cannot give us, however, the one clue by which to predict his foreign policies. History shows no exact and necessary correlation between the quality of motives and the quality of foreign policy. This is true in both moral and political terms.

We cannot conclude from the good intentions of a statesman that his foreign policies will be either morally praiseworthy or politically successful. Judging his motives, we can say that he will not intentionally pursue policies that are morally wrong, but we can say nothing about the probability of their success. If we want to know the moral and political qualities of his actions, we must know them, not his motives. How often have statesmen been motivated by the desire to improve the world, and ended by making it worse? And how often have they sought one goal, and ended by achieving something they neither expected nor desired?

Neville Chamberlain's politics of appeasement were, as far as we can judge, inspired by good motives; he was probably less motivated by considerations of personal power than were many other British prime ministers and he sought to preserve peace and to assure the happiness of all concerned. Yet his policies helped to make the Second World War inevitable, and to bring untold miseries to millions of men. Sir Winston Churchill's motives, on the other hand, were much less universal in scope and much more narrowly directed toward personal and national power, yet the foreign policies that sprang from these inferior motives were certainly superior in moral and political quality to those pursued by his predecessor. Judged by his motives, Robespierre was one of the most virtuous men who ever lived. Yet it was the utopian radicalism of that very virtue that made him kill those less virtuous than himself, brought him to the scaffold, and destroyed the revolution of which he was a leader.

Good motives give assurance against deliberately bad policies; they do not guarantee the moral goodness and political success of the policies they inspire. What is important to know, if one wants to understand foreign policy, is not primarily the motives of a statesman, but his intellectual ability to comprehend the essentials of foreign policy, as well as his political ability to translate what he has comprehended into successful political action. It follows that while ethics in the abstract judges the moral qualities of motives, political theory must judge the political qualities of intellect, will, and action.

A realist theory of international politics will also avoid the other popular fallacy of equating the foreign policies of a statesman with his philosophic or political sympathies, and of deducing the former from the latter. Statesmen, especially under contemporary conditions, may well make a habit of presenting their foreign policies in terms of their philosophic and political sympathies in order to gain popular support for them. Yet they will distinguish with Lincoln between their "official duty," which is to think and act in terms of the national interest, and their "personal wish," which is to see their own moral values and political principles realized throughout the world. Political realism does not require, nor does it condone, indifference to political ideals and moral principles, but it requires indeed a sharp distinction between the desirable and the possible-between what is desirable everywhere and at all times and what is possible under the concrete circumstances of time and place.

It stands to reason that not all foreign policies have always followed so rational, objective, and unemotional a course. The contingent elements of personality, prejudice, and subjective preference, and of all the weaknesses of intellect and will which flesh is heir to, are bound to deflect foreign policies from their rational course. Especially where foreign policy is conducted under the conditions of democratic control, the need to marshal popular emotions to the support of foreign policy cannot fail to impair the rationality of foreign policy itself. Yet a theory of foreign policy which aims at rationality must for the time being, as it were, abstract from these irrational elements and seek to paint a picture of foreign policy which presents the rational essence to be found in experience, without the contingent deviations from rationality which are also found in experience.

Deviations from rationality which are not the result of the personal whim or the personal psychopathology of the policy maker may appear contingent only from the vantage point of rationality, but may themselves be elements in a coherent system of irrationality. The conduct of the Indochina War by the United States suggests that possibility. It is a question worth looking into whether modern psychology and psychiatry have provided us with the conceptual tools which would enable us to construct, as it were, a counter-theory of irrational politics, a kind of pathology of international politics.

The experience of the Indochina War suggests five factors such a theory might encompass: the imposition upon the empirical world of a simplistic and a priori picture of the world derived from folklore and ideological assumption, that is, the replacement of experience with superstition; the refusal to correct this picture of the world in the light of experience; the persistence in a foreign policy derived from the misperception of reality and the use of intelligence for the purpose not of adapting policy to reality but of reinterpreting reality to fit policy; the egotism of the policy makers widening the gap between perception and policy, on the one hand, and reality, on the other; finally, the urge to close the gap at least subjectively by action, any kind of action, that creates the illusion of mastery over a recalcitrant reality. According to the Wall Street Journal of April 3, 1970, "the desire to 'do something' pervades top levels of Government and may overpower other 'common sense' advice that insists the U.S. ability to shape events is negligible. The yen for action could lead to bold policy as therapy."

The difference between international politics as it actually is and a rational theory derived from it is like the difference between a photograph and a painted portrait. The photograph shows everything that can be seen by the naked eye; the painted portrait does not show everything that can be seen by the naked eye, but it shows, or at least seeks to show, one thing that the naked eye cannot see: the human essence of the person portrayed.

Political realism contains not only a theoretical but also a normative element. It knows that political reality is replete with contingencies and systemic irrationalities and points to the typical influences they exert upon foreign policy. Yet it shares with all social theory the need, for the sake of theoretical understanding, to stress the rational elements of political reality; for it is these rational elements that make reality intelligible for theory. Political realism presents the theoretical construct of a rational foreign policy which experience can never completely achieve.

At the same time political realism considers a rational foreign policy to be good foreign policy; for only a rational foreign policy minimizes risks and maximizes benefits and, hence, complies both with the moral precept of prudence and the political requirement of success. Political realism wants the photographic picture of the political world to resemble as much as possible its painted portrait. Aware of the inevitable gap between good—that is, rational—foreign policy and foreign policy as it actually is, political realism maintains not only that theory must focus upon the rational elements of political reality, but also that foreign policy ought to be rational in view of its own moral and practical purposes.

Hence, it is no argument against the theory here presented that actual foreign policy does not or cannot live up to it. That argument misunderstands the intention of this book, which is to present not an indiscriminate description of political reality, but a rational theory of international politics. Far from being invalidated by the fact that, for instance, a perfect balance of power policy will scarcely be found in reality, it assumes that reality, being deficient in this respect, must be understood and evaluated as an approximation to an ideal system of balance of power.

2.3.3 Third Principle—Interest is Always Dynamic

Realism assumes that its key concept of interest defined as power is an objective category which is universally valid, but it does not endow that concept with a meaning that is fixed once and for all. The idea of interest is indeed of the essence of politics and is unaffected by the circumstances of time and place. Thucydides' statement, born of the experiences of ancient Greece that "identity of interests is the surest of bonds whether between states or individuals" was taken up in the nineteenth century by Lord Salisbury's remark that "the only bond of union that endures" among nations is "the absence of all clashing interests." It was erected into a general principle of government by George Washington:

A small knowledge of human nature will convince us, that, with far the greatest part of mankind, interest is the governing principle; and that almost every man is more or less, under its influence. Motives of public virtue may for a time, or in particular instances, actuate men to the observance of a conduct purely disinterested; but they are not of themselves sufficient to produce persevering conformity to the refined dictates and obligations of social duty. Few men are capable of making a continual sacrifice of all views of private interest, or advantage, to the common good. It is vain to exclaim against the depravity of human nature on this account; the fact is so, the experience of every age and nation has proved it and we must in a great measure, change the constitution of man, before we can make it otherwise. No institution, not built on the presumptive truth of these maxims can succeed.

It was echoed and enlarged upon in our century by Max Weber's observation:

Interests (material and ideal), not ideas, dominate directly the actions of men. Yet the "images of the world" created by these ideas have very often served as switches determining the tracks on which the dynamism of interests kept actions moving.

Yet the kind of interest determining political action in a particular period of history depends upon the political and cultural context within which foreign policy is formulated. The goals that might be pursued by nations in their foreign policy can run the whole gamut of objectives any nation has ever pursued or might possibly pursue.

The same observations apply to the concept of power. Its content and the manner of its use are determined by the political and cultural environment. Power may comprise anything that establishes and maintains the control of man over man. Thus, power covers all social relationships which serve that end, from physical violence to the most subtle psychological ties by which one mind controls another. Power covers the domination of man by man, both when it is disciplined by moral ends and controlled by constitutional safeguards, as in Western democracies, and when it is that untamed and barbaric force which finds its laws in nothing but its own strength and its sole justification in its aggrandizement.

Political realism does not assume that the contemporary conditions, under which foreign policy operates, with their extreme instability and the ever presents threat of large-scale violence, cannot be changed. The balance of power, for instance, is indeed a perennial element of all pluralistic societies, as the authors of The Federalist papers well knew; yet it is capable of operating, as it does in the United States, under the conditions of relative stability and peaceful conflict.

If the factors that have given rise to these conditions can be duplicated on the international scene, similar conditions of stability and peace will then prevail there, as they have over long stretches of history among certain nations.

What is true of the general character of international relations is also true of the nation state as the ultimate point of reference of contemporary foreign policy. While the realist indeed believes that interest is the perennial standard by which political action must be judged and directed, the contemporary connection between interest and the nation state is a product of history, and is therefore bound to disappear in the course of history. Nothing in the realist position militates against the assumption that the present division of the political world into nation states will be replaced by larger units of a quite different character, more in keeping with the technical potentialities and the moral requirements of the contemporary world.

The realist parts company with other schools of thought before the all-important question of how the contemporary world is to be transformed. The realist is persuaded that this transformation can be achieved only through the workmanlike manipulation of the perennial forces that have shaped the past as they will the future. The realist cannot be persuaded that we can bring about that transformation by confronting a political reality that has its own laws with an abstract ideal that refuses to take those laws into account.

2.3.4 Fourth Principle—Abstract Moral Principles Cannot Be Applied to Politics

Political realism is aware of the moral significance of political action. It is also aware of the ineluctable tension between the moral command and the requirements of successful political action. And it is unwilling to gloss over and obliterate that tension and thus to obfuscate both the moral and the political issue by making it appear as though the stark facts of politics were morally more satisfying than they actually are, and the moral law less exacting than it actually is.

Realism maintains that universal moral principles cannot be applied to the actions of states in their abstract universal formulation, but that they must be filtered through the concrete circumstances of time and place. The individual may say for himself: "Fiat justitia, pereat mundus (Let justice be done, even if the world perish)," but the state has no right to say so in the name of those who are in its care. Both individual and state must judge political action by universal moral principles, such as that of liberty. Yet while the individual has a moral right to sacrifice himself in defense of such a moral principle, the state has no right to let its moral disapprobation of the infringement of liberty get in the way of successful political action, itself inspired by the moral principle of national survival. There can be no political morality without prudence; that is, without consideration of the political consequences of seemingly moral action. Realism, then, considers prudence-the weighing of the consequences of alternative political actions-to be the supreme virtue in politics. Ethics in the abstract judges actions by its conformity with the moral law; political ethics judges action by its political consequences. Classical and medieval philosophy knew this, and so did Lincoln when he said: I do the very best I know how, the very best I can, and I mean to keep doing so until the end. If the end brings me out all right, what is said against me won't amount to anything. If the end brings me out wrong, ten angels swearing I was right would make no difference.

2.3.5 Fifth Principle—Difference Between Moral Aspirations of a Nation and the Universal Moral Principles

Political realism refuses to identify the moral aspirations of a particular nation with the moral laws that govern the universe. As it distinguishes between truth and opinion, so it distinguishes between truth and idolatry. All nations are tempted-and few have been able to resist the temptation for long-to clothe their own particular aspirations and actions in the moral purposes of the universe. To know that nations are subject to the moral law is one thing, while to pretend to know with certainty what is good and evil in the relations among nations is quite another. There is a world of difference between the belief that all nations stand under the judgment of God, inscrutable to the human mind, and the blasphemous conviction that God is always on one's side and that what one wills oneself cannot fail to be willed by God also.

The lighthearted equation between a particular nationalism and the counsels of Providence is morally indefensible, for it is that very sin of pride against which the Greek tragedians and the Biblical prophets have warned rulers and ruled. That equation is also politically pernicious, for it is liable to engender the distortion in judgment which, in the blindness of crusading frenzy, destroys nations and civilizations-in the name of moral principle, ideal, or God himself.

On the other hand, it is exactly the concept of interest defined in terms of power that saves us from both that moral excess and that political folly. For if we look at all nations, our own included, as political entities pursuing their respective interests defined in terms of power, we are able to do justice to all of them. And we are able to do justice to all of them in a dual sense: We are able to judge other nations as we judge our own and, having judged them in this fashion, we are then capable of pursuing policies that respect the interests of other nations, while protecting and promoting those of our own. Moderation in policy cannot fail to reflect the moderation of moral judgment.

2.3.6 Sixth Principle—Autonomy of International Politics

The difference, then, between political realism and other schools of thought is real, and it is profound. However much the theory of political realism may have been misunderstood and misinterpreted, there is no gainsaying its distinctive intellectual and moral attitude to matters political.

Intellectually, the political realist maintains the autonomy of the political sphere, as the economist, the lawyer, the moralist maintain theirs. He thinks in terms of interest defined as power, as the economist thinks in terms of interest defined as wealth; the lawyer, of the conformity of action with legal rules; the moralist, of the conformity of action with moral principles. The economist asks: "How does this policy affect the wealth of society, or a segment of it?" The lawyer asks: "Is this policy in accord with the rules of law?" The moralist asks: "Is this policy in accord with moral principles?" And the political realist asks: "How does this policy affect the power of the nation?" (or of the federal government, of Congress, of the party, of agriculture, as the case may be).

The political realist is not unaware of the existence and relevance of standards of thought other than political ones. As political realist, he cannot but subordinate these other standards to those of politics. And he parts company with other schools when they impose standards of thought appropriate to other spheres upon the political sphere. It is here that political realism takes issue with the "legalistic-moralistic approach" to international politics. That this issue is not, as has been contended, a mere figment of the imagination, but goes to the very core of the controversy, can be shown from many historical examples. Three will suffice to make the point.

In 1939 the Soviet Union attacked Finland. This action confronted France and Great Britain with two issues, one legal, the other political. Did that action violate the Covenant of the League of Nations and, if it did, what countermeasures should France and Great Britain take? The legal question could easily be answered in the affirmative, for obviously the Soviet Union had done what was prohibited by the Covenant. The answer to the political question depends, first, upon the manner in which the Russian action affected the interests of France and Great Britain; second, upon the existing distribution of power between France and Great Britain, on the one hand, and the Soviet Union and other potentially hostile nations, especially Germany, on the other; and, third, upon the influence that the countermeasures were likely to have upon the interests of France and Great Britain and the future distribution of power. France and Great Britain, as the leading members of the League of Nations, saw to it that the Soviet Union was expelled from the League, and they were prevented from joining Finland in the war against the Soviet Union only by Sweden's refusal to allow their troops to pass through Swedish territory on their way to Finland. If this refusal by Sweden had not saved them, France and Great Britain would shortly have found themselves at war with the Soviet Union and Germany at the same time.

The policy of France and Great Britain was a classic example of legalism in that they allowed the answer to the legal question, legitimate within its sphere, to determine their political actions. Instead of asking both questions, that of law and that of power, they asked only the question of law; and the answer they received could have no bearing on the issue that their very existence might have depended upon.

The second example illustrates the "moralistic approach" to international politics. It concerns the international status of the Communist government of China. The rise of that government confronted the Western world with two issues, one moral, the other political. Were the nature and policies of that government in accord with the moral principles of the Western world? Should the Western world deal with such a government? The answer to the first question could not fail to be in the negative. Yet it did not follow with necessity that the answer to the second question should also be in the negative. The standard of thought applied to the first–the moral question—was simply to test the nature and the policies of the Communist government of China by the principles of Western morality. On the other hand, the second—the political question—had to be subjected to the complicated test of the interests involved and the power available on either side, and of the bearing of one or the other course of action upon these interests and power. The application of this test could well have led to the conclusion that it would be wiser not to deal with the Communist government of China. To arrive at this conclusion by neglecting this test altogether and answering the political question in terms of the moral issue was indeed a classic example of the "moralistic approach" to international politics.

The third case illustrates strikingly the contrast between realism and the legalistic-moralistic approach to foreign policy. Great Britain, as one of the guarantors of the neutrality of Belgium, went to war with Germany in August 1914 because Germany had violated the neutrality of Belgium. The British action could be justified either in realistic or legalistic-moralistic terms. That is to say, one could argue realistically that for centuries it had been axiomatic for British foreign policy to prevent the control of the Low Countries by a hostile power. It was then not so much the violation of Belgium's neutrality per se as the hostile intentions of the violator which provided the rationale for British intervention. If the violator had been another nation but Germany, Great Britain might well have refrained from intervening. This is the position taken by Sir Edward Grey, British Foreign Secretary during that period. Under Secretary for Foreign Affairs Hardinge remarked to him in 1908: "If France violated Belgian neutrality in a war against Germany, it is doubtful whether England or Russia would move a finger to maintain Belgian neutrality, while if the neutrality of Belgium was violated by Germany, it is probable that the converse would be the case." Whereupon Sir Edward Grey replied: "This is to the point." Yet one could also take the legalistic and moralistic position that the violation of Belgium's neutrality per se, because of its legal and moral defects and regardless of the interests at stake and of the identity of the violator, justified British and, for that matter, American intervention. This was the position which Theodore Roosevelt took in his letter to Sir Edward Grey of January 22, 1915.

To me the crux of the situation has been Belgium. If England or France had acted toward Belgium as Germany has acted, I should have opposed them, exactly as I now oppose Germany. I have emphatically approved your action as a model for what should be done by those who believe that treaties should be observed in good faith and that there is such a thing as international morality. I take this position as an American who is no more an Englishman than he is a German, who endeavors loyally to serve the interests of his own country, but who also endeavors to do what he can for justice and decency as regards mankind at large, and who therefore feels obliged to judge all other nations by their conduct on any given occasion.

This realist defense of the autonomy of the political sphere against its subversion by other modes of thought does not imply disregard for the existence and importance of these other modes of thought. It rather implies that each should be assigned its proper sphere and function. Political realism is based upon a pluralistic conception of human nature. Real man is a composite of "economic man," "political man," "moral man," "religious man," etc. A man who was nothing but "political man" would be a beast, for he would be completely lacking in moral restraints. A man who was nothing but "moral man" would be a fool, for he would be completely lacking in prudence. A man who was nothing but "religious man" would be a saint, for he would be completely lacking in worldly desires.

Recognizing that these different facets of human nature exist, political realism also recognizes that in order to understand one of them one has to deal with it on its own terms. That is to say, if I want to understand "religious man," I must for the time being abstract from the other aspects of human nature and deal with its religious aspect as if it were the only one. Furthermore, I must apply to the religious sphere the standards of thought appropriate to it, always remaining aware of the existence of other standards and their actual influence upon the religious qualities of man. What is true of this facet of human nature is true of all the others. No modern economist, for instance, would conceive of his science and its relations to other sciences of man in any other way. It is exactly through such a process of emancipation from other standards of thought, and the development of one appropriate to its subject matter, that economics has developed as an autonomous theory of the economic activities of man. To contribute to a similar development in the field of politics is indeed the purpose of political realism.

It is in the nature of things that a theory of politics which is based upon such principles will not meet with unanimous approval-nor does, for that matter, such a foreign policy. For theory and policy alike run counter to two trends in our culture which are not able to reconcile themselves to the assumptions and results of a rational, objective theory of politics. One of these trends disparages the role of power in society on grounds that stem from the experience and philosophy of the nineteenth century; we shall address ourselves to this tendency later in greater detail. The other trend, opposed to the realist theory and practice of politics, stems from the very relationship that exists, and must exist, between the human mind and the political sphere. For reasons that we shall discuss later the human mind in its day-by-day operations cannot bear to look the truth of politics straight in the face. It must disguise, distort, belittle, and embellish the truth-the more so, the more the individual is actively involved in the processes of politics, and particularly in those of international politics. For only by deceiving himself about the nature of politics and the role he plays on the political scene is man able to live contentedly as a political animal with himself and his fellow men. Thus it is inevitable that a theory which tries to understand international politics as it actually is and as it ought to be in view of its intrinsic nature, rather than as people would like to see it, must overcome a psychological resistance that most other branches of learning need not face *(Morgenthau 1978: 4–15).*

2.4 Kenneth Waltz—Neorealism

Neorealism or structural realism is a theory of international relations that says power is the most important factor in international relations. It was first outlined by Kenneth Waltz in his 1979 book Theory of International Politics. Associated in particular with the American political scientist Kenneth Waltz, neorealism was an attempt to translate some of the key insights of classical realism into the language and methods of modern social science. In the Theory of International Politics (1979), Waltz argued that most of the important features of international relations, especially the actions of great powers, could be explained solely in terms of the anarchical structure of the international system. Although Waltz's position was not original, in systematizing it and attempting to establish it on empirical grounds he simultaneously reinvigorated realism and further detached it from its classical roots *(Neorealism—Encyclopedia Britannica).*

Waltz recognized early on that classical realism was problematic. In particular, the philosophical anthropology on which it was based was impossible to prove or disprove—it rested simply on inherited beliefs about human nature that, to his mind, lacked scientific credibility. The 'evidence' on which it was based was not a systematic body of evidence and analysis, but rather sets of religious or philosophical speculations. As such, Waltz was convinced, it would not stand as a theory.

Waltz signalled his discomfort with the underpinnings of classical realism in Man, the State and War, but it was only in Theory of International Politics, published two decades later, that he set out the alternative. In the meantime, others had also rounded on the realists, asking similar questions as Waltz about its underpinnings and its plausibility, but supplying rather different accounts of what international theory should look like. In the 1960s and 70 s, the classical realists were hounded by behaviouralists, systems analysts, game theorists, neofunctionalists and institutionalists, and pushed out of the theoretical mainstream. Thinkers like Morton Kaplan, Anatol Rapoport, Ernst Haas, Joseph Nye and Robert O. Keohane came to the fore, displacing the realists and shifting the core concerns of the field away from issues of human nature and power politics.

What Waltz did in this context was remarkable: almost single-handedly, he resuscitated realism, amputating those parts that were clearly dysfunctional, giving it the transfusions of new thinking that it needed, and returning it, revivified, to the fray. Theory of International Politics shifted realism away from metaphysical speculation on human nature and onto firmer ground by removing any need for a philosophical anthropology to explain why international relations are as they are. Instead of a contentious account of 'man', Waltz substituted a structural account of the international system that borrowed heavily from the theory of the firm in classical economics.

Waltz's structural realism attracted criticism from the start, and continues to do so today, almost twenty-five years after Theory of International Politics was published. But it is impossible not to acknowledge that it decisively shifted the terms of debate in international theory, returning realism to the mainstream, where it has remained ever since. In the 1980s, 1990s and 2000s, the field was defined by a series of arguments between the realists and their critics, as first the neo-liberal institutionalists and then various bands of constructivists, feminists, postmodernists and critical theorists lined up to attack Waltz and his students *(Hall 2013)*.

Neorealism differed from classical realism in two important respects: methodology and level of analysis. In terms of method, realism was reconfigured as a rigorous and parsimonious social-scientific theory drawing in particular on microeconomics. Regarding level of analysis, Waltz argued that traditional realist arguments about domestic institutions, the quality of diplomacy and statecraft, national morale, and human nature were largely irrelevant. He conceived of states as unitary rational actors existing in a self-help system. Concerned above all with survival and operating with imperfect information, states are conditioned by the logic of the system into similar patterns of behaviour. The international system is defined by remarkable continuity across space and time, and the trajectory of international relations is explained by the distribution of power across units in the system. Waltz argued that the most stable arrangement was bipolarity, or a balance between two great powers.

Both Waltz's conception of international relations and his substantive arguments proved influential, and debates between neorealists and their critics dominated the field for much of the 1980s and'90 s. Although a competing school of neoliberal institutionalists dissented from Waltz's claims about the difficulty of cooperation under anarchy, they nevertheless adopted his methods and many of his assumptions. Neorealists, meanwhile, eventually split into "defensive" and "offensive" camps. Defensive realists, following Waltz, argued that because states tend to seek security, a stable international equilibrium is possible via balancing. Offensive realists argued that states seek to maximize power rather than security, making equilibrium harder to achieve.

Neorealism has had numerous detractors, including many who were sympathetic to classical realism. Neorealism has been faulted, for example, for neglecting the insights of history, sociology, and philosophy; for falsely claiming scientific validity; for failing to account for systemic transformations in international relations (including the end of the Cold War and the advent of globalization); and for an allegedly self-defeating analytical reductionism. Nevertheless, it has remained a powerful research program in the study of international relations *(Neorealism—Encyclopedia Britannica)*.

Defensive realism, which is frequently referred to as "structural realism," came on the scene in the late 1970s with the appearance of Waltz's Theory of International Politics. Unlike Morgenthau, Waltz does not assume that great powers are inherently aggressive because they are infused with a will to power; instead he starts by assuming that states merely aim to survive. Above all else, they seek security. Nevertheless, he maintains that the structure of the international system forces great powers to pay careful attention to the balance of power. In particular, anarchy forces security-seeking states to compete with each other for power, because power is the best means to survival. Whereas human nature is the deep cause of security competition in Morgenthau's theory, anarchy plays that role in Waltz's theory. Waltz does not emphasize, however, that the international system provides great powers with good reasons to act offensively to gain power. Instead, he appears to make the opposite case: that anarchy encourages states to behave defensively and to maintain rather than upset the balance of power. "The first concern of states," he writes, is "to maintain their position in the system." There seems to be, as international relations theorist Randall Schweller notes, a "status quo bias" in Waltz's theory. Waltz recognizes that states have incentives to gain power at their rivals' expense and that it makes good strategic sense to act on that motive when the time is right. But he does not develop that line of argument in any detail. On the contrary, he emphasizes that when great powers behave aggressively the potential victims usually balance against the aggressor and thwart its efforts to gain power. For Waltz, in short, balancing checkmates offense. Furthermore, he stresses that great powers must be careful not to acquire too much power, because "excessive strength" is likely to cause other states to join forces against them, thereby leaving them worse off than they would have been had they refrained from seeking additional increments of power (Mershaimer 2001: 45–46).

There are four key differences between classical realism and neorealism. First, classical realist locates the roots of international conflict and war in an imperfect human nature while neo-realists maintain that its deep causes are found in the anarchic international system. Second, the state is ontologically superior to the system in classical realism, in contrast to neorealism, allowing more space for agency in the former approach (Hobson, 2000: 17). Third, classical realists differentiate between status-quo powers and revisionist powers while neorealism regards states as unitary actors (Schweller, 1996: 155). Fourth, neo-realists attempt to construct a more rigorous and scientific approach to the study of international politics, heavily influenced by the behaviourist revolution of the 1960's while classical realism confine its analyses to subjective valuations of international relations (Georg and Sorensen, 2007: 75).

2.4.1 Defining Power

Morgenthau and Waltz both see the international arena as a competitive and hostile stage where power is the main currency. That is why the concept of power is at the heart of their analysis of international politics. John Mearsheimer (1995: 91) summarizes the orthodox view on how power is defined within the realist paradigm in the following statement: "Realists believe that state behaviour is largely shaped by the material structure of the international system". This quotation however deeply misrepresents Morgenthau's definition of power. This is evident when Morgenthau states that: "Power may comprise anything that establishes and maintains the power of man over man .... from physical violence to the most subtle psychological ties by which one mind controls another" (Morgenthau, 1965: 9). For Morgenthau, the most important material aspect of power is armed forces, but even more significant is a nation's character, morale and quality of governance (Morgenthau, 1956: 186). The validity of this reading of Morgenthau is further enhanced when he contends: "power .... tends to be equated with material strength, especially of a military nature, I have stressed more than before its immaterial aspects" (Morgenthau 1965: 9). Michael Williams (2005:109) is thus right when he claims that the closest affinities to Morgenthau's extremely broad understanding of power are to be found in the works of Michael Foucault and Pierre Bourdieu and not in the narrow and materialistic conception of power realism often is accused of.

Waltz offers a considerably thinner definition of power or capabilities than Morgenthau. His estimation of power includes the following components: "size of population and territory, resource endowment, economic capability, military strength, political stability and competence" (Waltz, 1979: 131). Even though Waltz evidently privileges material factors, non-material dimensions of power are also present in his theory as manifested by his emphasis on political stability and competence. The reason for Waltz's predominant emphasis on materialism is due to his commitment to,'scientific' realism. Consequently, Waltz limits his definition of power to mainly tangible variables as they are much easier to quantify.

There are thus vast differences between Morgenthau and Waltz in their definition of power. The formers' understanding of power poses a fundamental anomaly to the orthodox view since'soft' power trumps 'hard' power in Morgenthau's account. In this respect, Waltz's position is far easier to reconcile with the traditional view. Indeed, Waltz's rather narrow conception of power is predominantly, but not entirely, materialistic.

2.4.2 Why Do States Struggle for Power?

There is a wide consensus within the literature that classical realists and neorealists answer this fundamental question in opposing ways. Classical realism supposedly emphasizes human nature while neorealism locates causation in the anarchic international system (Brown, 2005: 92). Morgenthau's explanation is mainly, but no solely, confined to the first image which he bases upon a fixed and universalistic account of human nature. The first principle of political realism makes this point clear: "politics, like society in general, is governed by objective laws that have their roots in human nature" (Morgenthau, 1956: 4). According to Morgenthau, the struggle for power at the international level is largely the result of animus dominandi, the 'political mans' urge to dominate others, a concept influenced by Nietzsche's metaphysics on the 'will to power' (Peterson, 1999: 100–101). However, Morgenthau goes beyond human nature and moves up to the second level of analysis. He regards the state as a collective reflection of political man's lust for power and the unit which carries out its impulses at the international stage. The state is thus the referent object of Morgenthau's theory and the agent pursuing power in international affairs, highlighting Morgenthau's dependence on the unit-level. The third image is also present in Morgenthau's account of the struggle for power. Anarchy is not the deep cause of power competition but a vital permissive force. The absence of world governance means that there are no constraints on man's basic desires, reflected in state behaviour, to dominate others (Shimko, 1992: 290–293). In a hierarchic order however, the pursuit of power would be abolished as the animus dominandi would be constrained by a global leviathan (Morgenthau, 1956: 477). Hence, human natures innate desire to dominate others which is the driving force of state behavior can only take place as long as the international system remains anarchic. Through this narrative, Morgenthau also eloquently links all three levels of analysis together.

Kenneth Waltz, nevertheless, regards Morgenthau as a first image theorist and criticizes his approach on three accounts. First, Morgenthau's account of human nature is entirely hypothetical since we cannot empirically verify what the true human nature is. This in turn makes it impossible to assess the validity of his thesis (Waltz, 1959: 166). Second, Morgenthau's essentialist conception of human nature is problematic since a constant cannot explain variation. To paraphrase Waltz: if human nature was the cause of war in 1914, it was by the same token the cause of peace in 1910 (Waltz, 1959: 28). Third, Waltz accuses Morgenthau of reductionism since the latter tries to explain the whole by the sum of its parts. Reductionism fails to account why the patterns of international politics constantly reoccur even though the actors and their character are in a constant change (Waltz, 1979: 65, 74).

To overcome what Waltz regards as deficiencies in Morgenthau's work he attempts to locate causation at the systemic level instead. Indeed, Waltz contends that the anarchical international system inevitably leads to the logic of self-help and power politics. According to Waltz (1979: 87) states who struggle for power are simply following the dictates of the international system in order to survive in an international order where there is no global leviathan to offer them protection. By providing this explanation, Waltz tries to restrict himself to the systemic level and avoid 'reductionism'. Waltz however fails with this attempt as his theory is dependent on the unit-level in order to function. As Richard Ashley and Alexander Wendt have pointed out, Waltzian structuralism presupposes state preferences. International anarchy cannot possibly impel states to struggle for power if they do not share any ambitions (Guzzini, 1998: 129). Waltz is seemingly well aware of this point and makes interference at the second level of analysis by assuming that states pursue strategies for survival, in order to operationalize his theory (Waltz, 1979: 91). This motivational desire alone cannot however generate power competition. Randall Schweller convincingly argues that in an anarchic system where all states primary goal is survival, the units would have no incentive to pursue power at all since that would risk undermining their principal goal: survival. In Schweller's words: Waltz constructs "a world of all cops and no robbers" and must therefore make further interventions at the unit-level and bring revisionist goals into his analysis in order to trigger power competition (Schweller, 1996: 91–92). Reductionism thus seems to be unavoidable, even for Waltz.

As this section has shown, Morgenthau assigns the deep causes of power struggles to the first image while Waltz attributes it to the third image. However, both scholars make use of other levels of analysis as well. Without incorporating both systemic and unit-level explanations neither Morgenthau nor Waltz would be able to explain why states pursue power. The difference between the two lies in the fact that Morgenthau's 'bottom-up approach' takes human nature as the starting point and moves up the levels of analysis, while Waltz 'top-down approach' begins at the third image and slowly move down to the unit-level, without ever reaching the individual level. Contrary to the conventional wisdom then Morgenthau's classical realism cannot be seen as a strict first image theory and Waltzian neorealism is not a purely systemic theory.

2.4.3 The Critical and Normative Dimension of Power Politics

There are different opinions on the role normative and critical analysis plays in classical and neorealism. Some claim that both strands of realism overlook this dimension of politics (Burchill, 2001: 99), others argue that this aspect of theorizing in only apparent in classical realism (Lebow, 2007: 53) while a third strand maintains that realists of all kinds are driven by a normative and critical agenda (Sorensen and Jackson, 2007: 77). This section aims to bring some clarity to this important issue.

Critical and normative analysis shines through in the work of Morgenthau. Following Hannah Arendt, Morgenthau makes a distinction between the vita contemplativa and the vita activa, the first concept corresponds to truth and the second to power. In Morgenthau's world the two realms are at odds with one another as they are oriented towards different goals. While truth tries to unmask power for what it actually is, in order to open up space for normative and critical challenges to the status-quo, power tries to cloak itself and pretend to be the bearer of truth and justice in hope of maintaining the existing order. Morgenthau argues that the task of the scholar is to speak truth to power and expose it for what it actually (Morgenthau, 1970: 14–15). This is the task Morgenthau undertakes when he relentlessly attacks rational liberalism for uncritically accepting relations of domination by cloaking it under the banner of 'rationality' and 'harmony of interest' (Williams, 2005: 96). Rational liberalism then only reinforces the status-quo which Morgenthau claims to be contrary to the purpose of political science as a discipline designed to unsettle power and bring about change (Cozette, 2008: 8).

Morgenthau's approach in Truth and Power is also fully consistent with his key principle: "interest defined as power". This is because Morgenthau has an extremely broad understanding of power as has already been demonstrated but also an almost boundless definition of the national interest. This is evident in the following passage of Politics Among Nations: "The goals that might be pursued by nations in their foreign policy can run the whole gamut of objectives any nations have ever pursued or might possible pursue" (Morgenthau, 1965: 8–9). Echoing Weber, Morgenthau thus argues that prudent and ethical behaviour can be a part of the state objective. Indeed, good foreign policy "complies both with the moral precept of prudence and the political requirement of success" (Morgenthau, 1965: 7). Yet, Morgenthau clearly recognizes that states may choose not to act in such manner since moral principles do not serve as effective political restraints (Williams, 2005: 187).

Even though Waltz has spoken truth to American power since at least the 1970's, his theoretical work is dry of critical and normative engagement (Halliday et. al., 1998: 373). Waltz's lack of interest in normative and critical analysis does not however stem from a belief that theories should solely explain as one would expect (Waltz 1979: 6). Other explanations must therefore account for Waltz's antipathy towards critical and normative theorizing, here are two plausible renditions. First, Waltz's theory maintains that structure determines the behaviour of the units within it. Consequently, only structural changes are able to affect international outcomes in world politics (Waltz, 1979: 108). Hence, there is very little room for agency in Waltz's world and it would be superfluous to engage in prescriptions when it is systemic factors that ultimately decide state behavior. Waltz is open to the prospect of change in the structure of the international system but regard it as a formidable challenge, unlikely to happen any time soon (Waltz, 1986: 329). Second, Waltz wrote his book during the height of the Cold War which was characterized by bipolarity between the two great powers of the time, the United States and the Soviet Union. Since Waltz (1964: 881–909) contends that the bipolar distribution of power is the most stable and peaceful form of international order he was contempt with the status-quo and had therefore no reason to challenge it. These two explanations might account for Waltz disinterest in critical and normative analysis.

This final theme has demonstrated a sharp division between Morgenthau's and Walt's writings. While the former openly engage with critical and normative analysis the latter do not address these concerns at all. If we only consider the writings of Morgenthau and Waltz, Richard Ned Lebow's proclamation seems to be correct: only classical realism is preoccupied with the normative and critical dimension of politics *(Pashakhanlou, 2009).*

2.5 Realism, Liberalism and Constructivism in Transboundary Water Relations

Realism and Liberalism are rationalist approaches, assuming interests to be fixed in interactions, with variation only in strategies states use to attain their preferences. These theories suggest that cooperation is conditioned to different extents by objective material parameters, discounting the potential for change residing in social aspects of international relations.

2.5.1 Realism in Transboundary Water Relations

Realism is highly applicable to analysis of transboundary water relations. This theory of International Relations depicts international politics as an anarchic realm where the main actors, i.e. states, assumed to be strategically rational, pursue the essential goal of survival, specifically territorial sovereignty and integrity. Because states can never fully ascertain whether others are defensively motivated—that is, attempting to maximize their respective levels of security to protect what they have already attained, or offensively driven to attain more than what they have, they inherently mistrust each other and prefer to be as selfsufficient as possible (Waltz 1979). States in this 'self-help' system thus experience irremediable degrees of insecurity that compel them to maximize relative gains and capabilities (Grieco 1993), thereby transforming most of their mutual interactions into zero-sum games. Consequently, international politics is competitive and war-prone.

Realist thought, developed to explain great-power politics, does not map precisely onto the contours of river basin relations revolving around available supplies of a localized natural resource. Interestingly, though, the symmetrical array of littoral states ringing a common lake or flanking a boundary river exemplify 'common pool resources'. For these natural goods, relevant consumers cannot be excluded, or at least at high cost, from enjoying the available benefits, but consumption is rival, in the sense that each state's use subtracts from the total benefits available to everyone else (LeMarquand 1977, 9). Thus, common pool resources' politics bear some analogical resemblance to great powers' zero-sum security competition. The substantive distinction between the two domains lies in the fact that, unless rivals can agree on an optimal assignment of usage rights, restraints and responsibilities, they are more likely to destroy the resource than each other, thus illustrating the renowned 'tragedy of the commons' (United Nations 2006, 209).

In contrast to common pool resources' configurations, private goods are both rivalrous and excludable. Common pool resources might even be 'privatized' through legal or technological means of exclusion. While Waterbury (2002, 10) asserts that upstream storage does not obliterate the commons' dimensions of a transboundary watercourse, as water must eventually be released, salient upstream actions asymmetrically and unreciprocally diminish the quantity and quality of water available downriver, to the practical extent of excluding downstreamers from access (LeMarquand 1977, 10, Matthew 1999, Williams 2003). Indeed, Homer-Dixon (1999, 137–141) describes 'simple scarcity conflicts' as those occurring over scarce, vital and physically capturable resources, such as water.

Thus, salient upstream–downstream constellations unsurprisingly lend themselves to protracted riverine rivalry. It is not infrequently remarked upon that the 'English word rival comes from the Latin rivalis, meaning one using the same river as another' (United Nations 2006, 215). This rivalry should intensify to block unilateral construction of upstream hydrological installations, which pose the potential for excluding downstreamers from enjoying the myriad benefits stemming from the freer flow of water (Naff and Matson 1984, 193). Therefore, users in downstream areas, where historically prior development tends to occur (McCaffrey 1990, 235), have obvious incentives to try to forestall upstream actions via linkage strategies that draw on power resources from outside the water-related issue-area (Keohane and Nye 2001). Moreover, political leaders also harbour fears of losing social prestige and power at home lest their traditional reputations for delivering water to citizenries come under the sort of serious challenge posed by another state's hydrological developments (Allan 2002, 215–217).

Offensive Realism underscores that antagonism between great-power rivals is likely to resemble a 'security dilemma' that escalates to war because the two sides cannot necessarily differentiate between defensive and offensive capabilities, let alone motives for using these instruments. Apart from the obvious fact that upstream–downstream antagonism is based on more pronounced geographical asymmetries of position and interest, which tends to reinforce extant degrees of inter-state mistrust, especially in situations where shared hydrological data is in scarce supply, downstream-state actors are correspondingly ill-equipped to distinguish key intrinsic economic operations of upstream installations, especially where the latter permit substantial water diversions, from potential instrumental uses of these mechanisms to accomplish larger political goals (as suggested in Naff and Matson 1984, 184, Gleick 1993, 86–89).

2.5.2 Liberalism in Transboundary Water Relations

Despite their predominant propensity towards conflict, upstream–downstream interactions virtually never escalate to the point of inter-state 'water war' and cooperation is prevalent to varying degrees (Deudney 1999, Homer-Dixon 1999,

Allan 2002, Williams 2003, Kibaroglu et al. 2005, Selby 2005, Conca 2006, United Nations 2006). Liberal International Relations theory, especially Neoliberal Institutionalism, which encompasses regime theory, argues that anarchy makes cooperation difficult but not impossible where states stand to obtain larger absolute gains than each could otherwise get from unilateral action (Keohane 1989, Baldwin 1993). In the prisoner's dilemma game that exemplifies the cooperation-underanarchy problematique, uncertainty centres on whether potential partners will honour an agreement. Cooperation is allowed by the fact that most states interact over an indefinite time period and can thereby respond to each other's behaviour in tit-for-tat fashion if they can also agree on how to define, detect and punish cheating and other forms of non-compliant behaviour (Axelrod and Keohane 1993).

Certain problems related to international watercourses lend themselves more easily to cooperative resolution than others. Salient geographical and hydrological characteristics facilitate, to a greater or lesser extent, the formation of cooperative international regimes to manage economic uses of different multi-state systems of freshwater (LeMarquand 1977, 7–11). Situations where the relevant actors enjoy a relatively more symmetrical relationship to a common supply of water and non-consumptive uses of water (i.e., those, such as flood control or hydropower, that return withdrawn water, in the same quantity and quality, to the river channel) prevail should be the most conducive to cooperative arrangements, as indicated by numerous agreements regulating joint uses of 'international rivers' that demarcate boundaries. Cooperation confronts slightly more formidable obstacles when upstream and downstream states are negotiating to apportion the costs of 'integrated development opportunities' involving the production of new public goods, such as flood control or hydropower, but becomes even more difficult in relation to the question of how to induce individual and collective restraint on the part of symmetrically arrayed consumptive users of a common pool resource before it is depleted. However, the hardest test for Liberal IR theory involves the resolution of 'upstream–downstream conflicts', where asymmetry of territorial position is compounded by the predominance of consumptive uses of water. In these cases, incentives for cooperation, assuming that upstream states posses a preponderance of military deterrence capabilities, may come from the upstream states' countervailing cooperative interests, for instance, in protecting economic and social values attached to occupation of downstream position in other disputed river basins or in bolstering a 'good neighbourly' image for the purposes of promoting larger economic and political goals *(Ibid: 10–12)*.

Territorial proximity raises the potential value of positive relations with downstream states. Upstream states now espouse 'limited sovereignty', which entails liability for 'significant' harm to downstream uses (Wapner 1998, 280), rather than 'absolute territorial sovereignty', and often engage in prior notification and consultation related to project construction. Embrace of the 'equitable and reasonable utilization' principle, reflecting recognition of the historically laggard pattern of development upstream, may also imply the need for ancillary data gathering and exchange efforts, which can mitigate the severity of competition and nurture habits of cooperation (Benvenisti 1996, 401). Indeed, Neoliberal Institutionalism, the direct successor to Regime theory, identifies the need for information as a core part of regime demand (Hasenclever et al., 33–34). In the larger context of trade ties and institutional integration, which lessen the economic and political exigencies of the perceived need for self-sufficiency or territorial conquest (Deudney 1999, 205- 207), upstream states may be more predisposed to limit their own allocatively inefficient consumption of water in agriculture. 'Win–win' forms of cooperation identify opportunities for assembling 'baskets of benefits' that enhance each party's absolute welfare gains by transcending issues of volumetric allocation to encompass financial flows, hydropower trade, data sharing and peace agreements, all of which nonetheless require institutional capacity-building with the assistance of such key outside actors as the EU, World Bank and the UN Development Program *(United Nations 2006: 224–231).*

2.5.3 Constructivism in Transboundary Water Relations

Perhaps innately aware of the aforementioned risk of rhetorical entrapment, the representatives even of powerful upstream states purposefully and carefully craft discourse suiting their interests in regime formation and collaborative action. As international water law presents a logical and salient discursive template by which regimes may be shaped in certain directions, and not others, for specific river basins, reaching a consensus agreement on the textual content of this law becomes as politicized a task as that of negotiating particular basin accords. The 1997 UN (framework) Convention on the Law of the Non-navigational Uses of International Watercourses passed only after arduous negotiation and never obtained enough ratifications to become effective. The document provided no practical guidelines on reconciling its competing master principles, 'equitable and reasonable utilization' (Article 5) and the 'obligation not to cause significant harm' (Article 7), or on resolving competing claims, and fewer basin accords embody either or both of these principles, as well as that of prior notification (Conca 2006, 110–118; United Nations 2006, 218).

In its earliest gestation, international water law barely transcended crude codification of asymmetrical positions, with upstream states favouring 'absolute territorial sovereignty' and downstream states embracing 'absolute territorial integrity'. The current prevailing theory of 'limited territorial sovereignty' (Kibaroglu et al. 2005, 20) signals progressive movement towards reasoned compromise, since it entails that the predominantly upstream development of 'equitable uses', which does not mean equal divisions of water (Gleick 1993, 106–107), needs to take downstream 'acquired rights' into account (Waterbury 2002, 28). The implied limitation on states' rights to exploit transboundary resources signals emergence of a shared understanding that individual states may be held liable for 'damaging other states ecosystems' (Wapner 1998, 280). Moreover, the fact that the Convention even contains an 'obligation not to cause significant harm' puts downstream interests on a level legal footing (Conca 2006, 100–101). Watercourse agreements that proscribe 'significant harm' also tend to provide for prior notification, data exchange, and peaceful dispute resolution, the latter two appearing more frequently in general, while accords enshrining 'equitable use' often include corollary water allocations (Conca 2006, 114–118).

Providing a weak foundation for articulating shared conceptions of a 'common' resource, international legal developments offer an even more precarious basis for substantively more complex collaboration within the holistic framework of 'integrated watershed management'. Most agreements are dyadic, even for multi-riparian basins. Fulfilling an 'obligation not to cause significant harm' can be consistent with preserving ecological values and human needs (Waterbury 2002, 29), but most of the few basin accords upholding this principle have not 'created significant entry points for environmental protection' (Conca 2006, 118). Some even argue that, precisely by enticing disputants to advance flexible negotiating positions, contrary to fixed rules that create deadlock, the vague standard of 'equitable use' may allow for periodic water reallocations that respond to newly emergent needs (Benvenisti 1996). Others similarly emphasize the value of non-binding 'contextual regimes' as the basis for 'international ecosystem law', which emphasizes 'future-oriented, flexible and adaptable frameworks that nonetheless allow for the elaboration of specific norms on individual issues' (Brunée and Toope 1997, 42). Here, third parties might supply not only material assistance, but also shared knowledge of 'best practices' and non-state-centric modes of discourse.

2.5.4 Realism, Liberalism and Constructivism in Turkey's Hydro Diplomacy

Realism in Turkey's Hydro Diplomacy

Turkey's water diplomacy fits the Realist paradigm in a number of respects. Disputes over the Euphrates and Tigris rivers occupy a prominent position on Turkey's water-related foreign-policy agenda because of these rivers' national prominence. While Turkey's total mean annual run-off amounts to 186 billion cubic meters (BCM), only 112 BCM is estimated to be cost effective to develop, and the Euphrates-Tigris accounts for nearly 47 percent of this latter figure. The country's water-use demands are also rising. The supply being utilized is expected to increase due to: population growth, which could lower Turkey's annual per-capita water supply from 1,500 cubic meters to 1,000 cubic meters between 2000 and 2030; the need to improve upon respective 55 and 36 percent municipal access rates to sewage and wastewater treatment services; and efforts to augment domestic hydropower to meet more of Turkey's increasing energy needs, estimated to reach 285 billion kilowatt hours (kWh) in 2010. By then, the Southeast Anatolia Project (GAP) is projected to harness Euphrates-Tigris rivers' water to supply nearly 10 percent of Turkey's energy and one-fifth of its irrigable land (Kibaroglu et al. 2005, 5–9). At the same time, Turkey's upstream position on both branches of this river basin offers commensurably advantageous access. Downstream concerns stem from the capacity of Turkey's five Euphrates dams to impound nearly three years' worth of annual average water supply.

The slowing of the GAP does not imply Turkey's concession of sovereignty over Euphrates-Tigris water. While Turkish governments abjure the principle of 'absolute territorial sovereignty' in favour of 'limited sovereignty', calling the Euphrates a 'transboundary' river imputes an exclusive right to exploit it until it flows into Syria. Former Prime Minister Demirel even stated that 'water is an upstream resource and downstream users cannot tell us how to use our resources', with others in authoritative positions echoing that the 'rivers concerned are not subject to international rules' (quoted in Bagis 1997, 577). The prevailing position is usually articulated more subtly. Since 1984, Turkish experts have consistently advocated the 'Three-Staged Plan for Optimal, Equitable and Reasonable Utilization of the Transboundary Watercourses of the Euphrates-Tigris Basin', which proposes to inventory all riparians' water and land resources before evaluating both sets jointly in order to determine actual water needs and to convene a joint body to assemble and exchange data on temporal fluctuations in the level of these needs (Kibaroglu et al. 2005, 61).

Liberalism in Turkey's Hydro Diplomacy

Despite the high profile of its riverine water controversies, Turkey has signed accords to allocate streamflow in common watercourses, establish joint technical bodies, fund construction projects, exchange data and provide prior notification and consultation in relation to its infrastructure. As expected, Turkey faces stronger issue-specific incentives to cooperate on freshwater usage in shared river basins where it is downstream, but has also committed itself to joint action with respect to the use of river water that originates on Turkish territory but later demarcates one of its international boundaries. Conversely, arrangements where Turkey occupies a purely upstream position seem less committal, but bear some similarity in certain substantive terms to other agreements. Moreover, as in similar cases elsewhere in the world, Turkey's water-related interactions with various neighbours in particular basins are influenced not only by the territorial configuration of the watercourse in question but also by the quality of its overall bilateral relations with those neighbours (Brunée and Toope 1997, 47; United Nations 2006, 220).

Downstream position provides a logical incentive to collaborate. Conversely, Turkey's downstream vulnerability on the smaller Orontes River, which also demarcates a 31-km section of the international boundary via a 1939 Franco-Turkish treaty, was until recently aggravated by tense relations with Syria and a long-standing dispute over Hatay province. However, the 1998 Adana Accord gave a new impetus to cooperation, manifested in a 2004 trade agreement implying Syrian recognition of Turkey's possession of Hatay and an accord creating a bilateral technical commission to study building a joint dam on the Orontes (see Scheumann/Tereci/Sagsen in this volume; Kibaroglu et al. 2005, 71). An important part of efforts to build this 'friendship dam' involves positive potential linkages to this area of energy cooperation (Turkish Daily News 2007).

Turkey has engaged in cooperation even where it enjoys upstream status. Even the highly competitive Tigris-Euphrates rivers feature tenuous cooperation. While signed in close proximity to a security accord, the 1987 Turco-Syrian Protocol nonetheless informally committed Ankara to a 50–50 allocation of Euphrates water to Syria. Moreover, before Ataturk Dam's 1990 filling, Turkish authorities engaged, though not to downstreamers' satisfaction, in prior notifica- tion, consultation and streamflow releases from other dams (Gleick 1993, 107–108). Some contend that Turkey's dams even provide the public good of flow regulation (Bilen 1997, 68–73, Allan 2002, 255–266). Information sharing has taken place, and, while it cannot overcome larger political tensions, the 1983–1993 Joint Technical Committee (JTC) meetings, where Turkey advocated its Three-Stage

Plan, expressed commitment to finding a cooperative solution. In low-profile settings, water scarcity may propel conservation and innovation efforts, such as those to reduce the three-quarters share of Turkey's water use in irrigated agriculture (Kibaroglu et al. 2005, 8).

Constructivism in Turkey's Hydro Diplomacy

Understood in an International Relations Constructivist mode, Turkey has exerted itself in two key ways vis-à-vis its transboundary waters. In relation to the Tigris-Euphrates rivers, it has tried to eschew a 'water rich' image, while implicitly accepting the risk, albeit low, that its advocacy of 'equitable and reasonable utilization', if accepted by Syria and Iraq as a basis for negotiating a permanent tripartite treaty, could transform an instrumental negotiating stance into a principled basis for committing Turkey to provide a certain flow of water downstream. In this vein of logic, Turkey's ongoing EU accession process may entail outside introduction of 'green' discourse at the expense of the technocratic language that constitutes the dominant frame within which its transboundary water uses have been developed and negotiated.

Several factors fostered Turkey's politicized 'water rich' profile. In proximity to announcement of the Three-Stage Plan, a 1984 government study overestimated excess runoff in Turkey's 26 drainage basins at two thirds of the total (Kolars and Mitchell 1991, 291, 294–295). Ozal's 'Peace Pipeline' proposal, a component part of the 1987 Protocol that also pledged to deliver 500 cubic meters per second of Euphrates water at Syria's border, also implied that Turkey could compensate for any permanent shortage there by supplying water from its wholly domestic Seyhan and Ceyhan rivers. Moreover, the 1989 GAP Master Plan underestimated future maximum Euphrates water consumption at 10.4 BCM, equivalent to 335 cubic meters per second (Kolars 1994, 75), thus dovetailing with the 1990 Syro-Iraqi demand of 700 cubic meters per second (Gruen 1993, 103–104). Finally, in 1991, eminent hydrologist Malin Falkenmark placed Turkish per capita water supply at 4,600 cubic meters per year, much higher than Syria's 1,300 (Gruen 2000, 3). Ankara later moved to undermine the language of plenty, as when the foreign minister stated in 1992 that, 'We are ready to cooperate in this respect [water], but I must point out that.... Turkey is not a country which has abundant water resources. We may soon face problems in meeting our own needs' (quoted in Beschorner 1992, 44). This discursive turn suggests that even powerful upstream states remain conscious of the need to attend to the normative legitimacy of their bargaining positions. While Turkey represents one of three states that voted against the 1997 UN Convention, its complaints about what it claims to be the undue importance attached to the 'obligation not to cause significant harm' and inclusion of mandatory dispute settlement have some broader intellectual resonance (Benvenisti 1996, Brunée and Toope 1997, Waterbury 2002).

Conversely, discourse may also impel Turkey towards more intensive cooperation. Turkish experts' consistent advocacy of the Three-Stage Plan, embodying their preferred technocratic language, is premised on a basic understanding that water scarcity is non-negligible and requires curtailing those downstream claims, based on non-scientifically formulated mathematical quotas, that Turkey can 'reasonably' expect to fulfill within the spirit of 'equitable utilization' (Kibaroglu et al. 2005, 61–62). If multilateral relations improve and basin societies become more receptive to freer and more transparent exchanges of ideas and data, downstream actors may become willing to invoke the principle of 'equitable and reasonable utilization' to defend values associated with environmental restoration of endangered ecosystems, like the Mesopotamian Marshlands in southern Iraq and their inhabitants' unique traditions, to the extent that an argument can be credibly made for how and which upstream activities are as damaging now as actions by Saddam Hussein's Baathist regime were in pre-2003 history (Kibaroglu et al. 2005, 32–36, 86–90).

At first glance, Realist theories provide a useful analytical framework for understanding Turkey's water diplomacy, the tenor of which predominantly reflects the mixture of material incentives for competition suggested by its respective geographical positions on various transboundary watercourse systems. For instance, the country's governments have displayed their greatest reluctance to relax their bargaining stance on the Tigris-Euphrates system, both because of the nature of issues specific to that basin and to compensate for a weaker position on the Orontes River. As Liberalism would anticipate, in the latter cases, extraneous economic inducements, especially in the form of trade ties, exist to some degree.

However, the overall quality of Turkish cooperation on this issue remains suboptimal. As constructivist analysis might suggest, this is in part the result of implicit discursive efforts to avoid having to play a role of basin-wide provider of Tigris-Euphrates water, which would be more normatively appropriate for a country with a 'water rich' identity. On the other hand, the discourse of 'equitable and reasonable utilization' could, albeit with low probability at present due to downstream-state actors' reluctance to embrace it (reflecting what seems to be a gaping deficit of shared social knowledge of the problem at hand), form a principled basis for conducting ongoing dialogue leading to agreement on more favourable apportionments of Euphrates-Tigris water to downstream states, but in explicit service of inchoate ecosystem values, the benefits of which might diffuse more widely to current and future populations at large *(Kibaroglu, Scheumann, Kramer 2011: 197–212)*.

In our opinion, Turkey is guided by the 'limited sovereignty' and sometimes even 'absolute territorial sovereignty' principles in the governance of transboundary waters. This is possible due to the fact that Turkey is an upstream country in the case of the Euphrates, Tigris, Kura, Araks, Corukh rivers and a downstream country in the case of the Orontes and Maritsa rivers. This means that Turkey has basically no problem as a downstream country. Turkey's main problem in the case of Maritsa River is flood prevention (abundance of water, not scarcity) and Turkey's dependence on the Orontes River is insignificant.

In the empirical part of the work, we are going to show the manifestations of realism/neorealism, liberalism and constructivism in the Euphrates-Tigris basin. However, before addressing Turkey's water policy in the Euphrates-Tigris basin, we consider it necessary to present in general terms what hydro diplomacy, hydro policy, water law (1997 UN Water Convention) are, etc. (general introduction) (Chapter 1).

We are going to use the example of Turkey in the following chapters to emphasize how that upstream country strives to become as self-sufficient as possible in the water sector in accordance with neorealism (Chapter 3), and how the downstream countries Syria and Iraq are trying to prevent it through various strategies (actions) (Chapter 5).

We will also emphasize that Turkey's hydro diplomacy corresponds to the realist paradigm in a number of ways, and in that context we will present the characteristics of the Euphrates and Tigris rivers, their importance not only for Turkey, but also for other riparian countries (Chapter 2), the importance of water disputes in Turkey's political agenda (Chapter 4). It will be presented how Turkey uses the water factor not only against itself, but also against the Kurds of Syria and Iraq (Chapter 5).

In the empirical part of the work, we will also highlight the manifestations of liberalism in Turkey's hydro policy, according to which states can gain greater benefits from cooperation than from unilateral actions, and we will fix that Turkey cooperates even it has upstream country status (Chapter 6). Turkey is a downstream country in the Orontes River Basin and therefore has a vulnerability, which slightly pushes it to cooperate with Syria, a middlestream hegemon country (Chapter 6).

It should be noted that Turkey, an upstream country, sometimes defending the right of "limited territorial sovereignty", thus feels responsible towards the downstream countries, despite its contradictions regarding river flow. As a result,

Turkey has signed accords to allocate streamflow in common watercourses, establish joint technical bodies, fund construction projects, exchange data and provide prior notification and consultation in relation to its infrastructure (Chapters 4 and 6).

Finally, we want to emphasize the evolution of Turkey's hydro policy over the decades, that is, the hardening and softening of Turkey's positions, analyze their motives. In particular, we would like to emphasize that the changes in Turkey's positions were mainly related to the degree of its strengthening/weakening, as well as the situation of downstream countries. When Turkey did not have a great advantage over Syria and Iraq (in the twentieth century) with the 8 points of power mentioned by Hans Morgenthau, it was relatively more tend to cooperate on water issues with those countries, it was less tend to use water as leverage against neighboring countries.

However, since the second decade of the twenty-first century, when Turkey continued its rise meanwhile Syria and Iraq were in a worse situation, Turkey began to use water more as leverage against neighboring countries. Realism and liberalism, as well as constructivism, thus precede and follow each other in Turkey's hydro policy. In this context we can say the same about offensive and defensive realism, which are also precede and follow each other. And it will probably continue in the future, depending on who will be the authorities of Turkey, as well as Syria and Iraq, and what will be the condition of those riparian countries.

3 Hydropolicy and Hydropolitical Interdependence

3.1 Water and Interdependence in World Politics

3.1.1 The Importance of Water

According to a UN report on the state of the world's water (2018), global water use has increased by a factor of six over the past 100 years and continues to grow steadily at a rate of about 1% per year. Water use is expected to continue increasing at the global level, as a function of population growth, economic development and changing consumption patterns, among other factors. The world population is expected to increase from 7.7 billion in 2017 to between 9.4 and 10.2 billion by 2050, with two thirds of the population living in cities. More than half of this anticipated growth is expected to occur in Africa (+1.3 billion), with Asia (+0.75 billion) expected to be the second largest contributor to future population growth. Over the same period (2017–2050), global gross domestic product (GDP) is expected to increase by a factor of 2.5 (OECD), although with large differences among and within countries. Global demand for agricultural and energy production (mainly food and electricity), both of which are water-intensive, is expected to increase by roughly 60% and 80% respectively by 2025 *(UN 2018: 10).*

At the same time, the global water cycle is intensifying due to global warming, with wetter regions generally becoming wetter and drier regions becoming even drier. These aspects of global change illustrate the need for swift planning and execution of strategic, reasonable and effective management and countermeasures against deteriorating water security. Global water demand will continue to grow significantly over the next two decades. Contemporary global water demand has

H. Gabrielyan, *Turkey's Water Policy as Part of the Political Strategy*, Politik, Wirtschaft und Gesellschaft im Spannungsverhältnis der Regionen Südosteuropa und Mittlerer Osten, https://doi.org/10.1007/978-3-658-44070-1_3

been estimated at about 4,600 km3 per year and projected to increase by 20%–30% to between 5,500 and 6,000 km3 per year by 2050. 70% of global water demand goes to agriculture, 20% to industry and 10% to households.

Agriculture accounts for about 70% of global water withdrawals, the vast majority of which are used for irrigation. Yet global estimates for annual irrigation water demand are fraught with uncertainty. This is not merely due to a lack of monitoring and reporting on water used for irrigation, but also to the inherently erratic nature of the practice itself. The amounts of water used for irrigation at any given time will vary with crop type and their various growing seasons, and also depend on cropping practices and variability in local soil and climatic conditions, not to mention any changes in the land area equipped for irrigation. The efficiency of different irrigation techniques will also have a direct impact on overall water use. This is what makes projecting future water demand for irrigation so difficult. For example, whereas have projected increases in global crop irrigation water requirements for 2050 to be somewhere between 23% and 42% above the level in 2010, the Food and Agriculture Organization of the United Nations estimated a 5.5% increase in water withdrawals for irrigation from 2008 to 2050.

Water use by **industry**, which account for roughly 20% of global withdrawals, is dominated by energy production, which is responsible for approximately 75%, with the remaining 25% of industrial water withdrawals being used for manufacturing. Projections by suggest the overall water demand from industry will increase across all the regions of the world, with the exception of Northern America and Western and Southern Europe. Industrial demand could increase with up to eight times (in relative terms) in regions such as Western, Middle, Eastern and Southern Africa, where industries currently account for a very small proportion of total water use. Industrial demand should also increase significantly (up to two and half times) in Southern, Central and Eastern Asia. According to the OECD (2012), water demand for manufacturing is projected to increase by 400% over the period 2000–2050. Global water withdrawals for energy production have been projected to rise by one-fifth over the period 2010–2035, whereas water consumption would increase by 85% driven by the shift towards more efficient power plants with more advanced cooling systems (that reduce water withdrawals but increase consumption) and increased production of biofuels.

Domestic water use, which roughly accounts for the remaining 10% of global water withdrawals, is expected to increase significantly over the 2010–2050 period in nearly all regions of the world, with the exception of Western Europe where it remains constant. In relative terms, the greatest increases in domestic demand should occur in African and Asian sub-regions where it could more than triple, and it could more than double in Central and South America. This anticipated growth can be primarily attributed to an anticipated increase in water supply services in urban settlements *(Ibid 2018: 11)*.

Water is first and foremost an essential biological need, a fundamental precondition for human life. Without an adequate input of potable water, the human body cannot survive or grow. Water is a symbol in many religions and cultures for purification and replenishment, and is regarded as something to rejoice over. Large amounts of water are also needed for personal hygiene, sanitation, and other household activities, including cooking, cleaning, and laundry. Furthermore, huge quantities of freshwater are needed for agriculture, fisheries, mining, industrial production, electricity generation, riverine navigation, maintenance of ecological assets and biodiversity, promotion of tourism, and many other societal demands. This multiple use potential of freshwater, especially transboundary water resources, combined with the certainly of growing water scarcities in many arid and semiarid regions of the world, makes hydropolitics between riparian states that share international river basins one of the most urgent, complex, and contentious issues that the developing countries and the international community will have no face and resolve in the next century. The resulting political, economic, social and environmental interdependencies give water resources the crucial potential to either foster cooperation or exacerbate conflict. Wherever nations share common water supplies, their ability to meet their water needs will be interdependent *(Elhance 1999: 3–4)*.

3.1.2 Hydropolitical Interdependence

We leave in an era of interdependence. This vague phrase express a poorly understood but widespread feeling that the very nature of world politics is changing. The power of nations—that age—old touchstone of analysts and statesmen—has become more elusive: "calculations of power are even more delicate and deceptive than in previous ages". Henry Kissinger, though deeply rooted in the classical tradition, has stated that "the traditional agenda of intemational affairs—the balance among major powers, the security of nations—no longer defines our perils or our possibilities.... Now we are entering a new era. Old international patterns are crumbling; old slogans are uninstructive; old solutions are unavailing. The world has become interdependent in economics, in communications, in human aspirations.

Interdependence affects world politics and the behavior of states; but governmental actions also influence patterns of interdependence. By creating or accepting procedures, rules, or institutions for certain kinds of activity, governments regulate and control transnational and interstate relations. Political leaders often use interdependence rhetoric to portray interdependence as a natural necessity, as a fact to which policy (and domestic interest groups) must adjust, rather than as a situation partially created by policy itself. They usually argue that conflicts of interest are reduced by interdependence, and that cooperation alone holds the answer to world problems.

In common parlance, dependence means a state of being determined or significantly affected by external forces. Interdependence, most simply defined, means mutual dependence. Interdependence in world politics refers to situations characterized by reciprocal effects among countries or among actors in different countries. To understand the role of power in interdependence, we must distinguish between two dimensions, sensitivity and vulnerability. Sensitivity involves degrees of responsiveness within a policy framework—how quickly do changes in one country bring costly changes in another, and how great are the costly effects? It is measured not merely by the volume of flows across borders but also by the costly effects of changes in transactions on the societies or governments. Sensitivity interdependence is created by interactions within a framework of policies. Sensitivity assumes that the framework remains unchanged. Sensitivity interdependence can be social or political as well as economic.

The vulnerability dimension of interdependence rests on the relative availability and costliness of the alternatives that various actors face. Vulnerability can be defined as an actor's liability to suffer costs imposed by external events even after policies have been altered. Since it is usually difficult to change policies quickly, immediate effects of external changes generally reflect sensitivity dependence. Vulnerability dependence can be measured only by the costliness of making effective adjustments to a changed environment over a period of time. Vulnerability is particularly important for understanding the political structure of interdependence relationships. In a sense, it focuses on which actors are "the definers of the ceteris paribus clause," or can set the rules of the game. Vulnerability is clearly more relevant than sensitivity. Vulnerability applies to sociopolitical as well as politico—economic relationships. Vulnerability interdependence includes the strategic dimension that sensitivity interdependence omits, but this does not mean that sensitivity is politically unimportant. Different types of interdependence lead to potential political influence, but under different constraints *(Keohane & Nye 2012: 10–16)*.

One of them is hydropolitical interdependence. Shared waters have the potential of generating highly complex relations, as the actions of one country can undermine the interests of its neighbors. This is what Elhance *(Elhance 1999: 13)* labeled hydropolitical interdependence. Disagreements over water usually take place on countries where there is a history of animosity and resentment, however, it must be pointed out, not always water will be the pivot for disputes that might arise. Generally, water constitutes an aggravating factor of a pre-existing framework of tension catalyzed by a scenario of high hydrological interdependence. Hence, it becomes more useful and feasible to study hydropolitics as one of the factors to be considered in security policies, a factor capable of generating additional stress in conflict situations, and not as the primary cause of their outbreak, though on occasion, it is presented as the later *(Krishna-Hensel 2016: 3–5)*.

Nature does not respect national borders; human beings seem incapable of managing their affairs without them. Nature has also not endowed every place or nation on earth with the same type and amount of resources. Here in lie the roots of likely interstate conflict and cooperation over essential and scarce natural resources. Hydropolitics is the systematic study of conflict and cooperation between states over water resources that transcend international borders. Hydropolitics in international river basins is a very complex, multidimensional, and multidisciplinary subject *(Elhance 1999: 3–4)*.

Thus, water is becoming more and more important in the world than oil, and water problem will worsen significantly in coming decades due to various issues, including the growth of the planet's population. Climate change is predicted to bring about an increase in the variability of water increasing problems in transboundary river basins. Downstream countries can be sensitive and vulnerable to midstream and upstream country's water projects on transboundary rivers. The likelihood of water wars in the world will increase, especially in water-scarce regions, such as the Middle East.

3.2 The Rise of Hydro-Diplomacy

3.2.1 Transboundary Water Governance

The more than 263 surface water basins shared between two or more states account for roughly 60 per cent of global freshwater flows and cover almost half the earth's land surface area. Added to this is the large number of transboundary aquifers, constituting the primary source of water for over two billion people in the world. The availability, distribution and control of freshwater resources have been at the centre of the human story since the start of the Neolithic revolution roughly 12,000 years ago. With the advent of the modern nation state and its attendant emphasis on sovereignty, self-sufficiency and rivalry, it comes as no surprise that interactions between states over shared watercourses have at times been tense and conflictual. Water, as a fugitive resource, respects neither political boundaries nor commonly accepted notions of fairness or equity. Variable in both time and space, water has defied the efforts of politicians, economists and engineers to tame its capricious nature. No wonder much of the literature has focused on the possibility of disputes over water spilling over into outright conflict between states. Water is an indispensible input to almost all human activity—manufacturing products, delivering services, producing food, transporting goods and sustaining life itself.

The fact that water cannot readily be substituted by other resources leads, in part, to the long-term cooperation between states over its management and development. Disputes over water do occur, but they very rarely develop into greater conflicts as this would jeopardize the use of the resource itself. Instead, states either reach a stalemate or deadlock over their shared waters, or manage to cooperate to some limited degree. This has been described by John Galtung as a 'negative peace'—merely the absence of violence, without further constructive collaboration. In cases of water scarcity, where the likelihood of disputes between states over shared waters may be greater, the corollary is that there is also more evidence of cooperation. This cooperation is promoted and enhanced by institutions, such as laws or agreements, organizations and customary practices, which have been developed either on a bilateral or a multilateral level between states. These institutions (formal or informal) offer a forum where disputes can be discussed and amicably settled and may lead to the sustainable development of shared water resources, making a contribution to national and regional socioeconomic development. In the context of global change these institutions are bulwarks against the pressures introduced through natural climatic variability, resource degradation from socioeconomic development and climate change. Indeed, assuming sufficient institutional development, transboundary waters can become avenues of cooperation between countries, contributing to socioeconomic development and regional integration.

In the Basins at Risk (BAR) study carried out by Wolf and colleagues it is proposed that 'the likelihood and intensity of conflict rises as the rate of change within a basin exceeds the institutional capacity to absorb that change'. Rapid changes in the institutional framework (such as key staff members leaving) or in physical factors (climate, water demand, demographics etc.) which outpace the institutional capacity to absorb such change are at the heart of most water conflicts. Thus, where a well-capacitated institution is in place (encompassing human resources, legislative framework, financial sustainability and political will, among other factors), the chances of being able to withstand the pressures of global change are enhanced. This can improve the potential for cooperation between basin states and even lead to the co-management and co-development of shared water resources, shifting the balance towards cooperative management and away from the lack of development associated with the stalemate situation of a 'negative peace'. This is an important aspect considering that various parts of the developing world are in the early stages of creating water infrastructure (dams, inter-basin transfers etc.) which will have transboundary impacts *(Earle, Jägerskog, Öjendal 2010: 1).*

The use and allocation of water in transboundary basins is both a source of tension and an opportunity to promote cooperative practices and build collaborative institutions. The extent to which these conflict risks can be managed and the significant cooperative opportunities realized will depend on the level of political engagement demonstrated by both basin countries and the international community. Water management in many transboundary basins is highly politicized and has a considerable impact on conflict prevention, regional stability, environmental peace-making and international governance. Therefore, transboundary water governance is a domain that should elicit great interest in the foreign policy community. Competition over shared waters should warrant strong interest from foreign policy makers. Foreign policy can help improve transboundary water governance, and transboundary water governance can give foreign policy makers a toehold for making progress on crucial foreign policy interests. Thus, encouraging greater cooperation over transboundary waters offers significant prospects for the resolution of political conflicts and greater regional integration. Transboundary waters constitute a promising entry point for diplomats aiming for high peace dividends. Transboundary basin management is frequently eclipsed by intra-basin politics, which in turn is often compounded by power asymmetries. In this context, a focus on technical solutions for shared basins is often not enough; it needs to be complemented by political engagement. Foreign policy makers can provide crucial support in this respect, even if their engagement also entails risks by inserting (perceived) outside agendas *(Pohl 2014: I).*

Transboundary waters need greater political and diplomatic engagement[1]. Yet they also require better harnessing of the synergies between 'high' and 'low' politics, and between foreign, development, economic, and environmental policies. Improving water use and/or adapting to the effects of climate change can help

[1] In our opinion, in some cases, hydro policy can not only significantly affect foreign policy, but also predetermine it. We can also say that hydro policy is closely linked to domestic policy and domestic politics can sometimes even predeterminehydro policy. We will see the assurances of all this in the last chapters by the example of Turkey.

prevent conflicts by sparing scarce resources and providing better livelihoods. Foreign policy efforts can make such work more effective by embedding it into broader transboundary cooperation and efforts at regional economic and political integration: greater scale and scope in cooperation lead to greater potential benefits. Yet to achieve such synergies across different sectors requires express political interest, not least in order to give bureaucracies sufficient incentive to invest in closer collaboration.

Foreign policy engagement on transboundary water governance is needed to contain the conflict potential of shared waters. Yet water may also present a 'bridging resource'. Joint water management across borders can further bilateral and regional cooperation. Water can serve as one of few paths of dialogue in otherwise confrontational relationships. The need to cooperate on water management might (be used to) generate the political space necessary to address other contentious issues. It could thus serve as a tool for achieving positive spill-overs in terms of regional cooperation. One example is the case of the Itaipu project between Brazil and Paraguay. The two countries could not agree on the border in the river, a certain stretch with various falls. In order to end this long-lasting border conflict, in 1973 they agreed to build a jointly owned hydropower facility. Uncharacteristically for decision-making on hydropower infrastructure, this decision was taken by the two foreign ministries and then implemented jointly by both countries. Joint water management across borders can further regional cooperation.

There are several foreign policy objectives connected to transboundary water governance: facilitating the containment and resolution of conflicts in the short term; managing resources so that conflicts are avoided in the longer term; and harnessing water cooperation mechanisms to promote regional integration. Yet for all three purposes, there is a lack of agency at the international level. As a result, the international community faces huge challenges when it comes to systematically taking early action to both respond to emerging crises and reinforce cooperation. Foreign policy makers should therefore help to strengthen and connect existing international and transnational institutions for coordination so as to allow for concerted foreign policy approaches. The end game of solving conflicts over water is to build the appropriate institutions to safeguard and extend cooperation. This quest for closer cooperation should simultaneously seek to enhance the cross-sectoral synergies between 'high' and 'low' politics such that water-related technical and economic opportunities are used (or better used) to strengthen political efforts to prevent and resolve conflicts and vice versa *(Ibid: 9–10)*.

3.2.2 Technical Cooperation

Negotiations over water depend on the characteristics of the resource. Surface water negotiations typically focus on allocations and flows; negotiations over groundwater typically focus on storage. Both resources are hydrologically linked despite governance instruments that manage the resources independently. Water conflicts and negotiations are not easily handled without the assistance of specialists who can interpret causal chains. Because science remains at the core of water conflicts, it might be a source of conflict as well as the means of resolving conflicts *(Earle, Jägerskog, Öjendal 2010: 125)*.

Technical efforts that improve local and national water management can significantly contribute to safeguarding international security, just as foreign policy efforts can significantly contribute to the development and well-being of riparian people by helping them avoid conflict and harness the opportunities that closer cooperation brings about. For technical cooperation to realize its full potential, it also needs political support to overcome inertia and vested interests, to ensure broad ownership and legitimacy, and to convince political decision-makers of the necessity and benefits of cooperation (and of the consequences of non-cooperation). In seeking to support and build on technical collaboration, greater engagement by foreign policy makers could provide added value in three ways:

1) First, in contrast to technical experts and/or development agencies, foreign policy makers have the mandate to get involved in the political issues that often underlie water conflicts and to help mediate disputes, especially where these issues pertain to inter-governmental conflicts.
2) Second and related, foreign policy makers can play a helpful role through their political leverage and ability to get access to the highest political levels. Few foreign ministers or heads of government want to discuss the political challenges of bi- or multi-lateral cooperation on transboundary waters with 'technical' experts. Yet successful water negotiations often necessitate substantial compromises across several sectors, which can only be made at the highest level, not at the level of the water or development policy minister.
3) Third, foreign policy makers can help host country decision makers to defend international compromises domestically. They might be able to offer additional political gains in other issue areas, draw on their public diplomacy resources to directly intervene in the debate, or help government counterparts to couch these compromises in domestically palatable discourses *(Pohl 2014: 11)*.

In short, technical solutions alone can rarely resolve political problems. In the case of the Nile, for example, Egypt has historically taken most of the Nile's waters. Concurrently, the country's water reservoir, Lake Nasser, is losing far more water to evaporation than a hypothetical reservoir in Ethiopia would. Yet an external actor seeking to ease tensions in the basin by focusing on saving water may easily be perceived by the Egyptian government as hostile to its interests because conserving water might seem to imply putting the onus of adaptation on Egypt's political economy (in particular regarding its water-intensive agricultural practices), as well as a loss of control by relocating a potential reservoir beyond its borders. To achieve real progress, any outside support in identifying possible benefits of (closer) cooperation therefore needs to be carefully embedded in complementary diplomatic and political engagement *(Ibid: 15).*

This dynamic was insufficiently taken into account by the donor community, whose approach reflected the somewhat naive belief that once the technical opportunities and potential 'benefits beyond the river' became clear, political agreement would be much easier to reach. Technical support can of course be immensely helpful for reaching agreement, but is by itself often insufficient. The donor community's lack of political perspective was evident, for example, in an imprudent letter drafted in 2009 in response to political manoeuvring between basin governments. The letter's call for an 'inclusive agreement' was interpreted by several riparian governments as partial and supportive of Egypt's stance. It would be grossly unfair to blame the resulting deadlock over the planned Comprehensive Framework Agreement (CFA) on such missteps on the part of the donor community, but greater diplomatic sensitivity regarding intra-basin politics could have helped to mitigate the fall-out.

Politics is key in other basins, too. In South Asia, both Pakistan and Bangladesh have been quick to blame India for 'stealing water' from the Indus and Ganges basins. With respect to the Indian-built Farraka barrage, for example, which is used to divert Ganges basin water that would otherwise flow through Bangladesh, the issue has repeatedly been raised when either Bangladeshi or Indian domestic politics needed a culprit or diversionary conflict. Similar dynamics appear in other international basins. If there is political interest in creating or preserving conflict or deflecting blame (or even just a habitual prioritisation of thinking in terms of the national polity), technical solutions to water governance issues are obviously of little help. The political context must become more accommodating for technical solutions to be helpful, which in turn demands political-level engagement of would-be interveners. Simultaneously, such dynamics challenge technical experts to make their proposed solutions as politically palatable as possible.

Yet this is not to imply that primary responsibility for transboundary basins lies with these external actors (major donor countries). In fact, they can only support the riparian governments that are the direct actors and vehicles of water conflict and cooperation. The latter's foreign policy makers are thus crucial to "adding value" in all of the three manners mentioned above. Moreover, they are the necessary interlocutors of foreign policy makers from the international community. While they are usually part of the political struggles that complicate greater intra-basin cooperation, they can play a critical role through their ability to mediate disputes and frame and defend compromise and cooperation. Thus, many recommendations also—and often primarily—apply to the foreign policy makers of the riparian countries within a particular basin (which may overlap with the 'international community', as is notably the case with of India and China with respect to the basins that they do not share) *(Ibid: 12)*.

Preventing conflict over water requires better understanding among the water, climate and foreign policy communities, as does using water as an instrument for greater overall cooperation. Training the respective communities to this effect is a necessary first step. More capable national institutions can directly contribute to more sustainable water management; they can also encourage national governments to 'risk cooperation', as policy makers will feel reassured about their ability to estimate its effects. Climate change is predicted to bring about an increase in the variability of water, adding urgency to the task of building trust and a shared understanding of the challenges in transboundary basins. Building capacity and supporting institutions that are conducive to intra-basin cooperation will require funding. The amounts necessary, however, pale in comparison to the costs of the physical water infrastructure—as well as to the hypothetical cost of the conflicts that they can help to prevent *(Ibid: II)*.

Water governance remains largely a topic for technical and development cooperation. To be sure, this is often also the most appropriate setting. Many of the issues and challenges in water governance are technical—from gathering and analysing data to planning the use of water resources and setting standards for environmental impacts. Moreover, the development policy makers that often support such technical work have created comprehensive tools for addressing and resolving conflicts over water. Yet there are limits to what technical cooperation alone can achieve in conflictive political contexts.

The management of transboundary waters is often eclipsed by politics, which in turn is frequently complicated by power asymmetries in the basin. This poses tough challenges for the water and development communities whose instruments are hardly honed for enticing powerful states to play a constructive role. Domestic interests in conflict and power struggles often drive water policy in transboundary basins—sometimes more so than contending interests between countries. In such a situation, explicit political engagement is needed to nudge riparian governments towards more cooperative behaviour. The same is true for what is often the ultimate objective of engagement on transboundary waters: having cooperation on water spill over into broader and deeper political cooperation. These crucial challenges demand whole-of-government approaches in which foreign policy makers can play a crucial role.

In short, foreign policy can help improve transboundary water governance, and transboundary water governance can give foreign policy makers a toehold for making progress on regional integration and conflict prevention. Water issues in these basins often involve volatile political dynamics. In the context of limited institutionalisation of political and regional processes, water disputes can contribute to or even trigger conflict, whether at the local or transboundary level. In these cases where basin relationships are unstable, hydro-diplomacy may be able to build on technical collaboration to facilitate stability and peace. Such collaboration can and should simultaneously be used to foster regional integration by supporting the spill-over of cooperative practices into other sectors, such that water may become the nucleus of more formal integration via legal rules and shared institutions *(Ibid: 2)*.

Yet environmental changes may also nudge governments and other stakeholders towards closer cooperation. They will make better, collective management of transboundary waters more urgent—to safeguard sufficient availability of water, but also to ensure that the measures undertaken by governments in the interest of water security do not undermine it elsewhere. The role of dams is particularly crucial in this respect. Dams are important for clean energy, irrigation and flood control, and they have served as focal points for sharing benefits, from South America via West Africa to South Asia. Yet when undertaken unilaterally and/or without regard to their environmental consequences—for fishing, agriculture, sediment transport, and water availability downstream,—they simultaneously constitute the most dangerous flashpoints of conflict over water. The benefits of collaborative management of transboundary waters therefore cannot only be counted in the direct economic gains, but also in the benefits of conflicts avoided. The need for and prospective benefits of hydro-diplomacy are thus on the rise. Yet political awareness of and agency on the coming hydro-political challenges are currently lacking, as are the mediation and negotiation skills necessary to address them. This is where foreign policy makers need to step up their efforts. They have a range of useful tools to help alleviate the political consequences of transboundary water governance problems, and to foster greater cooperation.

There is no silver bullet, but foreign policy-makers should use their political mandate and leverage to ensure that the (potential) benefits of cooperation are fully considered. They can help identify cooperative opportunities, reduce uncertainty around them, provide incentives for their realisation, and help frame issues such that cooperation becomes politically more attractive than unilateral action. These skills should become a bigger asset in the international community's arsenal for addressing transboundary water governance issues *(Ibid: 41)*.

Given the substantial financial investments on the technical side of water infrastructure projects, there is a strong case for investing more on the diplomatic side. Puny by comparison, such investments can yield significant benefits where they help countries reach agreements that realise the rewards of greater scale in cooperation or at least help them avoid the costs of conflict. This report discussed various forms that such investments can take: • capacity building in national water institutions and foreign offices, with specific attention to the links between water management and conflict resolution; • advocacy for bilateral and multilateral confidence-building processes, such as the promotion of joint (scientific) risk assessments and joint water monitoring systems; • preventive engagement, including offers to support unbiased fact finding to reach transparency on water data and policy and the lending of 'good offices' in emerging or simmering conflicts; and • strengthening of the existing institutions and legal instruments to enable both early warning and a clear pathway to early action All these instruments are individually useful, and investing in them will often amount to 'no regret' policies. Yet as helpful as they could individually be, their effectiveness will certainly benefit from internationally coordinated engagement. Such engagement needs to build on strong, political-level involvement by the foreign policy community. Ultimately, strengthening foreign policy for transboundary waters hinges on creating and reinforcing international institutions that can channel political will into coherent action *(Ibid: 42)*.

3.2.3 Hydrohegemons

Riparians are all members of the international systems of nations. They are supposed to engage as equals, but in practice power relations are asymmetric in all river basins. There is always a hegemon. In river basins where all the economies have advanced industrialized economies these riparians can engage as equals. They do not even need a legal framework to be able to adopt outcomes that are equitable and reasonable. For example, in the river basins of Europe the riparians on the Rhine—Switzerland, France, Germany, The Netherlands and Belgium and the international corporations that utilize the Rhine waters—have cooperated to remedy pollution and protect the resource. International water law would have accelerated the improved joint management but its absence has not prevented the introduction of improved water quality standards and other environmentally appropriate measures. EU economies and many other industrialized economies have put in place environmental regulation, including the regulation of international transboundary waters that is many times more binding and intrusive than those evolving in the UN system.

Every basin is different in its water endowments and in its economic and its political asymmetries. The Nile Basin has ten riparians, and Egypt—in this case a downstream riparian—has enjoyed the position of hegemon for the past two centuries. Egypt has always had a GDP per capita many times that of the other riparians. An oil-enriched Sudan is beginning to catch up and as a consequence the relations over water in the Nile Basin are changing rapidly. But while the conflictual politics may intensify, the way to remedy the water deficits in both Egypt and the Sudan will be the same as it has been for the last three or more decades. Virtual water 'imports' from outside the basin will meet the increasing water deficits.

When awareness of water scarcity is perceived as an existential threat that evidently requires a remedy to protect the resource—that is to securitize it in the national interest—then measures beyond usual politics are taken by the hegemonic riparian to capture water resources. Note that securitization of water does not necessarily have to be based on actual scarcity and that perceptions matter. The extraordinary measures taken by the hegemonic riparian to capture water resources can include constructing dams; filling reservoirs; groundwater pumping; or the blocking of such interventions by other riparians, or threats to do any of these *(Earle, Jägerskog, Öjendal 2010: 20–21)*.

Hydro-hegemony is hegemony active at the basin scale, and occurs where control over transboundary flows is consolidated by the more powerful actor. Hydro-hegemony is taken as 'hegemony at the river basin level, achieved through water resource control strategies … that are enabled by the exploitation of existing power asymmetries. In other words, the more powerful basin state can exploit its advantage in a number of ways to ensure the configuration is in its favour. But an advantage in power does not necessarily mean an inequitable outcome. The hydro-hegemon (HH) also has the ability to lead on the basin, and create a more optimal outcome for all parties. This essentially occurs when this is perceived to bring gains to the hydro-hegemonic riparian, namely in terms of additional allocation of water resources. Furthermore, the so-called weaker ('non-hegemonic' is the preferred term) states are not always as weak or optionless as they are credited to be. Deeper examination of each case reveals evidence of counter-hegemonic mechanisms employed by the non-hegemonic states, with the aim to change the outcomes of water control and allocation towards a more equitable configuration.

While the basin hegemon is typically stronger in all fields of the various forms of power, it certainly does not follow that the non-hegemonic riparians are 'powerless'. Non-hegemonic riparians have capacities of bargaining power in particular which can be the main element of counter-hegemonic strategy. Through increased use of bargaining power, the non-hegemonic riparians can in theory 'level the playing field', influence the regional agendas and negotiations, and might contribute to change the hegemonic configuration in the basin.

Four forms of power can be used to evaluate hydro-hegemonic situations: geography; material power; bargaining power; and ideational power.

- **Geographical power.** One of the most influential types of overt power is that of riparian position. It relies on the distinct advantage that geography provides to an upstream state to manipulate the flows, i.e. to dam or divert them. In the Tigris (more precisely in the Euphrates—author) Basin, various Turkish governments have been exploiting this position with the continued construction of the GAP project. Consideration of Egypt's downstream yet dominative position on the Nile, however, shows that geographic position can be less influential and determining than other fields of power.
- **Material power.** This most visible form of power includes economic power, military might, technological prowess and international political and financial support. India's ability to undertake a massive river interlinking programme, with little consideration of the upstream or downstream protestations from Nepal and Bangladesh, serves as an example. Asymmetries in material power can influence the control exercised over water, in particular when combined with bargaining and ideational dimensions of power.
- **Bargaining power.** This field of power refers to the capability of actors to control the rules of the game and set agendas, in the sense of their ability to define the political parameters of an agenda. It is also evident in the power of actors to influence the terms of negotiations and agreements, through their ability to provide and/or influence incentives that may encourage weaker parties to comply. The relations between actors are crucial in determining the applicability of bargaining power. If each is legitimate in the eyes of the other, an actor with much less capacity in the material dimension of power may still retain influence over the so-called stronger actor. Daoudy (2009), for instance, recognizes the leverage that Syria was able to generate from linking non-water

issues (e.g. regional security, political alliances) in its Tigris and Euphrates negotiations with the much 'stronger' Turkey.

- **Ideational power.** This dimension refers to 'power over ideas' which represents the capacity of a riparian to impose and legitimize particular ideas and narratives. In sum, ideational power allows the basin hegemon to control the perceptions of the allocative configuration of the societies both in its own country and in the neighbouring riparian countries, thereby reinforcing its legitimacy. An abstract conception, ideational power may be exercised through knowledge structures, sanctioned discourse and the imposition of narratives and storylines. Hegemonic riparians may manipulate the interaction with the neighbouring riparians through a number of tools, including lack of knowledge and data sharing, or the use of time, silence or ambiguity. A refusal by the Israeli side to share data on water use by Israeli settle residents in the Palestinian West Bank, for example, can be understood as hegemonic use of ideational power. In persistently delaying negotiations over its preferred 1959 treaty on Nile allocations, Egypt is operating in the realm of ideational power by being present at the negotiations table and yet playing with time to maintain its hegemonic position in the Basin. A further example of ideational power common to the Nile, Jordan, and Tigris and Euphrates Basins is based on the 'sanctioning of the discourse'. Arguments against equitable sharing based on state security have been so common that the governments transform the water issues into matter of top national security (securitization process) that can now be used interchangeably to silence and/or overplay certain issues, according to the hegemon's interests *(Ibid: 31–32).*

Not all power is equal. The visual ('pillars') component of hydro-hegemony theory suggests that each of the four fields of power carries equal weight, by virtue that each pillar is the same width. The testing of the theory suggests, however, that some dimensions of power are more influential than others.

First of all, riparian position (geography-based power) was found to be relevant only under certain conditions. Position, it was found, can be an advantage to an upstreamer primarily if combined with material, financial and geopolitical power (e.g. Turkey in the Tigris–Euphrates Basin). An upstream position in the absence of advantage in the other pillars was found to be less relevant in various hydro-hegemonic configurations (e.g. Ethiopia and Equatorial riparians are weaker riparians in the Nile Basin). Furthermore, the importance of geography-based power was considered negligible in the case of transboundary aquifers.

Second, it was suggested that material power be considered more case-specific. Material power was considered a significant element of power in the Middle Eastern part of MENA, but much less so in the North African parts. The finding reflects the strong asymmetries that exist between Middle East states in terms of economic, military and geopolitical powers, and access to external support. Egypt, Israel and Turkey have clear material power supremacy over their neighbours. Power relations between the four North African countries—Morocco, Algeria, Tunisia and Libya—are relatively more symmetrical.

Third, bargaining power was understood as a double-faced power resource, which both hegemonic and non-hegemonic riparians can make use of to strengthen their position. The main message was: non-hegemonic riparians (Syria, Iraq, Jordan or Ethiopia) are not as weak as one might think, because they can (and typically do) exploit their bargaining power to counterbalance weaknesses in other power dimensions. The case study on the Nile Basin provides a clear example of how the non-hegemonic Nile riparians have been using collective bargaining power to counter the hegemonic power in the Basin, and how this has contributed to levelling the playing field among upstream and downstream riparians.

Finally, the practitioners also confirmed that the less visible forms of power—especially ideational power—are key explanatory factors for asymmetric power relations in transboundary basins. The ability to influence perceptions, the agenda, the discourse, or the timing of negotiations and projects are highly asymmetric among riparians. Israel, for example, benefited from its superiority in ideational power to co-opt its Jordanian co-riparian through the terms of the 1994 Jordanian–Israeli Agreement, though whether it was a strategic or short-sighted move from the Jordanian perspective is debated. Israel also leveraged its ideational power—with limited success—by excluding the issue of Palestinian access to the Jordan River from the agenda, during the 2008 'Annapolis' round of negotiations. Seeking not to derail the negotiations, the chief Palestinian water negotiator initially consented to the exclusion (though it was later raised, but not resolved). Benefiting from a bilateral volumetric water agreement signed in 1959 with Sudan, Egypt was generally considered to be in a comfortable pivotal position that often allows stalling or delaying tactics that prevent a basin-wide agreement being reached. Through securitization tactics, Turkish governments had been able to overplay the importance of the Tigris–Euphrates waters for its national security and political economy to the international community. At the same time it perhaps rejects the idea that Syria and Iraq also have rights to develop the Tigris–Euphrates water resources for their own economic development. The lack of discussion on permanent water allocations in the Tigris and Euphrates Basin can in part be explained by the fact that basin hegemon Turkey has benefited from its advantageous upstream position to develop unilateral hydraulic projects. Failing to even recognize the Tigris–Euphrates as an 'international river', Turkish authorities do not need or are even inclined to promote multilateral water cooperation.

In reality, the fields of power are interrelated, and cannot be separated. Bargaining or ideational power have less traction without material power, for example. There was also a strong feeling that geographical power can indeed be a very strong source of bargaining power, when combined with the other dimensions *(Ibid: 35–39)*.

Riparian hegemons can be classified into two categories: **malign (laggards)** and **benign (pushers)** hegemons. Malign hegemons are hegemons interested in maintaining a non-cooperative order on the basis of their power resources allowing them to preserve a unilateral system that produces negative effects for other actors. Benign hegemons, on the other hand, are hegemons willing to provide cooperation systems to the issue-specific community and actively engage for a cooperative governance system. Hence, they are powerful actors that contribute larger shares of the costs of cooperation, provide public goods or side payments to other actors and resources for enforcing compliance. Transferred to the specific issue-area of shared watercourses, where the nature of the hegemon has so far been neglected by research, this indicates that in addition to the location of a hegemon, its benignity matters.

Benign hegemons are defined as powerful states in the river basin that engage in the establishment, the maintenance and the development of an RBO and support its work financially, technically and politically. Malign hegemons, on the other hand, are states that refuse the idea of institutionalized cooperation and employ their power resources for maintaining a unilateral system. While benign hegemons contribute to effective river basin governance, malign hegemons impede it. An example for the former is found in the case of South Africa in the Limpopo River Basin, where South Africa promotes institutionalized river basin governance financially and technically. The latter is the case of Turkey on the Euphrates–Tigris. Turkey is reluctant to jointly and cooperatively govern the Euphrates–Tigris' water resources for water management related as well as political reasons. Moreover, instead of cooperating over water resources it shares with downstream countries, it is even able to store water behind the dams it has built and withhold it for political reasons. In 1987/8, for instance, Turkey released tremendous amounts of water without warning or notice, which led to severe flood damage in Syria. Similarly, India acts as a malign hegemon on the Ganges. India's lack of commitment to joint river basin governance is, for instance, reflected in statements by Indian politicians, pointing out that India "can accidentally forget to provide data or at a most inconvenient time our equipment can break down", and that India "can simply stop the river for a couple of hours or slow it down" *(Schmeier 2013: 76).*

3.2.4 River Basin Organization

The existence of an RBO provides river basin riparians with a means to cooperatively govern the basin and to address water-related collective action problems. Whether such governance is effective does, however, depend on a number of factors, together constituting the causal chain of river basin governance effectiveness. RBOs are more effective if riparian states cooperate on issues other than water as well and if regional integration is high. RBOs are more effective if the policy level of the collective action problem at stake is low. RBOs are more effective in governing shared watercourses if power is distributed equally among riparians or if the hegemon is situated downstream and/or benign in nature. The vast majority of watercourses (49 out of 116) are shared by two riparian states only. On the other end of the spectrum, four river basins are shared by more than 10 states (the Congo by 13, the Danube by 19, the Niger by 11, and the Nile by 11 riparians). Overall, 67 RBOs are bilateral in nature, that is, they only consist of two member states. 52 RBOS are multilateral, including more than two states as their members. However, the fact that river basins vary highly in the number of their riparians—from only two riparians in bilateral basins such as all Canadian–US basins, the Kunene or the Rio Paz River Basins, up to 19 riparian states in the Danube River Basin—suggests that the pure number of participants in river basin governance processes alone can neither be an indicator for effective nor can it serve as a basis for deriving policy recommendations, especially for large basins. More important than the laterality of an RBO is its inclusiveness. Within the sample of 117 RBOs studied, only 55 RBOs include all riparians to the river basin, while 64 exclude at least one riparian from the institutionalized governance of the river basin, thus being non-inclusive in nature *(Ibid: 81–83).*

Fewer than half of the world's transboundary basins are subject to any formal agreement outlining how the resources are to be divided and managed. There are even fewer water bodies with institutionalised cooperation: only 116 out of 276 transboundary basins have ever had a river basin organisation (RBO). Yet most experts agree that an RBO is a key institutional formation for cooperation, policy coordination, risk management, and conflict resolution. Such institutions have been identified as more important than any physical 'water stress' indicators for peacefully coping with rapid changes in a given basin. This being said, the mere existence of a treaty is not enough to prevent conflict because such agreements often lack robust conflict management mechanisms; this is the case, for example, with the existing agreements in the Tigris-Euphrates basin. Even hitherto successful institutions may be at risk. The Indus Waters Treaty, for example, suffers from insufficient governance insofar as it contains no rules on how to adapt to the changes that climate change may bring about, and insofar as there is no integrated water management that could provide the necessary long-term solutions to rapidly growing scarcity. Non-cooperation might lead to costly conflicts. Very limited investments into transboundary institutions can yield considerable 'peace dividends' in the form of avoided hostilities. Since the difficulty of resolving conflicts rises as more stakeholders become involved, preventing these conflicts from arising in the first place is far more efficient than interventions at a later stage. Even small investments in transboundary institutions can yield considerable 'peace dividends'.

Beyond the weakness of institutional mechanisms and the question of what issues treaty terms do or do not cover—water quality, variability, conflict resolution, etc.—lies the issue of what parties are involved in the agreements. In both the Indus and the Tigris-Euphrates, the existing agreements do not include all riparians. This is particularly problematic in the case of the Tigris-Euphrates, where no tri-lateral accord brings together Iraq, Syria, and Turkey. Geographical incompleteness might undermine agreements' potential resilience and riparian states' ability to advance collective management in the face of climate change. Rising water demands and climate change-induced variability and uncertainty thus threaten the survival of existing water-sharing agreements while simultaneously making better, collective management more urgent. The extent to which each country securitises water—i.e., transforms water into a key aspect of its national security whose protection justifies the use of extraordinary means—will depend on national perceptions of how the country will be impacted by climate change, both in absolute terms and relative to its (potential) rivals. Deteriorations in position—whether actual or perceived—may in many cases increase political stress and help fuel conflict.

Current efforts to support international collaboration on transboundary waters are characterised by a relative underinvestment in the diplomatic pillar as compared with the techno-managerial pillar of cooperation. The international community's response to the issues surrounding internationally shared river basins has focused on the optimisation of water use and the encouragement of riparian states to sign international agreements and subsequently form international river basin organisations. The underlying idea has been to de-politicise transboundary water management issues, with a view to expanding the collective pie that can be shared rather than haggling over its distribution. Currently, there is too little investment into diplomatic efforts.

Yet relying on technically focused management institutions is not enough because basin management is often eclipsed by basin politics. Focusing on overall optimisation of water management assumes that all parties are genuinely interested in identifying and implementing the 'most rational' solution, in achieving compromise and absolute gains. Such a technical-economic mindset should indeed be the objective of third-party involvement in transboundary water governance issues. Yet we should not assume that all parties can easily be convinced to adopt this mindset at the outset. More fundamentally, we should not assume that a single, optimal, 'most rational' solution in fact exists. Countries and the constituencies within them may legitimately disagree as to which solution brings the 'greatest overall benefit'. This is because different solutions embody different trade-offs between benefits (hydropower generation, flood protection, irrigation) and—even more problematically—trade-offs or conflicts between different subjective values such as security, justice and fairness. When providing the benefit of flood control, how much risk is acceptable? When providing the reservoir for the benefit of water storage, which landscapes, or species, or ways of life must be protected and which may be sacrificed? When siting the dam for the benefit of hydropower, how many communities can be required to leave their ancestral homes? When designing the procedures to make these decisions, who may decide?

These questions simply do not have a single 'most rational' answer. Nor is it clear that the basin is always the appropriate scale on which to maximise utility. When both food and power produced within the basin are routinely exported beyond the basin (and food and power produced beyond the basin imported to it), why should these benefits be optimised at the basin level rather than another scale? A techno-economic approach is hence often insufficient as a means to achieve a utility-maximising mindset. Technical solutions alone cannot transcend the logics of domestic politics, relative gains or securitisation. Consequently, the 'ideal' of maximising benefits and benefit sharing should be the goal ofa third-party involvement. However, third-party foreign policy makers should not proceed on the premise that there exists just one technical-economic, utility-maximising solution that would achieve the greatest overall benefits for all (if only the parties were 'rational' enough to recognize the one true answer) *(Pohl 2014: 6–14)*.

Although disputes over water often represent real conflicting interests, they are also frequently used as an instrument for other political ends. To return to the Nile, conflict over water also serves as an instrument of identity politics. Egypt's and Sudan's resistance to the revision of colonial-era treaties on water division has led upstream countries to use the issue to bolster African solidarity against Arab countries. Behind these alliances lurks a struggle between the Egyptian and Ethiopian governments as to who enjoys pre-eminence in the region *(Ibid: 16).*

We can say the same about Syria and Iraq with some reservations, because these countries united against Turkey. For example, in 1983, the construction of the Ataturk Dam was undertaken without the Syrians and the Iraqis having been involved or merely consulted, even though the project affects them deeply, since it does and will modify the level of the river downstream of the construction, i.e. in Syria and Iraq. The filling of the Ataturk Dam in January 1990 hasn't been without consequences for Syria and Iraq. Thus, both Syria and Iraq are concerned about the Ataturk Dam on the Euphrates *(Allan & Mallat 1995: 206–207).*

Basin politics are often compounded by power asymmetries, begging the question of how to deal with riparian hegemons such as Turkey, Egypt, India and China, but also Nigeria or South Africa. These hydrohegemons frequently refuse to be drawn into cooperative multilateral basin fora, preferring to deal with weaker partners individually on a bilateral basis. Their absence from RBOs might in some cases help these institutions to function, especially where their flow contribution is not crucial for the river basin management. Yet because these hegemons loom large in the respective river basins, the international community's focus on the river management organisations falls short in political terms where a comprehensive settlement is the objective. Basin politics are often compounded by power asymmetries.

RBOs themselves often lack the mandate and clout to address these political issues. To be sure, this lack of political leverage is not inherent or automatic: during the Mauritanian-Senegalese conflict, the only means of exchange between the conflicting parties was the respective RBO—the OMVS—which engaged even on non-water related issues. Yet the important role that the OMVS was able to play only underscores the importance of adopting a broader, political approach to basin governance rather than focusing on facilitating technical cooperation mechanisms only. Politics may be harder when bringing the regional hegemon in, but there is no way to manage water issues in the long run without them. This implies the necessity of stronger political engagement: transboundary water governance is also power politics, and attempts to institutionalise cooperation often need the political support that foreign policy makers are well placed to provide *(Pohl 2014: 17–18).*

The lack of a designated agent to address questions of transboundary water cooperation is particularly palpable when it comes to engaging riparian hegemons. These hegemons often do not participate in the multilateral basin management institutions, but their shadow clearly looms large. The greatest challenge in this respect is the emerging role of China. China has become the biggest stakeholder on transboundary water issues, both through its control of the upstream waters of key international basins (such as the Brahmaputra, the Mekong or the Salween) and its economic, financial and political engagement regarding water infrastructure (and agriculture) in other countries. This external activity is most pronounced in the aforementioned basins in South East Asia (where Chinese-financed dams on the Mekong in Laos, for example, might have potentially damaging impacts on Cambodia and Vietnam downstream) but has effects far beyond.

China's traditional emphasis on sovereignty and non-intervention has translated, in the water domain, into an unwillingness to sign onto multilateral legal commitments such as the 1997 UN Convention on the Law of the Non-Navigational Uses of International Watercourses. Together with Turkey and Burundi, it was also one of only three countries that voted against the convention in the UN General Assembly. This convention, which enters into force in August 2014 after a long slog of few ratifications, is a framework convention setting out norms that should inform basin-specific agreements to be negotiated by riparians. Specifically, it provides for equitable and reasonable utilisation of shared watercourses, an obligation not to cause significant harm, regular exchange of data and information, the principle of prior notification of planned measures that may have significant adverse effects on another riparian, provisions on the protection and preservation of international watercourses, and peaceful settlement of disputes.

Hegemons are not necessarily impediments to cooperation; they can also facilitate it. South Africa, for example, has supported river basin organisations in Southern Africa by providing an example in terms of national water management plans and institutions. Brazil has facilitated the Amazon Cooperation Treaty and supported the respective river basin organisation. Similar dynamics unfolded in the Danube basin. The economically strongest basin countries, Germany and Austria, are situated upstream and use the river for wastewater discharge, hydropower, etc., while downstream countries depend on the river for their drinking water supply and other uses. Trust can only be built through transparency.

Multilateral and bilateral donors have facilitated and encouraged international treaties in many basins, along with the establishment of RBOs to support cooperative behaviour and contain conflict over shared waters. The World Bank-sponsored Indus Waters Treaty, the Mekong River Commission and the Nile Basin Initiative are probably the best known RBOs set up to promote cooperation between riparian states. Many RBOs continue to be financed primarily by international donors. With the 1997 UN Convention on the Law of the Non-Navigational Uses of International Watercourses, the international community has also created a framework agreement that can serve as 'model legislation' for basin-specific agreements *(Ibid: 27, 35, 11)*.

3.3 International Water law

3.3.1 Conflicts Over Transboundary Water

International relations over transboundary waters take place in a context of conflict and cooperation. Conflict and cooperation coexist. Conflict over transboundary waters is normal. There are four levels of conflict: non-politicized (level of water scarcity in the basin is low and no need for negotiations), politicized (level of water scarcity in the basin is moderate and contention normally based on constructed knowledge and not on processes observed science or economics), securitized (level of water scarcity in the basin is high and hegemon riparians can determine) and violized (level of water scarcity in the basin is very high and violent measures are prevented by processes in the international political economy—virtual water 'trade') *(Earle, Jägerskog, Öjendal 2010: 23)*.

Four seemingly incompatible theories and approaches have traditionally been put forward concerning the rights of co-basin states to utilize shared international freshwaters. These include the principles of 'absolute territorial sovereignty', 'absolute territorial integrity', 'limited territorial sovereignty' and the 'common management' approach. Each of these theories attempts to reconcile a particular position in relation to state utilization of international watercourses with the concept of territorial sovereignty as recognized and protected under general international law.

Absolute territorial sovereignty

The first principle, that of 'absolute territorial sovereignty', provides that a co-basin state may freely utilize waters within its territory without having any regard to the rights of downstream or contiguous states. Having absolute sovereignty over water resources while they are within its territory, a state may extract or alter the quality of these waters to an unlimited extent but has no right to demand continued flow from an upper co-basin state or to assert its rights against a contiguous state. This approach is closely associated with the so-called 'Harmon

Doctrine', named after the United States Attorney-General who first articulated the principle in 1895.

The doctrine has been referred to by the United States, Austria, Chile, the Federal Republic of Germany, Ethiopia and India. Even these states which have purported to rely on the principle of absolute territorial sovereignty in diplomatic exchanges have not acted accordingly. For example, India had asserted its 'full freedom' with regard to the utilization of the waters of the Indus but subsequently concluded the 1960 Indus Waters Treaty which provided for the equitable apportionment of these waters.

Indeed, it appeared that the Harmon had 'become a potent weapon in the hands of a downstream state accusing an upstream state of acting unreasonably'.

Absolute territorial integrity

The second principle, 'absolute territorial integrity', confers a right on a lower co-basin state to demand the continuation of the full flow of waters of natural quality from an upper co-basin state but confers no right to restrict or impair the natural flow of waters from its territory into that of a still lower co-basin state. This principle is the antithesis of the Harmon Doctrine and would effectively grant a right of veto upon a downstream or contiguous state, as its prior consent would be required for any change in the regime of the international watercourse. As might be expected, this approach has generally tended to find favour among lower riparian states as it would be likely to operate to retard upstream states in the development of their water resources. Like the Harmon Doctrine, the principle is based upon sovereignty but it would also appear to have a basis in the equality of states and so may be seen as being more compatible with the principle of sovereign equality as enshrined in Article 2(1) of the Charter of the United Nations. It can also be seen as being somewhat more in step with the general principles of international law relating to environmental protection and with general obligations to cooperate. This approach has its origins in riparian rights doctrines which had traditionally existed in national legal systems.

Limited territorial sovereignty/equitable utilization

The third approach, that of 'limited territorial sovereignty', which is usually articulated in the context of international watercourses as the principle of 'equitable utilization', entitles each co-basin state to an equitable and reasonable use of waters flowing through its territory. This principle may be understood as a compromise between the principles of absolute territorial sovereignty and absolute territorial integrity because the sovereignty of the upper basin state and the integrity of the lower basin state are restricted by recognition of the equal and correlative rights of the other state. The principle is based on the notion that international watercourses are shared resources in which there exists a community of interest among all co-basin states. The existence of a community of interest requires a 'reasonable and equitable' balancing of state interests which accommodates the needs and uses of each state. To permit flexibility, the concept of 'reasonable and equitable' is deliberately vague and can only be determined in each individual case in the light of all relevant factors, including of course considerations of human need and environmental protection. This principle, which is clearly the prevailing theory of international watercourse rights and obligations today, has its doctrinal origins in the sovereign equality of states, whereby all states sharing an international watercourse have equivalent rights to the use of its waters. However, it is not possible to apply this principle definitively to the resolution of abstract disputes. Its application in the resolution of actual disputes will depend on the particular circumstances of each dispute and watercourse. It is worth noting that the principle of equitable utilization plays a pivotal role in the development of customary international law with regard to the environmental protection of international watercourses. It provides for the establishment of factors which are to be taken into account in determining water utilization and allocation of shares in the resource, and thus provides a theoretical structure or framework within which consideration of ecological conservation and environmental protection can easily be conducted.

The principle of equitable utilization has also been recognized as an established principle of customary international law in all recent significant codifications of this area, including the Institute of International Law's 1961 Salzburg Resolution; the International Law Association's (ILA) 1966 Helsinki Rules on the Uses of Waters of International Rivers; the United Nations Environment Programme's 1978 Principles on Shared Natural Resources; and the successive Draft Articles on the Law of Non-Navigational Uses of International Watercourses adopted by the International Law Commission (ILC) and recommended by the Commission to the United Nations General Assembly as the basis for the 1997 UN Convention on the topic. The principle has recently been emphatically confirmed by the ILA with the adoption of the Association's 2004 Berlin Rules on Water Resources Law *(Ibid: 60–66).*

The concept of 'war over water', where nations engage in military conflict over finite water resources has received considerable attention through the media and other public forums. Given ever rising levels of local water stress, combined with the fact that there are 286 international rivers and 592 transboundary aquifers shared by 153 countries (UN, 2018a), it could be expected that water-related conflicts have been increasing and/or are likely to increase in the future. However, current evidence does not fully support this hypothesis. Conflicts are often difficult to attribute to a single reason; however, water is often one among several contributing factors. According to UN Water report 2019, water conflicts can arise because of several factors, including territorial disputes, competition over resources, or political strategic advantage. They can also be categorized based on the use, impact, or effect that water had within the conflict[2].

In other words, almost every country with land borders (i.e., that is not an island) shares some waters with its neighbours. These international basins cover 46% of the earth's land surface, including 65% of continental Asia, 60% of Africa, and 60% of South America (Africa alone has more than fifty basins that are shared by two or more states). The entire territory of some developing countries, such as Paraguay in South America and Uganda in Africa, is covered by international river basins (UN-Water 2014b), host about 40% of the world's population, and account for approximately 60% of global river flow (UN-Water 2008). Shared waters are therefore of critical importance for riparian states, i.e. the states that lie within a transboundary basin. Many important shared basins—the Nile, the Indus, the Ganges, the Euphrates-Tigris, the Amu Darya and Syr Darja, and the Mekong—overlap with regions characterised by substantial interstate and intrastate tensions and often a history of armed conflict. Consequently, when a developing country looks to alleviate its present or prospective water shortages by making more or better use of the water in its rivers, the chances are that those rivers also pass through a number of other countries. And those countries will almost certainly be concerned about actions by an upstream riparian neighbor that reduce the quantity or quality of the water in the shared rivers.

Conflicts over transboundary water can threaten international peace and security. After the menace of 'water wars' started to be prominently discussed in the early 1990 s, policy makers were relieved to learn from academic research that there were few historical precedents for such conflicts, and that shared water had instead more often induced cooperation. Analysing 1831 state to-state interactions on water between 1948 and 1999, researchers found that around two-thirds of these were cooperative and that none resulted in formal war. Many violent conflicts past and present have been connected to competition over water, particularly in the Middle East and the Sahel. Water issues often feed into other conflicts. Many international basins will face a strong increase in demand for water as a result of demographic pressures, industrialisation and urbanisation.

[2] We argue that it is quite topical for Turkey, water conflicts also arised because of several factors, including territorial disputes (Syria), competition over resources (Syria, Iraq), or political strategic advantage (Syria, Iraq).

Simultaneously, in many cases supply will in recede, due to both earlier mismanagement and the impacts of climate change. Climate change might decrease water supply in many basins through changes in precipitation and greater evaporation. Other basins may witness increases in floods and droughts, or shifts in the seasonality of rain or snowfall. And even as climate pressures may alter the amount and timing of water availability, climate stresses may also increase the demand for water, e.g. for irrigation and cooling. These changes have security implications at both the national and the international level.

First, insufficient or irregular access to water can imperil agricultural production and rural livelihoods, threaten municipal drinking water and sanitation, compromise electric power generation, and jeopardise public health, posing manifold security risks at the subnational level. Some affected states may find it difficult to share the costs of climate change in a way that is agreed by societal groups. Water scarcity may therefore reduce the perceived legitimacy of the government. Pastoralists in the Horn of Africa—who usually carry arms—may need to find new feeding grounds for their livestock, and impoverished farmers in Afghanistan may migrate to Kabul because their fields have been desiccated. Such scenarios are likely to (further) undermine social and political stability and enhance the risk of violent conflict. These risks are mirrored in the potential consequences of sea-level rises for farmers and people living in coastal communities in littoral zones and river deltas such as in Southern Bangladesh. These examples of water insecurity and conflicting interests at the subnational level can also have transboundary impacts if impoverished migrants or refugees fleeing natural catastrophes seek to cross borders, or if the resulting grievances draw in foreigners, e.g. via shared ethnic ties. In this way, water insecurity and climate change may put additional pressure on individuals, institutions and states that are already vulnerable *(Pohl 2014: 3)*.

Second, conflicting interests over the use of often-scarce water resources can also directly contribute to interstate tensions. Such conflicts may arise around the construction of dams on transboundary rivers. Recent examples that have captured headlines include the Grand Ethiopian Renaissance Dam in Ethiopia, the Xayaburi Dam in Laos, and the Rogun Dam in Tajikistan, all of which have raised tensions between riparian states[3].

The countries pursuing such projects argue that the new dams will enable them to generate renewable hydropower, enhance flood security, and increase

[3] We can also add Ataturk dam in Turkey, which has temporarily reduced the flow of water into Syria and Iraq by 75% and raised tensions between riparian states (Turkey, Syria and Iraq).

water storage to buffer against varying availability. However, downstream countries frequently fear these same structures could be used to control or reduce the water flowing to them, placing their own water needs at risk. Dams have many potential benefits—producing clean energy, facilitating irrigation and controlling floods. Yet they are also regularly flashpoints for conflict in transboundary basins because downstream countries fear loss of control and water availability and/or disadvantages for fishing, sediment transport, etc *(Ibid: 4)*.

Even in the absence of clear-cut 'water wars' so far, there are strong links between water mismanagement, the impacts of climate change, and risks of social and political instability. Such instability has the potential to contribute to both inter and intrastate conflicts, which in turn might become internationalised. With respect to the latter, the 1989 conflict between Senegal and Mauritania over the Senegal River is an example. What started as a local conflict between herders and farmers over decreasing water availability (at least partly caused by a hydropower project that altered the river's flow regime) turned into an international conflict between the two countries. As both countries deployed troops along the border, they broke off all diplomatic relations—except for those through the shared river basin organisation OMVS, which continued to act as a means of communication. This brings us to the salutary role that shared waters can also play. There are strong links between water mismanagement, climate change, and social and political instability *(Ibid: 6)*.

The changes and uncertainty that climate change entails for many basins might bring about new opportunities for cooperation. Climate change has repeatedly been described as a 'threat multiplier' for unstable regions around the globe. The impact of climate change is likely to be felt primarily through the water cycle, reinforcing many worrying trends regarding water scarcity, salinisation, alteration of seasonal flow patterns, and flood risks. If climate change were to result in conflict, it would thus probably be over water. The political risks resulting from extreme weather events became apparent, for example, in the way fundamentalist forces were able to politically exploit government failures in Pakistan after the massive floods in 2010.

Yet extreme weather events may also open up new opportunities. Though hugely destructive, cyclone Nargis in 2008 arguably helped to bring change to Myanmar as officials came to appreciate that the foreigners who pressed for access for relief efforts were well meaning after all. A similar dynamic unfolded a few years earlier in the aftermath of the 2004 tsunami in Aceh. The extreme weather events that climate change is making more likely might have such positive side effects elsewhere, too, in part by drawing political attention to such regions. And whereas political progress in the presence of disaster might be a bitter blessing, preparing for possible disasters might release the positive potential of concerted political engagement without the attendant catastrophe. Adaptation to climate change might thus help secure the political engagement necessary to mitigate and resolve conflict. Beyond this form of disaster diplomacy, efforts to adapt to climate change can create further opportunities. As the latest IPCC report underlines, water is both the issue most affected by climate change and also the one through which most adaptation has to be managed, even for other sectors. New funds for adaptation and discourses that stress the need to address impending deteriorations in the supply and quality of freshwater may simultaneously help to address the current mismanagement of water resources.

Although currently 'climate is sucking water dry' in terms of financing, as one diplomat put it, the discussion about loss and damage from climate change is all about water. The (shared) threat of climate change might also help to convince local opposition groups to support international deal-making on water issues. In this context, the significant financial resources earmarked for climate adaptation can (and should) also be used to enhance resilience to conflict. Climate change adaptation pressures can thereby generate positive spill-overs, serving as an entry point for building trust and engaging in politically thorny regions. In short, vulnerability to water and climate change may constitute not only threat multipliers, but also opportunity multipliers *(Ibid: 9–10).*

3.3.2 The Helsinki Rules on the Uses of the Waters of International Rivers

The need for an international law to govern the equitable sharing of water resources between countries emerged long ago. Efforts on the professional, nongovernmental, governmental, and intergovernmental levels have been exerted to achieve such law. The most important outcomes of these efforts are the two frameworks given by the 1966 Helsinki Rules and the 1997 United Nations (UN) Convention.

The International Law Association (ILA), a nongovernmental organization founded in 1873, has a consultative status with a number of UN agencies. ILA's work on international water law began in 1954. The general principle of ILA's work is contained in Article IV of the 1966 Helsinki Rules (ILA, 1967), which state that the equitable utilization principle governs the use of international drainage basin waters. The Helsinki Rules consist of 37 articles spread over 6 chapters and have played an important role in the codification and progressive development of this branch of international law (Bourne, 1998). States refer to these guidelines to the present day and some countries have recommended that elements of the Helsinki Rules be incorporated into the UN's framework convention on watercourses that was later developed in 1997.

In the late 1960 s, the UN decided to assign the international water law topic to its International Law Commission (ILC) for detailed study. In May of 1997, after more than quarter of a century of working on the topic, the U.N. General Assembly adopted a framework convention on the Law of the Non-Navigational Uses of International Watercourses. Although "an important set of draft rules," according to Stephen McCaffrey of the McGeorge School of Law, the Helsinki Rules do not address independent aquifers, but only those connected to a river. Accordingly, the United Nations decided in 1970 to create a more inclusive set of guidelines, which after more than twenty years of investigation by the International Law Commission resulted in the adopting of the Convention on the Law of Non-Navigational Uses of International Watercourses in 1997 *(Abu-Zeid 2001).* As the Helsinki Rules led to the creation of the United Nations' Convention on the Law of Non-Navigational Uses of International Watercourses (in the 20th century) and in 2004 (in the 21th century), it was superseded by the Berlin Rules on Water Resources, it is more reasonable to focus in detail on the UN Convention.

3.3.3 UN Convention on the Law of the Non-Navigational Uses of International Watercourses

The 1997 United Nations Convention on the Law of the Non-Navigational Uses of International Watercourses is the only treaty governing shared freshwater resources that is of universal applicability. It is a framework convention, in the sense that it provides a framework of principles and rules that may be applied and adjusted to suit the characteristics of particular international watercourses. This introductory note will describe the historical background of the convention and significant developments in its negotiating history. It will then summarize the key provisions of the convention and, finally, touch upon its influence on subsequent legal developments, including both treaties and jurisprudence.

The Convention was concluded on 21 May 1997, as an annex to General Assembly resolution 51/229. Its adoption brought to a close a process the General Assembly had initiated well over two decades earlier. On 8 December 1970, the General Assembly adopted resolution 2669 (XXV), entitled "Progressive Development and Codification of the Rules of International Law Relating to

International Watercourses". In that resolution, the Assembly recommended that the International Law Commission "take up the study of the law of the non-navigational uses of international watercourses with a view to its progressive development and codification." In fact, the General Assembly had shown that it recognized the importance of this field over ten years earlier, when it adopted resolution 1401(XIV) on 21 November 1959. In that resolution, the Assembly had indicated that it was "desirable to initiate preliminary studies on the legal problems relating to the utilization and use of international rivers with a view to determining whether the subject is appropriate for codification".

The International Law Commission began work on the international watercourses topic in 1974 pursuant to the General Assembly's 1970 resolution. Over the course of the next twenty years, the Commission's work was guided by a succession of five special rapporteurs: Richard Kearney, Stephen Schwebel, Jens Evensen, Stephen McCaffrey, and Robert Rosenstock. Following its usual practice, the Commission in 1974 circulated a questionnaire to United Nations Member States seeking their views on various issues related to the watercourses topic. In 1976, the Commission decided that it was not necessary to determine the scope of the expression "international watercourse" at the outset of its work; in fact, the Commission did not define this expression until it adopted on first reading a full set of draft articles on the topic in 1991. The definition adopted in that year is substantially unchanged in the Convention. In 1994, the Commission concluded its work on international watercourses, adopting a complete set of 33 draft articles on second reading. The Commission also adopted a companion resolution on confined transboundary groundwater, which recommended that States be guided by the principles contained in the draft articles in regulating this form of groundwater. The Commission submitted its final draft and the resolution to the General Assembly with a recommendation that a convention be elaborated on the basis of the draft articles.

On the recommendation of the Sixth (Legal) Committee, the General Assembly decided in 1994 to "convene a Working Group of the Whole... to elaborate a framework convention on the law of the non-navigational uses of international watercourses on the basis of the draft articles adopted by the International Law Commission." The convention was negotiated in the Sixth Committee, convening for this purpose as a "Working Group of the Whole" as contemplated by the Assembly's 1994 resolution. The Working Group met for three weeks in October of 1996 and two weeks in March and April of 1997. As already noted, the Convention was adopted on 21 May 1997.

The Convention contains 37 articles arranged in seven parts: Part I. Introduction; Part II. General principles; Part III. Planned measures; Part IV. Protection, preservation and management; Part V. Harmful conditions and emergency situations; Part VI. Miscellaneous provisions; and Part VII. Final clauses. An annex to the Convention sets forth procedures to be followed in the event that States have agreed to submit a dispute to arbitration.

While it is difficult to single out particular provisions of the Convention, based on the preparatory work in the International Law Commission, the negotiations in the Working Group and the significance of the principles involved, it may be said that the Convention's key provisions are contained in Parts I, II, III and IV. Part I contains the definition of the expression "international watercourse," which is obviously of central importance.

Article 2 (Use of terms) defines the term "watercourse" broadly as "a system of surface waters and groundwaters constituting by virtue of their physical relationship a unitary whole and normally flowing into a common terminus". It will be noted that, importantly, this definition includes groundwater that is hydrologically connected with surface water, which is in fact the case for much of the world's groundwater. The expression "international watercourse" is then defined as "a watercourse, parts of which are situated in different States" (McCaffrey 1997).

According to Article 2 "Watercourse State" means a State Party to the present Convention in whose territory part of an international watercourse is situated, or a Party that is a regional economic integration organization, in the territory of one or more of whose Member States part of an international watercourse is situated. And "Regional economic integration organization" means an organization constituted by sovereign States of a given region, to which its member States have transferred competence in respect of matters governed by this Convention and which has been duly authorized in accordance with its internal procedures, to sign, ratify, accept, approve or accede to it.

Article 3 (Watercourse agreements) and Article 4 (Parties to watercourse agreements) pertain to the signing of agreements on watercourses. "Where a watercourse agreement is concluded between two or more watercourse States, it shall define the waters to which it applies. Such an agreement may be entered into with respect to an entire international watercourse or any part thereof or a particular project, programme or use except insofar as the agreement adversely affects, to a significant extent, the use by one or more other watercourse States of the waters of the watercourse, without their express consent. Where a watercourse State considers that adjustment and application of the provisions of the present Convention is required because of the characteristics and uses of a particular international watercourse, watercourse States shall consult with a view to negotiating in good faith for the purpose of concluding a watercourse agreement or agreements. Where some but not all watercourse States to a particular international watercourse are parties to an agreement, nothing in such agreement shall affect the rights or obligations under the present Convention of watercourse States that are not parties to such an agreement" *(UN Convention 1997).*

Article 5 (Equitable and reasonable utilization and participation), contained in Part II, reflects the principle that is widely regarded as the cornerstone of the Convention, and indeed the law in the field: equitable and reasonable utilization and participation. It requires that a State sharing an international watercourse with other States utilize the watercourse, in its territory, in a manner that is equitable and reasonable vis-à-vis the other States sharing it. In order to ensure that their utilization of an international watercourse is equitable and reasonable, States are to take into account all relevant factors and circumstances. An indicative list of factors and circumstances is contained in article 6. Article 5 also sets forth, in paragraph 2, the principle of equitable participation. According to this principle, States are to "participate in the use, development and protection of an international watercourse in an equitable and reasonable manner". Thus, affirmative conduct may be required by this principle, which is a further elaboration of the implications of equitable and reasonable utilization *(McCaffrey 1997).*

Paragraph 1 of Article 6 (Factors relevant to equitable and reasonable utilization) provides utilization of an international watercourse in an equitable and reasonable manner within the meaning of article 5 requires taking into account all relevant factors and circumstances, including:

(a) Geographic, hydrographie, hydrological, climatic, ecological and other factors of a natural character;
(b) The social and economic needs of the watercourse States concerned;
(c) The population dependent on the watercourse in each watercourse State;
(d) The effects of the use or uses of the watercourses in one watercourse State on other watercourse States;
(e) Existing and potential uses of the watercourse;
(f) Conservation, protection, development and economy of use of the water resources of the watercourse and the costs of measures taken to that effect;
(g) The availability of alternatives, of comparable value, to a particular planned or existing use.

In paragraph 3 is written that the weight to be given to each factor is to be determined by its importance in comparison with that of other relevant factors. In determining what is a reasonable and equitable use, all relevant factors are to be considered together and a conclusion reached on the basis of the whole *(UN Convention 1997)*.

Another key provision of the Convention is article 7 (Obligation not to cause significant harm). This article requires that States "take all appropriate measures to prevent the causing of significant harm" to other States sharing an international watercourse. The emphasis on prevention is important, since it is often difficult to stop or modify an activity once it has begun, and it can be very complicated and expensive, if indeed it is possible, to remedy harm once caused. While there has been debate, both in the negotiation of the Convention and in the literature, about the relationship between the principles set forth in articles 5 and 7, the two are best seen as being complementary. The two articles work in tandem in the following way: if a State believes it has sustained significant harm due to a co-riparian State's use of an international watercourse, it will ordinarily raise the issue with the second State. In the negotiations that follow, articles 5, 6 and 7 in effect provide that the objective is to reach a solution that is equitable and reasonable with regard to both States' uses of the watercourse and the benefits they derive from it. The possibility that the solution may include the payment of compensation, to achieve an equitable balance of uses and benefits, is not excluded *(McCaffrey 1997)*.

According to Article 8 (General obligation to cooperate) "Watercourse States shall cooperate on the basis of sovereign equality, territorial integrity, mutual benefit and good faith in order to attain optimal utilization and adequate protection of an international watercourse". Article 9 (Regular exchange of data and information) provides regular exchange readily available data and information on the condition of the watercourse, in particular that of a hydrological, meteorological, hydrogeological and ecological nature and related to the water quality as well as related forecasts *(UN Convention 1997)*.

Part III of the Convention sets forth the principle of prior notification of planned measures and elaborates in some detail on the various aspects of that obligation. The essence of the principle is that if a project or other measures are planned in a State and those measures may have a significant adverse effect upon another State or States sharing an international watercourse, the State in which the measures are planned must provide timely notification to the other States of the plans. If the notified States believe the planned measures would be inconsistent with the requirements of articles 5 or 7, a process of consultations and, if necessary, negotiations follows which is intended to lead to an equitable resolution of the situation.

Part IV of the Convention deals with protection, preservation and management of international watercourses. It contains provisions on protection and preservation of watercourse ecosystems, prevention, reduction and control of pollution, and consultations concerning management of an international watercourse, among others. The importance of these provisions is perhaps obvious: watercourse ecosystems and watercourses themselves must be protected, preserved, and properly managed, if they are to support human and other forms of life.

The Convention and its preparatory work have had significant influence. Four months after it was concluded, the International Court of Justice referred to and quoted from the Convention in its judgment in the Gabcikovo-Nagymaros Project case. In part because of its provenance, the Convention is widely viewed as a codification of customary international law with respect to at least three of the obligations it embodies, namely equitable and reasonable utilization, prevention of significant harm, and prior notification of planned measures. These and other provisions of the Convention have influenced the negotiation of treaties concerning international watercourses, as can readily be seen from even a cursory review of recent agreements, for example, the Revised Protocol on Shared Watercourses of the Southern African Development Community (SADC) of 7 August 2000.

The 1997 United Nations Convention on the Law of the Non-Navigational Uses of International Watercourses represents an important contribution to the strengthening of the rule of law in this increasingly critical field of international relations and to the protection and preservation of international watercourses. In an era of increasing water scarcity, it is to be hoped that the Convention's influence will continue to grow *(McCaffrey 1997).*

3.3.4 Similarities and Differences Between the 1966 Helsinki Rules and the 1997 U.N. Convention

Similar to the 1966 Helsinki Rules, the 1997 UN Convention offers principles—such as equitable and reasonable use and no significant harm—with which states sharing an international watercourse are to conform when using international waters. The main difference between the 1966 Helsinki Rules and the 1997 UN Convention is that the Helsinki Rules pertain to the water in an "international drainage basin" while the UN Convention pertains to the water in an "international watercourse." While the definition of the two terms "drainage basin" and "watercourse," as mentioned in the excerpts of the articles shown above, may appear to be very similar, they are quite different when it comes to the use of the waters in a drainage basin versus the use of the waters in a watercourse. One major difference is that the Helsinki Rules would consider the water that falls on the drainage basin and is used before flowing into a common terminus as beneficial water use for the State in place, whereas the UN Convention would not consider any water use from outside of the watercourse as part of the water budget to be equitably utilized. Examples of beneficial unaccounted water uses in international river basins include rainfed agriculture and natural forests. The consideration of this issue has a very significant impact on states sharing rivers that traverse extremely different climate environments. Falkenmark (1999) stated that it is becoming more and more evident that what has to be shared between those upstream and those downstream in a river basin is not the water currently going in the river, as the UN Convention on Non-navigational Uses of International Watercourses suggests, but rather the rainfall over the river basin. Sustainable, water-dependent, socio-economic development will simply not be possible without taking an integrated perspective on all water-dependent and water impacting activities in a river basin and their relative upstream\downstream relations. Eckstein (1998) reported that the lack of a more comprehensive and hydrologically sound application of the UN Convention to interrelated water resources suggests that it was formulated without a firm understanding of hydrologic reality. The UN Convention may be viewed as providing guidelines pertaining to the use, management, and preservation of only a portion of the hydrologic cycle, especially when considered in the context of hydrologic reality. Eckstein (1998) draws attention to the fact that it is not uncommon to have related surface- and ground waters (such as a stream and an underlying aquifer) flowing in different geographical directions and toward different termini. Thus, under the UN Convention, any use or management scheme developed for the stream would not be bound by the UN Convention's principles with regard to the underlying ground water.

Direct beneficial use of rainfall is a substantial amount of water, which if properly assessed, could significantly switch the balance of equitable utilization formulas. The World Water Council (WWC) defines this water as Green Water, or soil water, which is the portion of rainfall that is stored in the soil and then evaporates or is incorporated into plants and organisms. In its World Water Vision 2000, the WWC estimates the annual global Green Water to be 60,000 km3, compared to only 40,000 km3 of Blue Water, which is defined as the portion of rainfall that enters into streams and recharges ground water. It is apparent how significant Green Water is in resolving water conflicts, not only because of its amount but also, because of how much Green Water contributes to food production. Sixty percent of global food production comes from the Green Water. Nevertheless, Green Water is transformed daily into Blue Water (the UN Convention definition of watercourse) by the effects of continuous urbanization or deforestation practices. A proper water resources assessment is an essential step for the equitable utilization of shared water resources. It provides the opportunity for cooperation among riparian countries of a river basin to develop the untapped water resources in the basin rather than compete over already utilized water resources. It defines each country's actual utilized water as extracted surface and ground water as well as any beneficial evapo-transpiration resulting from rainfall on the river basin. It accounts for all possible potential water resources in each country, within or outside the river basin, whether it's river runoff, ground water, direct rainfall, or evaporation losses that could be saved.

On the other hand, unlike the UN Convention, the Helsinki Rules include harm as one of the factors to be considered in the overall assessment, and not the equitable utilization, of water resources. This distinction is important since, under the Helsinki Rules, it is clear that a use that causes significant harm could be justified under the principle of equitable utilization. The same is not quite so evident in the approach adopted in the 1997 UN Watercourses Convention, although States could argue articles 5 through 7 of the UN Convention mean the same thing. In practice, adopting equitable use, compared with no significant harm, as the governing rule can yield quite different results. The no significant harm rule acts as a veto on future development and tends to protect the status quo, i.e., the prior appropriations of the State first to develop *(Abu-Zeid 2001)*.

3.4 Turkey's Transboundary Water Policy (Official Position)

Turkey's policy regarding the use of Transboundary Rivers is based on the following principles:

- Each riparian state of a transboundary river system has the sovereign right to make use of the water in its territory without giving "significant harm" to other riparians.
- Transboundary waters should be used in an equitable, reasonable and optimum manner.
- Equitable use does'nt mean the equal distribution of waters of a transboundary river among riparian states.

As regards the Euphrates and the Tigris rivers;

- The two rivers constitute a single basin.
- The combined water potential of the Euphrates and the Tigris rivers is sufficient to meet the needs of the three riparian States, provided that water is

used in an efficient way and the benefit is maximized through new irrigation technologies and the principle of "more crop per drop" at basin level.
- The variable natural hydrological conditions must be taken into account in the allocation of the waters of the Euphrates and the Tigris rivers.
- The principle of sharing the benefits at basin level should be pursued.

With respect to the utilization of the waters of the Euphrates and the Tigris rivers, Turkey has consistently abided by these principles and continued to release maximum possible amount of water from both rivers even during the driest summers thanks to the completed dams and the reservoirs in South-eastern Anatolia.

Conclusions (Official Version)

- First and foremost, Turkey views water as a catalyst for cooperation rather than a source of conflict.
- Economic development and spreading of prosperity to all people in the region will be the most effective means of creating a climate of peace and good neighborly relations in the Middle East.
- Transboundary waters should be used in an equitable, reasonable and optimum manner.

The looming water shortage at global level can only be addressed through a holistic approach and with technical and financial support by the developed countries, regional and international organizations and financial institutions (*Rep. of Turkey Ministry of Foreign Affairs, Turkey's Policy on Water Issues*).

3.5 New Approach for Analyzing Turkey's Hydro Policy

In our opinion, many aspects of realism still prevail in the 21st century. Particularly today the idea of state/national interest is also central, which is the main driving force of international relations, the main determinant of state behavior. As for neo-realism, a number of its provisions are of course still applicable today. We agree with Waltz, who criticized Morgenthau for generally separating the domestic and foreign policies of states. We also think that domestic and foreign policy should be viewed as one whole. Moreover, today a number of foreign policy steps of the state are based on its domestic political developments. That's why the domestic policy largely determines how its foreign policy is formed and implemented.

Finally, we would like to highlight one important circumstance that exists in non-democratic countries with kharisma leaders in the 21st century. There are many leaders in the world, some of them are selfish and driven by ambition. They want it all for themselves and they will go to extreme actions to get it. For example, today's leaders in Turkey, as well as in Russia (Erdogan and Putin), are making every effort to keep their power and leave a unique trace in history. Since Turkey is the subject of our discussion, we will focus more on Erdogan's personality. Besides, in Erdogan's case it is much more obvious than in Putin's. These leaders are guided by personal interests, which may partially coincide or may not coincide with the state interests of their countries.

Erdogan is trying to imitate the former powerful leaders of his country (Ottoman sultans), to repeat their actions, to realize their dream projects on the other hand he is in remote competition with some of them (Mustafa Kemal Ataturk). In this context, Turkey's current president's foreign policy is based on his neo-Ottoman aspirations, his drive to become the leader of the Islamic world, his desire to leave a deeper trace in the history of Turkey than Mustafa Kemal Ataturk. It is also for this reason that Turkey entered Syria in 2016 and then does not want to leave Syria (Erdogan wants to annex the north of Syria as Ataturk did decades ago). These are the three pillars of understanding Erdogan's domestic and foreign policy (neo-Ottomanism, leadership of the Islamic world, rivalry with Ataturk).

Erdogan's domestic policy also fits into the context of competing with Ataturk. In particular, we can mention the closure of Ataturk Airport in Istanbul (Turkey's largest airport at that time) and construction of a larger airport, which will probably be named Erdogan. In this context Erdogan converted Hagia Sophia museum in Istanbul into the mosque. The same we can say about the current attempt to build the Istanbul Canal (Erdogan announced he is ready to build Istanbul canal with state budget despite current economic difficulties).

We want to emphasize that Erdogan is ready to take any steps to retain his power, despite the fact that millions of people are suffering in his country. Buying S-400 systems from Russia is the best example of this. We argue that Erdogan bought them to protect his residence and aircraft from aviation during the subsequent military coup attempts (friend or foe identification system). Erdogan could buy Patriot systems from US—Turkey's NATO ally, thus not depriving his country of F-35 fighters and keeping his country free from shocks and sanctions. But he preferred do the opposite (for the S-400 system, the F-16 fighter of Turkish aviation is foe).

All this means that in order to understand the logic of the internal and external steps of modern Turkey, we must at first recognize the essence of its leader Erdogan. Recently (especially after the 2016 coup attempt) it became obvious that Erdogan is more guided by personal interests and considerations. And his personal interests as already mentioned may either partially coincide (Turkey's invasions to Syria) or not coincide (the shooting down of the Sukhoi Su-24M, purchase of S-400 systems) with his country's state interests. This means that in some cases Erdogan's personal interests prevail over Turkey's state interests.

If you fail to recognize Erdogan's essence, reveal his dreams and plans, the roots of these, you will not be able to understand and predict Turkey's steps in foreign policy and domestic politics. Erdogan's (human's/leader's) essence has become the most important factor in understanding today's Turkey. We are already dealing with a case where the head of state is trying, at all costs, not to advance the state/national interest, but his own. In fact, the idea of "Erdogan's Turkey" is centered not on the state/national interest but on the personal interest of the leader, which is the main driving force of state behavior. It does not fit into Morgenthau's realistic thinking.

We can also say the same about Waltz's neorealistic thinking, because this is not the case, when the structure of the international system dictates, delimits, restricts the behavior of the state (Turkey) or, on the contrary, it creates favorable conditions for the functioning of the international arena. In this context, "Erdogan's Turkey" with its hydro policy is probably a unique country in the 21st century (no country in the world is to use water for as many purposes as Turkey).

Regarding Turkey's transboundary water policy, we would like to pay attention to the fact that there is an extensive material on Turkey's water policy on the Turkish Foreign Ministry website. This shows the importance of water, water policy for Turkey. The second, Turkey accepts that transboundary waters should be used in an equitable, reasonable and optimum manner (Article 5 of The 1997 United Nations Convention on the Law of the Non-Navigational Uses of International Watercourses), but emphisis, that equitable use does not mean the equal distribution of waters of a transboundary river among riparian states. Therefore, Turkey voted against the convention in 1997 and asserts that each riparian state of a transboundary river system has the sovereign right to make use of the water in its territory without giving "significant harm" to other riparians.

For us can be acceptable Turkey's position, that equal distribution of waters of a transboundary river among riparian states is not possible as it is necessary to take into account the population of countries, the level of development of the economy (industry and agriculture), the level of urbanization, the quantity of water resources, unequal distribution of water in the riparian countries, the impact of climate changes, etc. For example, Turkey exceeds the population of Syria and Iraq together. We can say the same about Turkey's economy. Finally, the Tigris, for example, is abundance in Iraq at the expense of getting new tributaries than in Turkey. Moreover, in Iraq, the Tigris exceeds the Euphrates by water flow rate, whereas the opposite is in Turkey. Turkey asserts that the Euphrates and the Tigris constitute a single basin, taking into account that Iraq can partially compensate for the decline of the Euphrates flow with the waters of the Tigris. However, this does not work in Syria because Tigris doesn't enter Syria forming a 40-kilometer border between Turkey and Syria.

Turkey argues that the combined water potential of the Euphrates and the Tigris is sufficient to meet the needs of the three riparian States. But it should be taken into account that the population, economic (industrial, agricultural, domestic) indicators, level of urbanization of riparian countries change continuously. That's why if some volume of water can today be considered equitable and reasonable, then we can't say the same for tomorrow. On the other hand the 1997 Convention doesn't imply riparian countries to use water equally.

Thus, water can be both platform of conflict and cooperation for Turkey, in some cases be a 'bridging resource' (Friendship Dam on the River Orontes). We believe that this cooperation greatly depends on what kind of foreign policy Turkey is currently implementing. In case of Turkey water projects became more of a platform for conflict rather than cooperation, which is proved by the fact that Turkey hasn't signed the UN Convention (with China and Burundi). Meanwhile, it is known that there are many hegemony (upstream) countries in the world of water, for which the 1997 Convention is acceptable. We believe that the international community has done almost everything possible to ensure that participants of the 1997 Convention can solve their water problems in a civilized manner. At the time, we think that there are two main factors, which makes the convention's work flawed.

- There are a number of contentious points. Particularly, in some cases, disagreements can arise from the one hand to utilize an international watercourse in an equitable and reasonable manner, and on the other hand, without the causing of significant harm to other watercourse States. For example, if the upstream country will utilize an international watercourse in an equitable and reasonable manner, it can cause significant harm to downstream country (countries). In addition, problems may arise in clarifying the amount of damage, whether it is significant or not, and if yes, how much? Disagreements can also arise whether upstream country has taken all appropriate measures to prevent the causing of significant harm to downstream country (countries), or not?

- According to Article 3 "In the absence of an agreement to the contrary, nothing in the present Convention shall affect the rights or obligations of a watercourse State arising from agreements in force for it on the date on which it became a party to the present Convention. Watercourse States may enter into one or more agreements, which apply and adjust the provisions of the present Convention to the characteristics and uses of a particular international watercourse or part thereof". All this means that the treaties which concluded between the states of the watercourse and refers to the utilization of the international watercourses have a priority over the UN Convention *(see also Harutyunyan 2005: 8–9).*

In the 20th century, Turkey began to implement major water projects in the Euphrates and also the Tigris basin, which created a new situation in Syria and Iraq, although there was nothing unusual in Turkey's move. The issue can be analyzed from 3 perspectives, taking into account that in the case of the Euphrates, Turkey is an upstream country, Syria is a midstream country, and Iraq is a downstream country.

1) **Financial-economic.** After Turkey began to implement major water projects in the Euphrates basin, Syria and Iraq may have begun to realize that Turkey, like them, wants to receive additional volume of electricity, as well as agricultural products. In other words, from the financial and economic point of view, Turkey was doing the same as Syria and Iraq, which were also building reservoirs and canals in the Euphrates-Tigris basin. In any case, it became obvious that Turkey's construction of reservoirs in the Euphrates and Tigris basins, and the implementation of other water projects, would lead to a reduction in water flow of these rivers (Iraq's situation was even worse, because the flow of the Euphrates would decrease not only from the implementation of water projects by Turkey, but also by Syria).
2) **Legal-moral.** The UN Water Convention was adopted in 1997 and therefore it was not there during the construction of the first reservoirs on the Euphrates in Turkey and it is not possible to examine the issue from this point of view (even after the the adoption of the convention, Turkey did not join it, and the situation did not change in that sense). As for the moral side of the issue, Turkey has essentially not done anything new here. Syria started implementing large water projects in the Euphrates basin almost simultanesely as Turkey, and Iraq started this process before them. Moreover, Syria was doing the same thing in the basin of the Orontes River, which, unlike the Euphrates, flowed from Syria to Turkey.

3) **Military-political.** If not from the beginning, at least over time, Turkey, Syria and Iraq realized that water can be used as a political lever, trying to extract various concessions from the other side. In this context, the more the upstream or midstream country can control the river flow, the more it will be able to make the downstream and also the midstream country dependent. In addition, the reservoirs may have some military significance, especially during possible wars (Turkey planned to release the water from the reservoirs during the war and sink the Syrian tanks with it).

In our opinion this situation led to the fact that, in the 20th century, Turkey acted more in the position of a justifier and defender, trying to deny the "water accusations" of Syria and Iraq, while the last two countries acted on the contrary, from an offensive position. Thus, we can say that in the 20th century, Turkey adopted defensive realism, meanwhile Syria and Iraq adopted offensive realism. This situation completely changed in the 21st century, when Turkey switched to offensive realism in the governance of transboundary waters ('limited sovereignty' and sometimes even 'absolute territorial sovereignty' principles).

As a result, Turkey was accused of "water imperialism". In our opinion, Turkey's water policy in the Euphrates-Tigris basin in the 21st century may somewhat resemble a "2.5 water war", whose targets are Syria and Iraq abroad, and the PKK inside the country. Turkey's water problems with neighboring countries are part of the whole complex of problems. As mentioned above, water problems can arise for many reasons, including territorial disputes, regional competition, and so on. In the case of Turkey it is obvious for several reasons:

1) Almost all of Turkey's neighbors are previously entered into the Ottoman Empire and have a certain negative attitude towards Turkey.
2) Turkey has (had) a several historical-territorial issues with its neighbors (Syria).
3) In the 21st century Turkey pretends to a regional superpower, which forced it an aggressive water policy (Iran, as well as Syria and Iraq).
4) The population and economy of Turkey continue to grow, that's why Turkey reduces the flow of transboundary rivers to the neighboring countries (water stressed country).
5) Turkey intends to turn into a hydro-donor, taking advantage of the fact that Iran, Arab countries and Israel have serious water problems. Thus, Turkey wants to sell water to these countries, make them dependent and push forward its own ambitions.

The Pacific Institute's list of Water Conflict Chronology defines three such categories:

- **Trigger:** Water as a trigger or root cause of conflict, where there is a dispute over the control of water or water systems or where economic or physical access to water, or scarcity of water, triggers violence.
- **Weapon:** Water as a weapon of conflict, where water resources, or water systems themselves, are used as a tool or weapon in a violent conflict.
- **Casualty:** Water resources or water systems as a casualty of conflict, where water resources, or water systems, are intentional or incidental casualties or targets of violence.

Items are included in the chronological list when there is violence (injuries or deaths) or threats of violence (including verbal threats, military manoeuvres, and shows of force). During the period 2000–2009, there were 94 registered conflicts where water played a role (49 as a Trigger, 20 as a Weapon and 34 as a Casualty). The period 2010–2018 (up to May 2018) reported 263 registered conflicts (123 with water as a Trigger, 29 as a Weapon, and 133 as a Casualty). Although this might suggest an increasing trend in water-related conflicts overall, these data must be interpreted with caution, as much of the increase could be attributable to greater awareness (and reporting) of such incidents. The eruption of armed conflict in several regions of the world during the period from 2010 to 2018 may also have influenced this apparent trend *(UN-Water 2019: 17).*

Of course we agree with the the Pacific Institute's list of Water Conflict Chronology (Trigger, Conflict, Casualty), but at the same time we want to present our (own) model of water conflicts chronology. It also consists of three chronological stages and has the same names (Trigger, Weapon, Casualty).

- **Trigger**—When an upstream country (for example, Ethiopia—Grand Ethiopian Renaissance Dam or Turkey—Ataturk Dam) and even midstream country (Syria—Tabqa Dam) builds one or more major reservoirs, it can become a (pistol) trigger in its hands against the downstream country. The downstream country (for example, Iraq) is already beginning to fear that the upstream country (for example, Turkey) or even midstream country (for example, Syria) may one day "fire" on it (using part of the water collected from the reservoirs for irrigation, thus partially dehydrating itself).
- **Weapon—**When the fear of the downstream country becomes a reality—the upstream country or countries use the weapons in their hands to "shoot" at

him, i.e a significant portion of the collected water begins to be used for irrigation purposes (again the example of Turkey, Syria and Iraq).
- **Casualty (victim)**—When a downstream country (for example Syria and Iraq) suffers greatly from being "shot" by an upstream country (Turkey) and becomes casualty not having alternatives. This means it doesn't necessarily that the downstream country (for example, Armenia—in case of Aras river) become a casualty in such cases.

In 2009 The Pacific Institute developed a new format to better illustrate how conflict over water impacts history. The following are the current categories or types of conflict included by the institute:

- Control of Water Resources (state and nonstate actors): where water supplies or access to water is at the root of tensions.
- Military Tool (state actors): where water resources, or water systems themselves, are used by a nation or state as a weapon during a military action.
- Political Tool (state and nonstate actors): where water resources, or water systems themselves, are used by a nation, state, or nonstate actor for a political goal.
- Terrorism (nonstate actors): where water resources, or water systems, are either targets or tools of violence or coercion by nonstate actors.
- Military Target (state actors): where water resource systems are targets of military actions by nations or states.
- Development Disputes (state and nonstate actors): where water resources or water systems are a major source of contention and dispute in the context of economic and social development *(Lorenz Erickson 2013: 6–7).*

In the following chapters we will see many of those identified by the Pacific Institute. We believe that in the 20th century, Turkey began to build reservoirs, first of all about their 4 functions: irrigation (agriculture), hydropower (hydroelectric power plant, HEPP), water supply (domestic and industrial water supply), flood protection (flood control, environment). But over time, Turkey realized that water can be used as an effective lever against neighboring countries and and started using water for that purpose as well. It happened after Turkey saw the Arab world use oil as a political lever in the 1970s.

The fact that Turkey started using water for various purposes (except for the famous 4 reservoir functions) became obvious in the 21st century, which was due to the fact that Turkey began to aspire to a regional superpower or even be perceived as such, meanwhile neighboring countries had serious problems (Syria and Iraq). In the 21st century, Turkey's advantages over Syria and Iraq in the four forms of power (geography; material power; bargaining power; ideational power) have become more obvious. And Turkey, except for the famous four functions of dams, tries to solve its problems in additional 4 spheres by implementing water projects.

1) To get an effective leverage against neighboring countries, make them dependent countries and receive different types of concessions from them to advance own interests in the foreign political field up to the recognition of its territorial integrity by neighbor (Syria).
2) To solve domestic political problems, especially regarding the Kurdish issue, including demographic and elective issues up to Erdogan's victory in the presidential election through a ground military operation (Iraq).
3) To solve religious, historical and cultural various issues, to leave underwater unwanted cultural heritage (Armenians, Kurds, Romans), thus to try to get permission for repairing or building historic-cultural (ottoman) monuments in neighboring countries (Georgia).
4) To solve military various problems, to ensure its security (PKK), to obtain a permit from a neighboring country for military intervention (Iraq).

All this does not conform to the UN Water Convention and makes it clear why Turkey hasn't joined the convention. In the empiric part of our work we will analyse the evolution of Turkey's water policy in the Euphrates-Tigris basin in the 20th and 21st centuries, will show how the Turkey's hydro policy changed over time, how domestic and foreign developments affected the Turkish hydro policy and what is the interdependence between them? We will show that water projects provoked a chain reaction in the domestic and foreign policy of Turkey, and vice versa. As a result, in the 21st century Turkey became a unique country in the world, which, in addition to four famous functions, uses water for many other purposes, which grew over time and can still grow in the future. Turkey also became such a country due to its historical and geographical features too which we will describe in detail in the following chapters.

Historical and Geographical Overviews of the Euphrates-Tigris and the Orontes Basins

4

4.1 The Importance of Water in the Ottoman Era

4.1.1 The Problem of Drinking and Irrigation Water

Water has played an important role in the household, economic (agricultural) and military spheres in the Ottoman Empire and water issues have been in the spotlight of the authorities, which continues hitherto in the modern Republic of Turkey. The Ottoman Empire has faced a number of water challenges (supply of drinking water to cities, providing farmers with irrigation water and so on), and therefore began to build aqueducts, canal systems, cisterns, public fountainsand so on. But they weren't large storage water structures, with only some exceptions in Istanbul. Water supply for the capital city of Istanbul became a crucial question for the Ottoman Empire, as it was before that—during the Byzantine Empire (Istanbul became the capital 1.5 centuries after the establishment of the Ottoman State in 1299).

When the Ottoman sultan Mehmet Fatih conquered the capital of the Byzantine Empire Constantinople in 1453, the city's (Istanbul) population was 50,000. However, soon afterward the population of Istanbul increased 5 times in 25 years and 7–8 times in 50 years. During the Byzantine period tens of small reservoirs and pools were built to supply of fresh water to the capital of the empire. They contained a total of 1 million cubic meters (MCM) of water which could provide 200,000 people for 200 days (1 person—25 liters per day). However, given the rapid growth of Istanbul's population, those steps were not enough *(Yildiz & Ozbay 2012: 42)*.

H. Gabrielyan, *Turkey's Water Policy as Part of the Political Strategy*, Politik, Wirtschaft und Gesellschaft im Spannungsverhältnis der Regionen Südosteuropa und Mittlerer Osten, https://doi.org/10.1007/978-3-658-44070-1_4

Historian Halil Inalcik, referring to historian Barkan, reports that the population of the Ottoman Empire reached 12–12.5 million for 1.5 decade (1520–1535). According to historian Braudel, when the borders of the Ottoman Empire reached their peak at the end of the 16th century, the population of the empire was about 22 million (according to Barkan 30–35 million). The population of the Ottoman Empire in the early 1800s was estimated at 25–32 million. According to Inalcik, in 1906 the population of the Ottoman Empire was 21 million *(Ibid: 44–45).*

Meanwhile, the population of Istanbul and other major cities of the Ottoman Empire also grew. It means that consumption of water also grew in these cities. Mosques and baths consumed the most volume of water in the cities. During the Ottoman Empire, groundwater supply wasn't sufficient and a number of water lines were built to divert water from springs to public fountains. By the middle of the 16th century, the population of Istanbul was 350–400,000 and by the end of the 17th century—800,000. Istanbul thus surpassed London and Paris and became the largest city in Europe and the Middle East. By the early 1900s, the population of Istanbul was over 1 million. Puny by comparison, in 1950 the population of Istanbul hadn't yet reached 1 million—983,000 *(Ibid: 144–147).*

That's why eight small reservoirs were built to provide Istanbul with fresh water in 1620–1893. The height of seven of these hydro structurs was 10–17 meters and the height of one was 30 m (have a storage capacity of 1.7 MCM) which can be already described as a dam *(Ibid: 85–86).*

In general, the Ottoman authorities were able to solve Istanbul's water supply problems. Still, given that Istanbul's population continued to grow almost continuously, the issue of water supply in the city remains on the agenda hitherto. Not only Istanbul, but also the other major cities of the empire and especially Cairo had water supply problems. Cairo, which was in a difficult climate, received water through camels. If the number of camels carrying water for Cairo in the 15th century was 20,000, then in the 17th century the number of camels doubled *(Ibid: 115).*

And thereby the Ottoman authorities at various times took serious steps to solve the water supply problems of the cities and mainly solved these problems. The same can be said for providing farmers with irrigation water. 75% of Ottoman population lived in villages and engaged in farming and livestock. In 1914 56% of the national income in the Ottoman economy came from agriculture *(Ibid: 200).*

There were no systematic irrigation activities for a long time in the Ottoman Empire. In 1875, a severe drought affected the Konya region, therefore, the Ottoman government decided to build a diversion weir and irrigation channel in that region. The project, which was named as the Cumra Irrigation and Drainage

Project, was realized between 1908 and 1914 in Konya and became the first modern irrigation project in Anatolia[1].

As for the hydropower generation, it has a shorter history in Anatolia. In 1902, a small HEPP with installed capacity of 60 KW for lighting was established in Tarsus. In 1914, the production and distribution of electricity in Istanbul was started by companies which were founded with the special permission of the Ottoman Sultan. In 1923, at the time of the foundation of the Republic of Turkey, electricity was available only in Istanbul, Izmir and Tarsus with a total installed capacity of 29.7 MW. Usage of electrical energy for purposes other than lighting began after 1930 when industrial development started *(Kibaroglu, Scheumann, Kramer 2011: 67).*

4.1.2 Economic and Military Importance of Rivers

In addition to the sea routes, the Ottoman authorities attached great importance to rivers as important communication and commerce routes. Ottoman Empire located on 3 continents controlled a number of important rivers, including the greater part of the Danube and the Nile, as well as the Euphrates and Tigris, Kizil Irmak. A number of projects were initiated to these rivers have been put forward. For example, in the mid-19th century, the Kizil Irmak waterway project was put forward. The Ottoman authorities wanted use this river (the longest river in modern Turkey) to reach from the Black Sea to at first Kayseri, then to Sivas. It happened in the era of Sultan Abdul Hamid II-2 (1876–1909) *(Yildiz & Ozbay 2012: 130).*

The Ottoman authorities were likewise required to resolve the water issue also during wars and especially in the invasions of water scarce regions. Water scarcity posed serious challenges during the governance the Ottoman sultan Selim I (1512–1520 period), who undertook a number of campaigns to the east (Iran) and to the south (Syria, Palestine, Egypt). During these invasions, in the Ottoman army had 6,000 camels in the upplying the army's needs, including water demand *(Ibid: 142).*

In May 1534, two decades of tension between the Ottoman and Safavid empires finally boiled over. After securing a truce with the Habsburgs the previous year, Sultan Suleyman I left the Ottoman capital Istanbul and marched east toward the Caucasus, the region where he intended to strike his archenemy, Shah

---

[1] The English-language name Anatolia derives from the Greek Ἀνατολή (Anatolē) meaning "the East" and designating (from a Greek point of view) eastern regions in general.

Tahmasp I. After the sultan's departure, conjectures about what could happen following the military confrontation were many and varied. Maybe, people in his entourage thought, Samarkand, Khurasan, Turan would be next. No one could have predicted that, as the Safavid army retreated deeper into Persia and winter approached, Suleyman would abruptly end the chase and set his sights on Baghdad, which he would triumphantly enter before year's end. The Ottoman camp had even less inkling that the impending campaign would eventually unify the entire Tigris and Euphrates rivers under Istanbul's control. Without forethought, the Ottomans at the end of 1534 joined other natural and biological forces governing, and being governed by, the two longest rivers in West Asia *(Husain: 10)*.

Throughout history, large rivers have created opportunities for political expansion into the remote interiors of the continents. From central Italy, imperial Rome used the Rhone to penetrate Gaul and relied on the Rhine and the Danube to guard its settlements in Germania and Pannonia. The energy of the Tigris-Euphrates system conferred upon the Ottoman Empire a competitive advantage and a logistical edge over its rivals. Wind and river currents extended the distances over which Istanbul could field heavy artillery, food supplies, and troops along the eastern frontier. One of the reasons that the Safavid Empire—its chief opponent in the east—could not sustain a more formidable war machine was that the Iranian Plateau lacked navigable waterways comparable to the Tigris and Euphrates. Even though its total land area is three times larger than Iraq, Iran enjoys only half of its neighbor's surface flow. This hydrologic deficiency made the business of provisioning a large army with field guns much more difficult, forcing the Safavids to rely almost entirely on overland transport through the Zagros range. Ottoman armies in the east, as a result, tended to be better armed and fed than their Safavid rivals and could keep Iraq, with brief interruptions, under Istanbul's dominance throughout the early modern period *(Ibid: 33)*.

The Tigris and Euphrates formed lifelines for Ottoman defenses along the eastern frontier. Like the Danube in the west, they "made the frontier feel closer" to the imperial center. They channeled natural resources from areas of surplus to areas of need through the treacherous terrain of the Jazira desert. It was through these geographical arteries, carrying vital supplements pumped by the imperial heart, that Iraq stayed within the Ottoman body politic *(Ibid: 49)*.

To control water and land communications in the lower basin, Istanbul poured its resources into Baghdad and Basra. The two fortresses were the largest in Iraq and enjoyed a propitious location. In the south, Basra sat at the crossroads of four rivers (Shatt al-Arab, Tigris, Euphrates and Karun rivers) through which travelers and cargo from all directions passed. North of Basra, Baghdad stood at the point where the Tigris and Euphrates come closest together, separated by a mere twenty-five miles of land. As in Basra, locational advantage conferred resilience to Baghdad since its founding in the early Middle Ages *(Ibid: 45).*

The Ottoman system of water communication impacted the two ends of the drainage basin differently. In the north, it drove environmental change by adding pressure on livestock for their skins, on arable fields for their harvests, and on Earth's crust for its ore deposits. In the south, the influx of guns and grains transformed Ottoman fortresses into centers for organized violence, exercising the powers of life and death over their hinterlands. As armed confrontations with Safavid Persia broke out throughout the sixteenth and early seventeenth centuries, fortresses along the Tigris, in particular, became highly militarized and home to the largest Ottoman garrisons in the southeastern frontier. From them, military personnel and hardware flowed to smaller outposts. The fortress of Mosul, for instance, provided support to the Ottoman regiment in Kirkuk near the Zagros foothills. Samawa in the lower Euphrates relied on Baghdad, whose janissaries served in the small town by rotation. At the confluence of the Tigris and Euphrates, Qurna was a military dependency of Basra. Among its peers upstream and downstream, the Baghdad fortress stood as the most ominous display of Ottoman military might. The Tigris on the west and walls behind a moat on the east enclosed the city within an irregular pentagon dominated by ten towers, each equipped with six to seven pieces of artillery. In the middle of the seventeenth century, the renowned Ottoman traveler Evliya Chelebi counted 1,060 artillery pieces of different types and sizes stationed on the wall towers, behind the gates, and in the citadel. Only in Istanbul, Budapest, and a couple other places in the empire, he wrote, could one find artilleries as impressive as those guarding Baghdad *(Ibid: 49–50).*

The unification of the Tigris and Euphrates allowed Istanbul to rebalance natural resource disparity along its eastern frontier. It organized regular shipments of grain, metal, and timber from upstream areas of surplus in Anatolia and the Jazira (the stony plateau between the Tigris and Euphrates north of Baghdad) to downstream areas of need in Iraq. Northern grain in the form of wheat and barley supported larger garrisons in the south; metal in the form of armaments equipped the garrisons with gunpowder weapons; and timber in the form of rivercraft delivered both grains and arms. Some river rafts were even broken up for their timber to be redeployed in the south. For some 200 years, this imperial system of waterborne communication anchored the Ottoman presence in Iraq, enabling Istanbul to fend off foreign rivals, suppress domestic revolts, and exploit the organic wealth of the Tigris-Euphrates alluvial plain *(Ibid: 13–14).*

In control of the entire drainage basin after 1534, the Ottoman Empire retrofitted the Tigris and Euphrates with a network of docks, pontoon bridges, and boat construction facilities that allowed it to manage—and profit from—the movement of peoples and goods between Syria, Anatolia, Persia, and Iraq. More important, the imperial system of waterborne communication created heavily militarized and Sunnified fortresses that stabilized the Ottoman presence in the eastern frontier and held major threats to Ottoman hegemony in check. Without the Tigris and Euphrates, Ottoman rule in Iraq would have resembled its experience in the Arabian Peninsula or any other inland region that lacked useful transport rivers—far less concrete and contingent on the fickle goodwill of tribal and religious leaders. In fact, the main reason the governors of Baghdad were reluctant to take on the fundamentalist Wahhabi movement in Arabia during the late eighteenth century—despite being repeatedly admonished by Istanbul to do so—was the difficulty of provisioning an army in the middle of the desert *(Ibid: 54)*.

The desired outcome of state-sponsored boat-building activities in Birecik and Basra was to thwart the challenges to Ottoman hegemony in Iraq and the Persian Gulf. Three major players confronted the Ottoman Empire in the east and triggered most gunboat construction orders: one was maritime and European, another overland and Persian, and between them stood an amphibious Arab enemy. Each rival influenced Ottoman naval buildup along the Tigris and Euphrates *(Ibid: 62)*.

The Ottoman Empire depended on its fleet along the Tigris and Euphrates to fend off its attackers from Persia. While its eastern rival relied entirely on land troops, Istanbul could count on a more complex and effective armed force that included a navy. Despite a brief setback between 1623 and 1638, Ottoman armies ultimately prevailed and maintained their edge over Safavid armies.

For the Ottoman state's thorniest challenge in the east were not the empires of Portugal and Persia but rather peoples of more modest possibilities who, along with their herds, made a home for themselves in Iraq. Unlike the episodic encroachment of foreign powers, this domestic menace posed an omnipresent threat to the Ottoman order. What it lacked in technology and resources it made up for in mobility, flexibility, and a peculiar geography. "All the forts and villages are in the water," wrote the Ottoman governor of Basra about one of his riotous districts in 1565. "Capturing them by [conventional] battle and governing them are not feasible." The tribal population of Iraq squared off against the Ottoman state on its own marshy terrain and fought according to its own rules.

With the aid of the river fleet, the Ottoman army adapted to fighting on this unconventional landscape. Ottoman expeditions against insubordinate tribal groups tended to include a significant naval force. Beyond the needs of the battlefield, the Ottoman fleet was critical for policing and governing the area. In the words of Teixeira in 1604, Ottoman galleys in Basra "are for use in the river and thereabouts, to keep in order the rebellious Arabs, from whom they [the Turks] exact heavy tribute." To crush the Arab tribes at war and exact tribute from them at peace, Istanbul placed numerous small and large construction and renovation orders in Birecik and Basra as well as in Raqqa and Baghdad.

In short, security anxiety and conflicts with Portugal, Persia, and Iraqi tribesmen created incentives for the Ottoman Empire to maximize its naval strength and maintain a provincial squadron in the Tigris-Euphrates basin. The agitated state of affairs was unique to the early modern era, in which the river basin was dominated in its entirety by a Sunni Turkish empire in frequent conflict within every side—with Christian Europeans, Shiʿi Persians, and tribal Arabs of mixed Muslim persuasions. In other historical periods, a naval industry on the scale the Ottomans established was either unnecessary or impossible to set up. It was unnecessary when the river basin was remote from a ruling power's frontier conflicts, as was the case during the Umayyad and Abbasid periods (661–1258). Likewise, the Ottomans' comprehensive naval infrastructure could not have emerged without political cohesion, which the region lacked for most of its history *(Ibid: 65–66).*

4.1.3 Steamship Era

The importance of navigable rivers in the Ottoman Empire became especially obvious during the steamship era. In the second half of the 19th century navigable rivers became an important link between the seas and seaports on one side and the rich valleys of the continent on the other side. The rise of commerce in the world in the 19th century contributed bring navigable rivers to the forefront. Launching steamboats on the Danube River was an important experience for both Europe and the Ottoman Empire. After that the attention was also given to the Euphrates and Tigris rivers *(Ekinci 2007: 4–7).*

The English began explore the Euphrates and Tigris rivers for steamship communication in 1830–1831. At the time, the English were looking for a short way to India and thats why they wanted to launch steamships on the Euphrates and Tigris rivers. For example, they wanted from Persian Gulf via the Euphrates River to reach to Meskene (modern Syria) or Birecik (modern Turkey) and then to Iskenderun (modern Turkey) by railway.

The British Empire wanted to connect the Euphrates and Orontes rivers to each other via the canal, thus creating a short route from the Mediterranean Sea to the Persian Gulf. When the first railways were being built in Europe, there were also plans to build a railway in the Ottoman Empire. River communication was seen as a continuation of rail communication. The reason for this interest of the British Empire wasn't the rich lands of Mesopotamia but the finding of short and convenient roads to India and keeping them under control. According to their plan, that route would become an alternative way to India via Red Sea (the Suez Canal constructed between 1859 and 1869—auth.). In addition, the ships would be released from the threat of monsoons in the western part of the Indian Ocean and the Red Sea (seaway from Istanbul to Basra through Suez Canal by ferry took 35 days).

The positive results of the steamboat test on the Danube and Rhine rivers also inspired hopes to do the same on the Euphrates and Tigris rivers. Investigates showed Tigris River is more suitable[2] for steamships in Basra-Baghdad route than the Euphrates. First two steamships were named "Fırat" (Turkish name for Euphrates) and "Dicle" (Turkish name for Tigris) *(Ibid: 24–26).*

Although the first attempts were unsuccessful, the Ottoman Empire and Britain Empire did not back down and ultimately started steamship tours on the Tigris and the Euphrates. The steamships began to appear between Basra and Baghdad. However, it was also planned to carry out river communication in the directions of Mosul-Baghdad and Basra-Meskene. But the opportunities here were limited. For example, a powerful steamboat from Baghdad to Mosul could reach only several times a year during the watery (abundant) season. It was necessary to clear that part of the Tigris River for ensuring permanent traffic which needed a major investment. Such an investment was also needed in the case of the Euphrates, in the Basra-Meskene part *(Ibid: 108).*

Construction of Berlin-Baghdad Railway has had some impact on steamship communication in the Euphrates and Tigris rivers. It turned out that rail communication has a number of advantages over river communication. For example, the railway distance from Baghdad to Basra was 500 km, which train was overcoming in 1 day (20–30 hours), whereas the river distance from Baghdad to Basra was 800 km, and for steamships it lasted at least 4–5 days by under normal conditions and 7–8 days in the low water season. The river's bend, depth, as well as variation of their flows in different seasons are very important. If river navigation had justified itself, there would be no need to build the Mosul-Baghdad (400–500 km) or Baghdad-Basra railways. In addition, the railway could be built in

[2] We think that it has two main reasons. 1) In modern Iraq the Tigris surpasses Euphrates in terms of the volume of its flow, 2) Unlike the Euphrates, the Tigris flows through Baghdad, Central Iraq.

anywhere, while river communications were limited. On the other hand, steamboats on the Euphrates and Tigris were necessary not only to reach point A from point B, but also to reach the other bank of the river *(Ibid: 73).*

During World War I, the Tigris River was widely used for military purposes, especially for moving divisions from the Caucasian front to the Mesopotamian front. The Euphrates River was also used for military purposes *(Bash 2016).* In addition, the Euphrates and the Tigris played an important role in the political interests of Germany, an ally of the Ottoman Empire, as well as in German military command in the Ottoman army. The same can be said for the British command, as well as for Mustafa Kemal Ataturk, the founder of the Republic of Turkey *(Sarikaya 2018: 38).*

Even in the 21st century the idea of using the Euphrates as a navigable watercourse is up-to-date. Hamza Tashkeser, representative of Maritime Undersecretariat of Turkey showed his waterway project in 2011. He emphasized that, the length of the route to the Persian Gulf from the Mediterranean using the Suez Canal and the Red Sea is 5,700 km, however, in the case of the Euphrates River it will be 1,700 kilometers (Karkamis (Turkish-Syrian border)-Basra route). Compared to the sea route, the river route is more three times shorter. But there are 7 dams on this route, 3 of them in Syria (Tishreen, Tabqa, Baath), 4 in Iraq (Haditha, Ramadi, Fallujah and Hindiya). Hamza Tashkeser doesn't consider these dams as technical barriers because there are mechanisms to bypass dams in the 21st century, and as a result, the Euphrates River can indeed become a commercial and tourist route, which will be profitable the regional countries and not only (for the European countries, too) (Deniz Haber Ajansı 2011).

We argue that this project of Hamza Tashker could not be implemented in recent years due to the war in Syria and unstable situation in Iraq, as well as due to Turkey's neo-Ottoman policy. But we do not exclude that this project will be implemented in the future when all these problems are resolved.

Going back to the Ottoman times, let's note that, it seemed that launching steamboats on the Euphrates and Tigris would not pose a legal problem, as the Ottoman Empire controlled both banks of both rivers. However, launching steamships became not only the question of the Ottoman Empire and the British Empire, but also of Iran, due the Karun River coming from Iran was joining the Shatt al-Arab River. That's why British Empire wanted to coordinate the issue of steamship communication on the Euphrates and Tigris also with Iran. Disagreements between the two sides pertained to the sector, which was from south of the confluence place of Karun and Shatt al-Arab rivers *(Ekinci 2007: 45).* This shows that Iran's factor in the Euphrates and Tigris water projects was also in the Ottoman era.

Using of the waters of the Euphrates-Tigris Rivers was not a controversial issue during the Ottoman period, but immediately after the First World War, issues dealing with water rights began to emerge. During the mandate period, the Allies were concerned about water use but not enough to raise the potential for conflict. In 1920, the French and British signed a convention establishing consultative committees over the use of the two rivers. This was at the request of the French, who envisioned diverting the Tigris to irrigate vast areas of Syria. France also negotiated a bilateral treaty with the Republican Turks on October 20, 1921, which concerned downstream riparian rights and tapping the Euphrates for use by the city of Aleppo. The Treaty of Lausanne signed between the Allies and the new nation of Turkey on 24 July 1923 included the following provisions in article 109 regarding the uses of international water.

"In default of any provisions to the contrary, when as a result of the fixing of a new frontier the hydraulic system (canalisation, inundation, irrigation, drainage or similar matters) in a State is dependent on works executed within the territory of another State, or when use is made on the territory of a State, by virtue of pre-war usage, of water or hydraulic power, the source of which is on the territory of another State, an agreement shall be made between the States concerned to safeguard the interests and rights acquired by each of them. Failing an agreement, the matter shall be regulated by arbitration".

This article has been interpreted by some authors as "an explicit appreciation of the rights of the downstream parties." Other specialists have constructed it to mean that "Turkey should confer with Iraq before beginning any activities that may alter the flow of the Euphrates." In any event, the French renegotiated a second treaty—titled the Convention of Friendship and Good Neighborly Relations—on 30 May 1926, ratifying the previous agreement. A third Franco-Turkish protocol was signed on May 3, 1930 that committed the two nations to coordinating any plans to use the waters of the Euphrates. The outbreak of World War II ended further conversations about water in the Euphrates-Tigris basin *(Lorenz and Erickson 2013: 36–38).*

Thus, water was a subject of both rivalry and cooperation in the Ottoman era, which became obvious in the 20th and 21st centuries. Besides, big rivers in the Ottoman Empire have been taken as important transport routes, and this importance similarly is preserved today in the modern Republic of Turkey. The Ottoman Empire has also faced a number of water tough challenges (supply of drinking water to cities, providing farmers with irrigation water and so on), which continues hitherto in the modern Republic of Turkey. Finally, fresh water has played a very important role in the Ottoman Empire and water issues have been in the spotlight of the authorities, which continues hitherto in the modern Republic of Turkey.

4.2 The First Steps of the Republic of Turkey in Water Sphere

4.2.1 EIE

The decision to utilize water resources goes back to Mustafa Kemal Ataturk, the founder of the Republic of Turkey. During those years when the country was making efforts for change and improvement in all spheres the need for electricity came to the fore as the most critical and urgent one. Then, upon the order of Ataturk the Administration for Electricity (Elektrik Işleri Etud Idaresi, EIE in Turkish acronym) was established in 1936 as a step to use streams in the country for producing electricity. EIE responsibled for stream flow measurement, hydropower planning and design. The General Directorate of EIE was affiliated to the Ministry of Energy and Natural Resources, and it was the main agency responsible for hydrometric measurement (part of its responsibility lies with the DSI). The EIE conducts studies and surveys to explore the country's hydropower potential, executes engineering services and designs studies for dams and HEPPs. It also carries out studies for new and renewable energy sources (wind power, solar energy etc.) and it oversees and makes hydrological plans for Build-Operate-Transfer (BOT) projects (World Bank 2006, 5).

EIE started intensive studies with the "Keban Project" including the establishment of gauging stations along the Euphrates to examine the flow of the river and draw necessary conclusions. Geological and topographical studies on the Keban gorge started in 1938. Over the years, the information gathered by the gauging stations was very useful for constructing a dam in Keban (five such stations were built before 1943). Thus in the 1930s the foundation of the South East Anatolian project (Güneydoğu Anadolu Projesi, GAP in Turkish acronym) was laid. It is noteworthy that Ataturk was inspired by the USSR in this context. In 1934 USSR ambassador to Ankara told to Ataturk about the construction of a dam on the Dnieper. After that Ataturk told Finance Minister Celal Bayar that they also can build such a dam in Turkey too *(Topdemir 2009: 95, 103).*

4.2.2 DSİ

EIE gave weight to drillings along both the Euphrates and Tigris in the period 1950–1960. Upon the emergence of new needs, the General Directorate of State Hydraulic Works (Devlet Su İşleri, DSİ in Turkish acronym) was established under Act No. 6200 on 18 December 1953 and was organized in 1954. This led to the emergence of the idea of basin surveys in Turkey and consequently Turkey was divided into 26 water basins in which the DSİ launched its surveys and planning work. DSİ General Directorate is a prime government agency responsible for planning and constructing facilities for utilization of water resources and for mitigation the effects of water related disasters. Until 2007 DSI acted under the aegis of the Ministry of Energy and Natural Resources, but in August 2007 DSI has been attached to the Ministry of Environment and Forestry (MoEF).

DSİ mainly serves to 4 sectors;

- To supply domestic and industrial water to accommodation areas;
- To take measures against flood hazards;
- To realise irrigation projects;
- To develop hydroelectric energy potential.

By these applications, DSI plays an important role in economic development of Turkey. The main financial resources (98%) of DSİ come from the national budget.

DSI activities are mainly in four groups

1. Investigation and planning
    - Data collection and surveys,
    - Project planning
2. Design and construction
    - Agriculture
    - Energy
    - Services
    - Environment
3. Quality control
4. Operation

- Irrigation and flood control

Water resources are limited but water demand for agricultural irrigation, domestic and industrial usage, and hydroelectric energy generation is increasing day by day. DSI tries to meet all these demands if there are enough water amount in water storage facilities.

Scope of DSİ

DSİ develops technically, economically and environmentally sound projects (via either in-house staff or outsourcing) by the activities summarized below:

- Basic investigations and surveys;
- Gauging of stream-flow and groundwater;
- Soil analyses and classifications;
- Agricultural economy analyses;
- Geological, hydraulic, geotechnical, and geophysical surveys;
- Water quality analyses;
- Hydraulic structures modeling;
- Physical and chemical analyses of construction materials;
- Survey and planning for river basin development,
- Master Plan and feasibility studies,
- Project studies of water structures (irrigation and drainage, water treatment plants, flood control structures, etc.),
- Where necessary, execution of land expropriation as well as preparation of resettlement action plans;
- Prepare environmental impact assessment (EIA) reports;
- Propose inclusion of projects in the investment programs;
- Preparation of contract documents and implementation of bidding for the works to be contracted out to judicial persons;
- Supervision of constructions;
- Allocate water usage right to private sector's HEPPs,
- Transfer facilities to related agencies, that is, HEPPs to the electricity authority, water treatment plants to the municipalities, irrigation facilities to the irrigation organizations);
- Manage the facilities not transferred,
- Provision of machinery and equipment to implement the above work.
- Design of hydraulic structures *(DSİ: 1)*.

Dam construction policy
Dams construction in the Republic of Turkey began in the 1930s. The Cubuk-I Dam was constructed from 1930 to 1936 to meet water need of Ankara. In 1938, the Gyolbash Reservoir for irrigation was put into operation in Bursa. Construction of major reservoirs in the Republic of Turkey began in the 1950s. In 1955, the Elmali 2 reservoir was put into operation, in 1956 the Seyhan and Sariyar reservoirs, in 1958 the Demirkopru reservoir, and in 1960, the Hirfanli reservoir. By the way, the Saryaar Reservoir became the first reservoir of energy significance built in Turkey. The rate in dam construction has increased tremendously after 1950's, especially after the establishment of DSİ. In total, 120 reservoirs were built in Turkey by 1980. As of 2013, 593 reservoirs have been built in Turkey. It is planned to build 400 large reservoirs in Turkey in the 21st century. As a result, Turkey has become one of the world's leading countries in both the number of reservoirs it has built and the size of its reservoirs. Table 4.1 shows that, most reservoirs (218) were built in 1990–2000 *(Agiralioglu 2014: 121–122).*

Table 4.1 Reservoirs built in Turkey

Period	Number of built reservoirs
1936–1940	2
1941–1950	1
1951–1960	10
1961–1970	28
1971–1980	78
1981–1990	158
1991–2000	218
2001–2010	101
2011–2012	6
Total	**593**

Summing up this part, we want to mention that new Turkish Republic had a number of key issues (water supply, electricity generation, agricultural development, industrialization), that's why the water sector came under the authorities' attention more than 10 years after the republic was created. Population growth also increased the demand for electricity in Turkey, which made it necessary to implement water projects (in 1923 the population of Turkey was 13 million, in 1955—25 million, in 1975—45 million). Useful experience in building reservoirs abroad (USSR) has served as a guide for Turkey. But the pace of construction of reservoirs depended on Turkey's financial capabilities that were limited. However, technological progress in the world and attraction of investments opened new perspectives for Turkey in dam construction area.

4.2.3 The Water Sphere of Turkey

Contrary to the general perception, Turkey is not a country rich in freshwater resources. Water rich countries are those which have 10.000 cubic meters of water per capita yearly. This is well above the 1.500 cubic meters per capita in Turkey. Another point is that Turkey's water is not always in the right place at the right time to meet present and anticipated needs. Certain regions of Turkey such as the Black Sea region have ample but unusable freshwater, while some of the more heavily populated and industrialized regions such as the Marmara and the Aegean regions lack sufficient fresh water (*Rep. of Turkey Ministry of Foreign Affairs, Turkey's Policy on Water Issues*).

Annual mean precipitation in Turkey is 574 mm, which corresponds to 448 BCM of annual water volume in the country. A volume of 246 BCM water evaporates from water bodies and soils to atmosphere. 63 BCM of water leaks into groundwater, whereas 28 BCM is retrieved by springs from groundwater contributing to surface water. Also, there are 7 BCM volume of water coming from neighboring countries. Thus, total annual surface runoff amounts to a volume of (139+28+7) 174 BCM of water. Including 35 (63–28) BCM net discharging into groundwater (covering safe yield extraction, unregistered extraction, emptying into the seas, and transboundary), the gross (surface and groundwater) renewable water potential of Turkey is estimated as 209 (174+35) BCM. However, under current technical and economic constraints, annual exploitable potential has been calculated as 100 BCM of net water volume, as 83 BCM from surface water resources, as 3 BCM from neighboring countries, as 14 BCM from groundwater safe yield (*DSİ: 17*).

At present, 59 BCM water has been consumed in various sectors in Turkey; 43 BCM in the agriculture (irrigation—72%), 8 BCM in the water supply (domestic—14%), 8 BCM in the industry (industrial—14%). This sum accounts for development of 59% of the available exploitable potential of 100 BCM (total). In 2023, water consumption in various sectors in Turkey will reach to 100 BCM; 64 BCM in the agriculture (irrigation—64%), 16 BCM in the water supply (domestic—16%), 20 BCM in the industry (industrial—20%) *(Ibid: 19)*.

Turkey has dynamic economic development and rapid population growth. In recent decades Turkey has made great strides in water resources development for domestic use, irrigation, and flood control and power generation. So, dams may have more than one purpose, including flood protection, energy generation, irrigation, and domestic and industrial water supply. There are 869 dams in Turkey (349 large-scale, 520 small-scale). According to the standards of ICOLD, a dam is classified as a "large dam" if its height from foundation is 15 m or more as well as its height from foundation is between 5–15 m having reservoir volume 1hm3 or more. The total reservoir capacity of dams in operation is about 166 km3. But, usable potential of this amount is 72 km3 (*Ibid: 27*).

Turkey's energy consumption is rising significantly due to rapid urbanization and industrialization. Turkey, which is neither oil nor natural gas producer, plans to meet the rising energy need in several ways, including the increasing use of its indigenous sources and in that respect, hydropower (*Rep. of Turkey Ministry of Foreign Affairs, Turkey's Policy on Water Issues*). The geographical and temporal distribution of precipitation across Turkey is uneven. The western, central and south-eastern parts of the country tend to be drier then those in the north and north-east which receive copious amounts of rain. Turkey's major urban population concentrations and much of its fertile lands are found in water-deficit regions, a fact which complicates distribution for consumption. Moreover, precipitation varies dramatically from winter to summer, and has high seasonal and multi-annual variance (*Biswas 1994: 63*).

Turkey imports 80% of its energy needs as energy fuel materials such as natural gas, oil and coal. Turkey imports 92% of oil and %98 of natural gas, and 50% of coal, which accounts for 16% of the amount which Turkey has paid for total imported materials. $ 37 Billion has been paid for imports of energy fuels in 2017 (Turkey's total import in 2017 is $ 234 Billion). Besides, Turkey has no nuclear power plant in operation, which strengthens the role of hydro energy among other alternatives (*DSİ: 32*). At present, 30% of energy generation in Turkey depended on renewable energy source (hydroelectric %20, wind, geothermal, solar %9, and biomass %1) and the remaining 70% on thermal power (natural gas, lignite, coal, fuel oil, etc., which are fossil fuels) (*Ibid: 34*).

Hydro energy is a renewable, sustainable and clean energy in the other alternative energy sources. Being one of the renewable energy sources par excellence, non-exhaustible, non-polluting and economically more attractive than other renewable sources, hydropower has turned out to be an important contributor to the future energy mix of the country. The gross theoretical viable hydroelectric potential in Turkey is 433 Billion kWh (in Turkey, 216 Billion kWh Technical Potential will be viable via the technology advancing and price soaring). Turkey has 627 HEPP in operation with total installed capacity of 28,200 MW to be generate 98,200 GWh/year, which is 55% of the economically viable hydroelectric potential (the economically viable potential, however, is 180 Billion kWh) (*Ibid: 38*).

The dams and reservoirs built have enabled Turkey to save water from its brief seasons of rainfall to use throughout the year for various purposes, agriculture in particular. Rain-fed agriculture in Turkey is being realized almost to the maximum level. As a result, increasing agricultural productivity has become primarily dependent upon irrigation by using modern techniques (*Rep. of Turkey Ministry of Foreign Affairs, Turkey's Policy on Water Issues*).

Another function of the agricultural sector is to provide finance for economic development. The agricultural and industrial sectors have a mutual relationship in economic development. By demanding the produced inputs and consumer goods of non-agricultural sectors, developing agriculture helps non-agricultural sectors to develop. On the other hand, non-agricultural sectors help the agricultural sector to develop by demanding agricultural goods. Thus, the agricultural and industrial sectors are two markets that are in a bilateral relationship continuously and support each other mutually. Neither of the two sectors can be neglected in economic development.

Total annual food production in the world today seems to be on a satisfactory level in terms of meeting world food consumption needs. However, there are differences in the amount of food production per capita among the regions of the world. In developed countries, less than 7% of the general population is active in the agricultural sector, and a farmer and his family, besides thei own needs, can meet the food needs of 50 people who are active in non-agricultural sectors. Nevertheless, in developing countries, more than half of the population is engaged in the agriculture sector, but a farmer and his family can provide for only 2 people. Almost one third of Turkey's total area is arable land which is 24 million ha (surface area of Turkey—78 Million ha). Rain-fed Agricultural Area: 15.5 Million ha (65%), Economically Irrigable Area: 8.5 Million ha (%35). About 39 million tons of grains and other crops 30 million tons of vegetables and 18 million tons of fruits are ,yearly produced in Turkey (*DSİ: 79*).

As noted Mevlut Aydin—Director General of DSI in Ankara, a dam may have 4 functions; irrigation (agriculture), hydropower (hydroelectric power plant, HEPP), water supply (domestic and industrial water supply), flood protection (flood control, environment) (*Ibid: V*).

We agree with him, and don't exclude that in the beginning, these four factors (especially first three functions) were the motives for building dams in Turkey. But It is important to understand that then (especially in the 21st century) new functions emerged for Turkey's hydro policy.

4.3 Physical Characteristics of the Euphrates, Tigris and Orontes Rivers

Among the transboundary rivers worldwide, the Euphrates and Tigris Rivers are two of the most outstanding rivers in the world. The combined water potential of the rivers is almost equal to that of the Nile River. Both rise in the high mountains of north-eastern Turkey and flow down through Turkey, Syria, and Iraq and eventually join to form the Shatt-al-Arab 200 km before they flow into the Persian Gulf (its drainage area is 80,800 km2).

The Euphrates and Tigris Rivers account for 28% of Turkey's total water potential (Euphrates—17%, Tigris—11%). Turkey is divided into 26 surface hydrological basins, the largest of which is the Euphrates-Tigris Basin (176,143 km2). Both rivers cross the south-eastern region of Turkey which receives less precipitation compared with other regions of the country. Turkey contributes to about 90% of the average annual flow of 32 billion cubic meters (BCM) of the Euphrates; the remaining 10% comes from Syria (some sources (Kolars and Mitchell, 1991) even suggest that 98% of the Euphrates flow originates in Turkey). As for the Tigris, 52% of the total average flow of 49 BCM comes from Turkey, while Iraq contributes to all the rest. There is, however, a declining trend in the natural flows as a result of climate change. Total average flow of Euphrates and Tigris in Turkey is 55.4 BCM.

The Euphrates-Tigris-Shatt Al Arab river system constitutes by far the largest surface water resource in the study area. The Euphrates–Tigris River Basin is a transboundary basin with a total area of 879,790 km2 from the headwaters in the Taurus-Zagros Mountain Range to the Mesopotamian lowlands and the only outlet to the Persian Gulf, the Shatt al Arab (13% of the Middle East). The overall basin is also home to around 54 million people in Iran, Iraq, Syria and Turkey. Table 4.2 shows how the Euphrates-Tigris basin is divided territorially among the riparian countries.

Table 4.2 Country areas in the Euphrates-Tigris River Basin

Countries included	Area of country in basin (km2)	As % of total area of the basin	As % of total are of the country
Iraq	407,880	46.4	93.1
Turkey	192,190	21.8	24.5

(continued)

Table 4.2 (continued)

Countries included	Area of country in basin (km2)	As % of total area of the basin	As % of total are of the country
Iran	166,240	18.9	9.5
Syria	96,420	11.0	52.1
Saudi Arabia	16,840	1.9	0.8
Jordan	220	0.03	0.2

4.3.1 The Euphrates River

- **Basin facts**

The Euphrates River originates in Turkey, flows through Syria and joins the Tigris in Iraq to form the Shatt al Arab, which discharges into the Persian Gulf. The river has three riparians, but its basin is distributed among five countries: Iraq, Jordan, Saudi Arabia, Syria and Turkey. The Euphrates Basin covers about 440,000 km2 of which 47% (206,800 km2) is located in Iraq; 22% (96,800 km2) in Syria, and 28% (123,200 km2) in Turkey. Jordan (0.03%—132 km2) and Saudi Arabia (2.97%—13,068 km2) are considered basin riparians, but they contribute surface water only under very rare and extreme climatic conditions.

- **River course**

The Euphrates is the longest river in Western Asia with a total length of 2,786 km. It originates in the mountains of eastern Turkey, not far from the city of Erzurum in the Armenian Highlands. Its headwaters, the eastern and western tributaries Karasu and Murat, originate at an altitude of nearly 3,000 m above sea level (asl) and join to form the Euphrates at the city of Keban. The Keban Dam is located 10 km downstream in a narrow gorge. From here the Euphrates flows south, and is fed by small tributaries and wadis before it crosses into Syria at the towns of Karkamis, Turkey, and Jarablus, Syria. The river covers 455 km from the confluence of the Karasu and the Murat to the Syrian-Turkish border.

Three tributaries flow into the Euphrates in Syria. The Sajur, the Balikh and the Khabour Rivers are all fed by tributaries or groundwater from Turkey. These three sub-basins are therefore shared between Syria and Turkey. South of the Khabour, the Euphrates has no other tributaries in Syria or Iraq. However, a number of dry riverbeds suggest that seasonal tributaries in the Syrian Desert flow into the Euphrates. The river leaves Syria at Al Bukamal and enters Iraq at an elevation of 165 m asl. The Syrian stretch of the Euphrates covers 661 km.

- **Climate**

From its origin in Turkey until its confluence with the Tigris, the Euphrates crosses several climatic zones. Mean annual precipitation in the Euphrates Basin ranges from approximately 1,000 mm in the Turkish headwaters in the north to 150 mm in Syria and just 75 mm in southern Iraq. The climate diagrams for selected stations clearly illustrate this shift from a cooler Mediterranean climate to an increasingly hot and dry (arid) climate as the river progresses to the sea. The Euphrates originates in a mountainous Mediterranean climatic zone, which is characterized by hot, dry summers and cold, wet winters. In the mountainous headwater areas, precipitation predominates in autumn, winter and spring with a mixture of rain and snowfall in winter. Annual precipitation gradually decreases to the southwest to about 300 mm near the Syrian-Turkish border. The mild influence of the Mediterranean Sea further decreases inland and to the south. Rainfall is sparse in the arid climate of the Iraqi Lowlands (Mesopotamian Plain), with an annual average of 150–200 mm falling mainly in the winter months. Summers are dry and hot with daytime temperatures of up to 50°C.

- **Population**

The Euphrates Basin has an estimated population of about 23 million (in 2010), of which 44% (10,2 million) lives in Iraq, 25% (5,69 million) in Syria and 31% (7,15 million) in Turkey. Along its course to the Mesopotamian Plains in Iraq, the Euphrates continues in south-easterly direction, crossing desert uplands and narrow wadis until Ramadi. Near Hit, the river enters the alluvial lowlands of Mesopotamia, where it briefly splits into various channels. Further downstream, the river loses water to a number of desert depressions and canals, some natural and others man-made. Near the town of Fallujah, the river course veers to the north-east towards the Tigris, but then turns southward again. Here, parts of the river are diverted into canals, some of which drain into the shallow Lake Hammar, while others discharge into the Tigris. The Tigris joins the Euphrates from the east close to the city of Qurnah to form the Shatt al Arab River, which discharges into the Persian Gulf.

- **Hydrological characteristics**

Turkey provides about 89% of the total Euphrates flow generated from 28% of the basin area. By contrast, Syria contributes only 11% of total river flow generated from 22% of the drainage area due to comparatively less rainfall. Contributions by the remaining riparians are generally very small. Most of the Euphrates streamflow originates from precipitation in the Armenian Highlands, and in particular the Keban Hills. In Syria, the Sajur, Balikh and Khabour Rivers and some intermittent streams contribute water to the Euphrates. Their contributions depend on the intensity and volume of precipitation and, increasingly, on water use and drainage in upstream irrigation areas. In Iraq, there are no major surface water contributions to the Euphrates except for rare runoff events generated by heavy storms.

- **Flow regime & Annual discharge variability**

The mean annual flow for the entire period 1938–2010 of record is 26.6 BCM at Jarablus (Syria) and 27.1 BCM at Hit (Iraq). Maximum flow levels were recorded in 1969 with 40 BCM at Hindiyah (Iraq), 56.8 BCM at Jarablus, and 63 BCM at Hit. This contrasts with the lowest annual flow of 3.1 BCM at Hindiyah in 1974, 12.7 BCM at Jarablus in 1976, and 9 BCM at Hit in 1990. Historically, the natural annual flow of the Euphrates at the Syrian-Turkish border was around 30 BCM. However, data records over the last 70 years show a negative trend, indicating a decrease in mean annual flow to about 25 BCM.

The water discharged during the high flow period from March to July (a low-flow season—from August to February). The increased discharge during the high-flow period was generated by snow-melt from the Highlands. With the construction of large water engineering structures in upstream Turkey and Syria, the Euphrates flow regime has shifted towards less pronounced seasonal variation. Water use in the Euphrates Basin in Iraq, Syria and Turkey focuses on irrigation, hydropower and drinking water supply, with agriculture consuming the largest share of water (more than 70%). The Euphrates river flow regime before 1973 can be considered near natural as there was limited water regulation in the runoff-generating area in Turkey. The regulation of the Euphrates River is an extreme example of how human intervention can impact a river regime (because a large portion of Iraqi territory rarely exceeds 300 m in altitude, the topography limits the possibility of impounding the Euphrates behind large dams *(Kibaroglu, Scheumann, Kramer 2011: 281).*

- **Groundwater**

Along its course in Syria, the Euphrates River receives groundwater from aquifers in the western part of the river catchment. These include Eocene chalky lime stones east of Aleppo and a multi-aquifer system of Cretaceous to Neogene Aquifers in the eastern steppe in Syria. The discharge quantities are, however, insignificant in comparison to the total river flow. In the eastern part of the catchment in Syria, the Euphrates River receives important inflows from spring discharges, which feed the tributaries Balikh and Khabour. Syria and Turkey share the Jezira Tertiary Limestone Aquifer System, a productive limestone and dolomite aquifer of Middle Eocene to Oligocene age, which lies in the area between these tributaries on the northern edge of the Syrian Jezira. The aquifer systems annual recharge is estimated at 1,6 MCM; the recharge areas are located mainly on Turkish territory, while discharge occurs via two major springs in Syria.

Small-scale irrigation from river water in Iraq may produce minor quantities of recharge from irrigation return flow in shallow aquifers. In the west and south-west of the Iraqi Jezira, groundwater movement in the Miocene Fatha Formation is directed toward the Euphrates. In most parts of the Iraqi Jezira and the adjoining south-eastern Jezira in Syria, groundwater moves to internal drainage discharge zones such as Wadi Tharthar, Lake Tharthar and the Tawila Salt Flat. Groundwater flow in Paleogene to Neogene carbonate aquifers in the western and southern deserts of Iraq (Umm er Radhuma-Dammam [North]) is directed toward the Euphrates river plain. The groundwater from these aquifers discharges mainly in mudflats, sabkhas and through a series of springs that run parallel to the river course over a length of about 450 km on the edge of the Mesopotamian Plain. The main recharge areas of the aquifers are located in Iraq; minor subsurface inflows occur from outcrop areas of the Paleogene aquifers in Saudi Arabia. Alluvial deposits in the marshlands in the lower Mesopotamian Plain in Iraq create a shallow aquifer. Recharge mainly occurs during winter and through infiltration of Euphrates and Tigris river water. Generally, water flows into the groundwater during high flows when the water level of the rivers exceeds the groundwater table. Conversely, groundwater is discharged into the river during low-flow periods in summer. In the past, several springs discharged south of the Euphrates River and along the base of the western plateau in the marshlands. Groundwater from these springs, most likely emanated from the Neogene Aquifer System (North-West) *(UN-ESCWA, Chapter 1, 2013: 48–61).*

- **Shared tributaries of Euphrates River**

As already mentioned, The Euphrates River has three main shared tributaries: the Sajur and the Balikh/Jallab are shared between Syria and Turkey, while the Khabour sub-basin is shared between Iraq, Syria and Turkey. With an average annual discharge of 97 MCM, the Sajur is the smallest of the three tributaries. Originally, the Balikh/Jallab was fed primarily by the karstic Ain al Arous Spring, but it increasingly receives irrigation return flows from intensive agricultural projects, mainly in Turkey. The Khabour is the largest of the three shared Euphrates tributaries in terms of length and mean annual discharge.

However, annual flow has decreased dramatically over recent decades from 2,120 BCM before 1980 to 924 MCM around 2000, with values constantly decreasing sincethen. While the three Euphrates tributaries used to make up around 8% of annual Euphrates flow, today their contribution has dropped to 5% or less due to decreased flow of the Khabour. In all three sub-basins water is mainly used for irrigation purposes. All three Euphrates tributaries form shared basins between Syria and Turkey.

The Sajur River stems from the confluence of two streams in Turkey, the Ayfinar Deresi and the Bagirsak Deresi. It flows south-eastwards, entering Syria at Kusek and discharging into the Euphrates about 20 km downstream of the city of Jarablus. This confluence is usually flooded by the Tishreen Dam reservoir. The river has a total length of 108 km, of which 48 km lie in Syria and 60 km in Turkey. The Sajur River drainage basin covers 2,860 km2, 40% (1,150 km2) of which lies in Syria and 60% (1,710 km2) in Turkey. According to the Central Bureau of Statistics in Syria, the mean discharge of the Sajur was 3.1 m3/s between 2002 and 2006, which amounts to an annual mean of about 98 MCM. The Sajur River flow contribution to the Euphrates is almost negligible and represents just 0.39% of annual Euphrates flow.

Covering a total surface area of 13,600 km2, **the Balikh/Jallab** sub-basin is shared between Syria (38%—5,200 km2) and Turkey (62%—8,400 km2). The Jallab originates in the Urfa Heights in Turkey and flows south for 15 km before joining the Balikh River which originates in Syria. The two rivers form a tributary to the Euphrates with a total length of about 196 km, of which 107 km lie in Syria and 89 km in Turkey. The Jallab used to be an intermittent stream with an annual discharge of around 111 MCM. According to official figures, the Balikh has an average discharge of 6.8 m3/s (214 MCM/yr), with a maximum discharge of up to 35 m3/s during floods (1,104 MCM/yr). The Balikh River flow contribution to the Euphrates is estimated at around 0.86% of annual Euphrates flow.

The Khabour River is the largest of the three shared Euphrates tributaries in terms of length and mean annual discharge. The Khabour Basin is often described as the most complicated element of the Euphrates system as the river's different branches originate both in Syria and in Turkey. The Khabour Basin is shared by Syria and Turkey, with a small part of the basin in Iraq. The drainage basin covers a surface area of almost 36,200 km2, of which 28% (10,208 km2) lies in Turkey and 66% (23,747 km2) in Syria and 6% (2,244 km2) in Iraq. The Khabour River has a total length of 388 km of which 308 km lie in Syria. The river discharges into the Euphrates near Deir ez Zor. The Khabour River and its tributaries once played a significant role in determining the quantity and quality of Euphrates water, contributing up to 12% of annual Euphrates flow. However, other calculations suggest that the Khabour only contributed a 7% share, if one assumes that the natural annual flow of the Euphrates River at the Syrian-Turkish border was 30 BCM before 1973, and that the near-natural flow of the Khabour was around 2.1 BCM. Current values and shares are probably far lower, suggesting a flow contribution to the Euphrates River of 3.7% for the period 1980–2000. This contribution may have dropped further since 2000 *(Ibid, Chapter 2: 80–90).*

4.3.2 The Tigris River

- **Basin Facts**

The Tigris River originates in the Armenian Highlands in Turkey and flows southeast along a short stretch of the Syrian-Turkish border before entering Iraq. The river merges with the Euphrates River in southern Iraq to form the Shatt al Arab, which discharges into the Persian Gulf. The Tigris has four basin riparians: Iran, Iraq, Syria and Turkey. The basin extends over approximately 221,000 km2, of which 24.5% (54,145 km2) is located in Turkey, 0.4% (884 km2) in Syria, 56.1% (123,981 km2) in Iraq and 19% (41,990 km2) in Iran *(Ibid, Chapter 3: 107).*

According to Aysel Kibaroglu, the Euphrates and its tributaries drain an enormous basin of 444,000 km2, of which 33% lies in Turkey, 19% in Syria, and 46% in Iraq while the Tigris and its tributaries drain an area of 387,600 km2, of which 15% lies in Turkey, 0.3% in Syria, 75% in Iraq, and 9.5% in Iran *(Kibaroglu 2013).* According to a number of sources, the Tigris embraces an overall area of 470,000 km2, though its effective catchment area is estimated to be between 217,843 km2 and 373,000 km2 *(Dolatyar 2000, p. 121).*

- **River course**

The Tigris River is the second longest river in Western Asia, with a length of 1800 km (or 1850 km with 400 km in Turkey, 32 km on the border between Turkey and Syria and 1418 km in Iraq). The river originates in the Taurus Mountains in Turkey, south of the Armenian Highlands and the city of Elazig, which lies at an altitude of 1,500 m asl. It is formed by the confluence of two headwater tributaries, the Batman, which drains from an altitude of approximately 4,000 m asl, and the Botan. In general, the course of the Tigris is less meandering than that of the Euphrates. After covering a distance of almost 400 km in Turkey, it forms the Syrian-Turkish border for about 47 km and then flows through Iraq for more than 1,350 km. The Tigris Basin has a number of tributaries, most of which are shared by Iraq and Turkey or Iran and Iraq. Six main tributaries and several smaller rivers join the Tigris in Iraq.

- **Climate**

The climate in the Tigris Basin ranges from semi-humid in the headwaters to the north, to semi-arid close to the confluence with the Euphrates in southern Iraq. Mean annual basin precipitation is estimated between 400 and 600 mm. However, values of 800 and 150 mm have been registered in the upper and lower parts respectively. Mean precipitation in the Tigris Basin is significantly higher than in the Euphrates Basin (approx. 300 mm/yr). This difference can be attributed to the high precipitation rates in the Zagros Mountains in the east of the Tigris Basin, which contributes to Tigris stream-flow. Precipitation mostly occurs between November and April, with snowfall in the mountains from January to March. Given the semi-arid to arid climate in the lowlands of Iraq and Syria, evapotranspiration causes considerable water loss in the Mesopotamian region (the Euphrates, which is a longer than Tigris, flows through warmer climatic zones, so its evaporation is greater, meanwhile precipitation in the Euphrates Basin is less than in the Tigris Basin therefore Euphrates gets less water from precipitation than Tigris). Air temperatures in the Tigris Basin range from −35°C in winter in the Armenian Highlands to 40°C in summer on the Jezira Plateau (in terms of agriculture, the waters of the Tigris are less suitable than those of the Euphrates because they contain more silt and the main flow is very strong).

- **Population**

The Tigris Basin comprises a total population of approximately 23.4 million inhabitants, of which more than 18 million live in Iraq, 1.5 million in Iran and 3.5 million in Turkey. Only 50,000 people reside in the Syrian part of the basin.

- **Hydrological characteristics**

The Tigris River waters mainly originate in Iran, Iraq and Turkey. Syria does not contribute any significant discharge to the river. In the absence of measured water balance data, riparian contributions are expressed as ranges: upstream Turkey contributes an estimated 40–65% of the river's annual discharge, Iraq 10–40%, while Iranian headwaters and tributaries are estimated to contribute between 5% and 25% to Tigris river flow. The Tigris is mainly fed by precipitation that falls in the Armenian Highlands and Zagros Mountains in Turkey, near the country's southeastern border with Iran. While the Tigris headwaters lie in Turkey, most of its tributaries originate in Iran and join the Tigris in the Iraqi Lowlands.

- **Flow regime & Annual discharge variability**

The mean annual flow for the entire period 1931–2011 of record is 20 BCM at Mosul and 25.7 BCM at Kut (Iraq). Maximum flow levels were recorded in 1969 with 43.1 BCM at Mosul and 59.2 BCM at Kut in 1946. This contrasts with the lowest annual flow of 6.5 BCM at Mosul in 1999 and 4.2 BCM at Kut in 2001. The Tigris river flow regime can be considered natural before the 1970s, with limited water regulation in the runoff generation area in Turkey, Iran and Iraq upstream of Mosul. This natural flow regime shows a high-flow season from February to June and a low-flow season from July to January. The increased discharge during the high-flow period is typically generated by snow-melt and increased precipitation in the Turkish and Iraqi-Iranian mountains.

Compared to the Euphrates flow regime, the Tigris high-flow season is much longer and more pronounced due to higher winter precipitation over a much greater basin area. The gradual melting of snow cover in the headwater region of the Tigris River and its tributaries helps to maintain water levels. Peak discharge in the Tigris Basin generally occurs in April, a month before the peak of the Euphrates River. Minimum flow generally occurs in September.

- **Tributary contribution**

In contrast to the Euphrates River which has few tributaries, the numerous tributaries originating in the Zagros Mountains make significant contributions to runoff along the course of the Tigris River. Flow contribution to the mean annual flow volume of the Tigris from tributaries located between Mosul and Kut amount to an estimated 25 BCM. In the literature these contributions are often referred to as significant, accounting for 50% of the Tigris flow in Baghdad. The addition of 25 BCM to the near-natural mean annual flow volume of the Tigris at Mosul (approx. 21 BCM for the period 1931–1973) would be expected to produce a 46 BCM flow volume at Kut. However, the actual mean annual Tigris flow volume at Kut for the same period was around 32 BCM. There are various explanations for this surprisingly large difference, including hydrological measurement errors, and large-scale abstraction between Mosul and Kut for flood control or other purposes.

- **Groundwater**

Little is known about hydrogeological connectivity between Iraq and Turkey in the Tigris Basin. However, piezometric water levels in the Jezira Aquifer, which is located north-east of the Tigris Basin, suggest a hydraulic connection, with water flowing towards Turkey and possibly entering the country via outcropping aquifers. A minor inflow of groundwater may occur in the area where the river runs along Syria's northeastern border, with water flowing in from the unconsolidated Pliocene aquifer. The water of small springs issuing from aquiferous basalts or from underlying Pliocene conglomerates in that area is generally consumed before it reaches the Tigris River. As such, there are virtually no exploitable groundwater resources in the small Syrian section of the Tigris Basin. There is limited evidence that groundwater flows south-west from the southern part of the Taurus-Zagros Aquifer System towards Iraq. Additionally, it is assumed that some groundwater moves between Iraq and Iran in the south-western Mesopotamian Plain. It has also been suggested that the lower part of the Mandali-Badra-Tib Aquifer lies within Iraq, whereas the higher parts of this aquifer system are mostly located in Iran. In north-western Iraq groundwater from Neogene Aquifers discharges mainly into the Tharthar Depression (Wadi Tharthar and Lake Tharthar), extending west of the Tigris River. Natural conditions have changed due to the diversion of water from the Tigris into the Tharthar Depression, with Lake Tharthar presently recharging the Quaternary Mesopotamian aquifer south of the lake. Between Fatha and Tikrit in north-western Iraq, the Tigris River drains groundwater from the Neogene and Quaternary aquifers on both banks. Between Tikrit and Samarra, the effluent conditions along the river seem to be retained on its western bank only, while the eastern bank becomes influent. Groundwater moves in the Quaternary aquifer from the Tigris River to local depressions in the east *(UN-ESCWA Chapter 3, 2013: 108–112).*

- **Shared tributaries of the Tigris River**

The Tigris River Basin has several sub-basins that are shared between Iraq and Turkey or between Iran and Iraq. The main shared tributaries are the Feesh Khabour, the Greater Zab, the Lesser Zab and the Diyala. With more than 27 BCM, the Tigris tributaries significantly contribute to total Tigris river flow. The main contribution to discharge originates from the Greater and Lesser Zab Rivers, which contribute 40–60% of total Tigris flow in Baghdad. In general, the four shared tributaries exhibit similar flow regimes, with normal fluctuations of wet and dry years around the mean annual flow. Although the Lesser Zab and the Diyala have been dammed since the 1960s, there is currently no evidence of a regulated stream-flow regime.

The Feesh Khabour River (also known as the Little Khabour or Habur in Turkish) originates in Sirnak, in eastern Anatolia in Turkey. The river flows south into Iraq, flowing through Iraqi Kurdistan and then west through the city of Zakho. Downstream from Zakho, the river is joined by its main tributary the Hezil Suyu, which forms the Iraqi-Turkish border for approximately 20 km from here on. The river discharges into the Tigris at the three-country border between Iraq, Syria and Turkey. With a length of about 181 km, the Feesh Khabour River has a catchment area of 6143 km2, of which 57% (3477 km2) are located in Turkey and 43% (2666 km2) in Iraq. The mean annual flow volume at Zakho is around 2 BCM. The flow regime of the Feesh Khabour shows a distinct high-flow season with a peak in May and a low-flow season from July to December.

The Greater Zab River is the largest Tigris tributary in terms of water yield. Its headwaters originate in the Ararat Mountains in Turkey at an altitude of 4636 m asl. The headwater topography is characterized by steep slopes, with several tributaries and wadis (Khazir, Rubar-i-Shin, Rukuchuk and Rubat Mawaran Rivers) flowing into the Greater Zab. This perennial stream has a total length of 462 km and flows mainly in Iraq before discharging into the Tigris River 49 km south of Mosul. The Greater Zab and its tributaries cover a basin area of around 26,310 km2 of which 35% (9209 km2) is located in Turkey and the remainder (17,102 km2) in Iraq. Peak flows of the Greater Zab occur in May. The Greater Zab supplies the Tigris River with an average annual flow volume of 12.7 BCM measured at Eski Kalak and 12 BCM farther upstream at the Bekhme Dam.

Located to the south of the Greater Zab, **the Lesser Zab River** (also Little Zab or Lower Zab) originates in the north-eastern Zagros Mountains in Iran, near the Iraqi border. In the upper basin, the river flows through deep canyons where a number of tributaries such as the Banah and Qazlaga contribute to discharge. With a total length of around 302 km, the Lesser Zab joins the Tigris near the city of Fatha, 220 km north of Baghdad. The Lesser Zab covers a basin area of 19,780 km2, of which about 76% (15,033 km2) lie in Iraq and 24% (4,747 km2) in Iran. The average annual flow volume of the Lesser Zab at Dukan and at the downstream gauging station of Altun Kupri-Goma is about 6 BCM and 7.8 BCM respectively, with an average discharge contribution to the Tigris of around 191 m3/s and 249 m3/s for the two stations. Compared to the Greater Zab, peak flows generally occur earlier in spring (April), mainly as a result of lower snowfall levels and earlier snow-melt. Generally, the Lesser Zab flow regime shows the same dynamics and seasonality as other Tigris tributaries.

The Diyala River originates near Sanandaj in the Zagros Mountains in Iran, forming the Iran-Iraq border for over 30 km. With a total length of 574 km, 17 the river has a drainage area of 33,240 km2, of which 25% (8,310 km2) are located in Iran and 75% (24,930 km2) in Iraq. The Diyala joins the Tigris 15 km south of Baghdad. Its principal tributaries are the Tanjeru, Sirwan and Wand Rivers. Many of the Diyala's smaller tributaries are shared between Iran and Iraq. Measured at the Derbendikhan gauging station for the period of record 1931–2011, the Diyala River has a mean annual flow volume of 4.6 BCM. However, the river's total flow contribution to the Tigris is probably significantly larger as various tributaries are not taken into account at this upstream gauging station. The Diyala stream-flow is very similar to that of the Lesser Zab. It is characterized by peak flows in April and a low-flow season from July until November *(Ibid, Chapter 4: 128–139).*

4.3.3 The Orontes River

- **Basin Facts**

Also known as the Assi River, the Orontes is the only perennial river in Western Asia that flows north from Lebanon to Syria and Turkey and drains west into the Mediterranean Sea. Its flow regime shows typical winter peak flows due to increased precipitation, and summer low flows maintained exclusively by groundwater discharge. The river is mainly used for irrigation purposes with several agricultural projects planned in the three riparian countries. Water quality at the headwaters is generally good, but deteriorates in the middle and lower reaches of the river due to agricultural, urban and industrial activities. There is no basin-wide agreement between the three riparians, but there are several bilateral agreements in place on issues such as water allocation (Lebanon-Syria) and the joint construction of infrastructure (Syria-Turkey). Orontes Basin politics are heavily influenced by the status of Turkish-Syrian relations in general, and discussions over the sharing of the Euphrates River in particular.

The Orontes is also known as the Assi in Arabic, which means "rebel". This is because unlike most rivers in the region, it flows from south to north before draining into the Mediterranean to the west. The Orontes River originates in Lebanon and flows through Syria and Turkey before discharging into the Mediterranean Sea. The Orontes has two tributaries which are shared between Turkey and Syria: the Karasu and the Afrin. The latter originates in Turkey, passes through Syria and discharges into the Orontes in the disputed Hatay region in Turkey. The Orontes Basin area is estimated at 26,530 km2, of which 25% (6633 km2) is located in Turkey, 67% (17,881 km2) in Syria and 8% (2016 km2) in Lebanon (92% of the Orontes River flow comes from Syria, 6% from Lebanon, 2% from Turkey).

- **River Course**

The Orontes River forms the main artery in the Orontes Basin, which consists of several subbasins. The river has a total length of 404 km, of which 38 km lie in Lebanon, 280 km in Syria, 27 km along the Syrian-Turkish border, and 59 km in Turkey. It is the only river in Western Asia that flows to the north and drains to the west into the Mediterranean Sea. The Orontes River originates in Lebanon, not far from the city of Baalbek in the Bekaa Valley. It rises from the karstic Labweh Spring and flows north, entering Syria to the north-east of Hermel, where it flows through an area of intensive irrigation with a network of drainage canals for agricultural use. Farther downstream, the Orontes broadens into the dammed Lake Qattineh, and then crosses the wide Homs Plain. The river passes the cities of Homs and Hama before turning west across the fertile Ghab Valley over a distance of 40 km. The Orontes is mainly canalized in this reach. Before the river reaches Turkey in the province of Hatay, it meanders through Syria and subsequently forms the Syrian-Turkish border for almost 25 km. In Turkey, the river turns south-west and is joined by two tributaries, the Karasu and the Afrin, before finally reaching Antakya and discharging into the Mediterranean Sea near Samandag.

- **Climate**

The climate in the Orontes Basin is characterized by Mediterranean winter precipitation (snow on higher ground and rain elsewhere), which decreases in intensity and quantity as one travels inland from the Mediterranean coastal plain. Precipitation in the basin ranges from around 300 mm/yr (the mean annual rainfall at Aleppo, Syria, is 332 mm) to around 800 mm/yr, with highs in December and January and lows in June and July. Average annual basin precipitation is estimated at 644 mm. Summers are dry and hot. The mean annual air temperature on the coast is around 20°C (measured at Tripoli, Lebanon), decreasing to 17.2°C (measured at Aleppo, Syria) further east.

- **Population**

Estimates show that the Orontes Basin has a population of almost 5.7 million. In Lebanon, the population living in the basin is estimated at 381,000 people (7 %). The area of the basin situated in Syria comprises 4.2 million inhabitants (74 %), while more than 1 million people (19 %) live in the area of the basin that lies in Turkey.

- **Hydrological characteristics**

The sources of the Orontes River are karstic springs that lie at an altitude of 690 m in the Bekaa Valley in Lebanon. The river is mainly fed by groundwater (groundwater contributes up to 90% to stream-flow). Groundwater recharge depends on the snow cover in Mount Lebanon and the Anti-Lebanon Mountains. Generally, the Orontes Basin receives 400 to 500 mm of rain annually, which is characteristic of the Mediterranean climate. In Syria, small streams and springs originating in the Coastal Mountains to the west and Zawiyeh Mountains to the east contribute to the Orontes river flow. Additional water sources originate in the Ghab Valley. In Turkey, the Orontes River receives input from its two northern tributaries, the Afrin and the Karasu.

- **Annual discharge variability & Flow regime**

The mean annual flow volume for the whole Orontes Basin including both the Afrin and Karasu tributaries is estimated at about 1,200 MCM. The mean annual flow volume for the period between 1931 and 2011 was 410 MCM at Hermel,

Lebanon. At Darkosh at the Syrian-Turkish border, the mean annual flow volume was 949 MCM/yr between 1964 and 2011. The Darkosh records show a minimal, though statistically significant, negative trend. From Darkosh onwards, if not before, the Orontes can be considered a regulated river. The mean annual discharge at Hermel is 13 m3/s and farther downstream at Darkosh it is 30.1 m3/s. Despite data gaps, the latter shows a quite regular variability, with drier and wetter periods compared to the mean, and no extreme drought or flood periods. Available data for Al Omeiry station close to the Lebanese-Syrian border northeast of Hermel show a mean annual discharge of 6.4 m3/s. The difference in flow volume between Hermel and Al Omeiry (410 MCM/yr and 202 MCM/yr respectively) indicates that there is significant water abstraction from the Orontes River in this region, possibly for irrigation purposes.

Generally, the downstream station Jisr al Shughur (15,130 km2) exhibits a high-flow season from December to May and a low-flow season from June to November. The Orontes river regime cannot be considered entirely natural due to regulation on the main river stem by canals and dams, but it retains certain natural seasonal characteristics. The increased discharge during the high-flow period is typically generated by increased rainfall throughout the Mediterranean rainy winter season and by snowmelt originating in the mountainous basin areas during spring. The river flow regime is maintained entirely by groundwater discharge during the dry summer months as indicated by the upstream gauging stations at Hermel (1241 km2) and Al Qusayr (1890 km2), similar to a groundwater flow regime without pronounced seasonal variations.

- **Groundwater**

The largest contributor to Orontes river flow is the Ain Zarqa Spring in Lebanon with a mean flow of between 1120 and 13.6 m3/s. The longterm average discharge at the Hermel station (13 m3/s) just downstream from the Ain Zarqa Spring in Lebanon confirms these values. The annual amount of groundwater recharge in the Syrian part of the Orontes Basin is estimated at 1,607 MCM, of which 1,134 MCM discharges as spring flow and the remaining 473 MCM is stored in aquifers and eventually withdrawn from wells for irrigation and water supply.

- **Main shared tributaries—The Afrin & Karasu sub-basins**

The Afrin River, which is shared by Syria and Turkey, is a major tributary to the Orontes. The river originates on the southern slopes of the Kartal Mountains in Turkey, crosses the border into Syria and passes through the city of Afrin.

In the past, the Afrin naturally discharged into Lake Amik. Today the river is drained through the artificial Nahr al Kowsit channel and redirected towards the Orontes River. Infrastructure on the river includes the Afrin Dam in Syria, which was constructed in 1997 with a capacity of 190 MCM. The Afrin River has a total length of 131 km, including 54 km in Syria. An estimated 60 MCM/yr of the Afrin flow originates in Syria, but most of the flow volume (approx. 250 MCM/yr) originates in Hatay Province in Turkey. The Karasu is the second main tributary of the Orontes River. With a total length of 120 km, the river rises in Turkey and subsequently forms a small part of the Syrian-Turkish border. It discharges into the Orontes River at the confluence with the Afrin River north of Antakya. The annual flow volume of the Karasu is approximately 40 MCM/yr *(Ibid, Chapter 7: 228–232).*

Thus, Euphrates is the longest river in Western Asia, but Tigris has the largest flow in Western Asia. The annual flow of the Tigris is more due to the many and important number of tributaries. Unlike Tigris, the Euphrates hasn't a lot of major tributaries.This is probably why Euphrates and Tigris aren't considered as tributaries of each other.

In the case of the Euphrates and the Tigris, Turkey is the upstream country, which means that Syria (midstream country) and Iraq (downstream country) are sensitive and even vulnerable to Turkish water projects in the Euphrates-Tigris basin. Although Syria is upstream country for Iraq in the Euphrates basin, it is also not in a good position, as Tigris doesn't enter Syria. In the case of the Euphrates-Tigris basin, Iraq is simply dependent on Turkey, as well as Syria and Iran. It seems that Iraq is in the most vulnerable position (in the 20th century), but in truth Iraq has the Tigris River, which is more water-rich than the Euphrates in its territory. As a result, Iraq derives the majority of its freshwater from the two rivers.

In the case of the Orontes River, Turkey is a downstream and vulnerable country, meanwhile Syria is upstream country for Turkey (Syria is midstream country in truth since real upstream country is Lebanon).

4.4 Construction of the First Dam on The Euphrates in Turkey—Upper Euphrates Basin

It's known that the Keban project was on the agenda since 1930s to provide Turkey with sufficient and cheap electricity. In this context in the second half of the 1930s the geological and topographical works were commenced and flow monitoring stations were established on the Keban gorge. Map works of Keban water collection areas were completed in 1940. In the same year the first oil well was opened in Turkey (in Batman). But World War II and the ensuing economic difficulties delayed the implementation of Keban project.

4.4.1 Suleyman Demirel—The Architect of GAP

In 1949 EIE sent a delegation to the United States, which included young engineer Suleyman Demirel (who will become Prime Minister of Turkey several times, as well as President—auth.). In USA Turkish delegation visits Nevada province to get acquainted with Hoover reservoir on Colorado River. Then the delegation returned to Turkey with great impressions. In 1955 Demirel was appointed the second head of the DSİ (until 1960), and was to oversee the construction of a multitude of dams, HEPPs, and irrigation facilities. Demirel had seen how rivers are controlled in the US how they get electricity from rivers, how rivers irrigated fields, how dry up marshes, how organize potable water supply, and wanted to do the same in Turkey. As a result, 16 years after seeing the Hoover reservoir, Demirel embarked on a similar reservoir construction in Keban. Demirel wanted to build reservoirs and HEPPs to give people and land water, to provide clean drinking water for villages, to illuminate villages in the evenings, and to obtain cheap and sufficient electricity *(Turgut 2000: 48–49).*

According to him, due to the lack of water the villagers were constantly dreaming of the rain. 'Turkey is a country surrounded by seas on three sides, with countless rivers and streams, wide and fertile lands in which to grow various crops ranging from barley to tea. Despite this, rain is called god's compassion (in Turkish—rahmet). There is water in winter, but it is an undesirable period. When water needs, it does not exist. Turkey has three serious problems: floods, droughts and darkness (in the evenings). The dams are meant to solve these problems. The dams will collect winter waters, thus the valleys will be saved from the floods, homes will be saved from demolition, lands will not filled with stones and sand, i.e. will not become useless. The water stored in reservoirs will be used for industrialized agriculture. Dams will also provide electricity to our homes, streets, industry. If our rivers will produce 100 billion kWh, that would be equivalent to 100 million tonnes of coal. Dams should become monuments to the welfare of the Turkish population, providing income to the Turkish state',—said Demirel *(Ibid: 59–61).*

The average annual discharge of the Euphrates and Tigris rivers together is difficult to determine due to the large yearly fluctuation. According to the records for 1938–1980, there have been years when 68 km^3 were observed in the two rivers in the mid–1960s, and years when the amount was over 84 km^3 in the mid–1970s. On the other hand, there was the critical drought year with less than 30 km^3 at the beginning of the 1960s. Such variation in annual discharge makes it difficult to develop an adequate water allocation plan for competing water demand from each sector as well as fair sharing of water among neighbouring countries (UNDG, 2005)..

Turkish authorities argue that control of the Euphrates River will also benefit Syria and Iraq, because of Euphrates waters fluctuate greatly during droughts and floods (the upper flow of the Euphrates can be 28 times greater than the lower flow, and in the case of the Tigris—8 times) The first season of the drought was recorded in 1958–1962. In 1961, for example, the annual flow of the Euphrates dropped to 14.9 BCM, which is 47% of the average annual flow of the Euphrates. As a result, agricultural production in Syria and Iraq has declined. The second season of the drought was recorded in 1970–1975. In 1973, the annual flow of the Euphrates decreased to 18.8 BCM, which is 59% of the average annual flow of the Euphrates. As a result, agricultural production in Syria and Iraq has again declined. The Turkish side emphasizes that the construction of the Keban Reservoir has reduced the consequences of the drought for Syria and Iraq. For example, if the Keban Reservoir had not been built, in 1989—a severe drought year, Syria would receive only 20.8 BCM of water (66%) on the border with Turkey via the Euphrates. However, due to the Keban Reservoir, this amount of water increased by 4.7 BCM to 25.7 BCM (81%).

On the other hand, the Euphrates also flooded large areas. In 1969, the annual flow of the Euphrates was 56.4 BCM, which is equivalent to 178% of the average annual flow of the Euphrates. As a result, 100,000 hectares in Iraq remained under water, there were a large number of casualties and material losses. In 1988, the annual flow of the Euphrates was 57.7 BCM, which is equivalent to 183% of the average annual flow of the Euphrates. But this time due to the Keban Reservoir floods did not feel in Syria and Iraq. These are also big annual fluctuations. However, these fluctuations are much higher on a monthly basis, when the largest flow is recorded in April-May, and the smallest flow is in September. Monthly fluctuations can vary greatly, from 530% to 16%. So the reservoirs would regulate the flow of the Euphrates (before joining the Tigris, the Euphrates loses 70–80% of its water due to irrigation, evaporation and absorption *(Dursun 2006: 129).*

Unlike the Euphrates, the Tigris flows through central Iraq and into the capital, Baghdad. The water discharge of the Tigris in Baghdad is 40 BCM, 1/10 of which reaches the Persian Gulf. Like the Euphrates, Tigris also fluctuates between different years and seasons. For example, in 1946–1994, the average annual flow of Tigris on the Turkish-Syrian border was 16.2 BCM. However, in 1973 this figure dropped to 9.6 BCM (59% of the annual average flow), and in 1969 it increased to 34.3 BCM (212% of the annual average flow). In the spring of 1954, the Tigris floods severely damaged Iraq. So the dams would also regulate the flow of the Tigris *(Yildiz & Ozbay 2011: 39–41, 49).*

4.4.2 Construction of Keban Dam

Keban Dam site is in the 45 Km North West of Elazig, 65 km North East of Malatya and is located one of the most bottlenecks where the Murat and Karasu further down the 10 km merged. Euphrates river caused by mergers of the Murat river and Karasu at the point of this merger is the first proper dam site. Keban Dam was not the first dam built in the Republic of Turkey, on the other hand, it was the first dam on the Euphrates River.

The construction of the Keban Dam was estimated at $100–105 million. Turkey wanted to get a loan from the World Bank to construct the dam. This issue was also discussed during Turkish President Celal Bayar's visit to the US (in 1954). In 1957, the government led by Adnan Menderes discussed the possibility of obtaining a loan from France. And although steps were taken in the 1950s to obtain loans, technical works were done, in 1954, geological research was carried out in Keban, construction of the Keban Dam was not started. The military coup of 1960 did not hinder the implementation of the Keban Reservoir project, it was on the agenda again after the 1961 elections—in the 1962 financial budget discussions. As a result the Turkish authorities decided to allocate 5 million liras from EIE budget for Keban Dam project.

At the time, Demirel continued to attach great importance to the construction of the Keban Dam. In January 1962, Demirel announced that the Euphrates River carries 40 BCM of water annually to Syria, which is slightly more than the volume of water that the Nile brings to Egypt. 'If the Keban Dam stores more than 10 BCM of water, it will be 6 times bigger than Seyhan Reservoir and 2 times bigger than Hirfanli Reservoir. If the capacity of the Keban HEPP is 1000 MW and it generates 5 billion kW/h of electricity annually, this will double the volume of electricity consumed in Turkey. There are many mines around Keban and the electricity from the hydroelectric power will enable them to be exploited, chemical, heavy or fertilizers industries to be created, and thus new jobs will be created. For developed countries, rivers today are sources of prosperity, and happiness, while for underdeveloped countries, they are a source of hardship and suffering',—said Demirel *(Turgut 2000: 66–69).*

In 1962 a research commission for the Keban Dam was established in the Turkish parliament. Demirel considered it possible to build 3–4 reservoirs and HEPPs in the area from Keban to Karkamish, which will generate 18–20 billion kW/h of electricity. It was expected that installed capacity of the Keban HEPP would be 980 megawatts, which would generate 4.5 billion kW/h of electricity annually.

In 1961, the Euphrates Planning Department was established, which in 1964 presented its report on the Euphrates Basin. According to the report, construction of 80 reservoirs, 66 hydroelectric power stations and 68 canals, 1.6 million ha irrigation in the Euphrates basin was considered possible. The total capacity of the HEPPs would be 5306 megawatts, with annual production of 23 billion 875 million kWh *(Ibid: 81–86).*

At the same time, the issue of funding of the Keban reservoir remained unresolved. But the situation soon changed dramatically. In 1964, Demirel was elected leader of the Justice Party, and his party won the 1965 (October 10) parliamentary elections. As a result, Demirel became Prime Minister of Turkey for the first time (Demirel has become Prime Minister of Turkey 7 times in total). It is noteworthy that before the elections, the Justice Party had made three major election promises, one of which referred to the construction of Keban Dam.

After becoming prime minister, Demirel began quickly fulfill his promises. On December 6, 1965 the Government of Demirel announced the tender for the construction of the Keban Reservoir (perhaps thats why DSI considers 1965 the first year of construction of the Keban Dam—auth.). The agreement was signed in 1966 on February 19. Demirel regretted that the Keban Reservoir was not built earlier adding that Turkey first surveyed Euphrates for 20 years then discussed the issue of necessity to build Keban Reservoir for 10 years. Therefore, Turkey lost 30 years (*Ibid: 93*).

Here we can't agree with Demirel, because 30 years ago (in 1930s) Turkey's financial and technical capabilities, as well as the information about the Euphrates, were quite limited. In addition, after the founding of the Republic, the Turkish authorities had a number of priorities, which pertain to reforming various spheres of public life.

In 1966, Turkey concluded credit agreements with Germany ($20 million), the World Bank ($40 million), the European Investment Bank ($30 million), Italy ($10 million), and France ($12.5 million), and in the summer of the same year the construction of the Keban Reservoir began. Demirel believed that the construction of the reservoirs would increase the population of the region from 500,000 to 5 million, that the Keban Reservoir would become a starting point to build new dams on the Euphrates. In fact, Keban Dam became the first mega project of the

Republic of Turkey. The main objectives of the Keban Reservoir were to obtain electricity and develop the industry. As Demirel stated, if there is electricity, then there will be industry, and if there is no electricity, then there is no opportunity for industry. Demirel also stressed the importance of creating jobs. According to him, the construction of Keban Reservoir became an indicator of Turkey's progress, because of 15 years ago HEPPs with capacity 1000 kWh were built in the country, whereas the capacity of Keban HEPP will be 1000 MW. There was a saying among the locals about the construction of the Keban Reservoir—'The Euphrates strangled one Suleyman, but the other Suleyman came and strangled the Euphrates' ("Bir Süleyman geldi, Fırat'ta boğuldu, bir Süleyman da geldi, Fırat'ı boğdu"—in Turkish). One Suleyman is Turkish Prime Minister Suleyman Demirel—'The king of the reservoirs', who controlled the flow of the Euphrates by building reservoirs on the Euphrates and in Turkey. And the second Suleyman is Suleyman Shah—the grandfather of Osman I Gazi, the founder of the Ottoman state, who drowned in the river Euphrates in Syria in the 13th century *(Ibid: 97–102)*.

We would add that the tomb of Suleyman Shah in Syria was considered to be the only area in the world that was de jure outside of Turkey but owned by it. Article 9 of the Treaty of Ankara, signed by France and Turkey in 1921, states that the tomb of Suleyman Shah (at its first location) "shall remain, with its appurtenances, the property of Turkey, who may appoint guardians for it and may hoist the Turkish flag there". Initially, a symbolic garrison of Turkish soldiers were guarding the tomb (the remains of Suleyman Shah have been moved to other locations several times for various reasons before and after the start of the 2011 Syrian conflict).

The first turbine of the Keban HEPP was put into operation on September 9, 1974, the second—on October 22, 1975, the third—on March 2, 1976, and the fourth—on June 3, 1976. The first four turbines of Keban HEPP started producing 5 billion kW/h of electricity annually, equivalent to 1.5 million tonnes of fuel. In 1976, it was decided that the Keban HEPP should have 4 more turbines, with a total of 8 turbines. The 5th turbine was put into operation on November 15, 1981, the 6th—on February 17, 1982, the 7th—on May 25, 1982, and the 8th—on August 27, 1982 (according to DSI, the first four turbines of Keban HEPP were put into operation in 1974 and the remaining four in 1981—auth.). Thus, the total capacity of the Keban HEPP was 1330 MW, with annual production of 6 billion kW/h. The volume of foreign loans for the Keban Reservoir amounted to $150 million and the construction cost—$300 million. However, after the putting into operation of the first turbine, the Keban HEPP produced 150 billion kW/h of electricity by 2000, equivalent to $10 billion in price. In addition, fish farming has been widespread in the Keban Reservoir since 1977, with annual catches of various fish species reaching 1000 tonnes *(Ibid: 102–104)*.

According to Necati Agiralioglu, initial calculations showed that Kebani reservoir construction will cost US $ 310 million, equivalent to Turkey's exports in those years. As a result, the construction of the Keban Reservoir cost $ 360 million, which was equivalent to Turkey's imports *(Agiralioglu 2014: 125)*.

The Keban Dam is a combined rockfill and concrete gravity hydroelectric dam operated by DSİ. The dam is 1097 metres long and its crest is 207 metres above the level of the river-bed (848 metres above sea-level). The Keban Reservoir became the first reservoir with a height of more than 200 meters in Turkey. The storage capacity of Lake Keban is 30.6 km3 and the surface area of the lake is 675 square kilometres. Keban Dam Lake (Turkish: Keban Baraj Gölü), the reservoir created by Keban Dam is reputedly the fourth-largest lake in Turkey after Lake Van, Lake Tuz, and the reservoir created by the Ataturk Dam.

According to DSI Keban is by volume the second-largest dam in Turkey after the Ataturk Dam. Although the Keban Dam was not originally constructed as a part of GAP, it is now a fully integrated component of the project, which aims to stimulate economic development in Southeastern Turkey. The Keban Dam has played a big role in Southeastern Turkey's social and economic development and progression.

Thus, increasing electricity demand (also due to population growth) and failure to find oil reserves (large quantities of oil weren't found) prompted Turkey to build Keban Dam. A number of previous steps in Turkey's water sphere (establishment of gauging stations on the Euphrates, construction of smaller reservoirs on other rivers) were a great experience and were instrumental in building the Keban Reservoir. The Keban Reservoir became Turkey's largest hydroelectric project and is a major (initial) indicator of Turkey's progress in the water sphere. The Keban Reservoir also became GAP prelude, and Turkey after the construction of Keban Dam started to launch major water projects in Euphrates-Tigris basin. In the 1970s Turkey was already aware of the benefits of building large reservoirs on the rivers (the Turkish side had seen it both abroad and inside the country). That's why, before completing the Keban Reservoir project, Turkey started the construction of the next reservoir, the Karakaya Reservoir on the Euphrates and the implementation of the GAP in general. S. Demirel himself played a key role in Turkey's implementation of not only the Keban Reservoir project but also numerous similar projects in the Euphrates-Tigris basin. Demirel has been the prime minister of Turkey for about 10,5 years (at different times) generally and has been the president of Turkey for 7 years. The experience of the following years has shown that military coups are just delayed for a short period of time and don't cancel major water projects, as all Turkish governments understood the importance of these water projects.

4.5 Water Disagreements in the "Turkey-Syria-Iraq" Triangle in 1920–1975

The main riparian states of the Euphrates-Tigris river system are Turkey, Syria, and Iraq. Transboundary water politics in the Euphrates-Tigris river system have evolved with competitive power dynamics and cooperative institutional development. Iraq derives the majority of its freshwater from the two rivers. Although the Euphrates basin is one of seven in Syria, it is strategically the most important because of its existing and potential uses for agricultural and hydropower purposes. The Tigris-Euphrates basin is one of twenty-five basins in Turkey, but accounts for nearly a third of the country's surface water resources and a fifth of its irrigable land. The variation of the flow of these twin rivers from one season and one year to another is extremely high, and severe drought and destructive flooding have been common phenomena for thousands of years. The physical characteristics of the rivers necessitate the coordinated management and use of water resources within and among the states they pass through. They cause interdependencies among the riparian states, which call for a cooperative attitude to ensure more efficient use of the water in the region and the avoidance of serious conflicts.

Kibaroglu Aysegul and Scheumann Waltina analyzed the evolution of transboundary water relations and divided them over four consecutive periods. The first period (Rivers of Common Geography and History) coincided with nation building in the region, when the riparian states focused on their domestic need for socioeconomic development rather than the formulation of external water policies. The second period (Rivers of Competition) saw the advent of competitive transboundary water politics shaped by the initiation of uncoordinated, large scale water development projects. The third period (Rivers of Discord) was the most complex, given the link between transboundary water issues and nonriparian security issues. In the fourth period (Rivers for Cooperative Endeavors), the role of water bureaucracies in the reorientation of water policies from hostile to cooperative became significant.

4.5.1 The First Period—Rivers of Common Geography and History

Kibaroglu Aysegul and Scheumann Waltina observe friendly relations among the riparians from the early 1920s until the late 1950s, when each country's priority was the establishment of state bureaucracies and all had similar concerns and the same need for socioeconomic development. Throughout that period, planning was done largely on a country-by-country basis. None of the countries engaged in major development projects, which would have resulted in utilization of water by each to the detriment of the others. The Euphrates and Tigris linked the communities in the river basin as they had done for thousands of years, and the newly established riparian states had yet to clash over the use of the water.

At transboundary level, harmonious water relations reigned in the basin under a series of bilateral political treaties. The first legal arrangement among the riparians was an agreement signed by France and Turkey in Ankara on 20 October 1921 with a view toward promoting peace between the two countries. Under Article XII of that treaty concerning the "Distribution and Removal of Waters" it was agreed that "the city of Aleppo may also organize, at its own expense, a water-supply from the Euphrates in Turkish territory in order to meet the requirements of the district." Article 109 of the 1923 Lausanne Peace Treaty covers another legal aspect of the issue, stating that, if the fixing of a new frontier results in the river system of one state being dependent on facilities that were established before the war and are now located within the borders of another state, the parties concerned must conclude an agreement that is capable of safeguarding their respective interests and sovereign rights and that, in the absence of an agreement, the dispute will be settled by arbitration.

One of the most important legal agreements between Iraq and Turkey concerning water resources is the Protocol annexed to their 1946 Treaty of Friendship and Good Neighbourly Relations (Iraq and Syria gained their independence in 1932 and 1946 respectively). This protocol establishes a framework that sets out the two parties' respective rights and obligations in the Euphrates and Tigris river system. Above all, it emphasizes the urgency of installing flood control works on the rivers and underlines the positive impact that storage facilities sited on Turkish soil would have for both. The parties agreed that, if the most suitable sites were on Turkish territory, the entire cost would be met by Iraq. Permanent observation stations would be built, operated, and maintained by Turkey, with Turkey and Iraq sharing the costs equally. Turkey agreed to inform Iraq of its construction plans and, if it determined that it needed water for irrigation and hydropower purposes, separate negotiations would be held. In recognizing rights and obligations for both the upstream and downstream states, it seems peculiarly enlightened and not only for its time since contemporary bilateral water treaties such as the 1987 Protocol between Turkey and Syria and the 1990 Protocol between Syria and Iraq seem less balanced in their recognition of upper and lower riparian rights and obligations.

During this initial period, the riparian countries were mainly concerned with water supply for urban and rural populations. Bureaucracies with technical expertise were busy with the initial organizational setup and the planning of irrigation systems and dam construction. Transboundary waters were the subject of domestic planning and development exercises and had little to do with the foreign policy agenda. Those involved in transboundary water relations at that time were therefore mainly medium-level technocrats—advisers and professionals who prepared the technical ground for the drafting of the water-related clauses of the treaties, in whose conclusion the riparian diplomats acted as brokers.

4.5.2 The Second Period—Rivers of Competition

In the second period, water relations became competitive due to uncoordinated and unilateral projects carried out in the region. As the riparian states further consolidated their regimes between 1960 and 1980, they paid more attention to socioeconomic development based on water and land resources. Turkey had long been dependent on oil imports. Having been hard hit by the oil crises of the 1970s, the government embarked on a program of indigenous resource development that particularly emphasized hydropower and lignite schemes with the aim of minimizing the national economy's dependency on imported oil.

The Syrian economy has traditionally been dominated by agriculture. Exploration for oil did not begin until the early 1980s. Even though oil made a significant contribution to export earnings in the following decades as world oil prices fluctuated, Syria focused on agricultural development with the aim of achieving food self-sufficiency. These considerations were reinforced by political goals which, under the ruling Ba'ath Party, placed the emphasis on the development of rural areas and the organization of peasants as a political power base.

Since 1958, Iraq changed from being mainly an agricultural country exporting wheat, rice, and other crops to an oil-producing, semi-industrial nation forced to import most of its own food. Yet after the Iraqi government nationalized the oil companies in 1972 and began to receive more income from oil, the focus also turned to agricultural production. This led to an expansion of irrigated areas, with the aim of achieving food security for the Iraqi people.

The central water agencies of all the riparian countries designated the rivers for large-scale development projects. Because the water is not present where (on farmland) or when (in summer) it is most needed, the main riparian stats of the Euphrates-Tigris river system have launched large-scale irrigation projects, which have become the main bone of contention in transboundary water politics since the late 1960s. The initial aim of the projects was flow regulation designed to end the alteration of flooding and droughts. But ambitions in each country quickly grew to include hydropower generation and sharp increases in the use of river water for drinking and irrigation. Unilateral and uncoordinated water development projects by each party began to stress the river system's capacity. As the demand for water exceeded supply, water authorities in each country finally began reaching out to their counterparts in the others and they developed rather ad hoc processes of discussion and negotiation.

Kibaroglu Aysegul and Scheumann Waltina also note that above the level of the water bureaucrats, political rivalries stemming from conflicting national positions within the Cold War framework prevented any fruitful cooperation from taking root. Turkey's NATO membership and Syria and Iraq's ties to the Soviet Union did more than inhibit cooperation; they aggravated existing disputes over water and moved them progressively up the agenda of contentious issues until they were near the top for Turkey with each of the others. Ironically, despite similarly dependent relations with the Soviet Union, Iraq and Syria also were at loggerheads over water, as well as other issues implicated in their bitter regional rivalry, and there were moments when water use in the Euphrates river basin propelled the two regimes to the cusp of war.

In Turkey, the major objective was to irrigate the fertile lands in southeastern Anatolia, which make up one fifth of the country's irrigable land, using the huge water potential of the Tigris and Euphrates river basin, which accounts for 28.5% of the surface water supply. In this context, Turkey implemented the Lower Euphrates Project, initially a series of dams designed to increase hydropower generation and expand irrigated agriculture. Subsequently, in the late 1970s, the Lower Euphrates Project evolved into a larger, multisectoral development project, taking in the Tigris waters as well and known as GAP, which included twenty-one large dams, nineteen HEPPs, and irrigation schemes extending to 1.7 million ha of land.

The Euphrates river basin provides 65% of surface water supply in Syria and accounts for 27% of total land resources. Syria launched the Euphrates Valley Project under the Ba'ath Party. The government set a number of objectives to be met by the project: irrigation of an area as large as 640,000 ha; construction of the large, multipurpose Tabqa or Al-Thawra Dam to generate the electricity needed for urban use and industrial development; and regulation of the flow of the Euphrates to prevent seasonal flooding.

The main channels and tributaries of the Euphrates and the Tigris rivers account for almost the entire freshwater supply in Iraq, which pioneered and built its first dams in the 1950s: the Euphrates Dam in 1955–1956 to divert water to Lake Al-Habbaniya; and the Samarra Dam on the Tigris, completed in 1954, to protect against previously catastrophic floods. The Ba'ath Party, which came to power under Saddam Hussein's presidency in 1968, adopted the slogan "food security for the Iraqi people," which was to be accomplished through the development of irrigation. To that end, the Revolutionary Plan was developed. The Higher Agriculture Council attached to the presidency, the Soil and Land Reclamation Organisation attached to the Ministry of Irrigation, and many other new departments were established to carry out studies, to create designs, and to construct and maintain water projects.

Owing to the competitive and uncoordinated nature of these water development projects, disagreements over transboundary water uses surfaced in the late 1960s. During this period, transboundary water issues were regarded by each country's political leadership as falling within the middle range of economic and technical objectives, which could be handled by official technical delegations. Hence, water negotiations were held by technocrats from the riparians' central water agencies, accompanied by diplomats who advised and monitored the negotiations, particularly when international legal and political aspects were under discussion *(Kibaroglu 2013)*.

In the 1960s, the three riparians entered a new phase of their relationship over water, upon Turkey's decision to construct the Keban Dam on the Euphrates. In 1964, Turkey had initiated separate and joint meetings with Syria and Iraq to offer them up to date information on the construction of the Keban Dam. The downstream riparians, particularly Iraq, insisted on guaranteed flows (350 cubic meters per second at minimum) to be released by Turkey during the impounding period. Hence, a first meeting was held in June 1964 with Turkish and Iraqi experts attending. At the end of negotiations, for the first time, Turkey guaranteed to undertake all necessary measures to maintain a discharge of 350 cubic meters per second immediately downstream from the dam, provided that the natural flow of the river was adequate to supply this discharge. This was communicated to Syria and Iraq the same year.

Following this first technical meeting between Turkey and Iraq, a few more special meetings were held. Among these the most notable one—the first tripartite negotiation—was held in Baghdad in 1965 where the three delegations exchanged technical data on the Haditha (Iraq), Tabqa (Syria) and Keban (Turkey) dams. Turkey proposed the establishment of JTC, which would inspect each river to determine its average yearly discharge. The JTC would determine the irrigation needs of the three countries through joint field studies and would be authorised—by calculating the needs of the riparians for present and future projects—to prepare a statement of the main principles and procedures in order to facilitate an agreement on water rights. Although the idea was accepted in principle, immediate disagreements between Iraq and Syria regarding whether the meeting should focus only on the Euphrates or also include the Tigris River, produced a deadlock. In line with a Turkish proposal, Syria suggested that it would be beneficial to commission a JTC study of the water requirements of the irrigable lands, and subsequently to examine the possibility of covering possible shortages of water supplied by the Euphrates by diverting a part of the Tigris River's water to the Euphrates. Iraq strongly opposed this proposal and insisted on negotiating only on the waters of the Euphrates. The idea was laid to rest *(Kibaroglu, Scheumann, Kramer 2011: 283–284, 222).*

Here we would like to emphasize that this position of Iraq is understandable. In contrast to Turkey and Syria, for which the Euphrates is a more important river than the Tigris, in Iraq the situation is the opposite. This means that Iraq was ready to compromise more on the Euphrates but not on the Tigris. In addition, during the meeting, the three countries discussed issues related to the construction of three reservoirs (Haditha, Tabqa, Keban), all of which related to the Euphrates, not the Tigris River.

Until the 1970s no overt or covert conflict had ever evolved around water usage of the Tigris-Euphrates since water withdrawal was only partial. Since the beginning of the 1970s, when both Turkey and Syria embarked on their separate development of the river's resources, conflict situations have been constantly arising. The first crisis between co-riparians of the Tigris-Euphrates took place in 1974 as a result of a combination of several negative factors. It was a poor year for precipitation and it was the first year that both Turkey and Syria had begun to store water in the Keban Dam and Tabqa Dam, respectively *(Kliot 1994: 132).* As a result, 3 million farmers in Iraq were affected. Iraq says Syria has left the Euphrates flowing at less than a third (9.4 km3). However, Syria has denied this, claiming that it has kept the Euphrates flow at a level of 12.8 km3 per year *(Dursun 2006: 169).*

During the 1970s, delegations from the three countries gathered on several occasions to exchange information about technical issues relating to the reservoirs. No agreement was reached, and Turkey and Syria unilaterally determined the impounding programs for their reservoirs. The main theme of these technical negotiations was the impact of the construction of the Keban Dam in Turkey and the Tabqa Dam in Syria on Iraq's historical water use patterns. Those meetings didn't achieve the expressed aim of coordinating the water development and use patterns of the three riparians. Consequently, a political crisis occurred in the region in 1975. Turkey began impounding the Keban Reservoir at the same time that Syria was completing the construction of the Tabqa Dam—during a period of severe drought, as a result, the water flow into Iraq was reduced to a trickle. The impounding of the two reservoirs triggered a crisis. In the winter of 1974, Iraq suffered from a severe water shortage for which Iraq accused Syria of reducing the river's flow to intolerable levels while Syria blamed Turkey. The Iraqi government was not satisfied with the Syrian response, and the mounting frustration resulted in mutual threats that brought the parties to the brink of armed hostility. The Arab League failed in its mediation efforts, and Iraq mobilized its army near Syria's Iraqi border. A war over water was averted when, thanks to Saudi Arabia's mediation, Syria finally submitted to pressure and released additional quantities of water (200 MCM) from the Tabqa Dam to Iraq (it eased the situation but no agreement was signed). Syria agreed to keep 40% of available water from the Euphrates River and let 60% flow into Iraq. The main cause of this crisis was the mounting political rivalry and tension between the two Ba'athist regimes. In other words, it was not a water-sharing crisis per se, but rather the beginning of the use of water as a political lever in non-riparian issues *(Kibaroglu 2013)*.

We can add, that dispute between Syria and Iraq, exacerbated by drought which reduced the amount of available water even further, led to the recall of ambassadors, the breakdown of air communication and the concentration of troops at the border. At the same time, a number of incidents took place on the Turkish-Syrian border. Despite Turkey's announcement that the Keban Reservoir is being built to get electricity that it will not significantly reduce the Euphrates flow, Syria reacted very negatively to it. Why?

- Syria understood that the Keban Reservoir would collect about 31 BCM, that's why the Euphrates River's flow at the time would be reduced by filling that huge hole with water. At the same time, Turkey could determine the speed of the process of filling the reservoir with water, depending also on the position of the neighboring countries, on the level of their relations with Turkey.

- Although Turkey had stated that it would not use the water of the Keban Reservoir for irrigation, for Syria there was no any guarantee that Turkey would not attempt to do so years or decades later.
- Syria realized that evaporation factor of Keban Reservoir may have negative impact on Euphrates River flow. Evaporation increases water salinization and water loss in major reservoirs. According to some data, the rate of evaporation of water in the Keban Reservoir is about 0.5 BCM per year *(Sumer 2017).*
- Syria understood that with the construction of the Keban Reservoir, Turkey would be able to maintain the Euphrates River flow within 400–1000 m^3 in per second *(Chalabi & Majzoub 1995: 199–200).* Turkey considers that control of the Euphrates River's flow would help prevent floods, which will be useful for other countries in the Euphrates Basin as well.
- The process of filling the reservoirs of Keban and Tabaka coincided, with Iraq most affected as the most downstream country. That's why Iraq was deeply disappointed that Syria had reduced the Euphrates River and first of all blamed its upper neighbor Syria. According to Iraqi President Ahmed Hassan al-Bakr, about 3.5 million Iraqis find themselves in a very difficult situation as the Euphrates River flow falls. Syria, in turn, blamed Turkey to reduce the Euphrates River, emphasizing that the Euphrates River flow has decreased from 28 BCM to 13 BCM. According to Arun Elhance, the Euphrates flow entering Iraq was reduced from about 920 cubic meters per second to just 197 cubic meters per second *(Elhance 1999: 142–143).*
- Syria apparently realized that Keban Dam is just the first dam on the Euphrates, and after that Turkey can build new dams on the Euphrates (in Turkey the construction of Karakaya Dam on the Euphrates began in the 1970s). Perhaps in Syria they predicted that Keban Dam will become a trigger, the description of which was given in the previous chapter by The Pacific Institute and by us. This situation remains the construction of the Renaissance Reservoir on the Blue Nile by Ethiopia in the 21st century. Although Ethiopia has stated that the Renaissance Reservoir will be used for energy purposes only, it will not reduce the flow of water to Egypt, Egyptian authorities fear that the Renaissance Reservoir is just the beginning, and Ethiopia will build new reservoirs after that.
- During the 1967 Six-Day War Israel occupied Syrian territory on the Golan Heights and took control of significant water resources of that strategic plateau (in October 1973 Syria attempted unsuccessfully to retake the plateau). In our opinion, Syria has become more sensitive to water issues since then.

Thus, the above proves that disagreements over water usually take place on countries where there is a history of animosity and resentment, and generally, water constitutes an aggravating factor of a pre-existing framework of tension. A number of other factors were also at the heart of the water disputes arising within the same Turkey-Syria-Iraq triangle: historical, military-political, economic and etc.

For example, in the mid-1970s, the worsening water conflict between Syria and Iraq was facilitated by Iraq's agreements with Turkey and Iran. In particular, in 1973, Iraq concluded an oil agreement with Turkey that Iraqi oil by pipeline would reach the Mediterranean sea through Turkey (maybe it was also one of the reasons why Iraq did not hurry to accuse Turkey of dehydration and only blamed Syria). This fact angered Syria, which thought Iraq was thus neglecting its interests to form a common front against Turkey in the water issue (Syria naturally wanted Iraq's oil to flow into the Mediterranean via its own territory).

In March 1975, the Algerian Agreement was signed between Iraq and Iran to settle any border disputes and conflicts (such as the Shatt al-Arab, known as Arvand Rud in Iran), and it served as basis for the bilateral treaties signed on 13 June and 26 December 1975 (in the mid-1970s, Iran began supporting Kurdish rebels in northern Iraq, as Iraq refused to sign an agreement on the demarcation of the Shatt al-Arab). And Syria feared that resolving the problems between the two countries and especially the Kurdish issue would give Iraq the opportunity to speak with Syria on tougher terms, including on water issues. These side effects thus contributed to the deepening water crisis between Iraq and Syria.

On the other hand, there were also non-water factors in mitigating the water conflict between Iraq and Syria. This is in particular related to the agreement signed between Egypt and Israel, according to which Israel was to partially withdraw its troops from the Sinai Peninsula. Iraq and Syria criticized Egypt, saying the deal weakens the western front on the Sinai Peninsula and increases the danger on the Syrian front.

We agree with Aysel Kibaroglu, who thinks that in the region, water began to be used as a political lever, which later gained momentum. Turkey was in the best condition here, as the Euphrates and Tigris, as well as some of their tributaries, originated in its territory. Iraq is in the worst situation, as besides Turkey and Syria, there is also the Iranian factor (part of the Tigris tributaries originates from the Iranian territory).

We don't claim that in the 1960s, Turkey began building reservoirs in the Euphrates-Tigris basin primarily to gain political leverage over neighboring countries. We believe that Turkey began to build these reservoirs for the four main purposes outlined above (irrigation, hydropower, water supply, flood protection).

But at the same time, we believe that in time Turkey realized that the control of the flow of transboundary rivers is a serious leverage against downstream countries. And Turkey began to use the water leverage to achieve various goals, especially after it built a large number of reservoirs in the Euphrates-Tigris basin (GAP project). That process has become apparent in the 21st century.

4.6 Concluding Summary of the Second Chapter

Before discussing the water problems in the Republic of Turkey, we considered it appropriate to describe water importance and water projects during the Ottoman period. In this chapter we emphasize the similarities and differences between the water problems of the Ottoman Empire and the Republic of Turkey. For example, one of the differences was that the Ottoman Empire unlike Republic of Turkey faced the issue of providing the army with water during raids. The similarities are naturally much greater.

We describe in sufficient detail the geographical data of the Euphrates and Tigris, as well as the Orontes River and their tributaries, so that a number of circumstances will be clear in our future work. For example, how much riparian countries contribute to the flow of these rivers, how much riparian countries depend on these rivers, what are the maneuvering capabilities of them, etc. In addition, the geographical-historical features of the rivers have a unique place in defining the positions of the riparian countries. That's why we preferred to give a description of all that, before describing the construction of reservoirs in the Euphrates-Tigris and Orontes basins (in riparian countries).

In the second chapter we also talked about how quickly the Republic of Turkey was able to realize the importance of water and water major projects, we showed the influence of foreign countries on it in two aspects at once—1) to copy their experience (USSR, USA), 2) not to lag behind them (Iraq, Syria). We emphasized the important role of individuals (leaders) in Turkey (M. K. Ataturk, S. Demirel), as well as the existence of Turkey's economic problems (lack of oil and electricity) and the urgency of their solution.

We described how non-water factors affect both the emergence and resolution of water problems. By the way, we mentioned that these problems had a tendency to deepen, which in turn would lead to the implementation of new, major water projects. In the third chapter we are going to examine in detail those water projects. In addition, we have presented the origins of the first serious water disputes within the Turkey-Syria-Iraq triangle, which pertained to the construction of the first large reservoirs on the Euphrates and their filling with water. Nevertheless, the nature of the general (historical) relations between the three countries played a significant role in this.

It was then that the countries of the region began to view water as a serious lever for the downstream countries. It would still take on its full shape in the future, with new water projects being implemented, when the upstream or midstream country would be able to control the flow of transboundary rivers more. It will leave its rather serious mark on the water plans and projects of the parties, as well as on interstate relations in general, and on domestic life. We will describe all this in detail in the next chapter.

The Southeastern Anatolia Project—GAP

5

5.1 General Information About GAP

GAP is the largest scale and costliest project in the history of the Republic of Turkey, also the one most effectively implemented among regional development plans and programmes developed so far. With its integrated regional development approach and sustainable human development philosophy, the GAP has its high prestige in relevant international literature.

The project area covers 9 provinces (Adiyaman, Batman, Diyarbekir, Gaziantep, Kilis, Mardin, Siirt, Sanliurfa and Sirnak) located in the Euphrates-Tigris Basin and upper Mesopotamia plains. These GAP provinces constitute, on average, 10.7% of Turkey in both geographical and population terms. The surface area of the region bordering with Syria to the south and with Iraq to the southeast is 75,193 square kilometres which corresponds to 9.7% of Turkey's total surface area. Turkey has in total 8.5 million ha of economically irrigable land (7.9 million ha with surface water and 0.6 million ha with groundwater resources) and GAP's share in this total is 20% (almost one third of Turkey's total area is arable land which is 24 million hectares).

GAP Region, comprises 10% of Turkey's surface area, 20% of Turkey's agriculture potential, and 20% of Turkey's Technical hydroelectric potential. The total population at the 1985 census was 4,303,567 in the GAP region, accounting lor 8.5% of the Nation's total, 50,664,458 in 1985. The GAP region is one of less developed regions in Turkey, and its per capita gross regional product was 47% of the per capita gross domestic product of Turkey in 1985.

H. Gabrielyan, *Turkey's Water Policy as Part of the Political Strategy*, Politik, Wirtschaft und Gesellschaft im Spannungsverhältnis der Regionen Südosteuropa und Mittlerer Osten, https://doi.org/10.1007/978-3-658-44070-1_5

The objectives of the GAP include improving the level of income and life quality of local population by utilizing region's resources; eliminating development disparities existing between the region and other parts of the country, and contributing to national economic development and social stability by enhancing productivity and employment opportunities in the region.

In the 70'ies the GAP was considered as a programme geared to developing water and land resources of the region and it was planned to launch 22 dams—14 dams in the Euphrates basin and 8 dams in the Tigris basin (Table 5.1), 19 HEPPs—11 HEPP in the Euphrates basin and 8 HEPP in the Tigris basin (Table 5.2) and irrigation investments covering 1.82 million ha of land in the Euphrates-Tigris Basin. GAP's aim is to increase the irrigated land from 2.9% to 22.8% of the total area of the region. The total installed capacity of hydraulic power plants would be 7476 MW with annual energy production of 27 billion kwh. The total cost of the project was $ 32 billion.

DSİ implements the major part of the Project containing 13 sub-projects; 7 of which took place in the Euphrates basin and 6 of which in the Tigris basin (Table 3). The total water potential in Turkey's 26 basins is 186 BCM, 32 BCM of this is in the Euphrates and 21 BCM in the Tigris, total 53 BCM is located in this basin. However, the annual usable water potential is 112 BCM, of which 14 BCM are groundwater.

If GAP Project were completed, 2.2 Billion $—Irrigation benefit, 4 Billion $—Energy Benefit, 0.505 Billion $—Watersupply Benefit and total 6.705 Billion $ would be contributed to the National Economy and 1,270,000 people would be employed directly (Ministry of Industry and Technology of Turkey, Southeastern Anatolian Project, What's GAP?).

According to Timuchin Kodaman, Turkey wanted to receive $ 2.5 billion annualy from GAP irrigation projects and $ 5.3 billion annualy from GAP energy projects, total—$ 7.8 billion. GAP would also provide 3.5 (3.8) million jobs *(Kodaman 2007: 44)*.

Southeastern Anatolia has an economy based on dry farming whose main crops are cereals (the area grows some 11% of Turkey's total cereal production), pulses (the area grows 37% of Turkey's crop), industrial crops, oil-seeds and tuber crops. About 55% of the total land in the region is devoted to grain and 18.6% of it is lying fallow. Productivity is very low since the soil is inadequately watered. When the GAP is concluded some 1.6 million ha will be irrigated and the region will grow 4.1 million tons of beets, 1.3 million tons of oil-seeds, 117,900 tons of corn, 3.5 million tons of vegetables, 1.1 million tons of grapes, 685,000 tons of pistachio nuts and 660,000 tons of fruit. In addition, Turkey's total cotton production is expected to rise by 25 percent. The importance of GAP for Turkey can be summed up by the following:

- GAP will add 70% to Turkey's existing energy output.
- Gap will add 1.7 million ha to the current 3.2 million ha of irrigated land in Turkey (Istanbul Chamber of Commerce 1989).

The irrigation projects in the region will contribute Turkish lira (TL) 442 billion to the Turkish economy whereas the energy projects will produce an added value of TL 940 billion (Istanbul Chamber of Commerce 1989) *(Kliot 1994: 104, 108).*

The GAP, which originally started as a 'hydraulic mission'-type scheme, turned into a regional development project when the Master Plan designed in 1989 envisaged investments in agriculture, industry, transportation, education, health and rural-urban infrastructure. The project builds on the philosophy of sustainable human development committed to creating environments that future generations will benefit and capitalize on. The underlying strategy in the GAP encompasses fairness and participation in development, environmental protection, employment, spatial planning, infrastructure development, public-private partnership and people participation in investments. In the GAP Master plan made in 1989, the project was envisaged to be converted into an integrated development project and completed in 2005. In 1989 GAP Regional Development Administration was established. Thus, the GAP is implemented as a multi-sector and integrated regional development project on the basis of sustainable human development targeting enhanced competitive power of the region and stronger economic and social integration *(Ministry of Industry and Technology of Turkey, Southeastern Anatolian Project, What's GAP?).*

The importance of the GAP to Turkey beyond hydropower and/or foreign exchange is obvious, given the underdevelopment of the south-east and the government's desire to stabilize the area politically through significantly raising the population's level of living. According to the GAP Master Plan, the region is to become an 'Agro-related Export Base'. It is in the context of both its positive and negative consequences that the GAPmust be evaluated. The importance of hydroelectric development through the creation of major dams and power plants provided the initial incentive for the GAP. The accompanying potential increase in irrigated cash crops and their sale abroad was thought of as a means of paying for such monumental structures. However, as the project attained reality, questions concerning the impact of GAP on the socioeconomic structure of both its region and the nation were inevitable. This led, in turn, to the creation of the aforementioned Master Plan through the cooperation of the Japanese firm Nippon Koei Co. Ltd. and the Turkish firm Yuksel Proje, A.S. This consortium has defined the development objectives of the GAP as:

- 'To raise the income levels in the GAP region by improving the economic structure in order to narrow the income disparity between the Region and other regions.'
- 'To increase the productivity and employment opportunities in rural areas.'
- 'To enhance the assimilative capacity of larger cities in the Region.'
- 'To contribute to the national objective of sustained economic growth, export promotion, and social stability by efficient utilization of the Region's resources.' These objectives are to be met through development strategies:
- 'To develop and manage water and related land resources for irrigation, urban and industrial uses.'
- 'To improve land use by managing cropping patterns and establishing better farming practices and farm management.'
- 'To promote manufacturing industry with emphasis on agro-related ones and those based on indigenous resources.'
- 'To provide better social services to meet the requirements of local people and to attract technical and administrative staff to stay in the region.' (Master Plan, Vol. 1, pp. 2, 3).

It should be noted that hydropower development is not specifically cited in these overarching objectives. Nevertheless, it continues to play an important part in development planning as is shown by three alternative scenarios suggested by the Master Plan in order to achieve the goals stated above. The first posits that all irrigation areas in the original plan be completed by 2005; the second, that power generation be maximized 'subject to the implementation of priority irrigation schemes'; the third, that 'only priority irrigation and hydropower schemes will be implemented by 2005' (Master Plan, Vol. 1, p. 9). In view of the difficulties surrounding the first two scenarios, the Master Plan recommends the third scenario. The reaoning behind that suggestion is summarized as follows:

GAP's original schedule called for the irrigation of one million hectares of land with Euphrates waters, and 625,000 ha with Tigris waters by the year 2002. To achieve this goal would require putting 100,000 ha into production in the Euphrates basin each year beginning in 1993, and another 60,000 ha per year in the basin of the Tigris. The annual ability of the General Directorate of Rural Affairs (GDRA) to develop farmland at present is thought to be between 1000 and 3000 ha (Master Plan, Vol. 2, p. 3.5). The slow pace of land redistribution, enmeshed as it is in a web of local and national politics, is largely responsible for this delay. At the same time, the Ministry of Agriculture, Fisheries, and Rural Affairs (MAFRA), responsible for the introduction of hands-on aspects of irrigated agriculture, is facing a Herculean task. Its facilities are limited and the inertia of the traditional farming systems is great.

Agricultural inertia may delay the realization of profits from agriculture for a number of reasons. The training of farm workers and the initiation of farm managers into the nuances of irrigated farming and the importance of applying exactly the right amount of water at the right time to the optimum mix of crops is a slow process. By the same token the fine tuning of agricultural choices to the best set of crops, matching conditions of soil, exposure, temperature and market demands, must be worked out in agricultural research stations. Timing crops to the market and to the season of the year in order to catch demands at their peak also needs the development of additional skills. Finally, the proper packaging and marketing of crops, whether they are boxes of perishable fruit or bales of cotton, require even more expertise. All of these caveats are summed up by the Master Plan which states, 'The large discrepancy between the expected pace of irrigation development and the extremely limited capacity for on-farm works is a critical problem to be redressed' (Vol. 2, p. 3.5).

The second scenario, commitment to maximum hydroelectric production, is rejected by the Master Plan in view of the importance placed on the upgrading of economic and social conditions in the GAP region. Selling electric power at the expense of agriculture might benefit the nation but will fail to alleviate the poverty and its attendant unrest which are evident in the south-east.

The third scenario, the one recommended, essentially says 'take it easy', finish what has been begun, and let further investment and development be dictated by the pace of agricultural adjustments and social change. The practicality of this view cannot be denied. Nevertheless, such a course of action draws out the problems and decisions which river managers will have to face with increasing frequency in the years ahead.

Given such a situation, the GAP would have three significant negative impacts downstream: the depletion of downstream flow, the detouring of downstream flow, and the pollution of downstream flow. Depletion of flow would come from evaporation from reservoir surfaces, necessary evapotranspiration for crop production, and system and on-farm inefficiencies resulting in unsalvageable water loss. Water is lost through evaporation from reservoir surfaces.

A second possible problem is the detouring of significant quantities of water from the main channel through the Urfa Tunnels to the Urfa-Harran and Mardin-Ceylanpinar irrigation projects. This means—according to my maximum projection—that 2.456 BCM might be subtracted from the main stream, i.e. transboundary border flow into Lake Assad, only to be returned to the main stream via the Khabur and Balikh tributaries downstream of Syria's main power plants and irrigation projects. This flow will represent loss to Lake Assad, and as such will be another element in the water distribution and sharing equation to be solved by both Turkish and Syrian river management. Lake Assad must remain full in order to feed the turbines at the Tabqa Dam, and to ensure the full capacity of the siphon or offtake which provides the city of Aleppo with its water supply.

If reservoir water is used for irrigation there will be additional loss from evapotranspiration, though some return flow (RF) will occur in the system. With no irrigation, the Ataturk HEPP would have a firm discharge of 677 m3/s, firm annual energy production of 8190 GWh, and possible total annual production of 8705 GWh. Under full irrigation, firm discharge would be 375 m3/s, and firm annual production 4550 GWh (Master Plan, Vol. 2, table 5.4). It should be remembered as well, that some of the energy produced would be used to pump water to higher parts of the GAP fields. Crops can be transferred to industry, or processed and sold directly for domestic consumption or foreign exchange.

In every case electricity will be consumed to prepare the crops for sale. This electricity will come either from domestically produced hydropower or from thermal power (burning imported fuels). If water is used directly to produce electricity—with the minimum amount of agriculture possible—additional energy can be exported to earn more foreign exchange, which in turn will offset the purchase of petroleum. At the same time, political and environmental dissonance will be minimized downstream. If irrigated agriculture is emphasized, then electrical energy used to pump water to additional, higher fields, will add to the costs of agriculture. Thus, decisions will have to be made concerning the pay-off between agriculture and electricity. At the same time downstream dissonance is increased.

Thus, GAP managers will inevitably find themselves enmeshed in a nexus of competing demands. At stake will be not only the questions of more or fewer crops and what mix of crops to plant, but also questions of foreign exchange, petroleum imports, provision of cheap power for industry, and the assurance of sufficient and inexpensive food and in- dustrial crops for home consumption or sale abroad.

A third problem is the possible pollution of mainstream and tributary waters by the return flow from irrigated fields. It is certain that pollution of this kind will take place on the Euphrates and Tigris Rivers as more and more irrigation projects come on line. The Master Plan does not consider the international implications of this, and makes reference to drainage and salination in only one paragraph in its four volumes (Vol. 2, p. 5.6). Nevertheless, as river volume diminishes and water use increases, such problems will increase downstream. Syria may experience relatively little additional trouble regarding salination from Turkey, but its own soils are notoriously gypsiferous and saline, and their proper washing and cleansing could dump oppressive loads of dissolved solids on Iraqi fields. This problem is of less importance to Turkish river managers than either the detouring or the diminishing of river flow, but it must be kept in mind that reduced flow inevitably means greater concentrations of dissolved solids downstream *(Biswas 1994: 66–77)*.

The GAP's reservoirs (Table 5.1) and HEPPs (Table 5.2)

Table 5.1 GAP's reservoirs

	Euphrates Basin Dams		**Tigris Basin Dams**	
1	Ataturk D.& HEPP	In Operation	Batman D.& HEPP	In Operation
2	Birecik D.& HEPP	In Operation	Cizre D.& HEPP	In Design
3	Buyukcay D.& HEPP	In Planning	Dicle D.& HEPP	In Operation
4	Camgazi Dam	In Operation	Garzan D.& HEPP	In Operation
5	Cataltepe Dam	Under Const.	Ilısu D.& HEPP	In Operation
6	Gomikan Dam	In Planning	Kayser D.& HEPP	In Planning
7	Hancagiz Dam	In Operation	Kralkizi D.& HEPP	In Operation
8	Karakaya D. & HEPP	In Operation	Silvan D.& HEPP	Under Const.
9	Karkamis D.& HEPP	In Operation		
10	Kayacik Dam	Under Const.		
11	Kemlim Dam	In Planning		
12	Kocali Dam	Under Const.		
13	Sirimtas D.& HEPP	In Operation		
14	Kahta Dam	In Operation		

According to Nurit Kliot, GAP, the largest regional development project to be implemented in Turkey in 30–40 years, is a prestigious endeavour with a symbolic value for Turkey no less than that which the Egyptians attach to the Aswan High Dam.

In our opinion, there are a number of important reasons and contributing factors why Turkey put forward and started implementing the GAP project.

a) Reasons

Table 5.2 GAP's HEPPs

	Euphrates Basin HEPPs		Tigris Basin HEPPs	
1	Ataturk D.& HEPP	In Operation	Batman D.& HEPP	In Operation
2	Birecik D.& HEPP	In Operation	Cizre D.& HEPP	In Design
3	Buyukcay D.& HEPP	In Planning	Dicle D.& HEPP	In Operation
4	Erkenek HEPP	In Operation	Garzan D.& HEPP	In Operation
5	Karakaya D. & HEPP	In Operation	Ilısu D.& HEPP	In Operation
6	Karkamis D.& HEPP	In Operation	Kayser D.& HEPP	In Planning
7	Kocali D.& HEPP	Under Const.	Kralkizi D.& HEPP	In Operation
8	Sirimtas D.& HEPP	In Operation	Silvan D.& HEPP	Under Const.
9	Sanliurfa HEPP	In Operation		
10	Cagcag HEPP	In Operation		
11	Bulam HEPP	In Operation		

- Turkey had a great need for electricity, including for industrial development (water is also needed for industry). In the period between 1975 and 1982 Turkey's energy consumtion increased by 30%. At the same time, its total electricity consumption increased only by 24%. And HEPPs could provide a significant portion of that electricity (the volume of hydropower produced in 1979 amounted to only 7.7% of the total energy).
- The process of finding large reserves of oil in Turkey didn't yield serious results. In those seven years (1975–1982) petroleum consumption had increased by 18% and its annual import was nearly four billion dollars. Persistent exploration for new oil deposits continues to prove unsuccessful and Turkey's oil reserves at Batman, near Siirt, had only limited supplies of poor quality. These reserves, which are the northerly extension of the Arabian Gulf and Mosul deposits, are limited by extensive faulting and past volcanic activity, conditions common throughout Turkey. Thus, the situation of the oil sector in 1982 has not changed for the better in the last ten years.
- Turkey had also serious problems with other energy sources. Turkish coal reserves at Zonguldak on the Black Sea are deep, contorted, dangerous, and expensive to mine. As of 1989, Turkey produced 1,973,000 tons of coal but consumed 4,687,000 tons, the balance of which was imported. Some reserves of natural gas were found in Turkish Thrace. The role of natural gas remained insignificant (2.1% of total energy produced) although its import increased by over 1000%. In the area of lignite, asphaltite, geothermal energy, wood and

animal fuel (in Turkish—tezek) Turkey consumes what it produces, but such sources, with the exception of lignite, are unimportant.

- Turkey took into account the fact that HEPPs have a number of advantages over thermal power plants (TPP).

  1) Unlike TPPs, HEPPs don't require fuel and use water, which is a renewable source.
  2) Since HEPPs don't need fuel, the price of electricity produced by them is clear. Unlike thermal power plants, it doesn't depend on the price of fuel and its import from abroad.
  3) Unlike TPPs, HEPPs do not pollute the air.
  4) Unlike TPPs, HEPPs have a longer life.
  5) Unlike TPPs, HEPPs operating costs are less.
  6) The productivity of HEPPs is easily controlled by changing the speed of the water flow (the volume of water supplied to the turbines).
  7) The reservoirs constructed for hydroelectric stations can be used as recreation zones sometimes a truly breathtaking landscape is formed around them.
  8) The water in artificial reservoirs is usually clean, as impurities settle on the bottom. This water can be used for drinking, washing, bathing and irrigation.

- Turkey, which has richer endowment of agricultural resources in terms of cultivable land and availability of water than any Middle Eastern country, needed large-scale agricultural production, both for domestic consumption and export. That's whay Turkey had to build reservoirs, canals and water tunnels for irrigation its lands. GAP will double Turkey's irrigation land and hydroelectricity production and also increase the per capita income in the region by 50%.
- The population of Turkey continued to grow, which led to increase the demand for fresh water. If in 1955 the population of Turkey was 24 million, in 1980 it was about 45 million. The Turkish side naturally took into account that the growth rates of the population would be maintained in the future. Already in 1985, the population of Turkey reached 50.6 million, in 1990—56.5 million, and in 2000—67.8 million.
- The population of big cities in Turkey was growing rapidly at the expense of people from rural areas. Thus, the level of urbanization was increasing, which aggravated the water supply problems of those cities. In 1955, more than 71% of Turkey's population lived in villages and the rest in cities, meanwhile in 1975 58.2% of the population lived in villages and 41.8% in cities. It was also expected that the increase in urbanization would be maintained in the future. In 1985, the majority of the country's population (53%) lived in cities.

- The GAP, which originally started as a 'hydraulic mission'-type scheme, turned into a regional development project. In terms of socio-economic development, Turkey's east/south-east was significantly inferior to the country's west and center, and the GAP would contribute to the partial solution of this problem. This especially pertain to the development of infrastructure in the GAP region. This point may be contentious for Kurds, which we will discuss in 5th chapter.

b) Contributing factors

- 1973 Arab-Israeli war and the oil embargo imposed by the Arab countries caused a major energy crisis. In a short period of time, the price of a barrel of oil increased from $ 2.90 to $ 11.65 (in 2000 prices, it increased from 11 dollars to 39 dollars in one month). As a result, Turkey suffered greatly and thus received additional impetus to develop its hydropower potential *(Agiralioglu 2014: 145).*
- The second oil crisis was associated with the overthrow of the Shah regime in Iran in 1979 and the rise to power of Imam Khomeini, which caused panic in the oil market. Because of that, in 1978–1981 the price of one barrel of oil increased from $13 to $34 (in 2000 prices, it increased from $31 to $69 in one month) *(Bilen 2003: 137).*
- Perhaps Turkey was inspired by the idea of the Great Man-made River Project (GMRP) in Libya, which was conceived in the late 1960s and work on the project began in 1984. The GMRP has been described as the largest irrigation project in the Guiness World (Libyan Leader Muammar Gaddafi described it as the "Eighth Wonder of the World").
- Turkey did not want to lag behind Syria and Iraq (downstream countries) in implementing water projects.
- Turkey wanted to gain serious leverage over Syria and Iraq, to make those countries dependent on Turkey for water.
- Turkey may have wanted to take advantage of the Iran-Iraq war that began in 1980, as Iraq was the most downstream country and suffered the most from both Turkey's and Syria's water projects.

Finally, we want to add, that later, new factors related to the GAP emerged, with the help of which Turkey began to solve other problems. We will describe these new factors in later chapters. It means that over time, Turkey began to use its water projects more diversiform, to solve different tasks through them.

5.2 Water Projects in the Euphrates Basin

It was planned to irrigate more than 1.19 million ha within a framework of GAP project in the Euphrates Basin, capacity of HEPPs will be more than 5300 MW, power generation—more than 20 billion kW/h. These water projects (7 sub-projects of GAP) are presented in Table 5.3 *(Yildiz 2009: 67)*.

Table 5.3 Water projects in the Euphrates Basin

	Projects	Power capacity (MW)	Generation (GWh)	Irrigation area (ha)
1	Karakaya dam and HEPP	1800	7354	–
2	Lower Euphrates Project	2450	9024	718,844
3	Border Euphrates Project	852	3168	–
4	Suruc-Yaylak Project	–	–	113,136
5	Adiyaman Kahta Project	195	509	78,134
6	Adiyaman Goksu Araban Project	7	43	71,598
7	Gaziantep Project	–	–	144,064
	Individual projects	14,4	42	65,165
	Total	**5318,4**	**20,140**	**1.191.391**

5.2.1 Construction of Karakaya Dam

Euphrates Planning Authority was established in Diyarbekir in 1961, and the "Euphrates Basin Development Report" assessing the irrigation and energy potential of the Euphrates Basin was prepared in 1964. Besides, the "Lower Euphrates Development Report" was ready in 1966. In the meantime, studies of the Tigris Basin were carried out by the Diyarbekir Directorate of DSİ. These works made clear how to go on developing the Lower Euphrates and Tigris Basins, as a result, in 1977 it was decided to coin these two basin projects together as GAP project. GAP was formally established in 1980. The task of addressing the region of South-eastern Anatolia in the context of integrated regional planning and ensuring the coordination of relevant activities was assigned to the State Planning Organization (DPT—in Turkish acronym).

Construction of Karakaya's Reservoir on the Euphrates appeared on Turkey's agenda in the 1970s. This shows that Turkey did not want to wait for the completion of the Keban reservoir project, because knew how useful can be major dams. This was facilitated by the management of S. Demirel, who was aiming to build HEPPs on the Euphrates and Tigris and thus receive 30–40 billion kW/h of electricity annually *(Turgut 2000: 111)*. And it was no coincidence that during the reign of Demirel the volume of investments in the east of the country increased. If in 1963 the Eastern region (in Turkish—Doğu Bölgesi) accounted for 10% of the investments in Turkey, then in 1969—24% *(Ibid: 114)*.

In 1969 the Justice Party again won the parliamentary elections and Demirel again became Prime Minister. In 1971 Demirel's third government presented its plan to build a second reservoir on the Euphrates, the Karakaya Reservoir (Demirel formed his second government in 1969 and the third in 1970). The Karakaya Reservoir should thus become the second "golden bracelet" of the Euphrates (Central Euphrates Basin). But on March 12, 1971, a new military coup took place in Turkey that overthrew the Demirel government. Military coup not only delayed construction of Karakaya reservoir, but also significantly increased project cost. In 1975, Demirel again became Prime Minister and continued to implement major energy and irrigation projects *(Ibid: 123)*.

Karakaya Dam was constructed 166 km south of Keban Reservoir (Diyarbekir Province). The construction of the Karakaya reservoir began on October 18, 1976. On that day Demirel used a sentence that resembled a word game in Turkish—'Fırat akar biz de böyle bakar' ('Euphrates flows, we look at that). The HEPP generates power with six units of 300 MW, totalling the installed capacity to 1,800 MW. The first turbine at Karakaya HEPP was put into operation on March 18, 1987, the second—on July 9, 1987, the third—on October 27, 1987, the fourth—on March 5, 1988, the fifth—on June 10, 1988, the sixth—on March 9, 1989 (according to DSI, the Karakaya HEPP was put into operation in 1987—auth.). Karakaya HEPP thus surpassed the Keban HEPP and became Turkey's biggest HEPP. It generates 7354 billion kW/h of electricity annually.

It was also planned to build on the Euphrates the reservoir of Karababa (later renamed Ataturk Dam). According to Demirel, Turkey could generate about 21 billion kW/h of electricity by constructing 4 reservoirs and HEPPs on the Euphrates. 6 billion kW/h of electricity was generated annually from the Keban HEPP, it was expected to got 7.4 billion kW/h from the Karakaya HEPP, 5 billion kW/h from the Karababa HEPP and 2,5 billion kW/h from the 4th HEPP.

In addition, Demirel was planning to build three major dams on Tigris (Kralkizi, Batman and Ilisu) and receive 10 billion kW/h of electricity. Thus, the Euphrates' and Tigris' HEPPs would produce annually 31 billion kW/h. Demirel also wanted to build a number of canals to irrigate the 20 million-acre area by the waters of Euphrates and Tigris reservoirs. According to Demirel, the cost of all these projects will be 100 billion liras *(Ibid: 128–129).*

S. Demirel often compared Turkey with European countries and the US in order to express his vision of elevating Turkey to their development level. 'Southeastern Anatolia Region is 'Turkey's California', and it will become 'Turkey's Ruhr' with its future industrial plants',- he stated in the early 1970s. In the mid-1980s, he narrated how the efforts of the US government aiming to develop its water and land resources impressed him: 'I am the first Turkish engineer who was sent to western states in the US by the government to enhance my knowledge and skills in 1949. When I saw the Boulder (Hoover) Dam on the Colorado River in Nevada, I sat on a rock and watched it for three days. There, I saw a lot and then had the opportunity to apply them in my country',- said he *(Bilgen 2019).*

5.2.2 Lower Euphrates Projects

The Lower Euphrates Project, one of the 13 main irrigation and energy projects in the GAP Region, is the largest and the most comprehensive one. It includes the Ataturk Dam and HEPP, Birecik Dam and HEPP, Sanliurfa tunnels, Sanliurfa-Harran irrigation, Mardin-Ceylanpinar irrigation, Siverek-Hilvan pumped irrigation and Bozova pumped irrigation.

Ataturk Reservoir is the largest water project in Turkish history, the largest investment, the pride of Turkey, the sixth largest reservoir in the world, the largest reservoir in Europe. The location of the Ataturk reservoir was determined as a result of studies carried out in the late 1950s. This third "gold bracelet" of Euphrates is 180 km away from the Karakaya Reservoir. In 1978, it was decided to call the Karababa Reservoir the Ataturk Reservoir as it should become the largest reservoir in the country. Construction of the reservoir was scheduled to begin on October 29, 1980, on the 57th anniversary of the founding of the Republic of Turkey, and be completed in 1987. On September 12, 1980 there was a military coup in Turkey, which delayed the start of the construction of the Ataturk Reservoir *(Turgut 2000: 163–176).*

However, on October 28, 1983 the tender for the construction of Ataturk Reservoir and HEPP was signed. On November 3, 1983 Turkish President (leader of Turkey's 1980 military coup) Kenan Evren laid stone foundation for the construction of the Ataturk Reservoir (in 1981 K. Evren also participated to the start of Ataturk dam's derivation tunnels construction) and announced that the region will become the "Second Chukurova"[1] due to the Ataturk Reservoir *(Agiralioglu 2014: 208).*

The dam with volume of 48.7 BCM would cover part of the Adiyaman, Sanliurfa and Diyarbekir provinces. The process of filling the Ataturk reservoir with water began in January 1990. On July 16, 1992, the first turbine of the Ataturk HEPP put into operation, and on December 1, 1993, the eighth turbine. On July 25, 1992 the opening of Ataturk Reservoir took place, during which Demirel declared that the Ataturk Reservoir was a monument to the nation's pride (in 1991, Demirel again became Prime Minister of Turkey). Turkish President Turgut Ozal also took part in the opening of the Ataturk Reservoir, he also was a big supporter of the GAP and had visited the Ataturk Reservoir site several times before (T. Ozal studied electrical engineering at Istanbul Technical University, where he met the future Prime Minister S. Demirel).

The dam is a multi-purpose project for both hydropower generation and irrigation. The HEPP of Ataturk dam has 8 turbines, each with a capacity of 300 MW, with a total capacity of 2400 MW. It generates 8900 GWh of electricity annually, making it Turkey's largest HEPP. Each turbine has a rated discharge of $218.5m^3/s$ and head of 151 m. It was planned to irrigate 874,200 ha of water in the Ataturk reservoir, of which 142,000 were in the Sanliurfa-Harran valley, 158,000—in the Lower Mardin-Ceylanpinar valley, 192,100—in Upper Mardin, 180,300—in the Siverek-Hilvan valley, 55,300—in Bozova, 146,500—in Suruc. When irrigation projects will be completed, HEPP production will be reduced to 8.1 billion kWh, equivalent to saving 2 million tonnes of oil annually. It was expected that the Ataturk Reservoir and HEPP would cover the costs within 8 years at the latest. Ataturk dam's HEPP increased electricity production in Turkey by 1/3, and the reservoir increased irrigated land 15 times *(Turgut 2000: 163–176).*

Thus, the Ataturk Reservoir was built in 8.5 years (1983–1992), although the program provided for 10 years. According to Necati Agiralioglu, the premature completion of the construction of the Ataturk Reservoir was of great benefit to

[1] We want to emphasize that Chukurova, alternatively known as Cilicia, is a geo-cultural region in south-central Turkey, covering the provinces of Mersin, Adana, Osmaniye and Hatay. Most of the Chukurova region is a large stretch of flat, fertile land which is among the most agriculturally productive areas of the world. The Chukurova plain has some of the most fertile soil in the world in which 3 harvests can be taken each year. The region has the second richest flora in the world and it is the producer of all agricultural products of Turkey except hazelnut and tobacco.

Turkey. 'Ataturk Reservoir should produce 9.1 billion kWh per year. The price of 1 kWh of electricity is estimated at \$ 0.10 per year. As a result, Ataturk Reservoir generates \$ 910 million a year and \$ 30 per second. That is why it is not necessary to delay the construction of the reservoir for even a second. In general, the delay of the construction of Ataturk Reservoir's HEPP would cost the country \$ 30–300 per second. Construction of many reservoirs in Turkey has been delayed. Turkey's energy production has lost 76.3 billion kWh due to delays in the construction of only 20 reservoirs. In sum, it is \$ 7,63 billion (1 kWh = \$ 0.10). Meanwhile, the construction of the Ataturk Reservoir was completed 1.5 years earlier than planned, it was built in 8.5 years. Since the construction of the Keban Reservoir, which by its parameters is significantly inferior to the Ataturk Reservoir, took more than 10 years, a number of DSI experts thought that the construction of the Ataturk Reservoir would take at least 15 years',- he noted *(Agiralioglu 2014: 300–304, 267–268).*

According to head of General Directorate of DSI Mevlut Aydın, Ataturk Dam, which is also one of the largest in the world, can fulfill the water needs of Turkey for seven years. "The dam will fulfill the water needs of millions of decares of land, primarily in Sanliurfa, Harran, Mardin, Ceylanpinar, Siverek-Hilvan and Suruc plains. The total amount of land in GAP Project to benefit from Ataturk Dam is estimated to be 10 million decares and the dam is expected to generate \$2.5 billion income once the irrigation projects are completed. In terms of body size, the dam ranks fifth in the world and it is both Turkey's and Europe's largest hydroelectric dam. The reservoir created behind the dam, named Lake Ataturk Dam, is also the third largest in the world. The dam also contributes to local economy and food supply with its fish farms. The Ataturk Dam has alone contributed more than TL 150 billion to the Turkish economy over 26 years, according to 2019 data", he said (*Daily Sabah: 05.06.2019*).

Sanliurfa Irrigation tunnels are the name of a major irrigation tunnel constructed within a framework of GAP. The tunnels carry water from the Ataturk Reservoir to near the city of Sanliurfa. There are two parallel tunnels (T1 & T2), the length of each being 26.4 kilometers. The outer diameter of each tunnel is 9.5 metres and the inner diameter is 7.62 meters. The flow rate is 328 (2*164) m3/s (for comparison, the flow rate of Sakarya river is 225 m3/s). With these figures, the tunnels are the one of the largest tunnels in the world, in terms of length and flow rate. Thus, water reaches the Sanliurfa-Harran Plains, the largest irrigation area in the GAP Region, through the Sanliurfa twin tunnels system.

It was planned to irrigate 148,649 ha by tunnel waters in the valleys of Sanliurfa and Harran and 327,825 ha in the valleys of Mardin, Ceylanpinar and Viransehir. The first tender for the construction of tunnels was held in 1977, and the second in 1981. Turkish Prime Minister S. Demirel attended the start of tunnel construction in 1977 and announced that "Urfa tunnels are drilled through the ages, not mountains" (in Turkish—"Urfa tünelleri ile dağlar değil, çağlar delinmektedir"). The project cost $ 585 million *(Agiralioglu 2014: 162–165).*

The first tunnel was opened on 6 November, 1994. It was planned to irrigate 60,000 ha in the Harran Valley by tunnel water. Thus, the waters of the Euphrates River met for the first time with the arid lands of the Upper Mesopotamian plains. This time, S. Demirel was also here and announced that the construction of this tunnel was one of their dreams, adding that Harran had been waiting for the Euphrates for many years. According to Necati Agiralioglu, the total length of Sanliurfa tunnels was 52 kilometers, making it the longest irrigation tunnel in the world, 3 MCM of excavation was carried out in the tunnels, 1 million 150 thousand m3 concrete was poured and 70,000 tons of injections. Implementation of the tunnels' project lasted 17 years (1977–1994) instead of the planned 8 years due to economic and technical problems.

T1 & T2 tunnels thus carry water from Ataturk Reservoir to Sanliurfa, from where the 221-kilometer-long canal (204 m3/s) carries water to the valleys of Viranshehir, Kiziltepe and Mardin (224,530 ha). Two canals were also built—The Urfa Canal (40 m3/s) should irrigate 54,092 ha in the Urfa Valley, and The Harran Canal (84 m3/s) should irrigate 97,327 ha in the Harran valley. HEPP with capacity of 52 MW (2*26) was also built in Sanliurfa. It is capable of generating 124 million kWh of electricity per year *(Ibid: 257–261).*

5.2.3 The Border Euphrates Project

The Border Euphrates Project is laid out on the plain near to Syrian Border. Because of that heights of the Birecik Dam and the Karkamis Dam are not very big. However dams will use regulated water by other dams at the upstream. The area is semi-desert, because of that they will be used to supply irrigation water.

The Birecik Dam, one of the 22 dams of GAP, is located on the Euphrates River 60 km downstream of Ataturk Dam and 8 km upstream of Birecik town 80 km west of Province of Sanliurfa in the southeastern region of Turkey (about 30 km away from the Syrian border). It was purposed for irrigation and energy production. Birecik HEPP comprises 6 units of 112 MW nominal capacity, having a total installed capacity of 672 MW. Storage volume is 1,220 MCM and has a 62.5 m of height from the foundation. With mean annual flow of 963 m3/s the annual energy generation will reach 2.5 billion kWh. Hydrological risk is the risk related with reduced energy output caused by changes in river flows. This is mainly due to upstream facilities which can reduce flow and therefore output. Area of the reservoir is 56 km2. Irrigation area is 92,700 ha on Gaziantep and Araban plains.

The construction of the Birecik Dam on the Euphrates River that provides electricity and water for irrigation was started in 1993 (according to DSI—in 1985) and completed in 2000. Total project cost is 2,262 million DM (app. 1,114 million Euro), this capital was mainly provided by international investors. Birecik is the first major hydropower project that was financed on a BOT basis in Turkey. The dam was financed and built by a German-French-Belgian-Austrian consortium. The investment will be repaid through the sale of electricity during the 15-year operation period. Thereafter, the dam and HEPP will be transferred to the Turkish government. The Birecik hydro power project in Turkey demonstrates the effective role private companies can play in the planning, financing and construction of hydro power plants. The Government of Turkey thus wished to stimulate private sector involvement in electricity generation *(Gundes 2006: 268–269)*.

The Karkamis Dam and HEPP is the second unit in the Border Euphrates Project, which constitutes one part of GAP. The foundation of the dam was laid in 1996, and is 4.5 kilometres from the Syria border and 33 km downstream from the now completed Birecik Dam. They use the water of the Euphrates River which has already regulated at the upstream by other dams. In fact, Karkamis and Birecik dams are operated together. Karkamis Dam lake area lies in Sanliurfa and Gaziantep provinces. It covers a total surface of 30,000 ha between the E5 International Transporting Road and the Syria border. Construction of the Karkamish Reservoir was completed in 2000. Karkamis HEPP consists of six units producing 652 GWh/y with 180 MW installed capacity. Constructed as a clay-core earthfill dam, the Karkamis Dam and HEPP is a very important project being the first application of run of river type HEPP in Turkey. When the protective embankments on the right and left shore of the reservoir for this electrical power generating dam were built, the 336-meter level of the lake was raised to an operational level of 340 meters. The purpose was to protect the residential area and 433 ha of farmland below the lake. The project was completed by an Austrian Consortium including Turkish company—Yuksel Inshaat. The cost of Karkamis Dam and HEPP is $175 million (or $192 million) and is one of the smaller dams in GAP. Karkamis Dam is the last of the Euphrates in Turkey *(Yüksel İnşaat, Karkamış Dam and HEPP)*.

The evolution of the financing of Turkey's hydro-development programme is remarkable. The Keban Dam, farthest upstream, is a HEPP facility without agricultural water commitments. The first to be built on the Euphrates, its financing met with little difficulty. Work, beginning in 1968, was financed by the European Investment Bank, USAID, and the French, German and Italian governments. The total cost in 1974 U.S. dollars, the year it was completed, was about $85 million. In the years that followed, difficulty was experienced in finding international financing for the Karakaya Dam, next downstream and included in the GAP. Nevertheless, a combination of Turkish and foreign funds was eventually found and the dam completed in 1988. By the time contracts were tendered to the Dogus Insaat ye Ticaret A.S. for the Ataturk Dam, questions over the downstream impact of the GAP precluded the loaning of funds by the World Bank for its construction. However, in March 1985 the Export-Import Bank of New York and the Manufacturers Hanover Trust loaned Turkey $111 million for the dam. European banks have also provided at least $460 million for equipment, but the bulk of the funding for the Ataturk Dam has been provided by the Turks themselves. As of mid-1992 the total cost of the Ataturk project had reached TL 11,241,000 million (1$ = 7600 TL on 15 October 1992). The Birecik Dam is being financed by a new, experimental scheme BOT *(Biswas 1994: 62).*

Table 5.4 Parameters of 5 reservoirs built on the Euphrates

	Keban	Karakaya	Ataturk	Birecik	Karkamis
Height, m	210	173	169	62,5	29
Length, m	1097	462	1644	–	–
Total capacity, km3	31	9,58	48.7	1,22	0,157
Surface area, km2	675	268	817	56,2	28
Installed capacity, MW	1330	1800	2400	672	180
Generation, GWh	6000	7500	8900	2500	652
Irrigation area, ha	–	–	874,200	92,700	–
Construction date	1965–1975	1976–1987	1983–1992	1985–2000	1996–2000

Thus, Ataturk Dam is the key energy and irrigation project, the epitome of GAP and Birecik Dam is the first major hydropower project that was financed on a BOT basis in Turkey, which showed that the construction of new dams will gain speed. The upper reservoirs—Keban and Karakaya, are not used for irrigation purposes, which, in our opinion, had a number of reasons.

- The use of the Keban and Karakaya reservoirs for irrigation would have a negative impact on the lower reservoirs, first of all on the Ataturk reservoir (Ataturk HEPP).

- In this region, there are relatively few/no favorable areas for irrigation.
- Relations with neighboring countries would be further strained.
- The construction of canals and water tunnels is a time-consuming and costly process.
- Implementation of irrigation projects requires preparatory work with farmers.

By building reservoirs on the Euphrates, Turkey in that way began to control the flow of the Euphrates 100 percent. Turkey has gained serious leverage over Syria and Iraq, which strengthened their degree of resistance. In the 20th century major reservoirs were built primarily on the Euphrates (not on its tributaries) in Turkey. The main dams of the GAP were located on the Euphrates basin, and it could be argued that it has several reasons. a) The Euphrates Basin is larger than the Tigris Basin in Turkey (and in general): Euphrates is a longer river than the Tigris. b) The Euphrates is a more water-abundance river than the Tigris in Turkey (but not in Iraq). c) Irrigation areas are mainly located in or around the Euphrates Basin in Turkey. d) The Euphrates Basin is more convenient and accessible for water projects in Turkey (the Tigris Basin is more inaccessible).

5.3 Water Projects in the Tigris Basin

The Tigris River was the last major river system in Turkey to be developed, as geographic conditions in the basin made large-scale developments more difficult than in the Euphrates Basin, as already mentioned. Nevertheless, due to its upstream riparian potential, Turkey has started to make more use of the Tigris in recent years. Initial projects launched in the 1940s focused on hydroelectric power production and support for irrigated agriculture in the lower parts of the basin. Plans for dams, power plants and irrigation areas in the Turkish part of the Tigris Basin were first touted as the "Western Tigris Development Plan". At a later stage, GAP also included infrastructural development in the lower section of the Turkish Tigris Basin. Turkey has to date built eight large dams and eight hydroelectric power plants on the Tigris River and its tributaries as part of GAP. The project also aims to establish a reservoir system on the upper Tigris River for flow regulation. The Ilisu Dam Project lies at the heart of this system.

Due to its geographic position, Turkey controls about a third of the total Tigris flow and its influence on the river's water regime is constantly growing. Theoretically, Turkey could also use the Greater Zab headwaters, as this tributary originates in Turkey before it flows into Iraq. The region's topography, however, would make this a challenging endeavour *(UN-ESCWA 2013: 113–114)*.

It was planned that about 630,000 ha of water could be irrigated under the GAP project in the Tigris Basin. Capacity of the HEPPs to be constructed should have been more than 2100 MW and power generation more than 7 billion kW/h. These water projects (6 sub-projects on Tigris) are presented in Table 5.5 *(Yildiz 2009: 68)*.

Table 5.5 Water projects in the Tigris Basin

Projects	Power capacity (MW)	Generation (GWh)	Irrigation area (ha)
Kralkizi-Dicle Project	204	444	130,159
Batman Project	198	483	37,351
Batman-Silvan Project	240	964	245,372
Garzan Project	90	315	60,000
Ilisu Project	1200	3833	–
Cizre Project	240	1208	121,000
Individual projects	–	–	35,773
Total	**2172**	**7247**	**629,655**

5.3.1 Kralkizi-Dicle Integrated Project

Impounding of the Kralkizi and Dicle Dams of the GAP have started upon ceremonies held in 25 October 1997. Apart from many local businessmen and citizens, the ceremonies were conducted at the presence of S. Demirel, the State President; Hikmet Cetin, the Speaker of the Parliament; Prime Minister Mesut Yilmaz; State Ministers and some deputies. "The River Tigris has been running since the creation of our world; but for the first time it has been harnessed for the needs of people. All must be happy on this event" said S. Demirel. In his speech at the ceremony organized for the Kralkizi Dam, Demirel also remarked that the River Tigris is now at the service of the people within the framework the GAP. He added that the dam will start generating energy in 1998. In his speech, M. Yilmaz noted Turkey's need for new investments in the field of energy and gave the figure 31 trillion TL as the cost of the Kralkizi Dam which took 13 years to complete. Yilmaz said that the country needed 6.5 billion kWh of electric energy for the coming year and urgent measures had to be taken to meet this need. "*It is necessary to invest continuously in this sector and it is one of our priorities to take measures to avoid any energy gap in the near future*",- he added. After these speeches, the President of Turkey pressed the button and let the two dams start impounding.

Kralkizi Dam thus is one of the dams of GAP in Batman. The HEPP has a total installed power capacity of 94 MW. The dam was constructed between 1985 and 1997. The Kralkizi Dam is also functional as a storage for the waters of the Dicle Dam. Dicle Dam is also one of the dams of GAP and located 22 kilometres downstream of the Kralkizi Dam. Construction works were started in 1986. The project is for energy production and irrigation. The dam has an installed hydroelectric capacity of 110 MW, annual generation is 298 GWh and is designed to ultimately irrigate 128,080 ha.

These facilities are located within the provincial territory of Diyarbekir, at a distance of 50–80 kilometres to Diyarbekir city centre. Kralkizi-Dicle Project is an integrated project comprising the dams of Kralkızı and Dicle as well as Irrigation Facilities. With the Project, 130,159 ha of land on the right bank of the Tigris will be brought under irrigation. Out of the 130,150 ha of planned irrigation which will cover the plains of the central, Cinar and Bismil districts of Diyarbekir, 54,279 ha will be irrigated by gravity while 75,880 by pumping water. According to the results of the land classification work, 420,000 ha of land on the right bank is feasible for irrigation. Kralkizi-Dicle Project will also supply water to Diyarbekir for drinking, domestic and industrial purposes *(T.C. GAP Bölge Kalkınma İdaresi Başkanlığı).*

5.3.2 Construction of Batman and Garzan Dams

Batman Dam is one of the 22 dams of GAP, built on the Batman River, north of Batman, in southeastern of Turkey. It was constructed between 1986 and 1999. There is a hydroelectric power plant, established in 1998, at the dam, with a power output of 191.7 MW. The dam is designed to service an irrigation area of 37,744 ha (93,270 acres). The Silvan Dam is located upstream.

Garzan Dam is an embankment dam on the Garzan River 9 km northeast of Kozluk in Batman Province, Turkey. It is part of the Southeastern Anatolia Project and has a primary purpose of hydroelectric power generation and irrigation. Surveys for the dam were completed in 2008, construction began in 2009 and the dam began to impound its reservoir in October 2012. The power plant has an installed capacity of 49 MW. The irrigation works remain under construction and are expected to irrigate an area of 40,000 ha when complete.

Here we don't want to present the data of these reservoirs built on the Tigris and its tributaries, as we did it in case of the Euphrates Basin. We will do it at point 5.5 when we will present implementation of GAP in the 21st century, including the dams of Silvan, Ilisu and Cizre in the Tigris basin. We would like to emphasize again that geographic conditions in the Tigris basin are very complicated, more difficult than in the Euphrates Basin. In addition, Tigris is significantly inferior to the Euphrates in its discharge of water (in Turkey), that's why Turkey in the 20th century began to build reservoirs not only on the Tigris river, but also on its important tributaries (Batman, Garzan), unlike the Euphrates Basin. Thus, in the 20th century Turkey also began to take steps to control the flow of Tigris River, but this trend appreciably was intensified in the 21st century. Turkey wanted to strengthen its water leverage over Iraq (Tigris doesn't enter Syria), as a result Turkey began to control the Tigris for 60% in the 20th century. In any case, at the time Turkey has not yet built large reservoirs in the Tigris Basin for well-known reasons (the focus was mainly on the Euphrates Basin), which allowed Iraq to replace the reduction of the Euphrates River with the waters of the Tigris.

5.4 Water Projects in Syria and Iraq

5.4.1 The Euphrates Basin

Water management in the Euphrates Basin dates back 6,000 years when the Mesopotamian landscape was transformed by the introduction of irrigation networks to improve agricultural yield. More recently in the 20th century, the basin witnessed the implementation of extensive water resources development schemes, with the construction of dams, reservoirs and hydroelectric power plants. Today, water management in Iraq, Syria and Turkey focuses on hydropower, irrigation and drinking water supply. More than 70% of water in the Euphrates Basin is used for agricultural production. GAP in the upper Euphrates Basin in Turkey has drastically impacted the natural flow regime of the river in recent decades. The maximum storage capacity of the major dams and reservoirs (>144 BCM) on the Euphrates (in Turkey, Syria and Iraq) exceeds the natural annual flow volume of the river (30 BCM) by four to five times.

Development & use: Syria

Syria has constructed 165 dams with a total storage capacity of 19.6 km 3 on the Euphrates for the production of hydropower, irrigation and storage of water for drinking. Like Turkey, Syria did not start exploiting the Euphrates until the 1960s. Upon completion of the Tabqa Dam in the 1970s, the country developed ambitious plans for major irrigation projects along the Euphrates River. The Tabqa Dam, also known as the Euphrates Dam, was designed to meet Syria's primary irrigation and energy needs. Its construction led to the creation of Lake Assad, the country's largest water reservoir with a projected capacity to irrigate 640,000 ha of land. The third-largest dam on the Euphrates in Syria, the Baath Dam, was built in 1987, mainly to regulate flow from the upstream Tabqa Dam. The Tishreen Dam, located upstream of Lake Assad, was built in 1999 to generate hydropower.

Water resources in the basin are mainly used for a series of large irrigation projects. Syria has vastly expanded its irrigated area in recent decades: total irrigated area has increased from 652,000 ha in 1985 to 1.4 million ha in 2005, remaining constant since then. Overall, the Euphrates Basin comprises the largest share of cultivated area in the country.

One of the main water development projects in the Syrian part of the Euphrates Basin is the Great Khabour Irrigation Project, as part of which three dams were built on the Khabour River to produce hydropower and store water for irrigation. In 2010, about 59,550 ha of land were irrigated by the Khabour and Jagh Jagh Rivers. In addition, two development projects in the Balikh/Jallab sub-basins use water imported from Lake Assad, while waterfrom the Sajur River is also used for irrigation.

In the Syrian part of the Euphrates Basin, an estimated total of 325,000 ha of land were irrigated in 2000, with a further 325,000 ha of land earmarked for future irrigation projects. The annual volume of water required for the proposed projects is assumed to be about 5,180 MCM. This volume should be added to the 3,586 MCM used in operational irrigation projects. Official data states that 206,987 ha were irrigated by the Euphrates River in 2010 in addition to 59,550 ha from the Khabour and Jagh Jagh Rivers, amounting to almost 270,000 ha. Applying a commonly accepted rate for irrigation requirements, this suggests an irrigation water use of about 2,700 MCM from the Euphrates, Khabour and Jagh Jagh Rivers.

Lack of information on the current state of irrigated land in the Euphrates Basin in Syria makes it difficult to explain the difference between the 2000 and 2010 figures. However, it is likely that irrigated agriculture has declined in some areas. The disparity could also be the result of different methods of assessing and defining irrigated land.

Either way, the figures show that the scale of Syrian irrigation projects is comparable to that of GAP in the Euphrates Basin in Turkey in terms of irrigated area. However, it must be noted that in Turkey as well as in northern Syria (unlike arid south-eastern Syria or Iraq), agriculture is partly rain-fed with seasonal supplementary irrigation. Nevertheless, Syria depends largely on the Euphrates as more than 50% of the blue water used in the country is abstracted from the basin. While most of this is used for irrigation, the Euphrates also supplies drinking water to the cities of Deir ez Zor and Raqqah. Since 2006, Aleppo also draws its water from the Euphrates, with a pipeline running west from Lake Assad and supplying cities and villages along its route.

The Euphrates Valley Project
The Tabqa Dam was Syria's main development focus in the Euphrates Basin. Initiated in the 1960s, the project had multiple objectives including the expansion of the region's irrigated area to 640,000 ha, the generation of energy, and the prevention of seasonal flooding. The project comprised six irrigation districts which were all centrally supervised by the General Authority for the Development of the Euphrates Basin. However, after the initial plan failed, the government reduced the irrigated area objectives to 370,000 ha. The problems encountered included high gypsum levels in the soil and salinization caused by intensive irrigation.

Total area irrigated by the Euphrates River in Syria in 2010
Upper Euphrates (Aleppo)—75,468 ha
Lower Euphrates (Deir ez Zor)—33,952 ha
Middle Euphrates (Raqqah)—97,567 ha

Development & use: Iraq
Before Turkey and Syria developed an interest in the Euphrates, Iraq was the main user of river water. It was the first riparian to develop engineering projects along the river, irrigating more than five times as much land as Syria and nearly 10 times as much as Turkey in the Euphrates Basin. However, by the late 1960s Syrian and Turkish irrigation projects had outgrown Iraqi projects.

Built in the first half of the 20th century, the Hindiyah Dam and the Ramadi-Razzaza Regulator were constructed to prevent flooding and ensure year-round irrigation of crops via canal systems. The Haditha Dam is the largest dam along the Iraqi stretch of the Euphrates River with a maximum capacity of 8.2 BCM. It is located about 120 km from the Syrian border and regulates flow in addition to generating electricity. Iraq also constructed a complex network of canals on the Euphrates, diverting Euphrates water to reservoirs such as Lake Habbaniyeh and Lake Tharthar which store excess flood water.

Iraq irrigates a greater surface area along its part of the Euphrates River than Syria and Turkey. In the 1960s, Iraq extracted about 16 BCM between Hit and Hindiyah to irrigate around 1.2 million ha. While no recent statistics on irrigated area in Iraq are available, figures from 2000 suggest irrigated areas along the Euphrates River in Iraq added up to about 1.5 million ha. Other sources suggest that an area of 1 to 1.3 million ha was irrigated by Euphrates water. These estimates do not support the assumption that irrigated agriculture in Iraq had declined since the 1980s as a result of the Iraq-Iran war, economic sanctions and the two Gulf wars.

Total potential irrigable land in Iraq within the Euphrates Basin is estimated at 1.8 million ha. Another study states that 4 million ha of land are suitable for agriculture in the Euphrates Basin in Iraq.

The Third River or Main Outfall Drain
Also known as the Saddam River, the Third River flows from Baghdad to the Persian Gulf via the Khor Zubair Canal. Construction on the 565 km canal system was completed in 1992 after 30 years of work. As a main outfall, it collects drainage water from more than 1.5 million ha of land between the Euphrates and Tigris Rivers. The canals discharge into the extensive southern Hammar Marshes that are fed by the Euphrates and Tigris. The project was also set up to resolve the chronic salinity problem affecting farmland between the two rivers, by collecting saline drainage water and preventing it from flowing into the Euphrates. In 1995, around 17 million tons of salt reportedly flowed into the Gulf through the Third River *(UN-ESCWA 2013, Chapter* 1*: 64–66).*

5.4.2 The Tigris Basin

Development & use: Syria
Syria is a minor Tigris riparian as the river defines only a short stretch of the Syrian-Turkish border. The country only exploits the basin's water resources for small-scale agricultural activity and domestic use. However, in mid-2010, Syria launched the first phase of an irrigation project on the Tigris River. The project is based on a 2002 agreement between Syria and Iraq, which authorizes Syria to pump an annual 1,250 MCM from the Tigris River. The water is to be used to irrigate approximately 150,000 ha of land in Hasakah Governorate in the upper part of the Khabour Basin through an inter basin water transfer. The project also aims to generate hydroelectricity and strengthen the local economy by improving agricultural yield.

Development & use: Iraq
Iraq has a long history of water use in the Tigris Basin and was also the first riparian to develop irrigation projects, and construct dams, barrages and cross regulators on the river and its tributaries. Early engineering projects included the 1939 Kut Barrage and the 1956 Tharthar System Barrage, two water regulation projects with limited irrigation capabilities. The Tharthar Dam and Canal were constructed north-west of

Baghdad in the 1950s to protect it from flooding. The scheme diverts floodwater from the Tigris through the 64 km Tharthar Canal to the Euphrates River. Completed in 1977, the project is regarded as the cornerstone of Iraq's surface water management system.

A number of important reservoirs and regulating structures were built on the eastern tributaries of the Tigris between the 1960s and 1980s, including the Dukan and Dibis Dams on the Lesser Zab, and the Derbendikhan Dam on the Diyala. Other dam projects followed, including the Mosul Dam, which has one of the largest reservoirs in Iraq. It is mainly used for hydropower production, but also serves irrigation and flood control purposes.

The Tharthar Canal, which connects the Tigris to the Euphrates, is the cornerstone of Iraq's water development system. The Tharthar Dam has allowed Iraq to overcome water shortages in the Euphrates Basin by diverting water from the Tigris to the Euphrates via Lake Tharthar. The capacity of Lake Tharthar is twice that of the Ataturk Dam reservoir in Turkey and equal to the operating capacity of the Aswan Dam in Egypt. The Main Outfall Drain, formerly known as the Saddam River, was constructed to collect drainage water from more than 1.5 million ha of agricultural land between the Euphrates and Tigris Rivers. Iraq constructed several other canals in the Tigris Basin, including the East al Gharraf Drain and the Tigris East Drain, for the purpose of land reclamation and drainage. The main irrigation canal in the Tigris Basin is the 170 km Shatt al Gharraf which irrigates an area of 700,000 ha.

Agriculture

In the mid-1970s, Iraq irrigated approximately 5.6 million ha of land, of which almost 70% (3,825,000 ha) were located in the Tigris Basin. The river currently irrigates around 4 million ha of land in Iraq. The largest irrigation projects in the Tigris Basin in Iraq include the Kirkuk Irrigation Project in the Adhaim Basin, the North Jezira Irrigation Project and the East Jezira Irrigation Project. Launched in 1983, the Kirkuk Irrigation Project initially irrigated 87,500 ha, with plans to expand to a total of 300,000 ha. The North Jezira Irrigation Project was initiated in the early 1990s to supply approximately 60,000 ha with water from the Mosul Dam. The East Jezira Irrigation Project created irrigation networks on about 70,000 ha of rain-fed land near Mosul. The latter two projects were part of a scheme to irrigate 250,000 ha of land in the Jezira Plain. Iraq launched several other irrigation projects before the 1991 Gulf War, most of them focused on draining the Iraqi marshlands.

In recent decades, Iraq's agricultural and water resources policies have focused on land reclamation with the expansion of irrigation networks and drainage systems to improve soil productivity. As a result, an area of approximately 1 million ha was reclaimed, in addition to 1.5 million ha of semi-reclaimed land. Land reclamation projects in the Tigris Basin are situated in Kirkuk and Diyala Governorates and in the area south of Baghdad. In an attempt to rehabilitate agricultural infrastructure, the ministries responsible for water resources, irrigation and agriculture are planning to implement several integrated irrigation projects using both surface and groundwater resources. Planned projects include the reclamation of 920,000 ha by 2015 and the irrigation of 134,000 ha of new land in Kirkuk Governorate and in the eastern and southern Jezira. Irrigation rehabilitation projects have also been implemented on almost 800,000 ha.

The Mesopotamian Marshes
The area along the confluence of the Tigris and the Euphrates Rivers in southern Iraq was once home to the largest wetland ecosystem in Western Asia. However, by 2002, over 85% of the Mesopotamian Marshes had been destroyeda as a result of heavy damming and massive drainage projects in the second half of the 20th century. Historically, the marshes constituted a sequence of interconnected marshlands and lake systems. The heart of the marshes comprised three main areas: the Hammar Marshes south of the Euphrates, the Haweizeh Marshes east of the Tigris River and the Qurnah (or Central) Marshes situated between the two rivers. The Qurnah Marshes were the largest of the marshland formations. Before the marshes were drained, they acted as a natural wastewater treatment system for the Euphrates and Tigris Rivers, filtering out fertilizers before the water drained into the Persian Gulf.

The regular annual flooding of the Euphrates and Tigris inundated the marsh lowlands over an area of more than 10,000 km2. During low-flow periods, the area would shrink to a few thousand square kilometers. The damming of the Euphrates and Tigris during the 1970s diminished water flow to the downstream ecosystems. In the early 1990s, the Iraqi Government embarked upon a large-scale water diversion scheme designed to drain the southern marshes. The project was driven by the prevailing belief at the time that the Mesopotamian Marshes were a source of diseases such as malaria and an obstacle to human development in the area.

Originally the Mesopotamian Marshes were home to 250,000 Marsh Arabs. By draining the marshes, the Iraqi Government displaced the Marsh Arabs, who were regarded as opponents to Iraq's former regime. Today only 40,000 indigenous people still live in the region, adding a human dimension to the environmental disaster. The draining of the Mesopotamian Marshes also destroyed a unique freshwater ecosystem that once formed a habitat for wildlife and migratory birds, and supported coastal fisheries along the Persian Gulf coast. Today most of the territory has become barren land and salt crusts. In 2002, the marshes had shrunk to 14% of their original size. Only 35% of the Haweizeh Marshes remained, while the Central and Hammar Marshes had been almost completely drained. After the fall of Saddam Hussein's regime, locals began to destroy dikes. This was followed by joint restoration efforts by the Iraqi Government, UN agencies and other donors. Record precipitation in Turkey also contributed to the success of the initiative. By 2006, more than half of the original marshland area was flooded again. Today the damming of the Karkheh River in Iran is seen as a critical challenge, as the river directly feeds into the marshes. The construction of a levy along the Iran-Iraq border poses an additional threat to the area as it runs through the Haweizeh Marshes and disrupts natural flow in the ecosystem. Despite all the negative developments over recent decades, experts are hopeful and claim that the marshes have shown astonishing resilience to past drought *(Ibid, Chapter* 3: *115–117).*

5.4.3 Orontes River Basin

All three riparian countries use the water resources in the Orontes Basin for agricultural, domestic and, to a lesser extent, industrial purposes. However, Syria and Turkey have dominated water resource use in the basin with various development plans to increase irrigated surface area. In 2009, FAO estimated total irrigated area in the basin at 300,000–350,000 ha, of which 58% lies in Syria, 36% in Turkey and 6% in Lebanon. The annual water withdrawal for agriculture in the whole basin is estimated at about 2,800 MCM. The basin's sustainability is threatened by heavy exploitation of water resources and economic expansion, particularly in Syria and Turkey.

Development & use: Lebanon
At present, the use of the Orontes in Lebanon is limited to small-scale farming, fish farms and tourism. Total water use is estimated at 21 MCM/yr, of which around 23% is used for domestic purposes, and the rest for irrigation. Official figures estimate irrigated areas in the Lebanese part of the basin at 1,703 ha. Most of this land is irrigated by wells. It is likely, however, that these figures only refer to the perennial northern section of the Orontes River downstream of the Ain Zarqa Spring, which has also been the focus of Lebanese-Syrian cooperation. FAO estimates of irrigated area in the Lebanese part of the Orontes Basin are much higher (18,000–21,000 ha), possibly because they refer to the entire topographic catchment, including the agricultural areas around Labweh, Al Ain, Ras Baalbek and El Qaa.

The Lebanese Ministry of Energy and Water has plans to increase the exploitation of water resources in the basin. One of the projects under consideration is the Assi scheme, planned following consultations with the Syrian Government and aimed at developing water use for irrigation, domestic use and power generation in the regions of Baalbek and Hermel. The project is divided into two phases: the first phase includes a diversion dam with a storage capacity of 27 MCM near the Ain Zarqa Spring, three pumping stations and a network for the irrigation of around 3,000 ha. A second phase aims to construct a 37 MCM capacity dam upstream of the Hermel Bridge, with several pumping stations and a network for the irrigation of 3,800 ha, as well as a hydroelectric power plant providing approximately 50 MW of electricity per day. Altogether, the proposed irrigation schemes comprise a new irrigated area of 6,800 ha in the Hermel and Al Qaa area of the basin.

Progress Made on the Assi Project in Lebanon
The Assi Project was officially launched in 2004, with a Chinese contractor starting construction with a local partner in 2005. Phase 1 of the project was already well underway when Israel bombed the construction site during the 2006 Lebanon War. As the Lebanese Higher Relief Council was slow to provide compensation for losses suffered, the contractor demanded a renegotiation of the contract before resuming work. This has resulted in a dispute within the Ministry of Energy and Water about whether to cancel the contract and issue a new invitation to tender or to meet the current contractor's demands. The Lebanese Council of Ministers formed a special committee in 2011 to resolve this issue.

Development and use: Syria
Since the early 1950s, Syria has intensively developed water resources in the Orontes Basin. In terms of water use, the Orontes River constitutes the second most important river in Syria after the Euphrates, providing 20% of the country's total estimated water use volume.

According to official data, total annual water use in the Orontes Basin has increased from around 2000 MCM in 1992 and temporarily exceeded 3000 MCM in 2004–2005. Average annual use for the period from 1992 to 2009 was around 2,582 MCM. Agriculture is the largest water user, consuming about 1,977 MCM annually (77% of total water use), followed by domestic water use at 9% and industry at 8%.

Both groundwater and surface water are heavily exploited in the Orontes Basin in Syria, and average annual groundwater use for irrigation (1111 MCM or 56%) exceeded surface water use (886 MCM or 44%) during the period between 1992 and 2009.

In order to increase irrigation capacity, Syria has over the years built more than 40 dams in the basin. The total reservoir capacity of all dams in the basin reached about 950 MCM in 2006. A number of these dams, such as the Rastan, Qattineh, Zeita and Mhardeh Dams, have a large reservoir capacity. The Zeita Dam near the Lebanese-Syrian border is partly supplied with water diverted from the main stream of the Orontes in Lebanon through the left-bank Zeita Canal. Both this canal and the rightbank Jawsiyeh Canal are also used for direct irrigation of downstream Syrian lands. The two canals are located between the Hermel and Al Omeiry monitoring stations. Diversions through these canals may partly explain the decrease in long-term average annual discharge (approx. 200 MCM/yr) between upstream Hermel and downstream Al Omeiry.

Two main agricultural areas in Syria are supplied with water from the Orontes: the region between Homs and Hama, and the Ghab, a large, formerly swampy valley. The latter was systematically drained from 1950 onward to reclaim land for irrigated agriculture. The Ghab project included the expansion and deepening of the Orontes riverbed, and the construction of dams for flow regulation and irrigation water. An area of about 70,000 ha is irrigated as part of the project, which consumes around 330 MCM/yr of reservoir water and another 150 MCM/yr of groundwater. The region between Homs and Hama is partly supplied from Lake Qattineh via the Homs-Hama canal, which provides water to an area of about 23,000 ha. However, as the reservoir does not meet demand, it is supplemented by groundwater wells, which irrigate another 20,000 ha in this part of the basin.

The total irrigated area in the Orontes Basin in Syria has increased from approximately 200,000 ha in 1992 and temporarily exceeded 250,000 ha in 2004–2008. In the first half of the data period, irrigation with groundwater clearly dominated, but irrigation with surface water has gained momentum since 2004, possibly due to the construction of dams and other irrigation infrastructure or because of stricter regulation of groundwater abstractions. On average, an area of about 97,000 ha (43%) is irrigated by surface water, and 130,000 ha (57%) by groundwater.

Municipal and industrial use of the river is low due to water quality issues caused by untreated effluents into the Orontes River. These sectors are mainly supplied by groundwater, which is overexploited following the intensive drilling of wells. Average total annual groundwater use in the

Orontes Basin can be estimated at 1,466 MCM and surface water use at 1,115 MCM. The intensification of water use in the Orontes Basin in Syria has raised the question of long-term sustainability. For example, the average annual discharge of more than 20 springs in the Ghab Valley dropped from approximately 18 m3/s between 1965 and 1971 to 4.2 m3/s in 1995–1996. Water tables in some parts of the western Orontes Basin have dropped as much as 57 m in 10 years.

Development & use: Turkey

The most important dams in the Turkish part of the Orontes Basin are the Yarseli and Tahtakopru Dams, which are both located on tributaries of the Orontes. The

Tahtakopru Dam was built in 1975 on the Karasu River and has a maximum capacity of 200 MCM, with a reservoir area of 24.3 km2.

In recent years, a dozen new water resource development projects have been planned and implemented in the Turkish part of the Orontes Basin. These projects are designed to regulate the flow of the river and its tributaries for irrigation and flood protection purposes. They also aim to provide water for domestic use and for the generation of electricity. Once completed, the projects will irrigate an area of almost 100,000 ha, produce 180 GWh/yr of electricity and provide 37 MCM/yr of potable water.

In 2004, Turkey proposed the construction of a joint dam on the Orontes River in Syria to generate power and provide irrigation water to both countries. Five years later, in December 2009, Turkey and Syria signed a memorandum of understanding regarding construction of the Friendship Dam on the Orontes River. The two countries agreed to split the costs of the dam, which will benefit both riparians by protecting land and settlements from floods and droughts. It will also irrigate 13,334 ha of farmland and generate almost 16 GWh/yr of electricity (according to other data, the purpose of this dam would be to provide water to irrigate 20,000 hectares in Turkey and 10,000 hectares in Syria, to produce hydropower for Turkish and Syrian needs and to improve flood control). Although the details of the dam will be ironed out in the feasibility study, its height may reach 15 m and its storage capacity about 110 MCM. Of that total, 40 MCM will be used to prevent flooding and the rest for energy production and irrigation. The construction of the Orontes River Friendship Dam started in February 2011. It is unclear if construction is ongoing in view of the unrest in Syria which began in March 2011.

Lake of Antioch or Lake Amik

Before it was drained, the Lake of Antioch or Lake Amik was a large freshwater lake within the Orontes Basin in Hatay Province. Draining and land reclamation around the lake began in the 1940s, specifically for cotton production and to eradicate malaria. In the second half of the 1960s, DSI in Turkey initiated a major drainage project, channeling the lake's tributaries, the Karasu and the Afrin, as well as other rivers, directly to the Orontes River. By the 1970s Lake Amik had completely disappeared and its bed was being used as farmland in what is now known as the Amik Plain. Today, Hatay Airport is located on land that once lay at the bottom of the lake *(Ibid, Chapter 7: 115–117).*

The above summary shows that in the 20th century, Turkey was able to store 90–100 BCM of water in reservoirs built in the Euphrates and Tigris basins, Syria has developed a capacity of 12 BCM, and Iraq has a storage capacity of 100 BCM. The Euphrates gives life to three countries and the Tigris to only two (or in the 21st century Syria may add to them). As for the Orontes River, it is more important for Syria. The total irrigated area in the Orontes Basin in Syria is 200,000–250,000 ha, which means that the Orontes River flows through more irrigated areas in Syria than the Euphrates. The Orontes River was meant to be a river of peace between Turkey and Syria, but it failed for non-water reasons.

Turkey has a favourable climate compared with its co-riparians who have large arid areas. Before Turkey and Syria developed an interest in the Euphrates, Iraq was the main user of river water. It was the first riparian to develop engineering projects along the river. Iraq has a long history of water use in the Tigris Basin and was also the first riparian to develop irrigation projects, and construct dams, barrages and cross regulators on the river and its tributaries. Iraq has the second largest agricultural potential in North Africa and the Middle East, after Sudan. In Iraq, 80% of water is used for agriculture. Unlike Turkey and Syria, in Iraq the Euphrates and Tigris are connected by a (Tharthar) canal before forming the Shatt al-Arab River.

Downstream concerns stem from the capacity of Turkey's five Euphrates dams to impound nearly three years' worth of annual average water supply. If in the 20th century Syria, which heavily depends on the Euphrates, didn't pay attention to Tigris, in the 21st century Syria also wants to use the waters of Tigris. The scale of Syrian irrigation projects is twice as low as Turkey's planned irrigated lands of GAP in the Euphrates Basin. According to the Turkish side, Syria loses 50% of its irrigation canal water due to the hot climate *(Şen 1993: 462)*. In the 20th century Syria was more vulnerable to Turkish water projects, as Iraq was able to partially compensate for the reduction in the flow of the Euphrates through the waters of the Tigris (in Iraq, Tigris is more water-rich than Euphrates). In addition, Turkey didn't use much the waters of the Tigris. However, Iraq, a downstream riparian, received less water and water of lower quality from its upper-stream riparians. The beginning of implementation of water projects on Tigris in Turkey will become even more dangerous for Iraq in 21th century as it made more difficult for Iraq to compensate for the lack of Euphrates water with Tigris waters.

Major water projects on the Euphrates and Tigris rivers have a negative impact on the Shatt al-Arab river, reduce its flow as a result the salt water of the Persian Gulf pushes back the freshwater of the river. In Iraq, water was also used to suppress "internal enemy"—Marsh Arabs (in the 6th chapter we will see that Turkey also started to use water against its Kurds). Turkey's water projects in the Euphrates-Tigris basin also have a negative impact on Iran, creating conflict situations (details in Chapter 6).

5.5 Peace Water Pipeline

In 1986 Turkish Prime Minister Turgut Ozal had proposed a "Peace Pipeline" Project for the Middle East water problems. The project has drawn considerable attention and caused both negative and positive reactions. Political feasibility and financing of the project had been argued more than its technical feasibility. Preliminary studies on the project were initiated in 1986. The ultimate aim of the project was much beyond of the supplying some water to the countries. The project proposal mainly aimed to create a process of confidence building and a cooperation environment on water that will help to contribute to the stability and security of the region. The concept of transfering water from Turkey to the Middle East, to promote regional peace and economic development in the Middle East has been a constant in Turkish foreign policy since the late T. Ozal in 1986 proposed an extensive 'Peace Water Pipeline'. This was a $ 21 billion project to bring vast quantities of water from the Seyhan and Ceyhan Rivers via two pipelines to supply the major cities in Syria, Jordan, and the Arab Gulf states. The pipelines could convey 10 MCM of water every day, which was estimated as sufficient to meet the needs of 15 million persons.

The original project would divert the water from Seyhan and Ceyhan Rivers, both national rivers of Turkey, to the Arab Countries in the Middle East. Daily water transfer capacity of the project was 6 MCM that is only a part of mean total daily flows of the rivers after Turkey's use. The water would deliver through the peace pipeline is not intended to replace, but rather supplement current water supplies in the countries served. The Project has an estimated cost of US $ 20 billion. It foresees the use of local materials and labor in each country on the route of the water transfer line.

The Project consists of two pipelines.

- The first one called the Western Line has a length of 2,650 km and a daily water capacity of 3.5 MCM (40 m^3/s) or 1,277 BCM/year. The western line will start in Turkey, traverse the Nur mountains through a tunnel, continue to Syria (Aleppo, Hama, Homs and Damascus) and Jordan (Amman) and reach Saudi Arabia (Tabuk, Medina, Yanbu, Jeddah and Mecca). According to preliminary studies made about 30 years ago the cost of 1 cubic meter of water is US $ 0.84. Syria will be provided with 1.1 million m3 of water a day, and Jordan will be provided with 600,000 m3 a day (a shorter pipeline from the Seyhan or Ceyhan rivers to Syria and Jordan has been estimated to cost $ 5 billion in 1986).

- The Eastern or Gulf Line extends, after Syria and Jordan to Kuwait, Saudi Arabia (Jubail, Damman, Hofuf), Bahrain, Qatar, United Arab Emirates and Oman. The second branch, the eastern pipeline (or Gulf line) will pump water up to 900 m to cross the high Jordan plateau parallel to the Iraq-Jordan border. The route will then follow the trans-Arabian Pipeline (Tapline) to the Gulf. It is longer than the first one with a total length of 3,900 km. In the preliminary study, the daily capacity and the unit cost of water was determined as 2,5 MCM (29 m^3/s or 0.912 BCM/year) and US $ 1,07 respectively. The total investment cost of the Eastern Line is US$ 12 Billion. In sum, technical and economic feasibility of the Project was accepted by many experts 32 years ago. In regard to political feasibility, it had been generally argued that realization of this project would be difficult due to lack of confidence and trust among the countries over the pipeline route *(Yildiz 2018)*.

The Seyhan and Ceyhan have a total discharge of 39.1 MCM/day of which Turkey plans to utilize approximately 23.0 MCM/day for irrigation or hydroelectric power generation. A further 16.1 MCM/day which flows into the Mediterranean could be used in the Peace Pipe. Eleven pumping stations using a total of 900 MW will be needed on the western line and five pumping stations using 600 MW on the Gulf line. The scheme should take eight to ten years to complete and have an economic life of fifty years. The cost for the western pipeline is estimated at $8.5 billion and it is expected to provide 8 to 9 million people with up to 400 litres of water per person per day. An additional estimated 6 to 7 million people could be served with 400 litres per day by the eastern or Gulf pipelines which will cost $12.5 billion. Turkey will obtain $2 billion annual revenue from these pipelines. The average cost of water delivered has been calculated at $0.84 per cubic meter for the western pipeline and $1.07 per cubic meter in the Gulf pipeline, compared with $5 per cubic meter for desalinated water. Finance for the project will come from the International Bank for Reconstruction and Development (IBRD) and the Islamic Development Bank. Technically, financially and ecologically the project is feasible and the only obstacle is political. The rivalry and conflicts that exist among the prospective clients play an important role in the possibility for implementation. It is not clear how many of the states which are to benefit from the pipeline will be completely ready to rely on Turkish water provision *(Kliot 1994: 109–110)*.

The original Turkish proposal also envisioned making some of this water available to Israel. However, when some Arab states objected, Ankara modified its proposal, saying that Israeli participation would have to be deferred until after the conclusion of peace treaties between Israel and its Arab neighbors. It should be noted that unlike the Tigris and Euphrates, the Ceyhan and Seyhan rivers originate and flow entirely within the sovereign territory of Turkey before emptying into the Mediterranean Sea. The pipeline idea was rejected by the oil-rich Gulf states, which Turkey hoped would finance the giant project. Since Peace Water Project's initial presentation to public opinion and the parties concerned, it had received several political responses. While Jordan displayed, in general, a receptive attitude, Syria and Saudi Arabia adopted a negative one. The Saudis contended that desalination was a cheaper solution, since they could fuel flash distillation desalination plants with surplus gas produced *(Yildiz 2018)*.

The "Peace Pipeline" Project wasn't implemented due to its high cost (66% of the GAP project). The Arab countries considered it expedient to desalinate salt water of sea. The "Peace Pipeline" Project wasn't also implemented due to political differences between regional countries. Moreover these disagreements referred to Turkey-Arab countries, Israel-Arab countries, as well as the relations between the Arab countries. With the implementation of this project, Turkey would become a hydro-donor and gain serious water leverage towards the Arab countries. With the implementation of this project, Syria may well have a role to play in the regional water-sharing schemes. Any pipeline carrying water from the upper reaches of the Euphrates and the Ceyhan and Seyhan rivers are located in south-central Turkey would have to traverse Syrian territory.

The countries of the Arabian Peninsula didn't want to become dependent on Turkey for water, to strengthen Turkey, to give it the right to vote on issues related to the Arab world. Pipelines that will pass through 8 states and 23 regions are vulnerable to attacks during wars or terrorist attacks. The countries of the Arabian Peninsula didn't have any guarantee that Turkey wouldn't use the waters of Ceyhan and Seyhan in the future, thus reducing the volume of water intended for them. Maybe Arab countries also wondered why Turkey doesn't want to connect the Seyhan and Ceyhan rivers to the Euphrates via a canal or pipeline, thus increasing the flow of the river into Syria. In addition, the Arab countries maybe didn't fully understand why Turkey didn't connect the excess water of the Seyhan and Ceyhan rivers to the Orontes River. It is known that Turkey always accuses Syria of dehydrating Orontes.

5.6 Concluding Summary of the Third chapter

The third chapter presents the Southeastern-Anatolia project—GAP, Turkey's motives on it, the project's importance for Turkey, and the concerns of Turkey's neighbors from the GAP. The major water projects implemented by Turkey within the framework of the GAP in both the Euphrates and Tigris basins are presented separately. It is emphasized that Turkey first of all focused on the Euphrates, the reasons for that move are presented, and also why the Tigris basin remained in the background? In addition, this chapter covers the topic of the Peace Pipelines put forward by Turkey, which was quite an interesting project although it remained on paper.

The third chapter is the most crucial part in terms of water projects, as it includes the implementation of major water projects not only in Turkey, but also in Syria and Iraq. These projects are presented in detail, their impact on the rivers flow to neighboring countries. In addition, the reasons for Turkey's temporary choice for the implementation of these projects are described.

Of particular importance in Turkey is the construction of the Ataturk Reservoir on the Euphrates, both in terms of hydropower, irrigation and control of the Euphrates. It is still considered the largest reservoir in Europe, a masterpiece of Turkish engineering. The third chapter shows that to some extent, Turkey is lucky that the lands suitable for irrigation are located in the Lower Euphrates basin, in the areas bordering Syria. As a result, Turkey is only able to use the Keban and Karakaya reservoirs above the Ataturk Reservoir for energy purposes, as otherwise (for irrigation use) it (water shortage) will negatively affect the Ataturk HEPP. In any case, in the next, fourth chapter, we will see that the irrigation systems starting from the Ataturk Reservoir will have a negative impact on the capacity and productivity of the Ataturk HEPP.

According to Nurit Kilot, the implementation of the various projects of GAP is facing three major barriers. First, some of the projects on the Tigris are still in the planning stage and all the GAP projects are behind schedule; thus, the whole scheme looks certain to be seriously delayed. Keban was completed four years late, Karakaya three years behind schedule, and the same is true for the Ataturk, most of the delays being caused by financing problems (in our opinion, one of the three obstacles was the technical complexity of building of dams and HEPPs).

Second, the financial difficulties are enormous. The Keban Dam's cost was $85 million at 1970 prices, the Karakaya's total cost is estimated at $500 million (1981 prices) and the Ataturk Dam's cost is estimated at $3.0 billion (MEED 17 July 1981). The World Bank and, following their lead, most international funding agencies are not prepared to lend money for water projects involving possible infringements of international riparian rights unless the interested nations have come to an agreement. Thus, no funds are likely to be made available until Turkey can agree on the question of sharing the waters with its neighbours.

Third, downstream neighbours are reluctant to let Turkey take a sizable proportion of the Euphrates annual flow for irrigation purposes (MEED 17 July 1981). According to various estimates the GAP will reduce the Euphrates flow by approximately 30–50% (30–40% will be consumed by irrigation and 10% will be lost due to evaporation). By the year 2000 only 20% of the Euphrates flow will disappear but this could be very harmful to both Syria and Iraq (US Army Corps of Engineers 1991).

Eventually, they may consider legal or other international measures in order to convince Turkey to allocate more water to them. Turkey, on the other hand, claims that the experience with the Keban Dam shows that high volume water releases from the Ataturk Dam will be possible. Thus, according to this argument, the storage capacities it develops will benefit Turkey's co-riparians by alleviating flooding damages and by releasing water from the storages in years of drought (Tekeli 1990:15). Turkey has also suggested an increase in water supply for her neighbours via water pipes *(Kilot 1994: 108).*

There is also a general description of the water projects implemented by the riparian countries in the Orontes River Basin, which is also quite important from the point of view of understanding the Turkish-Syrian relations. This river creates assymetrical interdependence between Turkey and Syria, is also a bone of contention between Syria and Turkey like the Euphrates. In the 21st century it was called to become a symbol of Turkish-Syrian friendship, but that didn't happen until today. We will discuss all of this in more detail in Chapters 4 and 6. The presentation of the Orontes River water projects can also be used to understand Turkey's behavior as a downstream country.

In this chapter we emphasize that in the 20th century, the GAP further deepened Turkey's disagreements with Syria, contributing to Syria's support for the Kurdish armed struggle. We have also explained why the implementation of GAP in the 20th century didn't have a very negative impact on Iraq, unlike Syria. Due to the GAP, Turkey was able to control the Euphrates River 100%, gain an influential water lever towards Syria, which in turn began to support the PKK. In fact, the implementation of the GAP project in Turkey and the Euphrates Valley project in Syria significantly aggravated the Turkish-Syrian relations, which we are going to address in the next chapter, the fourth chapter.

In Chapter 3, we also note that in the 20th century, Turkey basically didn't turn its attention to the Tigris, which allowed Iraq to respond relatively calmly to Turkey's water projects on the Euphrates, as the Tigris is a much more important river for Iraq and Iraq was able to compensate for the lack of water in the Euphrates with the waters of the Tigris. On the other hand, it was obvious that after implementing the important water projects in the Euphrates basin, Turkey would also focus on the Tigris allow for 6 of the 13 major projects proposed under the GAP referred to the Tigris Basin. We will discuss all this in more detail in our next chapter, which is about the Turkey-Syria-Iraq triangular water conflicts. And GAP would be at the core of the water component of those conflicts, which is why a comprehensive presentation of the motivations and process for the implementation of this project is crucial to understanding the nature of the water conflicts and the positions of the riparian countries.

6 Water Conflicts Between Turkey, Syria and Iraq in 1980–2000

6.1 Water Quantity and Quality

Large volumes of water flowing in rivers are not easy to calculate and compare. To facilitate this, water quantity in this section will be given in billion cubic meters and flow rates in cubic meters per second (CMS). Water quality is a factor that is often overlooked in water basin research, but the impact of declining quality in the Euphrates-Tigris basin will be greater, and more immediate, than declining water quantity. Rivers will not literally "dry up," but water quality will reach a point where agriculture becomes impossible and human health is seriously affected. Statistics for water quality are even more difficult to research than for water quantity. For large agricultural projects such as the GAP in Turkey, irrigation water will inevitably return as groundwater or to the river itself as return flow. The water quality prognosis for the Euphrates-Tigris basin is precarious.

Groundwater is generally overlooked in the analysis of river basins, not merely because it is less evident, but because the data on it is less available. The measurement and monitoring of groundwater use is particularly difficult in the Euphrates-Tigris basin. In agriculture, water is a low-cost resource, and most regional farmers are using primitive methods of extracting groundwater. In Turkey, more progress has been made in measuring groundwater, but that has largely been focused on measuring the declining water tables and not on measuring each farmer's extraction. Turkey claims to have exploitable groundwater resources of 14 BCM per year, of which 90 percent is used and allocated. Turkey also claims that "there is no contamination in private areas and no over pumping," but this is contradicted by a number of global reports and one of the coauthors' travels through the GAP region *(Lorenz and Erickson 2013: 89–90).*

H. Gabrielyan, *Turkey's Water Policy as Part of the Political Strategy*, Politik, Wirtschaft und Gesellschaft im Spannungsverhältnis der Regionen Südosteuropa und Mittlerer Osten, https://doi.org/10.1007/978-3-658-44070-1_6

In a 2005 technical report for the Centre for Environmental Studies and Resource Management in Norway (CESAR), independent water quantity and quality data for the Euphrates River was publicly released for the first time. The dynamic model in this report used input data obtained in part from publicly available data and in part from "grab samples" taken from the river by those preparing the study. The study also included an analysis of power production in the GAP region and how it would be affected by changing water flow levels. The study concluded that maintaining a minimum flow level of 500 CMS at the Turkey-Syria border would only slightly reduce energy generation within Turkey. A reduction in irrigation volume from 10 BCM/year (the target volume) to 5.5 BCM/year would actually increase energy generation by about 9 percent, however. The report indicates the dynamic relationship between power generation and water flow, a subject that must be carefully calculated by Turkey but is still closely held as a national security matter. The CESAR report also reveals that agricultural return flow and high salt levels will be the most dangerous consequence of GAP development.

Approximately 25 percent of Iraq's population depends on irrigated agriculture for their livelihood and subsistence. Agriculture uses about 90 percent of Iraq's average annual water supply and is therefore critical to water development and management. Iraq can become the contemporary "California of the Middle East." Salination of a large part of the irrigated land results in reduced crop yields and high salinity of the rivers, creating problems in the municipal water supply as well as ecological problems that threaten the restoration potential of marshlands in the south. Increased salinization of the Tigris in southern Iraq has already been attributed to reduced flow due to upstream and northern tributary use.

Salinity has long been a significant but rarely measured threat in the basin. High salt levels pollute drinking water and can make agriculture impossible. Salt levels are related to water quantity; during low water levels, salt levels tend to increase, aggravating the situation. Freshwater is generally considered to have less than 1,500 milligrams per liter (mg/L) of TDS; brackish water 1,500 to 5,000 mg/L; and saline water more than 5,000 mg/L (the United States established a secondary water quality standard of 500 mg/L to provide for the potability of drinking water). Salination of much of the irrigated land results in reduced crop yields and high salinity in the rivers, which creates problems for the municipal water supply as well as ecological issues that threaten the restoration potential of the marshlands drained by Saddam Hussein. For example, although Saudi Arabia has only 95 CM per capita, it is able to maintain a high standard of living by the importation of "virtual water" and using desalination to create "new" water.

Although surface water is the main source of water supply in Iraq, groundwater is an essential source of supply in the desert areas (which cover about 58 percent of the country) and in some parts of the south. Today, Iraq is estimated to have approximately 200 BCM of groundwater, but the exploitable amount is estimated to be only about 1.2 BCM, based upon 2009 figures. Groundwater quality in the north and the east has been adequate for use as potable and irrigation water. In contrast, water quality is less than favorable in the south and west, and in many places groundwater development is already impossible. Even in areas where groundwater quality is acceptable, excessive pumping is likely to cause intrusion from saline sources nearby. Moreover, water quality can vary tremendously within the subsurface region, with higher salinity levels the deeper one goes. As of 1950, only a modest number of wells had been drilled in the northern, western, and central parts of Iraq. Between 1960 and 1980, more than 2,500 wells were drilled by different government organizations and foreign firms. The number of hand-dug wells may be several times greater than that of drilled wells, but reliable statistics are not available *(Ibid: 102–103, 113, 119–120).*

For Turkey, a number of UN reports predict major climate change–related impacts, with temperatures expected to rise by 2–3 degrees Celsius by the end of the century. Temperatures in the eastern regions of Turkey, which contain the headwaters of the Euphrates and Tigris, are expected to in- crease during summer seasons by 4 degrees Celsius by 2061. As a result, the amount of water in the Euphrates could eventually decline by 30 percent by the end of the century. In a more pessimistic report on annual precipitation and annual runoff in the Euphrates watershed, comparing the year 2000 with the year 2050, a 60 percent decline was predicted (see figure 3.3). 74 In an even worse scenario, the decline in the Tigris watershed is predicted to be more than 60 percent. If these figures are accurate, the amount of water reaching Syria and Iraq will show massive declines even without the impact of increasing population and the development of the GAP *(Ibid: 131).*

One of the major factors in computing water demand is population, and the future populations of the three countries dependent on the Euphrates-Tigris are comparatively easy to predict. The total population of these countries was less than 30 million in 1950 but had climbed to 106 million by 2000. This number was approximately 134 million in 2011 79 and is likely to be 150 million in 2020. These potential changes will pose problems for food security, especially for a basin that has no significant water-sharing agreements *(Ibid: 133).*

Water is essential to human life and the health of the environment. Water has two dimensions that are closely linked: quantity and quality. Water is never pure and is affected by community uses such as agriculture, urban and industrial, and recreation. Generally, the water quality of rivers is best in the headwaters, where rainfall is often abundant. Water quality frequently declines as rivers flow through regions where land and water use are intense and pollution from intensive agriculture, large towns, industry, and recreation areas increases. Water levels in Iraq's rivers have rapidly decreased to less than a third of their normal capacity. Water levels may fall further in the coming years due to declining precipitation. Therefore, in Iraq, the quality of water used for drinking and agriculture is poor. Point sources or dispersed sources such as urban, agricultural, commercial, and industrial wastes are main organic or inorganic water pollutants. It was estimated that this river transports about 48 tons of oil residues to the Arabian Gulf annually. The Arabian Gulf is also an extremely busy shipping line or oil transports, with accidental spilling being almost unavoidable.

Tigris–Euphrates rivers embodies over 95% of the total Iraq nation water demand presented in the form of the domestic, agriculture, industrial, and several others.

In 1977, the utilization of the Tigris–Euphrates rivers by the Turkish Government through the South-eastern Anatolia Project (GAP) (Unver 1997), has influenced these rivers' flow noticeably. The project constructed 19 hydraulic power plants and 22 multipurpose dams for land irrigation covers approximately 17,100 km 2. The storage capacity of this project was about 100 km 3, which is more than thrice the capacity of all the reservoirs in both Iraq and Syria *(Jawad 2021: 230, 286–288).*

As mentioned earlier, Kibaroglu Aysegul and Scheumann Waltina analyzed the evolution of transboundary water relations and divided them over four consecutive periods. The third, which they called "Rivers of Discord", was the most complex, given the link between transboundary water issues and nonriparian security issues. In the third period, from the 1980s until the late 1990s, political tensions among the parties insinuated themselves into every corner of the relationships and, thus, inevitably water issues moved into the realm of high politics *(Kibaroglu 2013).*

But before describing these issues, we want to show riparian contributions to the Euphrates-Tigris Rivers Basin (Table 6.1), as well as compare water potential of the Euphrates/Tigris basin and consumption targets of riparian states. The demand for water in the *Euphrates* and *Tigris watershed* can be thought of in two principal ways: first, a demand which can be satisfied because water is available, and second a demand which cannot be met owing to water scarcity. Until the 1960s the water demands of all three countries in this watershed could be satisfied with water to spare. Since then, as water demands in the upper part of the watershed have increased, the situation has changed and will continue to do so for the next two decades until all the planned irrigation projects are fully commissioned.

Several scholars have addressed the problem of demand for water over the years and all have reached the same conclusion, namely, that there is not sufficient water in the Euphrates River to meet the needs of the three countries with interests in the watershed. On the Tigris, the situation is less serious, but even here the most optimistic scenarios only register a flow into the Shatt Al-Arab of about 9.5 to 10.5 BCM when all the irrigation schemes are in operation. On the Euphrates, a maximum water demand in Turkey of around 21.5 BCM each year when all the irrigation projects are commissioned *(Kangarani 2005: 45).*

Table 6.1 Riparian Contributions to the Euphrates-Tigris Rivers Basin

Euphrates & Tigris Rivers	Turkey	Iraq	Syria	Iran	Total
Discharge (BCM/year) (%)	78.1 65.7	8.1 6.8	0.5 0.5	13.3 11.2	84.2 100
Drainage Area (%) (Km2)	20.5 170,000	46.0 469,000	9.0 77,000	19.0 37,000	100 819,000
River Length (%) (Km)	33.5 1630	51.0 2478	15.5 754	---- ----	100 4862

SOURCE: Macquarie 2004

- Turkey is the source area of the Tigris-Euphrates waters, contributing more than 70% of the united Tigris-Euphrates flow. Syria's contribution was estimated at 2%, Iraq's contribution at 3–8%, and Iran's contribution—at 13–16%. The Tigris-Euphrates discharge comprises 40% of the total water supply of Turkey as compared with 80–85% in Syria and 98% in Iraq. Syria contributes very little to the actual discharge of the Euphrates itself. Iraq has control over some 40% of the Euphrates basin but contributes nothing to its water budget. The Euphrates is not replenished with water of tributaries in Iraq, and Tigris—in Syria. The annual flow of the Orontes River in Syria is 1.2 BCM, of which 90% is used by Syria and the remaining 10% (120 MCM) by Turkey. In the case of Euphrates-Tigris and Orontes rivers, Turkey and Syria are in asymmetric (hydropolitical) interdependence, as Syria has more water dependence on Turkey than vice versa (the Euphrates is a much more water-rich and important river than the Orontes, the Euphrates and Orontes basins account for about 50% and 20% of the water use respectively in Syria). Contribution of the riparian countries in these rivers' flow is important, but not decisive.

6.1.1 Euphrates and Tigris

The water demand of riparian countries in the Euphrates basin is 1.5 times (about 17 BCM) higher than the water potential of the Euphrates (Table 6.2). So, it is impossible to meet this demand as far as the river's potential is concerned *(Kodaman 2007: 33).*

Table 6.2 Water demand of riparian countries in the Euphrates Basin

Country	Water potential (BCM)		Consumption targets (BCM)	
Turkey	31,58	88,7 %	18,42	34,94 %
Syria	4	11,3 %	11,30	21,43 %
Iraq	0	0 %	23,00	43,63 %
Total	**35,58**	**100 %**	**52,72**	**100 %**

A number of Turkish experts suggest that "Turkey's water demand is fair meanwhile Syria's and Iraq's are not". They emphasized, that 88.7% of the total water potential of the Euphrates basin originates in Turkey and the remainder, only 11.3% originates in Syria. Iraq's contribution to the runoff is nil. Though contribution of these two downstream countries to the water potential of the Euphrates is such a modest percentage, Syria demanded 22% of the water and Iraq 43%. Turkey envisaged utilising only 35% of the total flow, compared to its contribution of 88.7% (*SAM 1996*).

We can partly agree with them, because if we follow this logic, Iraq should not have the right to use Euphrates water at all (Table 6.2). In addition, this logic puts in the foreground the extent to which a country how much contributes to the waters of the Euphrates. However, the data on the territory and population of riparian countries, their climatic zones, the demand for water in these countries, and the degree of dependence of those countries on a particular Euphrates are much more important factors. That's why we don't say that the waters of the Euphrates should be divided into three equal parts (33.3%).

Table 6.3 Water demand of riparian countries in the Tigris Basin

Country	Water potential (BCM)		Consumption targets (BCM)	
Turkey	25,24	51,9 %	6,87	13 %
Syria	0	0 %	2,60	4 %
Iraq	23,48	48,1 %	45,00	83 %
Total	**48,72**	**100 %**	**54,47**	**100 %**

Table 6.3 shows that the current demand outstrips the existing water supply by about 6 BCM a year in the Tigris River. In almost all international river disputes, competing uses of the riparian states come into conflict "where the quantity and quality of the water is such that all the reasonable and beneficial uses can't be realized to their full extent" *(Erdem 2003)*.

We argue that that these data of Erdem regarding Tigris refer to the beginning of the 21st century, when the Ilisu Reservoir has not been built yet, as well as the Silvan and Cizre Reservoirs. This means that Turkey's demand for Tigris waters will increase sharply in the near future, which will further complicate the situation. This is the case with the Tigris and Euphrates rivers. The main the objections of the lower riparian states, Iraq and Syria, against GAP and Turkey's counterclaims are water quality and water quantity. Table 6.4 shows riparian contribution, length and drainage area of Euphrates River.

Table 6.4 Riparian Contribution to the Euphrates River Basin

Euphrates River	Turkey	Iraq	Syria	Iran	Total
Discharge (%) **(BCM/year)**	98.6 32.2	0.0 0.0	1.4 0.5	---- ----	100.0 32.7
Drainage Area (%) **(Km2)**	28.0 125,000	40.0 177,000	17.0 76,000	---- ----	85 444,000
River Length (%) **(Km)**	41.0 1230	35 1060	24.0 710	---- ----	100.0 3000

SOURCE: Macquarie 2004

Table 6.5 shows riparian contribution, length and drainage area of Tigris River.

Table 6.5 Riparian Contribution to the Tigris River Basin

Tigris River	Turkey	Iraq	Syria	Iran	Total
Discharge (%) (BCM /year)	65.0 33.5	13.2 6.8	0.0 0.0	21.7 11.2	99.9 51.5
Drainage Area (%) (Km2)	12.0 45,000	53.8 292,000	0.2 1,000	34.0 37,000	100.0 375,000
River Length (%) (Km)	21.0 400	77.0 1418	2.0 44	---- ----	98.2 1862

SOURCE: Macquarie 2004

On the Euphrates, a maximum water demand in Turkey of around 21,500 MCM each year when all the irrigation projects are commissioned. This seems a very high figure when it is remembered that the planned irrigation area on the Euphrates only amounts to 1,083,000 ha. With the water volume quoted this would seem to imply a water usage rate of 19,853 m3 per hectare or a much larger area under irrigation. A more realistic calculation would seem to be a figure of about 10,000 m3/ha, giving a total water demand figure of 10,830 MCM. Even if irrigation tariff of 12,000 m3/ha was used, a maximum demand of only 12,996 MCM is reached. On top of this there are, of course, evaporation losses from the major dams along the Euphrates, which amount to 1083 MCM. This gives a total of between 11,913 and 14,079 MCM, which is reasonably close to the figure quoted by Altinbile (in the case of the Euphrates, Turkey is trying to take much more water than is necessary to irrigate the declared lands to compensate for the evaporation losses of large reservoirs on the Euphrates).

For Syria, Kolars quotes a water demand of 11,995 MCM and Kliot, 13,400 MCM, while Altinbilek gives a total of only 5,500 MCM. Here the situation is much more difficult to assess, because everything depends on the size of the irrigated area which is eventually developed by Syria. It would seem that the total figure would be between 475,000 and 1,000,000 ha when all projects are completed. However, at the moment, it is difficult to be any more precise than this as the Syrian government has been extremely slow to begin the schemes, which were planned more than 20 years ago. Annual water demands for these irrigated regions would be 4,750 MCM (for the lower value of 10,000 m3/ha) to 12,000 MCM (for the higher value of 12,000 m3/ha). On top of this evaporation from the reservoirs along the Euphrates is 630 MCM each year (Table 6.6).

The question of water demand in Iraq becomes something of a theoretical concept. If Turkey and Syria extract the maximum expected volumes of water from the Euphrates, the discharge into Iraq will be reduced to around 5,000 MCM each year. Iraq needs more water for irrigation than Syria or even Turkey. Evidence suggests that even in the 1960s Iraq was extracting 16,368 MCM between Hit and Hindiyah to irrigate around 1,230,000 ha. It is also known that considerable irrigation was taking place downstream from Hindiyah at this time, though exact amounts are unknown. In 1970 only 400,000 ha were being irrigated along the Euphrates and 800,000 ha along the Tigris. However, these figures would seem to be incorrect. The irrigated area in Iraq in 1970 was 3,680,000 ha. The vast majority of this would be located in the Tigris-Euphrates basin.

Kliot quotes figures from the late 1980s and early 1990s which estimate the actual irrigated area along the Euphrates River in Iraq as 1.0 to 1.29 million ha. It is, however, acknowledged that at this time the irrigated area had been reduced as a result of the Iran-Iraq war of the 1980s. The total area on the Euphrates, which can be irrigated, is thought to be 1,833,000 ha. If this is a realistic figure it means that total water demand at some time in the future could rise to 24,379 MCM/y with an irrigation rate of 13,300 cubic metre/ha. For a rate of 15,000 m3 per hectare the total demand would rise to 27,495 MCM (Table 6.6).

Table 6.6 Revised water demand estimates for the Euphrates basin for the period after the year 2020 in MCM/y

Country	Irrigation Water Use	Evaporation	Total
Turkey	10,830–13,000	1,100	12,000–14,000
Syria	4,750–12,500	630	5,400–12,600
Iraq	24,400–27,500	600	25,000–28,100
Total demand	42,300—54,800		
Available water	31,800		
Balance	−10,500 to 23,000		

SOURCE: Beaumont, YALE F& ES Bulletin

Table 6.6 clearly shows that the potential water deficit on the Euphrates River after the year 2020 might be as high as from 10,500 to 23,000 MCM each year. Since there will be enough water in the river to satisfy the full needs of both Turkey and Syria, it will be Iraq which will be least able to satisfy its potential needs. On the Tigris the overall situation is similar. There is general agreement that water demand for Turkey will be between 6,700 and 8,000 MCM each year (Table 6.8). The calculations of the present author suggest that the likely water demand for the planned irrigation of 558,000 ha will be between 5,580 and 6,696 MCM/y (Table 6.8 and 6.7).

Table 6.7 shows revised water demand estimates for the Tigris River for the period after the year 2020 in MCM/y.

Table 6.7 Revised water demand estimates for the Tigris River for the period after the year 2020 in MCM/y

Country	Irrigation Water Use	Evaporation	Total
Turkey	5,600–6,700	630	6,200–7,300
Syria	0	0	0
Iraq	37,200–60,000	1,000	38,200–61,000
Total demand	44,400–68,300		
Available water	52,700		
Balance	+8,200 to −15,700		

SOURCE: Beaumont, YALE F& ES Bulletin

Evaporation from a total of nine proposed reservoirs, with a total surface area of 693 km2 is likely to add a further 624 MCM to the demand. This is based on an evaporation rate in these upland valleys of 900 mm/y. Syria's use of water from the Tigris remains something of an enigma. It would be possible to divert water from the Tigris and pump it into the upper Khabur. However, without the active support of Turkey it would only be possible to obtain significant quantities of water during the high flow period. What is certain, though, is that Syria's demand for water to be used within the catchments of the Tigris River itself will be small, as it does not have access to suitable land. Potential water demand in Iraq is high with estimates from 29,200 to 40,000 MCM/y (Table 6.8).

Table 6.8 Water demand and water availability on the Tigris in the period after 2020 in MCM/year

Country	Kolars	Kliot	Altinbilek
Turkey	6,700	7,200	8,000
Syria	0	500	0
Iraq	29,200	40,000	31,900
Total demand	38,700	47,700	39,900
Available water	49,200	48,000–52,600	49,570
Balance	10,500	300–4,900	9,670

SOURCE: Beaumont, YALE F& ES Bulletin

As with the Euphrates, it is exceedingly difficult to obtain accurate statistics as to the area of irrigated land. Kliot quotes a figure of 2 million ha being irrigated in the Tigris basin in the late 1980s and a total irrigable area of between 2.8 and 4 million ha. If these figures are correct, potential water demand could rise to values of between 37,240 and 60,000 MCM/y based on water tariff figures of 13,300 to 15,000 m3/ha.

Prediction of maximum evaporation losses for all the reservoirs in Iraq is difficult to calculate owing to the lack of data, but will be at least 1,000 MCM/y. Taking these figures for the Tigris as a whole suggests a surplus of around 8,000 MCM/y for the lowest figures, but a deficit of over 15,500 MCM/y if the higher values are utilized. If the newly calculated water demand data for the Euphrates and Tigris Rivers are summed, they provide an estimate of the overall balance for the basin in the period after 2020. The minimum data estimates point to a possible water deficit of 2,233 MCM/y. However, the maximum values reveal a huge potential deficit of 38,641 MCM. This, it will be noted, is greater than the average flow of the Euphrates River *(Kangarani 2005: 45–46*).

Water quality has become a serious issue on the Euphrates River: return flows from agricultural drainage cause salinity problems that are exacerbated along the river course. Agricultural development has a significant effect on water quality in the Euphrates Basin and is by far the largest source of pollution. The return flow from irrigation causes water pollution, which in turn affects potential downstream uses. Pollution from agricultural and domestic sources seriously affects water quality.

Equally important are natural causes for environmental concern in the sense that some residual characteristics common to both rivers exacerbate the deleterious effects of human pollution. Notable natural causes are the high rate of evaporation, sharp climatic variations, the accumulation of salts and sediments, poor drainage and low soil quality in the lower reaches of the Tigris and Euphrates rivers. In Iraq, the Euphrates suffers from severe salinity that increases along the course of the river. In addition, dumping of untreated sewage into the Euphrates and its tributaries joined to other forms of water pollution.

In Turkey, large quantities of good-quality water are diverted from the main course of the Euphrates at Lake Ataturk and taken through the Urfa tunnel and canal system to the extensive Urfa-Harran agricultural area in the upper Jallab/Balikh sub-basins. Return flows from this irrigation development are significant, entering Syria through the Jallab River and other streams near the town of Tell Abyad, around 90 km east of the point of inflow of the Euphrates River. These waters carry a considerable salt load and other pollution, which is ultimately discharged into the Euphrates River through the Balikh River near Raqqah, around 200 km from the Syrian-Turkish border. Water is also carried from Lake Ataturk through the Urfa tunnels to the Urfa-Harran project in the upper Khabour basin. This may be one of the reasons why Euphrates water quality at the Syrian-Turkish border has remained relatively unaffected by upstream Turkish development.

Either way, assessing the dynamics of the various tributaries along the Syrian-Turkish border is of paramount importance when trying to understand the overall hydrological status of the upper part of the basin, and especially the downstream impacts of Turkish agricultural development. Water quality would therefore be an important topic to address in future discussions between Euphrates Basin riparians *(Erdem 2003)*.

It is expected that Turkey will cause injury to its co-riparians in due time, with regard not only to the quantity of the Euphrates and Tigris water flow but also to the quality of the water. The return flow, comprising low grade water, will eventually constitute some 40% of the Euphrates flow to Syria and 25% of the Tigris flow to Iraq. Syria will continue to degrade the water of the Euphrates by shipping its own return flow to the Euphrates downhill to Iraq and some 50% of the flow to Iraq will be return flow by 2030. Thus, Iraq will have less and much more polluted water—a violation of her right to reasonable and just water use of the Tigris-Euphrates.

ILC Rules stress similar principles calling for the prevention of appreciable harm to other water-course systems. Turkey has very rich water resources which could be developed for irrigation, thus leaving large amounts of the Euphrates flow for her co-riparians. The Tigris-Euphrates discharge comprises 40% of the total water supply of Turkey as compared with 80–85% in Syria and 98% in Iraq. This factor should receive high ranking in the process of sharing the water of the Tigris-Euphrates basin. Perhaps more weight should be given to it to satisfy the principles of equity and justice than to the Turkish contribution to the water balance of the Tigris-Euphrates. The Helsinki Rules also refer to the prevention of water wastage and economy of use. There is enough evidence that there is wastage related to inefficient and poorly maintained irrigation systems in Syria but the situation is worse in Iraq. Turkey has referred to this matter by mentioning Syria and Iraq's wastage of water on non- or low-productive lands: Turkey carries out irrigation by channel system while Iraq and Syria use less sophisticated methods' *(Kliot 1994: 123)*.

6.1.2 Impact on the Gulf

A further complication may wait at journey's end for the combined waters of the two rivers, the Shatt al-Arab. The Gulf into which the Shatt empties is a shallow body of water with a circulation pattern requiring about three years. Its only opening is the Strait of Hormuz giving access to the Gulf of Oman. The Gulf has a rich and diverse marine life which supports the shrimp and pearling industries. Its coasts also support major desalination plants for Kuwait, Saudi Arabia, Bahrain, Qatar and the UAE. Its waters have a natural high salinity which is modified by the entry of fresh water from the Shatt, which also provides nutrients essential to the marine biota. If the flow of the Shatt is reduced as much as fifty per cent in the future, the water which reaches the Gulf will be considerably saltier than at present, and the ecology of the Gulf may be seriously affected. Higher salinities might also create additional problems for the desalination plants of the GCC. Although the impact on the Gulf is again of less immediate concern to Turkish management, its relation to the volumes of water maintained in Turkish reservoirs and flowing through Turkish fields can reflect upon Turkey's own problems. Thus, Turkey will find itself drawn with Syria and Iraq into river-associated relations with Gulf countries far from the rivers' headwaters *(Biswas 1994: 77–78).*

We also consider it important to first present the positions of Turkey, Syria and Iraq on a number of important water issues and then to describe their water conflicts. Table 6.9 describes the positions of Turkey, Syria and Iraq on a number of important water issues.

Table 6.9 The positions of Turkey, Syria and Iraq on a number of important water issues

	Turkey	**Syria**	**Iraq**
Permanent tripartite treaty	Doesn't want	Wants	Wants
Euphrates and Tigris rivers	Common basin	Common basin	Separate basins
Own doctrine	Absolute sovereignty of the country	Indivisible integrity of the river	Right to historical use
Orontes river	Be discussed	Not negotiable	No comment
GAP	Will increase cooperation	Will increase the problem	Will increase the problem
Desired flow rate (Euphrates)	500 m3/s	700 m3/s	700 m3/s
Solution	Three-stage plan	Sharing over quantity	Sharing over quantity

Turkey's position:

1. Turkey (as well as Syria) would like the Euphrates and the Tigris to be considered as one watershed, two branches of the same river. This would mean that one could agree separately with Syria on the Euphrates and with Iraq on the Tigris, because this would be an easy way of sharing the "one" river watershed.
2. Turkey considers the rivers as "transboundary" and not "international". This means that Turkey has more freedom on how to use the waters. As the rivers have their source in Turkey, it maintains that it has rights over them. If the rivers were considered as international, a trilateral agreement would have had to be signed before GAP could have been implemented. Conceding 500 m3/s (15.75 BCM) to Iraq and Syria is seen as an act of good neighbourliness, not a legal obligation. This "Turkification" of the two rivers, as described by some experts, gives Turkey the right to decide freely how much water it allocates to other riparian States, taking what it wants to meet its own needs.
3. Turkey nevertheless respects certain aspects of international law: not causing appreciable harm to "prior rights" of utilization; in other words, Turkey will not cause too much harm to users who have already been using the water. This avoids, or at least postpones, open conflicts. What does "appreciable harm" or "too much" mean, however?
4. Turkey proposes the principle of "comparative advantage". Thus, in agreement with others and based on technical considerations, water should be developed for the maximum benefit of all; in other words, this means a sectoral specialization. Turkey uses the water to develop irrigation, thus covering the nutritional needs of the countries of this watershed as well as supplying them with hydroelectric power; on the other hand, Iraq could supply Turkey with oil, a vital resource for Turkey's economy.

Syria's position:

1. The rivers should be considered as an "international" river, historic rights of usage are to be protected. No water development projects should be undertaken without the prior consent of the other riparian countries. Supply increase due to water development projects should be shared on an equitable basis. Although Syria takes a strong stand regarding these principles when it comes to negotiations with Turkey, she is more flexible in applying them in relation to the downstream, Iraq. This is largely due to the conflict-rich relationship between the two opposing Bath-parties in power in these two countries.

2. The rivers should be considered as one watershed. Syria has the total downstream rights on the Euphrates, Iraq on the Tigris.

Iraq's position:

1. The rivers should be considered as "independent"; each river should be shared equitably and independently of each other. This would ensure that Iraq has rights over the Euphrates equal to the other riparian countries. Utilization of the Tigris is linked to numerous problems:
a) The river traverses the North of Iraq, which is Kurdish territory. Should this area become more independent, it would mean that Baghdad would lose control over its water resources.
b) The Tigris River has a higher salt content than the Euphrates; this means that it is difficult to use this water without mixing it with less salty water from the Euphrates—especially for soils that are already naturally salty.
c) The majority of Iraqi irrigation schemes, as well as many villages, are situated along the Euphrates. The probable outcome in the long run will be for Iraq to transfer water from the Tigris to the Euphrates watershed within her boarders.
2. Concerning the legal status, Iraq has a similar position to Syria. In sum, Turkey's water security is clearly driven by not only economics, but also political motivations, regardless of proud claims to irrigate 1.7 million hectares by GAP. The technical stance taken by Turkey regarding water allocations is helpful, but any successful cooperative arrangement to share Euphrates or Tigris waters from Turkey will have to go further to address mutual regional security agreements first, followed by strengthening economic interdependencies. Interestingly, social and environmental concerns seem to take low priority in Turkey's development agenda. Concerns from downstream riparian focus on Turkey's projected use (withholding) of water and water pollution, threatening Syria and Iraq's water security *(Kangarani 2005: 30–31).*

In the 20th century, Turkey was able to control the Euphrates 100% due to building five reservoirs on the Euphrates. Syria and Iraq described Turkey's water projects in the Euphrates Basin as a threat, tried to prevent them, even internationalized the issue, but failed as a result. Even in the absence of international financial support at the urging of Syria and Iraq, Turkey was able to build the Euphrates reservoirs with its own financial resources. Turkey greatly used of the Iran-Iraq war in 1980–1988, Iraq's participation in that war to build the Ataturk Reservoir.

Nevertheless, Turkey, Syria and Iraq did not sign a trilateral agreement on the joint use of the Euphrates, one of the main reasons for which was the mutual distrust between them. Even in the context of the water crisis, there were certain elements of regional cooperation, for example, the establishment of the JTC, the signing of bilateral water agreements between Turkey and Syria, as well as between Syria and Iraq. Turkey's position played a key role in the absence of a trilateral agreement on the Euphrates-Tigris. Turkey wanted to sign separate agreements with Syria on the Euphrates and with Iraq on the Tigris. This position of Turkey is somewhat contradictory, given that Turkey considered the Euphrates and the Tigris to be as one watershed. As a midstream country, Syria followed a dual policy on the Euphrates toward Turkey and Iraq over the Euphrates. Iraq demands its rights to historical use of the Euphrates-Tigris basin, but it cannot be taken seriously by Turkey. The situation in Iraq in the Euphrates-Tigris basin is deteriorating not only because of Turkey and Syria, but also because of Iran's actions in the Kurdish autonomy in Iraq.

6.2 Water Conflicts in the Euphrates Basin

The emergence of water issues, which became a major concern of Turkish foreign policy, was to a large degree the product of Turkey's decision to utilize the waters of the Tigris and the Euphrates rivers for power generation and eventually also for irrigation. The downstream riparians, Syria and Iraq, immediately perceived Turkey's plans to develop these rivers as a threat. They turned to a variety of means to resist these plans. They argued that as the downstream countries, they had acquired rights of prior use, concluding that any plans Turkey had would be subject to their approval since Turkey's utilization would inevitably have an impact on their current use. During this time, a set of principles regarding the utilization of transboundary waters was being discussed and developed by the United Nations under the auspices of the International Law Commission. According to them, the waters of transboundary rivers were to be used equitably and optimally, and further utilization by one riparian should not cause appreciable harm on others. In practice, these principles were interpreted as protecting exclusively downstream countries since upstream countries were in a position to utilize the river waters without being dependent on the goodwill of those downstream. Sensing that the international environment was in their favour, Syria and Iraq both tried to internationalize their problems with Turkey. These efforts commenced initially when Turkey asked the World Bank and USAID for credits to help finance the Keban Dam in 1965. Syrian arguments at the time appear to have impressed these agencies. A Turkish government official who was involved in the negotiations complained: "During the construction of Keban, [International Cooperation Agency] ICA (USAID) confronted us as if it were Syria's attorney..."

In the subsequent years, Syria and Iraq continued their efforts to stop Turkey's projects by utilizing a multiplicity of means. They continued, for example, their efforts to stop international lending agencies from making funds available to Turkey with some success. Turkey was unable to find funding from the international lending agencies for the construction of the Ataturk Dam, and to the surprise of the lenders, proved capable of financing and constructing the dam with domestic sources *(Kibaroglu, Scheumann, Kramer, 2011: 185–191)*.

In 1980–2000, two major water conflicts were registered in the Euphrates Basin, one of which refers to the Ataturk Reservoir and the other—the Birecik Reservoir (Border Euphrates).

6.2.1 Ataturk Dam Crisis

JTC

Even though the regional political environment was not conducive to water cooperation in the early 1980s, the growing exploitation of the Euphrates through the construction of the Ataturk Dam in Turkey led to fresh calls for cooperation. Because the issues triggered by water development schemes along the Tigris and Euphrates are so complex and far-reaching, the three riparians had to find ways to structure their discussions. To this end, Iraq took the initiative in the formation of a permanent joint technical body. The first meeting of the Joint Economic Commission between Turkey and Iraq in 1980 led to the establishment in 1983 of the JTC, whose members included participants from all three riparians (Syria joined in 1983) assigned to lay down methods and procedures that would lead to the definition of a reasonable and adequate quantity of water for each country from both rivers.

The mandate given to the JTC was defined as determining the methods and procedures, which would lead to a definition of a reasonable and appropriate amount of water that each country would need from both rivers. The main items on the JTC's agenda were the exchange of hydrological and meteorological data, the sharing of information on progress achieved in the construction of dams and irrigation schemes in the three countries, and the discussion of initial plans for the filling of the Karakaya and Ataturk reservoirs.

Although 16 JTC meetings were held between 1981 and 1992, no consensus could be achieved for the settlement of disputes. The JTC could not fulfill its mandate and was not able to agree on any substantial resolution. Negotiations were suspended in 1993. The major issues that led to the deadlock related to both the subject and the object of negotiations: whether the Euphrates and the Tigris could be considered a single water system, or whether the discussions should be limited to the Euphrates. The wording of the JTC's final objective, i.e. reaching common terminology, was also problematic: whether to formulate a proposal for the 'sharing' of 'international rivers', or to achieve a trilateral regime to determine the 'utilisation of transboundary watercourses'.

Iraq and Syria consider the Euphrates an international river and insist on an immediate sharing agreement under which its waters would be shared on the basis of each country's stated water needs. On the other hand, Turkey regards the Euphrates and Tigris as forming a single transboundary river basin where the waters should be allocated according to the identified needs. A careful examination of the records of the negotiations among the riparian states, and their failure, shows that non-water issues (or, more precisely, the overall pattern of relations among the three countries) played a decisive part in the growth of tension and disputes.

However, the role of the JTC should not be underestimated; even if its meetings were infrequent and if it appeared that little substantive progress was made on the question of water allocation, it served as a useful channel of communication. Even though the JTC originated from the Joint Economic Commission, it focused on water allocation only. Its ultimate aim of ensuring cooperation and coordinated management of water resources could not be fulfilled because the riparians were persistently claiming their water rights *(Ibid: 284–286).*

International customary law on transboundary watercourses has been the point of reference throughout the negotiation process at the JTC meetings. The principles of equitable and reasonable utilization, of the optimum use of water resources between states, and of the avoidance of transboundary harm to both nature and human usage have been evoked by diplomats representing the three riparians. By their nature, principles of customary law do not constitute enforceable rules, nor are they subject to what concepts such as "equity" might mean in concrete situations. In this way, while interpreting the principles of international law concerning equitable utilization, the riparians adopted opposing and rigid positions, with Turkey insisting on its water needs being met, and Syria and Iraq demanding their unilateral shares and respect for their water rights.

The main argument of Iraq during the negotiations was over its 'acquired rights' or 'historical rights' which stem from the existing water installations and the ancestral irrigation systems. During JTC meetings Iraq refused to discuss the Tigris waters as the Tigris was regarded as Iraq's sovereign right. Thus, a Turkish offer to compensate for the scarcity in the Euphrates by the surplus in the Tigris was rejected. The Syrian stand was based on the codification efforts in the field of transboundary rivers. According to the Syrian arguments, the Euphrates and Tigris rivers are 'international watercourses' which should be classified as 'shared resources' and must be divided among riparian states according to a quota, on the basis of their declared demands.

During negotiations it emerged that the water potential was unable to meet the declared demands of the three riparians. And, more importantly, there were also uncertainties and inadequacies relating to the data on water and land resources. In response to Syrian and Iraqi demands to formulate urgent 'sharing arrangements' dependent on criteria put forward by them, Turkey proposed in 1984 the Three Stage Plan for Optimum, Equitable and Reasonable Utilization of the Transboundary Watercourses of the Tigris-Euphrates Basin, which involves: (1) compiling an inventory of water resources; (2) compiling an inventory of land resources; and (3) determining the optimum total water demands of each country for domestic, industrial and agricultural requirements *(Altinbilek 2004).*

Three Stage Plan

Since the water potential was unable to meet the declared needs of these three riparians, Turkey proposed the 'Three-Stage Plan for Optimum, Equitable and Reasonable Utilization of Trans-boundary Watercourses of the Euphrates–Tigris Basin', which envisaged a process of three consecutive stages which would result in the preparation of a master plan for allocating the water among the three countries. During the first stage, an inventory of water resources would be taken in the Euphrates-Tigris Basin. The associated activities would include collecting meteorological data and measuring river flows using the same standard instruments, and exchanging this information among the riparians. The second stage would comprise of the classification of soils and the determination of irrigation needs using the same standards and procedures. This would lead to the third stage where a master plan would be made for water allocation in the basin.

The Three Stage Plan encompasses joint inventory studies of land and water resources of the region and the estimation of water needs for the competing sectors, agriculture in particular. It was expected that this would provide the basis for optimum allocation of the available water resources related to the determined needs. With the Three Stage Plan, Turkey also called for the establishment of a joint body to collect, handle and exchange data regarding water and land resources so that annual and seasonal variations could be incorporated in the estimates made, in order to determine allocations. Along with reaching a set of agreed upon criteria in data-sharing, it was hoped that negotiations could move on to coordinating development projects and create joint projects. This plan was initially presented at a tripartite ministerial meeting in Ankara on June 26, 1990. However, the Turkish Three Stage Plan was coolly received by Iraq and Syria, and they continued to demand fixed water quotas.

Syria and Iraq use mathematic formulae to define their water quotas. Syria proposed that the co-riparians should declare their demands for each river separately, i.e. the Tigris and the Euphrates rivers. If the claims exceed a river's discharge, the deficit will be proportionally deduced from each share. The Iraqi mathematic formula is somehow different and admits that each riparian should declare its claims for the realised projects, for those under construction and, finally, for any that are planned. Each country's water quota would be defined subsequently, i.e. first for the projects in operation, then for those under construction, etc., with the realised projects having priority over planned projects.

Syria and Iraq thus insisted on an immediate agreement under which the waters of the Euphrates would be shared on the basis of the water rights claimed by each country. Both countries asserted that, as the annual average flow of the Euphrates River was around 1000 m3/sec, Turkey should keep only one-third of the flow for itself and allow the remaining two-thirds to be shared by Syria and Iraq. The JTC meetings, at which claims and counterclaims concerning the use of the rivers and the nature of customary international water law were voiced, did not make an effective contribution to the settlement of the regional water dispute. The JTC did not provide a platform for delineating the coriparians' priorities and needs as a basis for addressing regional water problems. In this respect, water use patterns and the riparians' related legislation and institutional structures never had a chance of being discussed at the JTC meetings. The most comprehensive offer Turkey has put forth in order to establish a basis on which Turkey, Syria and Iraq could cooperate in managing the waters of the Euphrates and the Tigris rivers has been the Three Stage Plan.

However, it was coolly received and then rejected by Syria and Iraq. Syria and Iraq stated that the Turkish three-stage plan could not lead to an equitable and reasonable solution. They accused Turkey of trying to seize the largest portion of Euphrates waters, which should be accepted as collective property. They insisted that the Euphrates and Tigris are separate international rivers.

Why were the downstream riparians not enthusiastic? We have already discussed two principles that they did not accept. To begin with, the plan treated the two rivers as forming part of the same basin while Syria and Iraq were interested talking only on the Euphrates, each for different reasons. Iraq is already assured of sufficient water from the Tigris and would therefore like to keep it out of the discussion. Syria, on the other hand, is interested only in the Euphrates since the

Tigris does not flow through its territory. It considers the Euphrates as its lifeline. Furthermore, the plan did not change the Turkish position that the waters might be allocated but not divided or shared. Yet the plan contained elements of a breakthrough that were ignored if not unnoticed by the downstream countries. As Kut observes:

"First, Turkey was proposing joint action to determine the common utilization of the waters by all three countries, thereby indirectly disclaiming full sovereignty over the rivers without calling it as such. Second, the plan was suggesting the application of high and appropriate technologies in order to minimize water requirements for agriculture, thus injecting the element of conservation as an essential solution to what is basically a problem of scarce resources. Together, the plan also proposed to regulate the flow of the Euphrates River according to seasonal needs of the downstream riparian countries—instead of keeping a steady flow which may not match the seasonal agricultural demand. . .".

The plan necessitated a change in the mind set with which water problems are taken up among the three countries. The interpretation of territorial sovereignty and territorial integrity would have to be moderated to accommodate the making of joint studies and the collection and sharing of standardized information. Further, the implementation of the principles of "equitable and reasonable utilization" of water resources and "not causing appreciable harm to other riparians" would constrain inflexible interpretations of sovereignty. These were points, that the lower riparians were not willing to concede. Rather, they chose to insist that Turkey should increase the amount of water made available to Syria to 700 cubic meters per second (58% of which would then be released to Iraq). It is not clear whether either of the countries is in immediate need of this water or would be able to utilize it fully if the water were made available. But, in anticipation of a future state of affairs when they might need more water and fearing that close international cooperation might undermine domestic authoritarian structures which are to a large extent sealed from international influences, and preferring to maintain a state of emergency to bring about national integration, governments have shunned cooperation and limited their position to insisting on increasing the amount of water released downstream.

Although an agreement was not reached over procedures or over water quotas, in 1987 and 1990, two bilateral accords were concluded which were largely products of the then prevailing political atmosphere. They were, however, not the results of JTC negotiations, but were initiated at the highest political levels. Both are acknowledged as interim agreements by all riparians and were not useful means of managing the transboundary river system equitably.

The Turkish-Syrian Protocol of 1987

In 1987, the Turkish-Syrian Protocol on Economic Cooperation was the first formal bilateral agreement reached on regional waters, its conclusion made possible by simultaneous negotiations on security matters and water. Turkish prime minister Turgut Ozal, the decisive the time, promised a water flow of up to 500 m3/s, or 15,75 km^3 per year, at the Turkish-Syrian border, with the intention of reaching an agreement with Syria on security matters.

The Turkish-Syrian Joint Economic Commission meeting on 17 July 1987 had an important effect on water issue negotiations. The Protocol on Matters Pertaining to Economic Cooperation, signed by Turkey and Syria at the conclusion of the meeting, incorporated provisions for water, the temporary nature of which was recognised. Article 6 of the Protocol reads as follows: During the filling up period of the Ataturk Dam reservoir and until the final allocation of the waters of the Euphrates among the three riparian countries the Turkish side undertakes to release a yearly average of more than 500 m3/s at the Turkish-Syrian border and in cases where monthly flow falls below the level of 500 m3/s, the Turkish side agrees to make up the difference during the following month (as a basis for comparison, the long-term average flow of the Euphrates is about 1,000 m3/s at the Turkish-Syrian border) *(Kibaroglu 2013)*.

In 1990 the flow of the river was interrupted for 27 days in order to partially fill the Ataturk Reservoir. As the Euphrates downstream flow diminished. Iraq and Syria formed an uneasy detente in order to attend tripartite ministerial meetings held in Ankara regarding the crisis. At those meetings, the Turks stated that the matter was a technical one; the Iraqis and the Syrians insisted that it was political. At that point, the ministers returned home. Shortly thereafter the invasion of Kuwait took place and the situation was put on hold.

During the Kuwait War when Premier Ozal was encouraged to shut off the river to 'punish' the Iraqis, he replied that the Turks would not use water as a weapon[1]. This was in some part contradicted by the next Prime Minister, Suleyman Demirel, in July 1992, when he stated. 'Water resources are Turkey's and oil is theirs (Syria and Iraq). Since we don't tell them, "Look, we have a right to half your oil", they cannot lay claim to what is ours. Therefore, we have the right to do (with "our" water) whatever we want.' This statement indicates Turkey's

[1] In 1988, Ozal stated, "We don't tell the Arabs what to do with their oil, so we will never accept the Arabs' demands for our water." And in 1996, former Prime Minister Tansu Çiller, expressing concern about the state of the water problem in the Near and Middle East and pointing to various actions directed against Turkey in the implementation of the GAP, noted that those who wish to share water resources must agree to the sharing of all natural resources, especially oil *(Mosaki 2005: 121)*.

ambition to exchange the waters of the Tigris and Euphrates for Syrian and Iraqi oil and gas.

From the Turkish point of view, the stakes have been raised, for the Ataturk Dam is not only intended to produce large amounts of electricity, but also as many as a million hectares of land are to be irrigated in the south-east with water from its reservoir. This was expected to generate large amounts of foreign exchange from the sale of new crops. High priority was also given to the potential that GAP has for raising the standard of living in south-east Anatolia. which in turn was seen as a way to anieliorate the discontent of the local Kurds who form a majority in the region.

Thus, the Turkish dream to harness the waters of the Euphrates River—one shared and contested by both Premier Suleyman Demirel and President Turgut Ozal—in order to allay Turkey's serious energy shortage has become translated into a matter of prestige for the two political parties involved. Also, it has become a matter of internal security vis-à-vis the Kurdish problem, as well as a source of international confrontations with downstream partners *(Biswas 1994: 49–50, 65).*

At the same time, a Mutual Security Accord was signed, setting out that each state would prevent activities against the other from originating in its territory and that criminals responsible for terrorist activities would be extradited. Ozal believed that the PKK would cease its attacks if Syria stopped supporting it. For a while, it seemed that Ozal's hopes had been fulfilled, but a dramatic upsurge in fighting between Turkish and PKK forces in 1988/1989 led to renewed Turkish concerns about Syrian support for the PKK (Iraq was frustrated that it was not included in the 1987 protocol and for this reason it did not allow Turkey to attack the PKK in Iraq and in 1988, Iraq suppressed its Kurdish uprising in February 1988, 60,000 Kurds fled to Turkey, further deteriorating their relationship) *(Kibaroglu & Scheumann 2013).*

Over the years, Turkey has made a number of statements that leave little room for doubting its 'first come, first served' approach to the waters of the Tigris and Euphrates. In 1992, for example, Turkey's Prime Minister Suleyman Demirel stated: 'Neither Syria nor Iraq can lay claim to Turkey's rivers any more than Ankara could claim their oil. This is a matter of sovereignty. We have a right to do anything we like. The water resources are Turkey's; the oil resources are theirs. We don't say we share their oil resources, and they cannot share our water resources.'

In recent years Turkey's tone has, in the words of The Economist, 'softened somewhat from outright belligerence to studied imprecision'. Nonetheless, despite the talk of collaboration over the use of the Tigris and Euphrates, the language is still uncompromising. Commenting on a series of dams that Turkey intends to build on the Uphort river, Turkey's Deputy Prime Minister Mesut Yilmaz told the Arab daily newspaper Asharq Al-Awsat in February 2001: "We have completed works in almost 50 per cent of the infrastructure and we are in the meantime working on the final stages, and we will extend the invitation to Syria to accept the inevitability of this project and to join negotiations on a rational use of waters. We are ready to deal fairly and generously, but the division of waters will not be equal, as the Euphrates, like any other Turkish river, should be basically used for serving the interests of the Turkish people".

Turkey's aggressive water politics were illustrated most dramatically in 1990, when Turkey blocked the flow of the Euphrates for 9 days whilst filling the reservoir of the Ataturk Dam. Both Syria and Iraq accused Turkey of failing to inform them of the cut-off, prompting Iraq to threaten to bomb all the Euphrates dams. Turkey's Ministry of Foreign Affairs rebutted such claims, arguing that its co-riparians had 'been informed in a timely way that river flow would be interrupted for a period of one month, due to technical necessity', and that, prior to impoundment, more water than usual was released downstream, in order to allow Syria and Iraq to store sufficient waters to carry them through the impoundment period.

Turkey also argued that the average flow downstream never fell below 500 m3/s—the minimum agreed under a 1987 Protocol signed between Turkey and Syria. This is disputed by both Syria and Iraq, which point out that the decision to release 'extra' water downstream prior to impoundment was taken unilaterally by Turkey and without sufficient notice. Syria also notes that whilst the average monthly discharge at Jarablus on the Turkish–Syrian border for the year 1989–90 may not have fallen far below the agreed 500 m3/s, the monthly discharge in January and February 1990 was far lower—321 m3/s and 320 m3/s respectively. The Mission reviewed the discharge data from the measuring station at Jarablus and found the Syrian case persuasive.

The Ataturk incident serves as a constant reminder to Syria and Iraq of the potential hold which the GAP project, even uncompleted, gives Turkey over its downstream neighbours. Turkey's three major dams on the Euphrates—Keban, Karakaya and Ataturk—have a storage capacity (some 90–100 BCM) which greatly exceeds the entire annual flow of both the Tigris and Euphrates put together. Should Turkey decide to cut off downstream flow completely, it would therefore have the means to do so for a considerable period of time. Inevitably, questions have been raised as to why Turkey should have built in such huge surplus storage capacity. Even if an agreement is reached on water sharing, assurances that downstream flow rates will be maintained will ultimately depend on Turkey's political ambitions in the region. Turkey's membership of NATO, its close relations with the US and its acceptance for application for membership of the EU all place it in a strong bargaining position vis-à-vis its downstream neighbours, particularly Iraq, which has been weakened economically and militarily by a decade of sanctions. Indeed, officials in both Iraq and Syria expressed the view that Turkey had taken advantage of the sanctions against Iraq—and its pariah status internationally—to push ahead with its GAP projects on the Tigris, on the assumption that opposition from Iraq (the major downstream co-riparian, since the Tigris only flows through Syria for 40 km) would be either ignored or muted *(Yildiz 2005: 71–72).*

The Syrian-Iraqi water accord of 1990

On the other hand, the Syrian-Iraqi water accord of 1990 designated Syria's share of the Euphrates waters as 42% (i.e. 210 m3/s) and the remaining 58% was allocated to Iraq as a fixed annual total percentage, which corresponds to a flow of 9 km3 /year at the border with Iraq using the figure of 15.75 km3 /year from Turkey. Syria and Iraq perceived the interruption to the flow of the Euphrates (from impounding actions at the Ataturk Dam) as the first of many similar disruptions resulting from The Southeastern Anatolia Project (GAP) activities, and consequently signed a bilateral accord in 1990. The Joint Minutes (1) read as follows: The Iraq water share on the border region between Iraq and Syria is 58% as a fixed annual total percentage (water year) of the water Euphrates River allowed to pass in Syria through the border with Turkey, and the Syrian share of water is the remainder quantity 42% of the water of Euphrates River allowed to pass through the border between Turkey and Syria.

However, the existence of these bilateral accords, both relating to only the Euphrates, could not be accepted as evidence of cooperation. Each agreement was bilateral and predominantly concerned with water quantity issues. The riparians could not agree on more comprehensive forms of cooperation that would adopt an integrated approach to the various aspects of water use and needs (quality, quantity, flood protection, preservation of ecosystems, and prevention of accidents) and might potentially facilitate negotiations by linking water management issues. The agreements lacked effective organizational backup, at least in the form of joint monitoring.

Most critically, both treaties failed to address fluctuations in flow, meaning that they contained no clauses referring to the periods of drought and flooding that occur frequently in the basin and cause drastic changes in the flow regime that require urgent adjustment to the use of the rivers. During that period, water relations among the riparian states were mostly handled at diplomatic level through the exchange of curt diplomatic notes. When diplomacy failed to ease the tensions, meetings were held at the highest level where the driving rationale was the pursuit of Turkey's, Syria's, and Iraq's strategic national objectives. Yet these strategic interests lacked sound and scientific foundations, particularly when they were most needed as water shortages grew and water quality deteriorated. Instead, rhetoric prevailed and all parties stressed the need to achieve food self-sufficiency, food security, or other social and regional development objectives, claiming them to be strategic national goals. Consequently, the riparians' negotiating strategies were incompatible and, not surprisingly, favored national claims *(Kibaroglu & Scheumann 2013)*.

In an atmosphere of distrust, sometimes even an honest mistake may be perceived as a hostile act. In 1997 during a religious holiday, the General Directorate of State Hydraulic Works, in anticipation of reduced demand for electricity, closed off some turbines in the Ataturk Dam on the Euphrates River. It failed to inform the Foreign Ministry to give the Syrians advance notice for what was a brief interlude of reduced flow. Vigilant protests were to follow immediately. Turkey released extra water after the holiday to demonstrate that this was an honest case of oversight and that no other interpretation should be conceived.

Distrust leads the political leaders of a country to perceive ill intentions on the part of other countries with which they have to interact, making it difficult for parties to perceive mutual benefits. Turkey's construction of dams on the Euphrates and Tigris rivers has a strong hydropower production component. This meant that at any given time, Turkey's own interest would dictate the release of a considerable amount of water downstream in order to produce electricity. This reality should assure the downstream riparians that the upstream riparian would suffer significant losses itself if it ever tried to impound most of the waters of a river. For example, a deputy director of the DSI explained in a written note to a British scholar that there were eight turbines in the Ataturk Dam, each of which needed 225 cubic meters per second to operate. Assuming that about six turbines would be operating at a given time, no less than 1,350 cubic meters per second would have to be released downstream. This is in far excess of the 500 cubic meters per second guaranteed in the 1987 Turkish-Syrian Protocol. Yet, even with this and other similar information, constant fears of damming the waters so none are left for the downstream countries are ever present.

6.2.2 Birecik Dam (Border Euphrates) Crisis

In 1990s Syria and Iraq also launched a campaign against Turkey among the Arab countries, arguing that the Tigris and Euphrates rivers had historically been Arab rivers which Turkey was wresting away from them. For example, when the credit agreements for the construction of the Birecik Dam on the Euphrates River were signed, Syria started lobbying against the construction of the dam in the Arab League and in December 1995 got Egypt, Bahrain, Kuwait, Oman, Qatar and the United Arab Emirates to call on Turkey to agree to equally share the waters of the Euphrates River with Syria. The arguments which were based on international principles regarding the utilization of transboundary waters, did not serve the interests of all Arab countries in the same way, however. Syria, for example, was the upper riparian on the Orontes River but had no interest in guaranteeing rights of prior use to the downstream country Turkey, a privilege it wanted to be observed on the Euphrates. The status of the riparians to the Jordan River was even more complicated. It proved easier to criticize Turkey by mobilizing feelings of enmity against her, derived from centuries of Ottoman rule and Turkey's parting ways with the Arabs to join the West (which was considered to be Arab betrayal).

The disagreements between Turkey and the other riparians continued during the filling of the Birecik Dam reservoir and the building of the Karkamis dam. Moreover, during the late 1980s, it became known that Syria would begin the construction of the Tishreen Dam near the Turkish border. The maximum depth of the dam reservoir was limited to 20 meters. On the Turkish side of the Euphrates River, a final dam, the Karkamis, had been planned as the last dam before the river entered Syria. In 1998, Turkey suggested to Syria that these projects should be combined, to build one dam together, rather than building two dams separately—one on each side of the border. The new dam would be 40 meters in depth and generate more power than the two independently built dams. The power generated would be divided between Turkey and Syria. Syria responded that the feasibility studies and the completion of construction plans would cause delays whereas it wanted to commence with construction works immediately. Turkey suggested that the two sides could form a technical committee and produce the needed studies in a short time, given Turkey's experience in dam design and construction. Syria chose to continue with its own project, however. Similarly, Turkey later proposed to Syria that a joint dam should be built in the region where the Tigris forms the border between the two countries for a short distance. The idea was similar to that of the Arpacay Dam: power and water for irrigation would be shared among the two riparians. However, on the Syrian side positive interest failed to materialize *(Kibaroglu, Scheumann, Kramer 2011: 186–189).*

From 1996 onwards, there were also some unfruitful efforts to restart JTC meetings. The water conflict over the Euphrates and Tigris rivers was temporarily frozen in 2003 due to a change of president in Syria and the occupation of Iraq by the Coalition Forces which ended the rule of the Baath regime.

6.3 Water Conflicts in the Orontes Basin

6.3.1 General Overview of the Orontes Basin Hydropolitics

The extensive literature on hydropolitics in the Middle East has focused on the Jordan River and on the Tigris and Euphrates rivers, overlooking the hydropolitics of the Orontes River. Concerning the Orontes River—also known as the Asi Nehri in Turkish and Nahr el-Assi in Arabic—most scholars have investigated relations between Syria and Turkey, rather than considering both Lebanon–Syria and Syria–Turkey relations. The Orontes River was the longest and the "chief" river of ancient Syria and the Levant in general. The Orontes River Basin is shared among Lebanon, Syria, and Turkey. These waters are a critical resource for the development of these co-riparians in terms of both water and national security.

In the Basins at Risk (BAR) project the Orontes River Basin was identified as "at risk" because ongoing and future large development projects may result in water scarcity conflicts. There has been an extensive hydraulic development in the Orontes Basin. The river is highly polluted in the midstream and downstream due to heavy industries such as cement and fertilizer plants, power stations and other industrial activities disposing of their waste in the river. In brief, the Orontes Basin is heavily exploited by the three riparian states with no clear integrated vision for the management of the river resources.

For Turkey, even though the river constitutes only 0.6% of its entire water potential, there are already some dams operating for both hydropower and irrigation purposes. Until recently, there has been a limited hydraulic development in the Turkish part of the Orontes Basin. However, currently several hydraulic development projects are being introduced by the Turkish government in the region.

In fact, the Orontes has two main tributaries, namely the Afrin and the Karasu streams, originate within Turkey. Furthermore, there are other small streams located in the Turkish part of the Orontes Basin. The Karasu River (the black river, 120 km) originates in Turkish territory and forms over a short distance the border between Turkey and Syria, while the Afrin River (131 km), which is one of the important tributaries of the Orontes Basin and has a larger water flow, crosses Syrian territory before flowing through the Turkish Amik plain. The Afrin stream, originates in Turkey and then enters Syria. After that, the flow re-enters Turkish territory from the Hatay region. In other words, the Afrin stream has an exceptional geographical character, which makes Turkey both the upstream and downstream riparian states *(Conker & Hussein 2019)*.

The Orontes River enters Turkey through the Amik Plain, flowing to the east and discharging into the Mediterranean Sea. The Amik plain was a lake with few natural drainage canals and used to flood nearby fields and villages. In the 1970s, DSI launched a project for drying the Amik Lake by draining its water and reclaiming the resulting land. Since then the Amik Plain developed into a significant agriculture asset for Turkey. Currently Turkey is engaged in the planning and implementation of 12 projects for the management of the Orontes and its tributary waters. The projects serve domestic and irrigation needs, protect from flooding and generate hydropower. Upon commissioning all projects, the irrigated land in the Turkish Orontes part is estimated at 100,000 ha and the generated hydro-power at 180 Gwh/year *(Ballabio, Comair, Scalet, Scoullos 2015: 92)*.

However, water quantity is not the only problem that Turkey has as a downstream riparian state in the Orontes Basin. Water flooding and water quality constitute even more significant problems for Turkey. According to Turkish water experts, the issue of flooding is one of the biggest challenges that Turkey encounters in regard to the Orontes issue. For instance, the unexpected collapse of the Zeyzoun Dam in 2002 had adverse effects on the Hatay region (The Great National Assembly of Turkey Minutes Journal 2003). Thus, considering Turkey's Friendship Dam proposal, apart from its symbolic importance in Turkish–Syrian relations, regulating the water flow and tackling floods were a priority for Turkey. Furthermore, water quality is another crucial issue for Turkey, given that there has been heavy exploitation in Syria. Due to these reasons, even though the Turkish government could deal with the water scarcity problem to some degree in the Turkish part of the Orontes, it still needed to cooperate with the upstream riparian states, primarily Syria, to deal with other water-related problems in the basin.

The Lebanese government has been planning the Assi scheme, aiming at building a diversion dam, pumping stations, an irrigation network as well as a hydropower facility *(Conker & Hussein 2019)*.

The Lebanese sector of the Orontes river watershed basin covers a total area of about 2,600 km2 in the northern part of the Bekaa Valley. In Lebanon, surface water irrigates approximately 87,800 ha of which 11,500 ha are located in northern Lebanon. Unfortunately, the available information on the area of land irrigated by the Orontes is contradictory. The Ministry of Energy and Water gives an estimation of 1,703 ha, whereas FAO refers to an area of 18,000–21,000 ha. These data show a big discrepancy which applies to the use of the Orontes waters in Lebanon. Lebanon uses about 21 MCM per year of water from the Orontes, primarily for irrigating about 1700 ha of land (up to 21,000 ha if considering the whole catchment area) and about 23% for domestic and municipal uses. On the other hand, measurements at the Lebanese Hermel station and at the Omeiry station on the Syrian-Lebanese border show an annual consumption of 202 MCM in the region. The Orontes flow generated in Lebanon is estimated at 410 MCM/year, hence the amount of water consumed by Lebanon—based on the previous measurement—corresponds to 50% of the river's flow. This fact is one of the reasons that urged the Syrian government to engage in negotiations and to sign an agreement, which legally regulates the Lebanese water share of the Orontes River *(Ballabio, Comair, Scalet, Scoullos 2015: 91)*.

Syria is classified by international standards as semi-arid to arid region with heavy dependence on agriculture in meeting the state's population food demand. The pressure on the water resources in Syria is also increasing due to the sharp rise in population. The Syrian population grew from 13 million in 1992 up to 21 million in 2013. Another distressing fact for the Syrians is that 70% of Syria's renewable water resources come from out of the country. 17 million or 81% of the Syrian population depend directly on transboundary water resources to meet their water demands. These facts reveal the importance of transboundary waters to Syria. As a semi-arid to arid country Syria has very limited water resources and only the coastal region and the Orontes Basin in the country are excluded from this classification *(Ibid: 84)*.

The dependence ratio of Syria on the Euphrates River is 50%, approximately 11% for the Tigris River and 11% for the Orontes River. This means that 11% of the water resources in Syria comes from the Orontes River and its basin which is heavily populated and cultivated. This is a very important point to consider when discussing the Syrian approach to the management of the Orontes River as a transboundary resource. Transboundary water resources thus play a major role in the water security in Syria, as they represent 72% of the country's renewable water resources.

Syria shares six main transboundary rivers with the neighboring countries Lebanon, Turkey, Iraq and Jordan. These rivers are the Nahr El-Kabir, the Orontes

River, the Kwaiq River, the Euphrates River, the Tigris River and the Al-Yarmouk River. Syria shares the Orontes, the Kwaiq, the Euphrates and the Tigris with Turkey, which makes the relation between Syria and Turkey rather unique. Turkey is the upstream country of all the shared rivers apart from the Orontes giving the country the upper hand in the management of these resources. Also, Syria shares the Orontes and Nahr El-Kabir with Lebanon, where Lebanon is the upstream country for the Orontes while Syria is the upstream country for the Nahr El-Kabir. Syria is also the upstream country for the Al-Yarmouk River. This discussion shows that Syria is not in a good position to negotiate as a downstream riparian state for all major shared water resources *(Ibid: 81–83)*.

For Syria, the Orontes Basin constitutes one of the most important water resources as it constitutes 13.6% of Syria's entire water potential, being the third largest sub-basin after the Euphrates and the Khabur basins in Syria. The Orontes is vital for Syria's agricultural development—one of the most strategic goals of the state during the Baath Rule—with a contribution to agriculture of 12.7%. Moreover, according to data before the 2011 Syrian War, the Orontes supplies domestic water needs of the Syrian cities of Hama and Homs, and it delivers 16.52% of the domestic water supply. Finally, it also meets approximately 40% of the industrial water needs. The high proportion of water for industry from the Orontes mainly stems from the fact that the main industries are located in western Syria *(Conker & Hussein 2019)*.

The Orontes basin was one of the first industrialized regions of Syria with the establishment in Homs of state plants such as the sugar factory in 1948 and oil refinery in 1957. Industrialization accelerated in the 1990s with the establishment of private factories in particular chemical and pharmaceutical plants. The agricultural and industrial development in the region, led to a strong growth in the population of the basin reflecting the large ethnic and confessional diversity of the country.

The agriculture sector provides more than 25% of the Syrian national income. More than 30% of Syrian labor force works in this field and more than 21% of the cultivated land is irrigated using transboundary water resources. Since 1940 the river has witnessed dramatic changes in its hydrological system. The first major change was the drying up of Lake Amik in the Hatay (Iskandaronatt) region due to the draining of the lake and the diversion of its tributaries directly into the Orontes River. By 1970 the lake dried totally up and the land was reclaimed for agricultural activities. The drying of the Ghab marshlands in Syria constituted the second major hydrological change. Between 1958 and 1968, Syria initiated a marsh drainage project resulting in the reclamation of 46,000 ha of land. Both projects caused a dramatic increase in the river basin's irrigated land. The Orontes riverbed was enlarged and deepened, and dams were built to regulate the flow of the river and to provide water for irrigation.

Two main agricultural areas in Syria are supplied with water from the Orontes: the region between Homs and Hama and the Al-Ghab region. An area of about 70,000 ha is now being irrigated as part of Al-Ghab Project project, consuming around 330 MCM/year of reservoir water and another 150 MCM/ year of groundwater. The Al Ghab Irrigation Development Plan initiated in the late 1950s was the first agricultural achievement of the Ba'ath Party after it took power in 1963. Farmers cultivating irrigated lands in the Orontes basin were among the main beneficiaries of the agrarian reform and the centralized agricultural policy until the second half of the 1970s. Then the Euphrates River basin development program became the national priority for irrigation projects.

The region between Homs and Hama, on the other hand, is partly supplied from the Qattineh Lake via the Homs-Hama canal, providing water to an area of about 23,000 ha. Since the reservoir does not meet the demand, it is supplemented by groundwater wells, which irrigate another 20,000 ha in this part of the basin. The total irrigated area in the Orontes Basin in Syria has increased from approximately 155,000 ha in 1989 Turkey's foreign policy orientation in the water context and the Orontes Basin, to 200,000 ha in 1992 and 215,000 ha in 2008, while occasionally exceeding 250,000 ha in the period between 2004 and 2008. On average, an area of about 97,000 ha (43%) is irrigated by surface water and 130,000 ha (57%) by groundwater. Part of the groundwater used is derived from fossil aquifers. The extent of the pressure on these resources, particularly in the Ghab region, puts the sustainability of water resources in the whole Orontes River Basin at risk. Another region which significantly increased the use of groundwater for irrigation purposes is the Province of Idlib *(Ballabio, Comair, Scalet, Scoullos 2015: 68–69).*

The intensification of water use in the Orontes Basin in Syria has raised the question of long-term water sustainability. Water tables in some parts of the western Orontes Basin have dropped as much as 57 m in 10 years. The total irrigation water need in the Syrian part of the Orontes Basin is indicated in the amount of 3,586 BCM, a number well above the annual discharge capacity of the Orontes.

Syria has heavily developed surface (and ground) water resources in the Orontes Basin. In the 1950s, this basin was the key to achieving food security in Syria as the Orontes and coastal regions constitute the only regions of Syria outside the semi-arid and arid areas. This condition explains the importance of the Orontes region as a very promising land resource for agricultural development. For this reason the utilization of the Orontes River started under French Mandate and at the beginning of Syrian independence in the 1940s. The Al Ghab Irrigation Development Plan is the first development phase. The second development phase was initiated by Presidential Decree No.3/1972 and involved the construction of a number of dams and flow regulators. Data from the Ministry of Water Resources (previously Ministry of Irrigation) give account of the construction of 41 dams on the Orontes River and its sub-basins: 2 hydropower plants (Al-Rastan and Mahardeh), 20 irrigation dams, 1 dam used for both domestic and irrigation purposes known as Dam 17 April in the Aleppo governorate, 6 flood prevention dams, 3 percolation dams and 9 dams used for livestock. According to a World Bank study of 2001, the Orontes provides 20% of Syria's total water use and the agricultural sector consumes 85% to 90% of the Orontes River waters *(Ibid: 90–91)*.

6.3.2 The Broader Political Context of Lebanon–Syria Relations

In order to understand the hydropolitical relations on the Orontes Basin, it is necessary to contextualise them in broader political relations. This section provides general background on Lebanon–Syria political relations, focusing on the period of the hydropolitical bilateral treaties, from the end of the Lebanese Civil War until 2005, the year of former Prime Minister Rafik Hariri's assassination.

The Lebanese Civil War lasted from 1975 until 1990. The civil war ended with the Charter of National Reconciliation, also known as the Taif Agreement, 4 was agreed on and signed by the surviving members of the 1972–1976 Lebanese Parliament. According to the Taif Agreement, the 40,000 Syrian troops in Lebanon in 1989 had to be redeployed in the Bekaa valley within 2 years from the implementation of the agreement. Nevertheless, according to many Lebanese politicians, Syria violated the agreement by deciding not to withdraw or redeploy its troops; however, according to Syria, the agreement meant withdrawing the troops 2 years after confessionalism was eliminated. The US and the international community did not interfere with Syrian influence in Lebanon, also because Syria supported the US alliance against Saddam Hussein in 1990–1991. This resulted in an implicit US acceptance of the Syrian role in Lebanon. In fact, in 2005 there were still 14,000 Syrian soldiers in Lebanon. Only after Hariri's assassination in 2005 and UN and international pressure, Syria withdrew all of its troops in April 2005. Before 2005, the Syrian influence in Lebanon was institutionalised, and Syria played a heavy role in Lebanese politics, shaping and determining Lebanese politics, policies and decisions. This role led to many controversies such as the assassination of President Moawad. According to Gambill, Syria kept portraying Lebanon as an unstable country needing Syrian stewardship to maintain stability and peace. Lebanese politicians saw the Syrian presence in the country as a "necessity" while Syria saw it as an "obligation". While Lebanon was aspiring to more independence from Syria, in practice Lebanese politics became more and more tied, intertwined and influenced by Syria. This special relationship was institutionalised by several bilateral agreements and treaties such as the Treaty of Brotherhood, Cooperation, and Coordination and the Defence and Security Pact, both signed in 1991. This agreement shows and reflects the special relationship between Syria and Lebanon, interlinking their economies and strengthening their cooperation.

In fact, the former treaty provides the formal basis for cooperation in different sectors, including water. This treaty also established the Lebanese–Syrian Joint Committee for Shared Water, and it allowed for discussions and drafting of the future 1994 bilateral agreement on the distribution of the Orontes River water originating in Lebanese territory.

In order to maintain its influence and role, Syria agreed to fulfil the demand of Lebanon to some extent, for instance, in the water sector, while not responding to the Lebanese requests of more political independence. As highlighted by Jörum and Pipes, this agreement is to be seen and contextualised within the general historical views that the Syrian government had of Lebanon perceiving Lebanon as part of its territory and zone of influence, part of the "Bilad al Sham" (historic greater Syria); Syria had been controlling Lebanon and Lebanese politics in different ways, considering it almost as a semi-domestic context for decades, exerting its hegemonic political control over Lebanon, including in the water sector. Exactly in this broader context, the 1994 agreement is situated and reflects how a hegemon can impose its will to the weaker party. However, the Syrian influence over Lebanon has been decreasing in the past two decades.

6.3.3 Lebanon–Syria Hydropolitical Relations on the Orontes Basin

Discussions between Lebanon and Syria for an agreement on the Orontes River have been taking place since the 1940s. In 1972, the Lebanese and Syrian governments agreed to allocate 80 MCM per year to Lebanon from the Orontes River. The agreement was signed by both parties in 1972. It is very important to note that this agreement is not limited to the river, but it also covers water use in the basin. Unfortunately, due to the circumstances in Lebanon and Syria and the political complexity, the agreement was never implemented. The agreement still has a special importance for the Orontes river management as it represents the first document in which Syria recognizes the river as an international river. Syria always considered the Orontes River as a national river discharging into the Mediterranean Sea through the Syrian land. The special relations between Syria and Lebanon led to this special deal, since Syria was using for a very long time the same argument with Turkey. This fact will be discussed in details in the section on the Syrian-Turkish cooperation over the Orontes.

However, the agreement never entered into force as the Lebanese Civil War started a few years later, and in 1976 Syria occupied the area of the sources of the river, which are in Lebanon, during the Lebanese Civil War (1975–1990). Hence, Syria controlled the use of the Orontes River waters in Lebanese territory. In 1991, Lebanon and Syria ratified the "Brotherhood, Cooperation, and Coordination Treaty", supporting bilateral cooperation in different sectors, including water. Within this cooperation, a bilateral commission prepared a draft agreement, building on the 1972 agreement, which was the basis for the 1994 agreement *(Conker & Hussein 2019).*

In fact, on the 20th of September 1994 a bilateral agreement (the "Agreement on the Distribution of the Orontes River Water Originating in Lebanese Territory") for sharing the Orontes River was signed by the Minister of Energy and Water in Lebanon and the Minister of Irrigation in Syria. The agreement regulates water use of the Orontes River between the Lebanese Republic and the Syrian Arab Republic. The major points of the agreement are the following:

- The agreement recognizes the Orontes River as "shared waters".
- The agreement defines the river's headsprings and their boundaries together with the average annual discharge of an average year flow.
- The agreement allocates a share of 80 MCM/year of the Orontes flow to Lebanon and 340 MCM/year to Syria, provided that the river's resources reach no less than 400 MCM/year (at the Hermel Bridge gage).
- It was agreed that in case the annual discharge of the river falls below 400 MCM, Lebanon's share will be reduced to 20% of the river flow.
- A special Joint Technical Committee composed of experts from both countries is formed to manage the river flow within Lebanese territory. The Joint Technical Committee is to be financed by Syria.
- The parties' commitment to the agreement will be evaluated by a joint arbitrary committee. If the committee fails to resolve any conflict then the problem will be transferred to a higher committee.

- Syria will be notified about any further river installations and related usage and about all water extraction from existing wells which will be considered part of Lebanon's 80 MCM/year share.

The agreement describes in great details the river flow and the related Lebanese share. It divides the annual river flow into four different phases of several months each and establishes specific flow allocations for each phase *(Ballabio, Comair, Scalet, Scoullos 2015: 95–96)*.

Concerning groundwater resources use, the agreement prohibited the construction of new wells. However, no similar restrictions were imposed on wells in the Syrian side. In the agreement, there are no mentions of the possibility for Lebanon to build dams, diversion works or other infrastructure development, preventing the possibility to store water in the winter—when it is less useful for irrigation—to be used in the dry seasons and for the development of the Kaa and Hermel regions.

In a nutshell, the 1994 agreement clearly shows the institutionalised asymmetrical balance of power between the two countries in terms of what is allowed and what is not allowed and in terms of water allocation to Lebanon and Syria. The 1994 agreement, however, was signed soon after the end of the civil war in Lebanon, and with the 1991 ceasefire the Syrian army entered into Lebanese territory, resulting in a heavy Syrian influence on the decisions of the Lebanese government. Hence, the 1994 agreement was perceived as not favourable to Lebanon and as reflecting "the strength of Syria's position in Lebanon" *(Conker & Hussein 2019)*.

Many Lebanese analysts considered the agreement unfair on Lebanon, claiming that it had been reached under the Syrian political influence on the country. The agreement became a very controversial issue and critics argued that it suffered from the following drawbacks:

- The agreement gives the Syrian authorities the right to observe, measure and control the Orontes River over Lebanese territories which would undermine the Lebanese sovereignty.
- The agreement allocates more than one third of the Lebanese water share from the Orontes river flow to the winter period which would prevent Lebanon from benefiting from this share for irrigation and development purposes.
- Lebanon does not dispose of any water structures to store Lebanon's share for better management. On the other hand, the agreement prevents Lebanon from obstructing the river flow, which means that Lebanon will not be allowed to build dams.

The agreement remained a very "hot" topic in the Lebanese media, leading to negotiations between the two governments, whereby the initial agreement was amended following direct contacts between the Head of the Lebanese Parliament Nabih Barri, the Lebanese Prime Minister Rafik Al-Hariri and the Syrian President Hafeth Al-Assad. These consultations and the high level negotiation reflect the importance of transboundary water resources for both countries, the strong role of politics in the issue, and the fact that at certain stages decisions related to transboundary resources in Syria are limited to the Head of State due to the high sensitivity of the subject. As a result of these efforts, the original 1994 Agreement was amended in 1997 by adding an annex that identified four sub-basins as "closed basins" as well as a main spring, which were to be excluded from Lebanon's annual share as settled in the 1994 Agreement *(Ballabio, Comair, Scalet, Scoullos 2015: 96–97)*.

Therefore, the agreement was renegotiated in 1997, when Lebanon started recovering from civil war and became more independent from the Syrian influence compared to 1994. On 11 January 1997, an addendum was attached to the 1994 agreement, envisioning the exclusion of five sub-basins of the Orontes River—Yammouneh, Marjhine, Jabal al-Homr and Orghosh as well as the Labweh Spring—from the Lebanese share of 80 MCM per year. According to the addendum, these five sub-basins are to be considered "closed" basins and not common sources; in other words, they are within Lebanon and not part of the transboundary basins—hence the exclusion from the 1994 agreement. This amendment increased de facto the allocation of the basin's water to Lebanon. The Lebanese government, in this instance, made use of issue-linkage to convince the Syrian counterpart to accept the changes to the 1994 agreement, emphasising that the "1994 [agreement] may constitute jurisprudence for Israel. This may affect the rights of Lebanon to waters in the Hasbani–Wazzani River Basin, a main tributary of the Jordan River".

The agreement over the Orontes and Nahr El-Kabir Rivers between Syria and Lebanon meant for Israel that Lebanon had resolved all issues concerning its shared water resources in northern Lebanon and that the next step would concern the southern Lebanese waters shared with Israel. In this context, the destruction of the Orontes Dam by Israeli attacks during the 2006 aggression provides strong evidence of the Israeli dissatisfaction with this agreement *(Conker & Hussein 2019)*.

Lebanon thus is very vulnerable to Israeli attacks, since the first dam constructed on the Orontes (60% complete) was destroyed by Israel during the Hezbollah-Israeli war of July 2006. This attack contributed to the internationalization of the conflict, by introducing a third party (Israel) which does not share the waters of the Orontes River with Syria and Lebanon. It will be interesting to follow the position of Israel in the future, as this hostile act against Lebanon can be seen as a message to the Lebanese authorities which are planning to build a dam on the Hasbani River, a tributary of the Jordan River shared with Israel. Israel may want to warn Lebanon about the consequences of building a dam on its other transboundary river *(Ballabio, Comair, Scalet, Scoullos 2015: 200).*

Given the increasing independence from Syrian influence, and the fact that both the Lebanese and Syrian governments signed the 1997 UN Convention on the non-navigational uses of international watercourses, they decided to form a committee to revise the 1994 agreement and the 1997 addendum. As noted by Comair et al., the Lebanese delegation prepared for the negotiations by identifying several linked issues to convince the Syrian counterpart to reach a more equitable agreement for both countries. Among these linked issues, for the Lebanese negotiators future relations with Israel on the Jordan River Basin were also a point to be considered: "a 'win–win' hydro-diplomatic situation between the two riparian countries will strengthen Lebanon's position regarding possible negotiations with Israel"; "build ties between Lebanon and Syria in the hope of establishing a future bilateral agreement between Lebanon and Israel". The new 2001 amendment envisioned an 80 MCM per year share for Lebanon plus 16 MCM from wells, and the construction of a diversion dam and of a storage dam to allow Lebanon to expand its agricultural activities. However, in December 2001 the Syrian negotiators rejected what was agreed upon in that year claiming that the new version would negatively impact the Syrian economy of the communities along the Orontes. Also in this occasion, the Lebanese negotiators used issue-linkage as a technique to increase their bargaining power and convince the powerful counterpart, Syria, to accept the new amendment. The issue-linkage deployed by the Lebanese included:

Negative effects on a major part of the Shiite population in the region, who lives beneath the threshold of poverty and may revolt against Syria; the fact that all the Lebanese communities were in favor of the newly revised agreement; the position of Israel which might see this as an opportunity to impose the same negotiation terms on the Jordan River. The latter could have had the following consequences: non-restitution of the Golan Heights and non-recovery of the water shares belonging to Syria *(Conker & Hussein 2019).*

Furthermore, Syria deliberately linked most of the items in the final agreement to the UN Convention for two reasons: first to give the agreement an international recognition and secondly to use this agreement as an example of cooperation in the Middle East, especially for Turkey. Turkey requests an extension of the agreement to include all the riparian states. However, such a request will put

Turkey in a very weird position as Syria, in turn, will be asking Turkey to reach a similar agreement for the Euphrates River. For this reason the agreement between Lebanon and Syria is criticized by Turkey, though not that loudly *(Ballabio, Comair, Scalet, Scoullos 2015: 101)*.

In January 2002, the presidents of the two countries met in Beirut and decided to sign the decision of the previous year; the new agreement was therefore ratified in the same year and is currently the valid bilateral agreement on the Orontes River between Lebanon and Syria. In the following years, Lebanon started construction which included: the diversion dam near Ain Zarqa Spring, pumping stations and the irrigation network (phase 1) and a dam near Hermel Bridge and a hydroelectric power plant in the Hermel and Al-Qaa areas (phase 2). A Chinese company, contracted for phase 1, started working on the dam in 2005, but the works had to be stopped the following year when Israel bombed the site during the 2006 war. The reconstruction of the diversion dam has recently been restarted. This shows that as Syria's influence fades away from Lebanon, the Lebanese elites have been active in using issue-linkages techniques and strategies to increase their power also in the water sector, including on the Orontes River Basin. Nevertheless, since the ongoing Syrian war projects on the Orontes are on hold, and therefore, it is difficult to estimate what and how future scenarios will look like.

Looking at the evolution of the Syrian-Lebanese transboundary agreements, decision makers in 1994 were involved in a "win-lose" negotiation or zero-sum game since the treaty was signed under Syrian influence, where there was no concern for management of storage and diversion infrastructure. As seen from the optimization results, the 2002 Agreement is considered to be very close to a "win-win" solution or positive-sum game between Lebanon and Syria, since the total water (96 MCM/year) allocated to Lebanon (80 MCM from the river and 16 MCM from wells) is very close to the optimized Lebanese share of 27%. However, to arrive at a reasonable agreement that considers the principles of the UN Convention, Turkey should be involved in future negotiations.

6.3.4 Untangling the Political Context of Transboundary Water Relations: The Case of Syria and Turkey on the Orontes Basin

The historical background and broader political context played a vital role in Syria's hydropolitical relations with Turkey on the Orontes Basin. During the water talks between Ankara and Damascus concerning the Euphrates and Tigris, the Turkish government wanted to also discuss the Orontes issue, but Syrian officials turned down this request. The complicated character of the Orontes case between Turkey and Syria allows for insightful conclusions given the existing power asymmetry between Turkey and Syria, which was reflected in the Euphrates and Tigris Basin. Ozden Bilen, former head of DSI, describes Syria's water policy on the Orontes vis-à-vis Turkey as "… a very deaf attitude towards the justified demands of the downstream countries". He summarises Syria's policy on the Orontes as "mine is mine, but yours is negotiable". Syria's reluctance to even discuss the issue is heavily criticised by Turkish governmental documents. For example, Syria's inconsistent policy was criticised for making the comparison between the Euphrates and Tigris and the Orontes basins in policy reports (Ministry of Foreign Affairs 1996).

In this instance, the Syrian government has used non-cooperation with the downstream riparian states as a bargaining power tactic to maintain its de facto control on the Orontes Basin. But what has driven the Syrian government to adopt such a defiant approach, which could be easily exposed by Turkey? The main answer of this question lies within the historical territorial dispute between Turkey and Syria over the Alexandretta (Hatay) province *(Conker & Hussein 2019)*.

The differences between Syria and Turkey regarding water resources are not the only cause of conflict between the two countries. Another major disagreement is a territorial dispute over the Hatay (Iskandaronatt) region. This dispute has a major impact on the sharing of the Orontes River, because according to the Syrian claims over the region the river is to be considered a national river. In other words, Syria does not have to negotiate with Turkey over the Orontes River. The Syrian claims to Hatay are based on the fact that until 1939 the region was a part of the Syrian Republic. Syria does not recognize the Turkish annexation of the region the way it was performed under the French occupation (Mandate) of Syria. Consequently, Syria considers all resulting rights for Turkey over the Orontes River as illegal. Based on this discussion, both parties do not have a shared status for the shared resources, where Syria considers the Orontes River as flowing within Syrian territories, only Turkey considers the Orontes as a transboundary water resource calling for equitable use of the river.

On the other hand, Turkey sees the Euphrates as an "International River" which in the Turkish perception means that—due to the limited contribution of Syria and the absence of any contribution from Iraq to the river's resources—the two countries have the right to share the river waters but no right to claim equitable use. In this context, it is important to clarify that the international water diplomacy terminology does not make any distinction between the two wordings

"International Rivers" and "Transboundary Rivers", which contradicts the Turkish position. So no real achievements can be claimed over the Orontes and the Euphrates until the two countries agree on the status of the two rivers *(Ballabio, Comair, Scalet, Scoullos 2015: 102–103).*

The Syrian ruling elites were always dissatisfied by the post First World War order. In fact, the Syrian elites perceived today's Lebanon, Jordan and Palestine as part of the "historic Syria". The Alexandretta province was also an indispensable part of the envisaged "Greater Syria". In the eyes of the Syrian elites, cession of the Alexandretta province to Turkey by the French Mandatory Authorities was a betrayal carried out by the West. Syria has never officially given up its claims over the province.

The Alexandretta issue was the main obstacle in the Turkish–Syrian hydropolitical relations regarding the Orontes River. For the Syrians, the river does not constitute a transboundary water setting as it flows through the Alexandretta, which was supposed to be within Syrian territory. For Kout, from the Syrian Ministry of Irrigation, the Orontes River "originates in Lebanon runs through the territory of Syria from south to north and drains into the Mediterranean Sea" without mentioning Turkey. In an interview with the Turkish academic Ozis, he explained, "When we tell our Syrian counterpart 'let us discuss the Orontes issue too'; he replies if you can provide to grant asylum in Turkey, then I can discuss the issue. Otherwise, the moment I discuss the Orontes, I cannot return to Syria anymore'". Therefore, the Orontes issue remained unsolved between the two riparian states in the context of this historical background and a direct issue-linkage with a non-water issue.

Other issues have also made Syria and Turkey "distant neighbours" for decades. First, the historical legacy inherited from the late Ottoman Empire period, informed mutual identities. On the one hand, the Ottoman Rule is considered as a decay in Arab historiography and inspired Arab nationalism. The end of the Ottoman era is regarded as the emancipation from "Ottoman imperialism". On the other hand, when the Arabs joined the First World War, this was considered as a betrayal among the late Ottoman elites, many of whom then became the founders of the republic of Turkey.

Second, Turkey and Syria had opposing positions during the Cold War, coming to the verge of war in 1957. On the one hand, Turkey received financial and technical assistance from the West (primarily the United States) to fund its large-scale hydraulic development projects. On the other hand, the Syrian government, under the Baath Party rule, adopted the Soviet model of large-scale dams, irrigation networks and reclamation projects.

Third, the issue of the Euphrates and Tigris Basin became another hydropolitical conflict area as of the 1960s. Particularly, when Turkey introduced the Southeastern Anatolian Project (GAP), one of the leverages used by Syria to undermine the project was supporting armed groups. Moreover, Syria's sanctuary to the PKK during the 1980s and 1990s further worsened relations. As the PKK posed a threat to Turkey's territorial integrity, Syria's direct support and sanctuary to Abdullah Ocalan, the leader of the PKK, brought the countries to the verge of war in 1998.

Rarely, do midstream riparian countries emerge as "hydro-hegemons" in the transboundary water settings? However, Syria (at least until the Syrian War started in 2011), as the midstream riparian state, appears to be a hydro-hegemon in the Orontes Basin. Here, two questions must be addressed to justify the assertion. First, why should we consider Syria as a hydro-hegemon in the basin? Second, how has the Syrian government consolidated and maintained its hegemony in the basin. With respect to the first question, the following geographical–hydrological and political factors give an advantage in the basin. First, the lion's share of the river basin is located in Syria. Approximately, 72% of the entire river flows within the Syrian territory. Thus, given the strategic importance of the Orontes River in Syria's agricultural, industrial and domestic use, the river basin has been heavily exploited by Syria, which gives the Syrian government a significant exploitation potential.

At the same time, the utilisation of the river in both the Turkish and Lebanese parts is relatively limited. Therefore, Syria has far greater exploitation potential and motivations to exploit the river basin for various purposes. Second, Syria has had strong political influence backed by the military presence in Lebanon for decades, which has enabled Syria to enjoy a highly favourable status quo in the Orontes Basin, vis-à-vis its relations with Lebanon. The 1994 Water Agreement between Syria and Lebanon shows the asymmetrical power relations between the two riparian states. The agreement endowed Syria a firm control of water in the basin. It is also worth noting that Turkey has been excluded in this process as a riparian state of the Orontes Basin.

With respect to the second question, the Syrian government has successfully followed a dual-game policy to maintain the status quo in the basin. First, Syria has established a highly asymmetrical status quo in the basin via agreements concerning its relations with Lebanon by using its strong political influence. Second, given its relative upstream position and high exploitation potential, Syria has used non-cooperation with the strong downstream riparian state as a bargaining power tactic in bilateral negotiations with Turkey to exclude the strong downstream riparian state. Even though the Turkish side has repeatedly raised the Orontes issue in water negotiations, the Syrian government has refused to negotiate. For example, Turkey, Syria and Iraq could not reach an agreement on tripartite talks for the Euphrates due to Syria's refusal to link the Orontes River issue with the Euphrates during the first rounds of water negotiations in 1965. The issues were once again brought by Turkey to the negotiation table in 1993 in bilateral talks between Turkey and Syria, but the Syrian side once again refused to negotiate. Thus, Syria's persistent refusal to negotiate the issues with Turkey created resentment on the Turkish side. Syria's comparative transboundary water policy concerning the Euphrates and the Orontes was portrayed as inconsistent in the Turkish official documents (Ministry of Foreign Affairs 1996). Finally, the fact that Turkey is excluded from the 1994 treaty also confirms that Syria has used non-cooperation with the strong downstream riparian as a bargaining power tactic to maintain the status quo. Therefore, we argue that this dual-game policy adopted by the Syrian government did not only enable Syria to maintain the status quo in the basin, but it was also the main reason why there has been no regional approach including all three riparian states.

In this regard, the Alexandretta province has always been considered by the Syrian ruling elites as "the stolen province", denying Turkey of any claim on the basin. Furthermore, water relations with Lebanon concerning the Orontes have almost been treated as a "semi-domestic" matter *(Conker & Hussein 2019).*

6.4 Concluding Summary of the Fourth Chapter

In the fourth chapter, we describe the water conflicts of the riparian countries, dividing them into two parts. In the Euphrates-Tigris basin there is a problem not only of water quantity, but also of water quality. The positions of Turkey, Syria and Iraq on the issue of transboundary rivers are presented, their similarities and differences are shown by comparison (the Euphrates-Tigris basin is generally much more important for Syria, and Iraq in particular, than for Turkey).

The fourth chapter describes the annual flow of the Euphrates, Tigris, Orontes, contribution of riparian countries to the river basin, and their demand for water. The result of all this shows that the water demand of the riparian countries exceeds the annual flow of transboundary rivers. Moreover, it is becoming more and more obvious. In the same way, the problem of water quality of transboundary rivers is becoming more severe as these rivers become more and more polluted.

Chapter 4 describes the interconnected water conflicts over the Euphrates and Orontes rivers. The Tigris River is missed for two main reasons. 1) In the 20th century The Tigris Basin was not in the center of Turkey's attention, Turkey did not implement major water projects in the Tigris Basin. 2) Tigris does not enter Syria, so it was not used by him (in the 20th century). Thus, most of the waters of the Tigris were used by Iraq in the 20th century. We emphasize that the reduction of the Euphrates-Tigris river flow leaves its negative mark on the Shatt al Arab, which may cause concerns both in Iran and in the Gulf countries.

Chapters three and four show that in the 20th century, there were three major water crises around the Euphrates waters: the first involving the construction of the Keban, the second the Ataturk, and the third the Birecik reservoirs. The biggest of them is the crisis around Ataturk Reservoir, which was the largest reservoir in the region. In addition, Turkey planned to use the water of the Ataturk Reservoir extensively for irrigation. Lack of mutual trust between the riparian states did not allow the three countries to sign a trilateral water agreement. These water conflicts come to confirm the thesis that such conflicts mainly arise between countries that have historical, political and other types of problems with each other.

The implementation of large-scale water projects in the Euphrates-Tigris basin greatly affected the local Kurds, which we will discuss in detail in Chapter Five. This particularly refers to the launch of the Kurdish Armed Struggle (PKK): Turkey's use of a water card against Syria, and Syria's use of a PKK card against Turkey.

Chapter 4 also describes in detail the differences between the riparian countries around the Orontes River. The example of the Orontes River is significant because Syria, as a midstream country, is a hydro-hegemon, which is one of the a unique phenomena in the world. In the case of the Orontes River, the existence of a historical problem (Alexandret Sanjak) exacerbated the water conflict. Syria's use of Orontes River has also had a significant impact on deepening water disputes between Turkey and Syria over the Euphrates.

In particular, the Turkish side claims that Syria was the first to start dehydrating the Orontes River, that Turkey later started implementing water projects on the Euphrates. The issue of the Orontes River is quite important from the point of view that Turkey, unlike the Euphrates and Tigris rivers, is a downstream country, although in the 20th century Syria did not recognize it as such.

The Syrian government had persistently refused to negotiate the Orontes issue with Turkey for decades, excluding Turkey with any bilateral or trilateral negotiations. Syria could show flexibility and negotiate with Turkey over the Orontes basin given that two imortant tributaries of the Orontes originate in Turkey. In other words, Syria could negotiate with Turkey not over the Orontes River, but over the Orontes River Basin. This dual-game policy followed by Syria is one of the primary reasons why there have been no trilateral cooperation initiatives in the basin.

7 Water Projects and the Kurds of Turkey

7.1 The Situation of the Kurds in Turkey and the Birth of the PKK

After the collapse and partition of the Ottoman Empire at the end of World War I, the Kurds were promised the possibility of an independent state in articles 62 and 64 of the Treaty of Sevres, signed on August 10, 1920. But there was to be no Kurdish state. The main reason for this was the emergence of a strong Turkish nationalist state in the aftermath of the war and the subsequent suppression of Kurdish nationalist revolts in 1925, 1930 and 1937–38 *(Olson 1997: 168–193).*

Between 1920 and 1938 alone, Turkey faced 17 Kurdish rebellions, three of them, those of 1925, 1930, and 1937, being major ones *(Heper 2007: 1–2).* The uprisings were harshly put down and a host of laws were enacted to wipe out Kurdish history and identity. Kurdish village names were changed to Turkish ones, the word Kurdistan—until then used to denote a geographical region—was expunged from books and the language itself was essentially banned *(Marcus 2007: 18).*

The Turkish government coined the term "Mountain Turks" to refer to the country's Kurdish population. Republican Turkey's Kurdish policy was outlined by Mostafa Kemal Ataturk, the nationalist founder of modern Turkey, and has been followed by his successors. One of Ataturk's most loyal associates, Turkish Prime Minister Ismet Inonu, encapsulated Kemalist Kurdish policy: "Only the Turkish nation is entitled to claim ethnic and national rights in this country. No other element has any such right." This has made the status of the Kurds in Turkey markedly different from that of the Kurds in Iran and Iraq, where their

H. Gabrielyan, *Turkey's Water Policy as Part of the Political Strategy*, Politik, Wirtschaft und Gesellschaft im Spannungsverhältnis der Regionen Südosteuropa und Mittlerer Osten, https://doi.org/10.1007/978-3-658-44070-1_7

ethnic identity and equality have been recognized by law, if not always by practice *(Entessar 1992: 81)*.

In the 1924 constitution, the terms "citizenship" and "citizen" had been equated with Turkishness. Accordingly, the document stated that one had to be a Turk to become a member of parliament and the like. Certainly, Kurds could qualify as "Turks," but only at the expense of denying their own ethnic identity. Here then the seeds for eventual Kurdish dissatisfaction were planted: In a state now officially defined as "Turkish" the Kurds were not Turks, and only by giving up their ethnicity could they be treated as Turks. The news media ceased referring to them as Kurds.

With the population exchanges with Greece that followed the establishment of the republic in 1923, the Kurds, de facto, became the single largest unrecognized minority with the potential to threaten the state. In fact, Kurdish resistance to the extension of Ankara's political, economic, social, and cultural role began. At times violent, this resistance has been continuous and has remained a major preoccupation of successive governments in Ankara *(Barkey and Fuller 1998: 10)*.

Turkey's repression of Kurdish ethnic identity was so complete and Kurdish fear and exhaustion so high after the failed rebellions that a British diplomat traveling through the Kurdish region in 1956 noted: "I didn't catch the faintest breath of Kurdish nationalism which the most casual observer in Iraq cannot fail to notice."

But Turkey could not close itself off from Kurdish nationalist activities in other countries nor from domestic shifts that encouraged a new, liberal approach to civil and political rights. These factors helped spark change in Kurdish views of themselves, their demands, and the best methods to reach their goals *(Marcus 2007: 18)*.

The period after the repression of the Dersim revolt up to the 1960s is considered as the "quiet years" in the Kurdish question. Following the 1960 coup, Turkey experienced dramatic changes both as a result of domestic transformations, such as rapid urbanization, limited democratization, increased income equality, and domestic political polarization, and of external developments, such as Cold War rivalry and its impact on frontline states like Turkey, the Kurdish question, and the political nature of its actors. Different associations and activist circles emerged in the eastern cities of Turkey with the goal of bringing attention to the "Eastern question." *(Bilgin and Sarihan 2013: 102)*.

In 1960, the Turkish military staged a coup to halt what was seen as Prime Minister Adnan Menderes's increasingly autocratic rule. Ironically, the coup, which had the backing of the educated elite, ushered in the most liberal period the people had known. A group of academics was invited to draw up a new constitution. The resulting document enshrined broad freedoms to form associations, publish, organize trade unions, and call strikes—all limited since the founding of the republic.

This expansion of Turkey's democracy coincided with the rise of a more educated and cosmopolitan Kurdish population. The first generation born after the Kurdish rebellions had come of age, and they did not carry with them the same fears and memories of the army's harsh put-down of the uprisings that helped silence their parents. More Kurds were attending university, where they were exposed both to new ideas and other Kurdish youth. At the same time, Kurdish peasants seeking a way out of economic hardship were moving to the cities, where they were more likely to hear grumbling about economic inequality between Kurds and Turks and whispers of a new Kurdish political agitation at home and in Iraq *(Marcus 2007: 19).*

Besides, Kurds no longer needed Turkish intellectuals and activists to explain to them what the agenda was or how to make revolution. Not only had the activism of the late 1960s and early 1970s sparked a violent political awakening in Kurds, but also the state's own assimilationist policies had in some cases awakened exactly what it was trying to wipe out.

Ankara hoped that offering educational opportunities to Kurds would hasten their assimilation by teaching them the Turkish language and history as if it were their own. In 1961, special regional boarding schools were established to remove Kurdish children from their home environment and educate them in a wholly Turkish one. But this had the unintended effect of boosting Kurdish identity. Young men, who before would have had no choice but to drop out of school and work in the family fields or hawk wares in a dusty town, were offered spots in regional boarding schools. Here they could receive an education through high school and could even qualify for university.

Instead of remaining locked in their small village or town, with little exposure to what was happening in the rest of the country, let alone the world, they were thrust into a new environment of ideas, debates, and other Kurdish students. "The goal of [these schools] was to turn the children into Turks, but because of that there was a reaction," said Ramazan Ulek, a Kurdish boy from a poor family in the southeast who was educated in such schools. "Before, none of us had left our villages and suddenly we had a chance to see the world and how it worked." *(Ibid: 26–27).*

Some Kurdish activists tried to test the new liberal atmosphere directly but they were disappointed. The state moved quickly to shut down cultural magazines and Kurdish-language newspapers, charging the editors and writers with communism or separatism *(Ibid: 19)*.

Kurdish radicalism burgeoned in the late 1960s. The end of the 1960s were a period of great political upheaval in Turkey and PKK future leader Abdullah Ocalan, like many other young men and women, was unclear where to turn. Not yet a Kurdish nationalist, he was beginning to recognize that there was a Kurdish problem and that something needed to be done about it. After reading a book entitled The Alphabet of Socialism, he decided that he was a socialist.

But Ocalan was unsure how to combine his developing Kurdish political identity with his socialist ideals. The fact that Ocalan was nearly 20 years old before he started to think about his Kurdish identity in any political way was hardly unusual for a Kurdish man or woman growing up in Turkey during this period *(Ibid: 17–18)*.

In March 1971 Kurdish movement suffered yet another setback when, once again, the military intervened in Turkish politics and installed a government headed by Nihat Erim. The WPT and DDKO were outlawed, their leaders and activists were imprisoned, and the military initiated a new round of sustained attacks on Kurdish villages resulting in their destruction and/or the deportation of their residents. It was not until the restoration of parliamentary democracy and the coming to power of an elected civilian prime minister, Bulent Ecevit, in January 1974, that the Kurds were able to reorganize themselves politically. The rejuvenated Kurdish movement had a broader social base and was "more radical in its demands" than the 1960's Kurdish movement.

A number of factors contributed to the radicalization of Kurdish political parties in the 1970s. As Martin van Bruinessen, a Dutch anthropologist, noted, the most significant factor in the radicalization of Kurdish movement was Kurdish urbanization–the massive voluntary and involuntary migration of Kurdish villagers to cities–and the inability of the strained Turkish economy to absorb them into mainstream life. Kurdish migrants to the cities of western Turkey became aware of the great disparities that existed between the western region of the country and their own eastern region—in living standards, economic development, educational opportunities, access to health care facilities, and overall quality of life. Although agriculture remained a major source of revenue for the eastern region, Kurds also became acutely aware of their region's importance to Turkey as the only producer of oil. For all intents and purposes, the region did not benefit from petroleum production, as the bulk of petroleum production revenues were exported to other parts of the country. In 1971, petroleum production generated \$2.5 million, and the following year it generated \$10 million. Less than 5% of revenues generated, however, were spent for the development of the Kurdish region.

Moreover, as the number of Kurdish secondary-school and university students increased, students became more politicized and sensitive to legal and social discrimination against Kurds. Leftist student radicalism pervaded Turkish educational institutions, and younger Kurdish migrants became the conduit through whom awareness of issues of class struggle, underdevelopment, exploitation, and imperialism "spread outside narrow intellectual circles…. Urban eduacated teachers and students returning to their villages brought new political ideas, in simplified form, to the countryside and attempted to mobilize the peasants." Kurdish mobilization faced new dangers in the 1970s, however. Revision of the country's penal code and constitution in 1971 made it easier to prosecute those who were active in the Kurdish movement. Nevertheless, until the imposition of martial law in Kurdish regions in 1979, various coalition governments that ruled Turkey during much of the 1970s were relatively ineffective in implementing a sustained and efficient repressive policy toward their Kurdish minority.

Another factor contributing to the leftward drift of the Kurdish movement in Turkey was the alienation of the Kurdish population from the "progressive" ruling circles. For example, before coming Turkey's prime minister in January 1974, Bulent Ecevit campaigned in the east and promised the Kurds that if his RPP won the elections, he would address the underdevelopment of Kurdish areas. However, when Kurds, including his supporters, raised the issue of Kurdish autonomy, Ecevit reacted harshly, in the same fashion as his predecessors. The Turkish left was the only segment of society that recognized the Kurdish predicament and called for an end to the Kemalist policy of forced assimilation and oppression. Differing objectives and tactics, however, strained relations between the Kurdish and Turkish left. For Kurds, the goals of socialist revolution and Kurdish nationalism were not incompatible; they had to be pursued simultaneously. The Turkish left, on the other hand, considered Kurdish insistence on ethnic recognition as counterproductive, divisive, and ultimately detrimental to the survival of the political left. They contended that ethnic recognition would be achieved under the proletarian leadership of a socialist Turkey. The two sides parted company and the Kurdish left sought to organize separate political parties *(Entessar 1992: 90–92)*.

The relative political freedom that characterized the Turkish political scene during the 1960s and 1970s allowed for the emergence of various leftist groups among the Turkish and Kurdish intelligentsia *(Ibid: 89)*. The most prominent and effective Kurdish organization to emerge during the leftist "renaissance" of the

1970s was the PKK. In November 1978 Ocalan inaugurated the PKK into existence at the meeting in Fis village. The PKK originated, when a small group of Kurdish university students in Ankara organized the Ankara Democratic Patriotic Association of Higher Education. Their original activities focused primarily on gaining official recognition for Kurdish language and cultural rights. The principal leader and driving force behind the association was Abdullah (Apo) Ocalan, a former student in political science at Ankara University.

The PKK, like the Komala in Iran, blended Marxism-Leninism with a strong dose of Kurdish nationalism. It advocated the establishment of a Kurdish Marxist republic in southeastern Turkey, with the ultimate aim of creating an independent Kurdistan that unites Kurdish regions throughout the Middle East. What separated the PKK from other Kurdish organizations was the party's unequivocal advocacy of total Kurdish independence. Other Kurdish groups in the Middle East either called for Kurdish autonomy (KDPI, Iraqi-KDP), or equivocated on the issue of total independence (SPTK, KUK) *(Ibid: 94).*

The PKK's activities, as well as those of other political parties and movements, came to a stop with military coup in September 1980 *(Ibid: 95).* At four a.m. on September 12, 1980, Turkish state radio began broadcasting military marches as an announcer read a statement from Leader, 1975–1980 General Chief of Staff Kenan Evren declaring the military takeover. Soldiers fanned out to the houses of the top politicians to arrest them. Parliament was abolished and martial law was imposed throughout the country. Over the next three years, tens of thousands of leftists, Kurds, and rightists would pass through the courts and prisons, torture of detainees would become routine, and all democratic opposition would be muzzled. The constitution would be rewritten yet again, the philosophy of the country's founder Ataturk would be promoted anew, and the universities would be restructured to stop them from ever turning into political arenas again. Yet when the country returned to democratic rule in 1984 (the November 1983 elections resulted in the victory of Turgut Ozal's Motherland Party), the PKK was just gearing up for its first flamboyant attack (in August 1984) *(Marcus 2007: 50–51).*

If something was to blame for the military and political establishment's surprise when the PKK attacked, perhaps it was that the generals had done too good a job remaking Turkey. In Turkey's reestablished democracy, Kurdish activists—whether in exile, in prison, or free in Turkey—saw no reason to believe there was room for them to operate. There also was no reason to think that even their basic, ethnic identity would be recognized. The new constitution the military rulers prepared stated that every citizen of Turkey was a Turk, another named the state language as Turkish, and another said that this article could never be changed.

Under the law governing political parties, it was not allowed to claim that minorities existed in Turkey, nor was it permitted to "protect [or] develop non-Turkish cultures and languages." In fact, Kurdish could not be taught or used at all under the military regime's special law 2932, which specifically banned all uses of the Kurdish language without actually mentioning the word Kurdish. Such a fearful approach to anything Kurdish was not new, what was new was the maze of constitutional articles and legal additions that sought to forestall even minimal cultural expressions of ethnic identity.

Kurds never officially existed inside Turkey, but in the 1960s and 1970s, they slowly had organized groups, published magazines and books, and elected local officials with nationalist bents. All this was destroyed in the 1980 coup. In the new Turkey the generals were fashioned, Kurdish cultural, linguistic, and political identity was eradicated by law. The simplest expressions of cultural identity—giving children Kurdish names, singing Kurdish songs, and certainly, speaking Kurdish in state offices— was seen as a separatist act. Kurds as Kurds ceased to exist in the official, public realm, to the point that a Turkish journalist visiting a Kurdish village two months after the PKK's attack was only able to write that the people there spoke Turkish with great difficulty. But of the language they did, in fact, speak—Kurdish—there was no mention. The ban on Kurdish-related activities was so complete that the ruling powers could be forgiven for having forgotten that there was, in fact, a Kurdish problem in Turkey *(Ibid: 85).*

The junta endeavored to further impede the promotion of Kurdish language and culture. In addition to the constitutional prohibitions against the use of the Kurdish language, the Turkish penal code was revised to criminalize expressions of Kurdish ethnic identity. These, along with the existing ban on the use of the terms "Kurd" or "Kurdish", further radicalized the Kurdish movement and its most visible supporter, the PKK *(Entessar 1992: 96).*

For many Kurds, the 1980 military administration had a lot in common with the repressive regime of the 1930s; not only mass closure of Kurdish newspapers and "culture halls," but renaming of the Kurdish towns became a common practice during the military administration. During the early 1980s, although all political parties had Kurdish members, the "Kurdish question" suddenly disappeared from the political agenda under strictly authoritarian censorship. In trying to wipe out all political-activist outlets in Turkey, the coup administration unwittingly created a political vacuum in the Kurdish areas, which eventually led to the emergence and rise of the violent PKK. Despite the fact that the military yielded power to civilians in the 1983 elections, it still performed a supervisory role in the party-political system. This control was partly eased after the 1987 elections, after which the Kurdish question once again became one of the top agenda issues in Turkish politics, but this time with the PKK in the picture *(Bilgin and Sarihan 2013: 186).*

After the 1980 coup and the arrest of several thousand Kurdish militants and nationalists, many remaining PKK members left Turkey and set up cells inside the neighboring countries of Syria and Iraq. During the summer of 1984, the PKK announced the formation of the HRK and, from bases in northern Iraq, carried out a number of attacks against Turkish army units and police stations located in villages in southeastern Turkey. The Turkish army reacted by immediately dispatching heavy armored units into Kurdistan but, for the most part, failed to capture the PKK guerrillas who launched the attacks *(Entessar 1992: 98–99).*

In 1984 the PKK began Viet-Cong style guerrilla attacks on Turkish security forces, government personnel and facilities, and Kurdish feudal elites that supported Ankara. Although initially the group was largely ignored by Ankara, which viewed them as little more than a handful of rural bandits, the attacks grew progressively more daring and sensational. In 1984–1985, the government's response to mounting PKK activity was also hampered by disputes among the political and economic elite in Ankara.

Although the PKK's military "victories" never went beyond killing a few dozen security personnel at a time, usually during ambushes and raids, the media impact of such actions put into question the state's capacity to deal with the group and maintain its rule. Support for the PKK snowballed, and by the late 1980s and early 1990s the PKK had acquired the characteristics of a mass uprising *(Romano 2006: 50–51).*

The PKK planned to wage its struggle in 3 main stages. The first stage was called Strategic Defense, during which he had to form guerrillas, organize and conduct propaganda among the people (also armed propaganda), create a positive background to replenish his ranks, make himself known both inside the country and abroad. The second stage was called Strategic Balance, during which he should take control of a number of parts of the region, create liberated zones, expand the number of militants (bringing them to the level of battalions and regiments), expand his logistical base and weaken the state forces as much as possible. The PKK intended to achieve all this in the late 1980s and early 1990s. The third stage is called Strategic Attack. At this stage, the PKK should have already had a guerrilla army, formed its structures in the cities and earned the support of the people of the region. Then he should have carried out open attacks on the security forces in the region and defeated them, overthrow the state order, aiming to take the entire region under his control, including the cities. For the PKK, the end result would be the creation of an independent Kurdish state (Northern Kurdistan) and then its unification with other Kurdish areas and the creation of a complete Greater Kurdistan. The PKK attacks on 15 August 1984 in Eruh (Siirt) and Shamdinli (Hakkari) were the first armed actions half a century after the Kurdish uprisings of the 1920s and 1930s and created a new situation in the south-east of the country. In the 1980s, PKK support in Kurdish-populated areas of Turkey was so strong that the Turkish side had to change even the essence of the GAP by pushing for GAP zone's developing plan *(Alan 2016: 16–17, 11)*.

Although GAP did originally start purely as an energy and irrigation project intended to realize the potentially rich water and land resources of the region, it had been expanded to enter the fields of rural and social development by 1989 *(Jongerden 2007: 48)*. Turkey expected the GAP project would help to curb the power of the PKK by increasing the prosperity of the predominantly Kurdish population in the southeast *(Hinnebusch and Tur 2013: 128)*. In 1989 the mayor of Nusaybin caused a sensation (and lost his job) by telling the Reuters correspondent that about 95% of his townspeople were happy to support the PKK *(McDowall 2007: 429)*.

The PKK reached its peak between 1991 and 1993. Ankara was caught unprepared for the kind of challenge the PKK offered. This was not to be one of the many small bands or groups that had appeared and disappeared over the years, but rather one that had a well-defined political agenda and could exercise unparalleled discipline. The PKK, in line with its political agenda, has divided itself into three elements. The party itself—that is, the PKK—is the foremost organ. In 1985 it created ERNK[1] to bolster its recruitment, provide intelligence, and engage in propaganda activities in Turkey and abroad. Finally, the third leg in its structure is ARGK[2], formed in 1986 *(Barkey and Fuller 1998: 22)*.

The early 1990s was the peak of PKK attacks against Turkey since the effects of the Gulf War, such as the waning of Saddam's authority north of the 36th parallel, had allowed it to improve its capabilities *(Ibid: 129)*. As a result of PKK attacks and clashes between the PKK and the Turkish security forces 20,181 people have been killed between 1984 and the end of 1995 including 5,014 civilians *(Kirisci and Winrow 1997: 126)*.

The government has steadily increased its military presence in the provinces under the emergency rule. According to the International Institute for Strategic Studies, the normal level of Turkish troop deployments in the area was around 90,000. This number had risen to 160,000 by June 1994. By the end of 1994,

---

[1] The National Liberation Front of Kurdistan (Kurdish: Eniye Rizgariye Navata Kurdistan, ERNK).

[2] Liberation Army of Kurdistan (Kurdish: Artêşa Rizgariya Gelê Kurdistan, ARGK).

taking into account also the part of police, special forces and village guards[3], there were 300,000 security forces deployed in eastern and south-eastern Turkey. The size of the security forces in the area remained roughly the same during 1995. Apparently, approximately one-quarter of the total manpower of NATO's second-largest army was deployed in the area against the PKK. In contrast, according to government figures at the end of 1994 the PKK fighters numbered only 4,000 to 5,000 *(Barkey and Fuller 1998: 148).*

According to US Department of State records, in the 1990s, the PKK had 10,000 to 15,000 full-time members; 5,000 to 6,000 of them were in Turkey. The rest of the members resided in Iran, Iraq, and Syria. The same records indicated that the PKK might have employed an additional 60,000 to 75,000 part-time militants. From 1984 to 1999, PKK instigated 95 major attacks on Turkish forces, which killed 5,824 security forces and 5,320 civilians, a total of 11,144 people.

The Turkish government defined the PKK's actions as a threat to Turkey's territorial integrity, and strongly denounced the establishment of an autonomous Kurdish region. In 1987, Turkey declared a state of emergency (OHAL) in the southeast region. OHAL created a post of a regional governor with additional powers and ability to combat the PKK more effectively and more quickly and included restriction of freedoms (such as freedom of protest) for the Kurdish

[3] The controversial village-guard system was introduced in April 1985 because of the enormous logistical difficulties of ensuring security in the mountainous and rural areas of eastern and south-eastern Turkey. The aim was to enable villages to defend themselves against attacks from the PKK. Originally it was believed that the village-guard system would provide income to areas that were economically depressed. Ismet G. Imset in his book (The PKK: 20 years of separatist violence, in Turkish—PKK: Ayrılıkçı Şiddetin 20 Yılı) has likened the village guard-system to the Ottoman Hamidiye regiments which functioned between 1905 and 1908. The role of those regiments was 'to discipline the nomadic people of the region' and maintain 'the loyalty of Kurdish tribes to the central authority'. As in the case of the Hamidiye regiments, the government has used the village-guard system not only to improve security in the rural areas but also to determine the loyalty of the villagers. Villages or tribes who have refused to join the system are suspected of being PKK sympathizers. However, over the years the village-guard system has become a source of serious complaint. Sadik Avundukoglu, a member of the Parliamentary commission investigating 'mystery killings', has even argued that the abuses committed by the village guards helped to swell the ranks of the PKK fighters. In spite of frequent calls for its abolition, the number of village guards increased from just under 18,000 in 1990 to 63,000 by August 1994 when the Interior Minister announced that there would be no further additions *(Ibid: 129–130).* The village guards are well paid for their work, receiving approximately $100 a month, and, with this representing their only source of income, they have reason to want to see the conflict perpetuated *(Barkey and Fuller 1998: 148).* In our opinion, emerge of village-guard system was also the result of Turkey's policy to divide Kurds into two parts and thus to control them better (divide and rule policy).

people. The "supergovernors," as they were called, had authority to use asymmetrical and unlimited force against the PKK and its supporters. For example, the supergovernors, in order to cut off the supply lines of the PKK, ordered the relocation of a number of Kurdish families and eradication of many Kurdish villages. In the years between 1984 and 1999, Turkish security forces destroyed approximately 3,000 villages and displaced approximately 3 million people in the region. The Turkish government spent $160 billion to overcome the PKK between the years 1984–1999 *(Bilgin and Sarihan 2013: 88–92).*

The Turkish Armed Forces had been applying methods of conventional warfare, based on an outmoded doctrine. The cold war had come to an end, but even after the fall of the Berlin Wall, the military strategy of the Turkish army was continued to be based on the doctrine of static territorial defense by a standing army against a coherent mega-threat (an invading Soviet Army, centrally organized and clearly identifiable). The war with the PKK didn't fight the doctrinal remnants of the cold war, however, and the army was rapidly losing control. The PKK guerrilla didn't fight classic pitched battles. Instead, it was characterized by poly-centricity (the 'people's army' had no center, but was composed of innumerable relatively independent units, clustering with and separating from other units whenever deemed necessarily); multi-directionality (the guerrilla army was difficult to localize and there was no front, its militants were permanently on the move and giving the impression of being able to attack at any time and any place); and multi-dimensionality (not all party militants were guerrilla, many were active in the political 'front' and within civil society organizations such as trade unions). Ozal proposed a reorganization of the Army so as to be able to wage an asymmetric war—which constituted a revolution in the Turkish military and military philosophy of the time.

When the PKK began its guerrilla campaign, the organization had no more than a couple of hundred armed fighters—within ten years this number had increased to 15,000–20,000. This figure alone indicates the success of the guerilla war against the Turkish State and its Army, and which forced Ozal to propose his radical counter-strategy. The PKK was not, of course, employing a military innovation in the use of the guerrilla option; on the contrary, guerilla warfare has a long tradition, history is replete with examples of its successful (and unsuccessful) employment, and there were several recent and ongoing guerilla conflicts at the time to serve as models *(Jongerden 2007: 50–52).*

In the 1960s and the 1970s, the eastern and southeastern Turkey continued to be comparatively poor and, consequently, the Kurds as Kurds were represented only in the radical leftist movements in that country. Kurdish students attending major universities frequently came up with demands for the development of the regions they came from. However, on the whole, they were not engaged in propaganda calling for independence. Although these students felt that their regions were ignored by Ankara, there has not been a widespread Kurdish nationalism in Turkey, either in the early Republic or later *(Heper 2007: 111)*.

The emergence of the PKK in 1984 as a revolutionary organization in quest of Kurdish independence marks a major new phase in the evolution of the Kurdish national movement, entering a stage of sustained armed struggle now of over thirteen years' duration—the longest Kurdish rebellion in modern Turkish history *(Barkey and Fuller 1998: 21)*.

From the outset, the PKK has proclaimed its goal to be the creation of a unified, independent Kurdish state, and thus it has made no secret of its pan-Kurdish aspirations. The PKK sought not only independence, but also a political and social revolution among the Kurds in order to transform their society's feudal structure. It described itself early on as Marxist-Leninist and adopted the generally left-wing anti-imperialist rhetoric of the period to oppose "imperialism," including "Turkish imperialism" in Turkish Kurdistan. The PKK's program mirrored the slogans of the extreme Left: Kurdistan with all four of its segments, controlled by Turkey, Iraq, Iran, and Syria, represented the weakest link in "capitalism's chain," and the fight against imperialism was a fight to save Kurdistan's natural resources from exploitation. The PKK adopted a tight paramilitary structure and Leninist "democratic centralism" that essentially denied any internal debate or any transparency of organization and activity—features that largely have remained intact today, even if Marxism-Leninism has been abandoned in keeping with the new post–Cold War environment *(Ibid: 23)*.

The PKK issue also became trans-state, which we will discuss in detail in the third sub-chapter.

The trans-state nature of the ethnic conflict between the Turks and Kurds was clearly illustrated by the agreement signed in October 1984 between Turkey and Iraq which allowed the armed forces of both states to enter each other's territory in hot pursuit of rebel units. In practice, only Turkey chose to exercise this right, mounting four cross-border operations involving the army and the air force before the agreement was abrogated by Iraq in 1988 at the end of the Iran-Iraqi war *(Kirisci and Winrow 1997: 130)*.

With the foundation of the PKK and its terrorist acts beginning in the early 1980s and subsequent escalation in the 1990s, the Kurdish issue became Turkey's most important security problem. Domestically, the legitimacy of the Turkish state was tested and military expenditures weakened the already problematic economy.

Internationally, Turkey's foreign policy both vis-a-vis regional actors and superpowers such as the US and USSR (and later Russia) was defined by this problem *(Hinnebusch and Tür 2013: 128).*

The PKK insurgency, or the 29th Kurdish rebellion as it is occasionally called, differed from the previous revolts for its extreme leftist ideology and intolerance of opposition, which left many Kurds alienated, albeit quiet. As Michael Gunter argues, Turkey reached a point of no return as a result of the concept of Kurdish nationalism advanced by the PKK. For the Turkish state, it is now impossible to deny Kurdish existence like it did the 1930s, or even in the 1960s, or ignore Kurdish demands as it did in the 1980s and 1990s.

Cengiz Candar argues that what differentiates the PKK from the earlier Kurdish organizations is not its resilience or the longevity of the insurgency, but rather its goals. Ocalan and his friends adopted an armed struggle approach from the outset. Their fundamental goal was to "liberate" the Kurdish people living in the region between Turkey, Syria, Iraq, and Iran and build an independent greater Kurdistan. The idea of a unified, independent Kurdish state established through armed struggle, Candar states, was unprecedented in the history of the Kurdish movement *(Bilgin and Sarihan 2013: 7–9).*

The revolutionary romanticism of the PKK was mainly shaped by the examples of the armed struggles of leftist groups sweeping the planet, from Latin America to Indochina, during the late sixties and all throughout the seventies. The victorious end of prolonged war in Vietnam by the Vietcong fighters, independence won by insurgents in Zimbabwe, Angola, and Mozambique during the period that PKK came into existence served as sources of inspiration for the Kurdish organization. Consequently, the PKK fought for a Kurdish nation-state but in a larger geopolitical space than its birthplace, Turkey. Its focus was—though that has changed in the 1990s—for a nation-state in "Greater Kurdistan." However, for more than a decade, its impact was very marginal among Iranian and Iraqi Kurds.

As a matter of fact, for nearly two decades, the PKK, despite its reputation of being a pan-Kurd movement, aiming for the independence of "Greater Kurdistan," remained mainly as Turkey's Kurdish movement. In the wake of the end of the Cold War, the PKK is forced to modify its demand for independence. It is vacillating between a federal settlement and vaguely defined autonomy. It became increasingly clear to everyone that a territorial dismemberment of Turkey through the PKK's armed struggle is impossible. The Turkish side learned by painful events of the last three decades that the policy of denial and assimilating the Kurds is untenable. That policy eventually collapsed and the necessity to address the grievances of the Kurdish people is better understood *(Ibid: 70–71).*

The PKK conflict in Turkey is commonly estimated to have killed around 40,000–50,000 people since 1984. The overall toll of the conflict is difficult to determine given the limitations on accurately verifying death claims. Over the years, Turkish media and academia have all too often simply cited overall death toll figures voiced by politicians and military representatives. As described Noah Arjomand, an academic at Columbia University, even these figures varied: in December 1997, Suleyman Demirel, then Prime Minister, said 37,000 people had been killed in the insurgency; in January 2005, then Prime Minister Recep Tayyip Erdogan said the PKK had killed 40,000; in September 2008, the chief of general staff said it was 44,042; in February 2013, a parliamentary commission report estimated the total death toll at 35,576.

We want to emphasize that there is also an opinion that Turkey has suffered the most losses in the fight against the PKK after the First World War (Milliyet 2012). The above proves that the Kurds have been subjected to political persecution in Turkey since the establishment of the Republic. Their basic rights were violated, the repressions didn't stop, which radicalized the Kurdish movement, then pushed it to start an armed struggle. Especially the military coup of 1980 and the violence that followed, the adoption of restrictive laws left the Kurds with no choice but to resort to armed struggle. However, not only political and assimilationist repressions against the Kurds, but also economic reasons and the coercive migration yielded to start an armed struggle. The last two factors will be described in the next sub-chapter.

7.2 Kurdish Migration and Impact of GAP

Hundreds of thousands of Kurds abandoned the land as a result of the massive mechanization of Turkish Kurdistan in the 1950s, joining those who had been resettled during the revolts of the 1920s and 1930s, and those whose pastoralism had been deliberately disrupted by the state during the 1930s. Most of these, for example, the deportees from Dersim, had been integrated into the industrial proletariat of Malatya, Adana, Sivas and Kaysari. Many Kurdish conscripts also sought their fortune in western Anatolia to which they were routinely posted, after their discharge. Indeed, although military service was generally unpopular and evaded, some Kurds enlisted in order to learn Turkish and thus be equipped to live in the West where jobs could more easily be found.

Most of those leaving rural areas in the 1950s and after sought employment in a local town, and only moved beyond Kurdistan subsequently. Thus, by the mid-1960s they were converging mainly on Diyarbekir (25% of migrants), Elazig

(16%), Siirt (15%) and Urfa (8%). The population of Diyarbekir grew prodigiously over the years, from 30,000 in the 1930S to about 65,000 by 1956, 140,000 in 1970 and 400,000 by 1990. Of those migrants who moved beyond Kurdistan, approximately 41% went to Istanbul, 18% to Ankara, 15% to Adana and 4% to Izmir. Over the years the number of migrants greatly increased, and the fact that they tended to live in close proximity with each other established permanent strongholds of Kurdish identity across the republic. In due course the existence of these communities was to make the Kurdish question a visible reality even for the citizens of Istanbul, 800 miles away from Kurdistan.

It might be thought that the beginning of major emigration from Turkish Kurdistan would have led to a measurable decline in population growth in the east. However, the statistics indicate that the Kurdish community had a significantly higher birthrate than Turks. This had first become noticeable by a comparison of the republic's first two census figures, for 1927 and 1935. Between 1940 and 1965 the Kurdish population of those provinces where they constituted a majority doubled, while the Turkish minority increased by barely 80%. Government statistics for the latter year indicated that while 41% of the republic's population was under the age of 15, in Kurdistan the figure was 48% *(McDowall 2007: 403–404).*

The areas traditionally inhabited by the Kurds have been the least developed parts of Turkey. The eastern and south-eastern regions where most Kurds currently live have the lowest scores for two socio-economic indicators. Illiteracy rates of 35.5 and 44% for these regions in 1985 were much higher than elsewhere in Turkey. Similarly, the number of medical doctors per thousand people in 1990 was lower in the less-developed eastern and south-eastern regions than elsewhere *(Kirisci and Winrow 1997: 126).*

The Turkish authorities, denying the existence of the Kurdish problem, have always maintained (and still maintain) that "the problem of the South-East is only socio-economic." They have always stated that the main goal of GAP is to develop the region and improve the living standards of the population. The average per capita income in the Kurdish region is about $500 per year, while the average for Turkey is about $2,000. That's why it is planned to raise the standard of living of the population, whose incomes are 4 times less than in Western Turkey *(Mosaki 2001: 201).*

The Turkish authorities call the Southeastern Anatolia Project "Turkey's window to the future", "the future of all Turkey", the "project of the century" that will revive "the whole of Mesopotamia". Olchay Yunver, the then chairman of the GAP Regional Development Administration, told the Anatolian news agency on June 3, 2001, "This project is aimed at the renaissance of Upper Mesopotamia in the 21st century." And Badraddin Karaboga, the chairman of the Diyarbekir-based

Association of Industrialists and Entrepreneurs of the Southeast, believed that after the completion of the GAP project, the Mesopotamian Plain will become an economic ridge of the Middle East." *(Mosaki 2005: 47).*

An important factor for starting the development of large-scale hydro projects in the territory of Turkish Kurdistan was Turkey's lack of significant reserves of oil and other energy resources. In the 60s, the country imported about half of the consumed energy resources, and 25% of the country's electricity was produced on imported energy raw materials. In the 70s, the cost of Turkish oil imports rose sharply, and it became very urgent for Ankara to reduce its dependence on expensive Arab oil. So, if, for example, in 1970 Turkey imported 3,835 thousand tons of oil and oil products worth $ 64.8 million, then in 1979 it already imported 11,758 thousand tons worth $ 1.7 billion. In the late 70s, the value of Turkey's oil imports was about a third of the country's exports *(Ibid: 49).*

Meanwhile, over the 70s, the share of crude oil produced in Turkey in the total consumption of the country has significantly decreased—from 50 to 28%. The growing needs of the developing Turkish economy for energy resources, geopolitical and geo-economic ambitions also forced Turkey to look for alternative energy sources *(Ibid: 50).*

Turkish President Suleiman Demirel once remarked that "the result of Britain's policy that divided the Middle East is that Turkey's borders begin where oil ends." At the same time, for Turkey, Kurdistan oil was almost the only source of liquid fuel produced in this country. The territory of Kurdistan gave Turkey more than 99% of its oil. Only a tiny fraction is mined not here in Kurdistan, but in Thrace. All in all, from 1954 to 2001, almost 115 million tons of oil was produced on the territory of Turkish Kurdistan, which is more than 99% of Turkey's oil production. During 1990–2001, more than 42 million tons of oil was produced in Turkish Kurdistan.

In doing so, special attention should be paid to the sectoral breakdown of the investments made. So, for example, if in the energy sector the planned total investments in GAP as of the end of 2001 were realized by almost 80%, in agriculture this figure was only 17%. It is obvious that the Turkish authorities were interested in GAP primarily from the point of view of the electricity potential of Kurdistan, and not its agricultural development *(Ibid: 55).*

It should be noted that the physical and geographical conditions of Turkish Kurdistan are very convenient for the creation of a large number of reservoirs. Numerous mountain gorges and depressions contribute to this. At the same time, the evaporation of water, unlike, for example, the Syrian reservoirs formed in the desert, is minimal. As a result of the implementation of the GAP the territory of the Diyarbekir—Urfa—Mardin triangle will become agrarian, and the territory of the Diyarbekir—Gaziantep—Keban triangle—the hydro-strategic and electric power ridge of the region *(Ibid: 56)*.

The production of electricity at the hydroelectric power stations built within the framework of the GAP with a total installed capacity of 7476 MW will reach 27.345 billion kWh per year (excluding 6 billion kWh annually produced at Keban, where the dam and the HEPP were built before the start of the GAP, producing at that time almost 2/3 of all Turkish hydropower). These figures significantly exceed the share of electricity consumed by Turkish Kurdistan—about 5% of all electricity in Turkey. Electricity generated in Kurdistan under the GAP, which Turkish authorities claimed to be 50% cheaper than electricity generated elsewhere in Turkey, fueled Turkey's economic boom and industrial growth in the 1990s.

Meanwhile, Turkish Kurdistan continued to experience power shortages. For example, during a trip to Diyarbekir and Mardin in late May 1998, then Turkish Deputy Prime Minister Bulent Ecevit admitted that one of the problems faced by entrepreneurs who want to invest in the economy of Southeast Anatolia is the lack of electricity and low voltage. So, if the annual per capita electricity consumption in Turkey was 625 kWh, then in the East—350 kWh. It is noteworthy that in Turkish Kurdistan, there was a shortage of not only electricity, but also water. According to Abdurrahman Kurt, head of the Justice and Development Party in Diyarbekir, many villages and districts in Diyarbekir did not have adequate access to drinking water *(Ibid: 66–67)*.

It is clear that Kurdistan's hydro resources are invaluable wealth for Turkey. However, large-scale projects also have significant negative environmental impacts. For example, Professor Alaaddin Taisun believes that Southeast Anatolia suffers from severe erosion and becomes arid. In his opinion, at least 5 million hectares of land are subject to erosion. The environmental situation is exacerbated by the abrupt change in the Euphrates and Tigris flows, which turn these rivers into standing reservoirs *(Ibid: 70)*.

However, the real motive of the authorities is the desire to change the ethno-demographic appearance of this region, destroying traditional Kurdish settlements under the pretext of building giant hydraulic structures, forcing the Kurds to migrate to the western regions of Turkey and resettling ethnic Turks from other regions of the country to the Kurdish regions.

The program of "modernization, raising the standard of living of the population and creating new jobs in the Southeast" is aimed at changing the socio-economic structure of the Kurdish society, the socio-geographical landscape of Kurdistan, at stimulating migration processes that are unfavorable for the "fertile Kurdistan" and geo-economic isolation and marginalization of the extreme mountainous southeastern part of Turkish Kurdistan, which is not self-sufficient and poor in terms of resources, but very important from the point of view of docking all parts of the divided Kurdistan *(Ibid: 49)*.

In reality GAP revealed that government either failed to understand the economic dimension of the Kurdish question, or that its intentions were primarily to do with wringing whatever wealth it could from the south-east for the benefit of the rest of the country. For, as GAP master plan itself admitted, within the region, 8% of farming families owned over 50% of the land, while 41% held between 10 and 50 dunums and 38% held no land at all. Of the large landowner families, a substantial proportion was absentee, content to allow inefficient farming as long as they obtained an adequate income from their lands. Without a fundamental reform it was inconceivable that the majority of the farming population could benefit from GAP. The last attempt at land reform, in 1978, was abortive thanks mainly to the fear of the main parties in Ankara that it would destroy the patronage system that delivered their votes. Plans to create state run enterprises and smallholder co-operatives seem more likely to drive large numbers off the land. Furthermore, it was difficult to see how a largely illiterate population would be able to benefit from capital-intensive agriculture or agro-industry, let alone the ancillary sector that would grow up to service it. The Kurds had neither capital nor education *(McDowall 2007: 447)*.

According to the project's critics, the GAP is intended to undermine the Kurdish population's cohesiveness through massive displacements. Border security appears to be another inherent objective, since it would result in separating Kurds in Turkey from their compatriots in northern Iraq and Syria. Yet, though aiming to promote societal security through socioeconomic development, these policies paradoxically provoked local and international reactions when 382 villages and 88 sub-villages were flooded, and an estimated population of 197,732 villagers, the majority being Kurdish, was displaced.

Displacement resulting from large water projects is generally perceived as a source of great socioeconomic impoverishment, while constituting a human rights issue for the individuals and collectivities involved. The Turkish government has relocated these people without employment opportunities in shelters that resemble, according to human rights advocates, prison camps rather than actual villages. This policy has encouraged an exodus to slums in large cities such as Istanbul. The consequences of rural migration are dramatic for families, which are driven out of their land and often left with no compensation, but do not dare to challenge the situation for fear of being targeted as sympathizers of the PKK. In parallel, social structures based on rural traditions are disappearing in favour of a complete state centralization and the emergence of new classes with interests different from the concerns of villagers in the region. The paradox is an increase in regional wealth, accompanied by socioeconomic inequalities, to which are added environmental and cultural consequences *(Hinnebusch and Tür 2013: 136).*

Far from being a panacea for the ills of the region, by 1998 only 42% of local people were aware that GAP was a development project, and over 10% thought it was merely a TV channel. Only 11% of those polled had either short or long-term expectations of GAP. In fact, the economic gulf between western and eastern Turkey widened during the 1990s. One reason was the war, but another was the decline in per capita spending by the government in the east and south east during the decade. One of the more remarkable features of the conflict was that after fifteen years of bitter and savage war, the conflict had not descended into an inter-communal one. The danger of this eventuality had been greatly increased by the progressive outflow from the Kurdish region of both economic migrants and dispossessed fugitives from military operations.

Displaced people faced police surveillance and harassment. Indeed, these slum areas became extensions of Kurdistan, where active nationalists, passive 'assimilationists' and willing adherents of the Turkish Republic all jostled together. By mid-1996 the Turkish human rights association, Mazlum-Der, claimed that Adana, Mersin and Antalya, hitherto predominantly Turkish towns, now had a Kurdish majority. Indeed, its president told a parliamentary commission the following year: 'In cities like Adana, Mersin and Antalya, Turkish and Kurdish districts are emerging. Turks cannot enter the Kurdish district and vice versa. One should realize, that with a little provocation this will lead to very serious social clashes' *(Ibid: 448–449).*

As a result of the GAP and the flooding of many regions, the Turkish authorities were destroying traditional Kurdish settlements and forcing their residents to move to other regions of the country (mainly to the western part of Turkey). Although the Turkish authorities have consistently stated that the implementation of the GAP is aimed at "modernizing and industrializing the Southeast" and "entering Southeast Anatolia into an era of unprecedented wealth and prosperity," as a rule, residents whose property and houses have been submerged were not compensated no loss, leaving them homeless *(Mosaki 2005: 49).*

For example, during the construction of the Ataturk Dam, 116 Kurdish villages were destroyed and 55 thousand people were evicted, and during the construction of the Birecik Dam 47 settlements were demolished and more than 30 thousand people were evicted. Several tens of thousands of people were also evicted during the construction of the Karakaya dam *(Ibid: 73).*

As a result of the implementation of the GAP, ancient settlements of world historical and cultural significance and architectural monuments, including the masterpieces of antiquity, were being destroyed. For instance, the Birecik Dam flooded part of one of the unique monuments of the Greco-Roman civilization in the eastern part of the Mediterranean basin—the ancient city of Zegma (Gaziantep province), founded by one of the commanders of Alexander the Great, Nicador I Seleucidus, in the Euphrates valley around 300 BC on the ruins of the state of Alexander the Great. The latter also crossed the Euphrates at this point, going to Persia. In Gaziantep and Adiyaman alone, 72 large cultural and historical monuments were destroyed during the construction of the Ataturk, Khanchagiz, Kayachik, Kemlin, Doganpinar, Karkamish and Birecik dams. The reservoir at the Ataturk Dam flooded the city of Samsat with its ancient and medieval cultural and historical monuments. In the 1st century BC Samsat was the capital of the Kingdom of Commagene *(Ibid: 74).*

In general, as a result of the implementation of GAP Project, hundreds of Kurdish settlements with a total area of several thousand square kilometers have been flooded. At the same time, the Turkish government, as a rule, did not fulfill its promises to pay compensation to residents of the flooded areas. People who were forcibly evicted were often left homeless and without means of subsistence. For example, when the town of Halfeti and the adjacent 47 villages (by the way, a unique archaeological area) were flooded by the Birecik dam, the population that lost all its property instead of the 4 billion liras promised in 1998 received only 400 million liras. In addition, it should be borne in mind that forced settlers, as a rule, a led traditional household and was not adapted to life in large cities. Thus, the marginalization and lumpenization of Kurdish society took place.

The Turkish authorities were actively changing the toponyms of the Kurdish region. At the same time, ethnic Turks from the country's high-density Black Sea regions were moving into the "river region," as Suleiman Demirel calls the region of Southeastern Anatolia, and migration from elsewhere in Turkey was encouraged. In general, migration from the Kurdish provinces to the western regions of Turkey maked at least half a million people annually. A special role in encouraging the migration of the non-Kurdish population to Southeast Anatolia was given to the increase in the region's GDP.

Therefore, Kurdish leaders reasonably call GAP a modern instrument of the Turkish "policy of conquest", which presupposes the "assimilation" of the Kurdistan Region and Kurdish society, the destruction of the ecological identity of Kurdistan. Irrigation is not carried out in the interests of the Kurdish population, which is deprived of the opportunity to fully engage in agricultural labor (as only 11% of irrigation canals have been built farmers cannot get the required amount of water, they are forced to sell their land), and electricity is supplied to the industrially developed west of Turkey *(Ibid: 79–81).*

The notion that a small group of politically highly motivated but relatively poorly equipped guerrilla fighters could defeat the second largest armed forces in NATO in a prolonged war seems incredible. But various attempts by Turkish politico-military organizations to prosecute a counter-insurgency guerrilla campaign against the separatist PKK during the second half of the 1980s had failed dramatically, resulting in the deaths of their leaders and main cadre, and by 1990 the 'liberation of Kurdistan' by the PKK had become not at all unthinkable. The Turkish Armed Forces were rapidly losing control of an undeclared war. They only managed to regain control several years later, after a reorganization of the army and the implementation of a radical (counter-insurgency) war doctrine. The 'new' war was characterized by a harsh resettlement practice, with forcible, wholesale evictions accompanied by summary executions, the slaughter of livestock and the burning of villages. The objective, it is argued, was not merely retaliation, and nor was it a negative side-effect of the war or collateral damage. It was not even a temporary clearance of the countryside in order to break the guerrilla. Rather, the resettlement program constituted a concerted attempt by the Turkish military to bring about a conclusive transformation of the regional settlement structure. Its rationale was spatial contraction leading to environment deprivation. The small rural settlements of the Southeast were regarded as the 'negative environment' that fostered the PKK guerilla, and the immediate aim of the Turkish Armed Forces was to solve this problem by changing the spatial ground of the war. The destruction of rural society was simply considered part of the solution *(Jongerden 2007: 43–44).*

Shortly before his death, President Turgut Ozal sent Prime Minister Suleiman Demirel a plan (a top-secret letter) to "resolve" the "Kurdish issue in Southeast Turkey." The plan covered "political, social and economic aspects, as well as the problem of terrorism" and primarily provided for the encouragement and "organization" of migration of Kurds to Western Anatolia and from villages to cities. In accordance with this plan, it was predicted that as a result of the "regulation" of migration flows, the population of the Kurdish region will be from 2 to 3 million people.

Former US Ambassador to Turkey Morton Abramowitz, in the foreword to the book of American researchers Henry Barkey and Graham Fuller "The Kurdish Question of Turkey", wrote that shortly before the death of Turkish President Turgut Ozal (that is, in February—March 1993), he asked Ozal that the Turkish authorities are going to do with the Kurdish problem, to which the Turkish President replied that half of the population of the Southeast has already left their homes for economic reasons, and investments in this region are not going due to high risks. Therefore, Ozal said then, the solution is for the remaining population of the Southeast to leave the region as well *(Mosaki 2005: 80–81).*

Turgut Ozal had been Prime Minister of the Republic of Turkey between 1983 and 1989, the period in which the PKK had developed into a force capable not just of causing the Turkish state problems, but of actually winning the struggle for independence from Ankara and achieving the establishment of a Kurdistan. In 1989 he ascended the presidency, as the PKK rose to the height of its power, effectively controlling great swathes of 'Turkish' territory. Ozal, as much as anyone was aware of how grave the situation had become. His letter, with the proposals, symbolizes the birth of a new war in Turkey. The following parts of the letter are taken from a translation published in 2002 by KHRP (KHRP 2002: 118–22):

'With the evacuation of mountain settlements, the terrorist organization (PKK) will have been isolated. Security forces should immediately move in and establish complete control in such areas. To prevent the locals' return to the region, the building of a large number of dams in appropriate places is an alternative (both official and non-official figures indicate that some 93% of the displaced people wish to return to their villages). Given a tendency for the locals to migrate to the west of the country, it would appear that only 2 to 3 million people will inhabit the region in the future. If this migration is not regulated, only the relatively well-off portion of the population will have moved and the poor will have been left behind. Thus, the area will turn into a breeding ground for further anarchy. To prevent this, the migration must be regulated by the state. A planned, balanced migration, including members from all segments of society, to predetermined settlements in the West is essential. In addition to committing terrorist acts, [the PKK] is spreading wide-spread, effective propaganda with the purpose of intimidating and ultimately brainwashing the local people to win them over to its side. Counter-propaganda to strengthen local support for the state, to boost morale, and correct disinformation is of crucial importance.

Such cities as Adiyaman, Diyarbekir, Urfa, Mardin, Siirt, Elazig, Malatya, Erzincan, Erzurum, Kars, Ardahan, and Igdir must be turned into centers of attraction for the local population currently settled in the countryside. This should be done through special incentives for investors. Thus, the evacuation of the countryside will have been facilitated. If mistakes are not committed, and inconsistent, unnecessarily hurried action is not taken, the fire in the Southeast will die out in five to ten years, with the weakening of nationalist sentiment and the decrease of foreign involvement (Because the fire has undoubtedly been started and fuelled by foreign powers which desire to prevent Turkey from using its historic opportunity to accomplish its aim of becoming a powerful nation'.)

President Turgut Ozal's proposal was marked by some striking features. First, the problem was defined as a spatial problem. A direct relationship was made between an effective combat of the PKK and the evacuation of villages and hamlets in the troubled areas and the resettlement of their populations. The clearing of the countryside was supposed to contribute to an isolation of the PKK, and the development of large infrastructure projects, such as dams, to prevent the return of deportees and a recovery of an environment hospitable to insurgency. Second, a relationship was drawn between an effective war against the PKK and knowledge about the people living in the insurgent areas. Knowledge about people was supposed to contribute to the practicing of control over them. The transformation of the insurgent region and its population into knowable objects became a growing interest of the authorities after 1989. The task of turning the region and its population into object of 'knowledge' was mainly allocated to the so-called Southeast Anatolia Project, GAP *(Jongerden 2007: 43–48).*

Additionally, the GAP administration had experiences with resettlement projects (for the construction of eight dams in the region, 336 settlements had been or were to be evacuated, affecting, according to government statistics, about 181,000 people living in approximately 25,000 households, to rural or urban resettlements or else receiving compensation payments) *(Ibid: 112).*

In our opinion, Saddam Hussein's policy towards the Marsh Arabs may have served as a basis for Turgut Ozal's this plan. Saddam Hussein also punished by water rebellious marsh Arabs, who have resided continuously in the marshlands for more than 5,000 years and whose ancestors were Sumerians. On 28 February 1991, the day the Gulf War ended, a Shiite revolt began in Basra. For a few years, Shiite rebels kept up a low-level insurgency, using what was left of the Marshes as a sanctuary, but they did not survive for long *(Thesiger 2008: 3–8).*

The repression against the Marsh Arabs since 1988 has been motivated by a combination of factors. In addition to the fact that Marsh Arabs are Shi'a, Iraqi authorities have targeted them because the remote terrain of the marshlands provided refuge for political opponents of the regime and because, in 1991, Marsh Arabs themselves took part in rebellion against the Baghdad government. The marshlands also contain great wealth: they are today recognized as the site of some the richest oil deposits in the country *(HRW 2003: 1).*

In 1992, Saddam Hussein ordered the rapid construction of an immense canal to drain the area (a 6,000-square-mile area of wetlands). Based on British ideas from the 1950s, a 565 km long canal between Euphrates and Tigris, the so-called Saddam or Third River, was constructed in order to desalinate the Euphrates water. During the 1990s, still bigger parts of the marshes were drained, which means that prior to the war in March 2003 an estimated 93% had been destroyed. The only partly intact marsh straddled the Iran-Iraq border and was fed by river flows beyond Iraqi control. However, this area is also highly vulnerable due to dams in Iran and Turkey.

According to UNHCR (1995), around half a million people lived in the area at the end of the 1980–88, Iran-Iraq war. HRW, on the other hand, estimates that 250,000 Marsh Arabs lived there in 1991. Although an estimated 90% of the marshes had disappeared; Marsh Arabs could accept resettlement somewhere else in Iraq; or they could escape. Again, the numbers are not in agreement. While HRW (2003) has suggested that app. 40,000 remained in the area, a UN report from June 2003 stated that 'Today few Marsh Arabs (perhaps only 10,000) are living in their traditional marshlands' (UNOHCI, 2003: 5). This report further estimates that 100–200,000 Marsh Arabs are internally displaced persons, while up to 100,000 have left the country as refugees, with 40–50,000 of them living in Iran, which has the biggest Marsh-Arab refugee community. A survey conducted by AMAR after the 2003 war shows that 73,000 marsh dwellers were forcibly relocated by the Baath regime and restrained in different locations within the marsh area *(DIIS 2004: 11).*

Thus, the migration of Kurds to Turkey was caused by both military-political and socio-economic factors. After the Kurdish uprisings of the 1920s and 30s the Turkish authorities forcibly evicted them to the central part of the country. However, the scale of those migrations, as well as the movements of Kurds in the 60–70s incomparable with the quantitative indicators of migration that took place in the 80–90s and the beginning of the 21st century.

The main reasons for the migration of Kurds during this period were: 1) the armed conflict in Turkish Kurdistan between the Turkish army and the Kurdistan Workers' Party and, in connection with this, the destruction of over 4 thousand villages and settlements in this region; as a result, several million people were forced to leave their homes; 2) the socio-economic backwardness of Kurdistan, a high level of unemployment (in some regions it reached and reaches 60%), the impossibility of absorption of labor surplus resources of Kurdistan by the regional economy.

The Turkish authorities deliberately did not build industrial enterprises in Kurdistan that could absorb the region's surplus labor resources, didn't create the appropriate social infrastructure, forcing the local population to migrate to the west. The authorities assumed that by evicting the Kurds from Kurdistan and settling them with immigrants from other regions, primarily from the Black Sea region, in this way the Kurdish problem could be solved *(Mosaki 2012: 96–99)*

In 1930s Field Marshal Fevzi Cakmak, Chief of the General Staff, sent a circular to all military units to the effect that all decisions on such matters as road construction, electrification of certain areas, and starting of new factories could be implemented only after obtaining permission from his Office. Field Marshal Fevzi Cakmak served as chief of the general staff for 22 years, from 1922 to 1944. During those years, both officers and officials sent to the southeast were given licence to suppress the Kurds so that they would not again rebel against the state. Consequently, Kurds were subjected to harsh and humiliating treatment, which in turn contributed to further unrest among the Kurds *(Heper 2007: 139–141)*.

And the Kurds, who migrated outside Kurdistan, as predicted by the Turkish authorities, will soon assimilate, becoming Turks. Thus, the Kurdish movement will lose demographic (patriotic Kurds fighting for their rights on their land), natural geographic (physical and geographical conditions of Kurdistan, allowing permanent armed struggle) and material (Kurdish villages are traditionally 'bases' for supporting the rebels with the necessary resources) base to resist violent Turkization.

Modern migration flows of Kurds in Turkey are intra-regional and inter-regional in nature (we do not touch upon the participation of Kurds in international migration here).

Intra-regional migration consists mainly of resettlement from villages to cities, from small towns to Kurdistan megacities such as Diyarbekir, Van, Urfa, Gaziantep.

Inter-regional migration includes the resettlement of Kurds from Kurdistan (both from rural areas and from cities) to other regions of Turkey, primarily to the largest industrial and service centers in Western Turkey, as well as to the Mediterranean, Central Anatolia and the Black Sea region and even to the territory of the (self-declared) Turkish republic of Northern Cyprus. Up to half of the population migrated from a number of provinces of Turkish Kurdistan.

7.2.1 Intra-regional Migration of Kurds

In Turkish Kurdistan since the 1980s there was a significant scale of intraregional migration—from rural areas to cities and from small towns to large ones. This has greatly increased the pressure on the already underdeveloped infrastructure of the latter, turning them into huge zones of poverty. It should be emphasized once again that a significant part of migration (both intra-regional and outside the Kurdish region) was caused not only by socio-economic reasons, but also by the actions of the authorities. This refers to the conflict in Turkish Kurdistan, during which several thousand villages were destroyed, which made several million people internally displaced. As you know, the most violent hostilities took place in the late 1980s and 90s.

Residents were driven from their homes and the most significant increase occurred in the population of Diyarbekir and Van. So, according to the 1990 census, the population of Metropolitan Diyarbekir (Big Diyarbekir, Big City) was 380 thousand people, and according to the 1997 census—already 750 thousand. In 2010, 970 thousand people lived in this metropolis. Moreover, in 1930 the population of the city was 30 thousand, in 1956—65 thousand, in 1960—80 thousand, and in 1971—140 thousand people.

Thus, for 1930–2010 the population of Diyarbekir increased 32 times. For 37 years (in 1960–1997), the number of residents of Diyarbekir increased 9.5 times, and South-Eastern Anatolia only 3.2 times (from 2.05 million to 6.6 million); Diyarbekir province—3.4 times (from 400 thousand to 1.36 million people). The annual population growth in Diyarbekir has exceeded 10%. About 2/3 of the city's population moved there due to the destruction of villages. The already backward infrastructure of the city (roads, water supply, energy system, sewerage system, health care system, etc.), whose area was less than 8 thousand hectares, could not withstand such an influx of internally displaced persons. Therefore, the city was undergoing a process of "ruralization". Many areas of the city have acquired significant features of rural settlements. Housing difficulties for newly arrived migrants led to massive illegal construction. Migration has become a real social disaster. In these cities a huge army of the lumpen proletariat and marginalized strata was formed.

7.2.2 Interregional Migration of Kurds

Interregional migrations of Kurds acquired enormous proportions in the 1980s and 90s, although in much smaller volumes were observed earlier. They included three types: 1) departure of the local elite from the largest Kurdistan centers, primarily Diyarbekir, to the Turkish megacities; they were mainly representatives of the commercial bourgeoisie and large landowners; 2) migration to the western, Mediterranean, Central Anatolian and even the Black Sea provinces of immigrants from Turkish Kurdistan for economic reasons, due to lack of work; 3) internally displaced persons—former residents of villages that were destroyed as a result of the conflict.

According to the 1990 census, 9.4 million people (de facto) lived in Eastern and Southeastern Anatolia (Turkish Kurdistan). According to the same census, the population of this region at that time was around 13 million people, which means that over 3.6 million people, or about a third of the total population of the region, migrated from their native places (there was almost no migration to this region). In some areas, up to half of the population migrated. For example, 53% of the population left Tunceli, about 50% of the population left Erzincan, Kars—45%, Siirt—42%, Erzurum—36%, Mardin—35%. The lowest migration rate was observed in Diyarbekir, Urfa, Van, Batman, Sirnak and Hakkari—from 15 to 20%. Only in Istanbul, the number of Kurds, who come from certain cities of Kurdistan, already exceeded the population of these cities.

Economic migrants and internally displaced persons have penetrated practically all regions of Turkey—both in the largest industrial and service centers of the country, and in small cities and even in the countryside. However, most of them still settled in cities. A significant part of Kurdish migrants was employed in unskilled labor. Kurds were massively represented in such areas as harvesting various agricultural products (including women), the transportation sector (drivers), workers (in construction, factories and factories), small trade, etc.

7.2.3 Results of Migration of Kurds

The migration of millions of the Kurds in Turkey led to the following results.

1. The level of urbanization in the formerly agrarian Turkish Kurdistan has grown, which has become comparable to the general Turkish indicators. About two thirds of the population of Turkish Kurdistan lives in cities. However, urbanization has taken on ugly forms.
2. The share of Kurds outside of Turkish Kurdistan has become very high, reaching and even exceeding half. That is, half or more than half of Turkey's Kurds started to live outside the Kurdish region. In the largest megalopolises, the number of Kurds has increased by a thousand times. So, if in 1934–1935 the number of people who speak the Kurdish language has only slightly exceeded 2 thousand, but now, according to various estimates, from 3 to 5 million Kurds live in Istanbul. In many areas, Kurdish settlements have become compact. In the Mediterranean province of Icel (Mersin), about half of the population is Kurds, in Adana, over a third. In a number of regions, the Kurds constitute an absolute majority.

3. The Kurdish problem has transformed from a regional-national problem—from the Kurdistan problem in Turkey into a general Turkish problem. It received its territorial and demographic dimension in those areas where the Kurdish factor was completely absent earlier. In various regions of Turkey, interethnic clashes began to be observed, developing into massive Kurdish pogroms.
4. In the new Kurdish quasi-diaspora, local features that largely characterize Kurdish society are being erased, and a common Kurdish identity is being strengthened. The Kurds often call Mersin "little Kurdistan", comparing it to Cyprus for the Turks. In Mersin, people from almost all Kurdish provinces are represented—Hakkari, Diyarbekir, Bitlis, Van, Siirt, Mardin, Sirnak, etc., as well as almost all dialects of Turkish Kurdistan. There were areas in this province that were almost entirely inhabited by Kurds. Even minibuses running in the Kurdish areas of Mersin were painted in the colors of the Kurdish flag (green, red and yellow). Kurdish weddings in Mersin were turning into a kind of folklore festivals *(Mosaki 2012: 96–99).*

By August 1994, barely two years since wholesale evacuations were started, it was estimated that the population of Adana had grown from 900,000 to 1.5 million, and that of Mersin from 550,000 to about one million (*McDowall 2007: 441).*

Thus, Turkish Kurdistan first gained attention for its oil and then for its water resources, which can be considered the most strategic resources in the 20th and 21st centuries, respectively. However, oil and water resources did not bring happiness to the Kurds, on the contrary, they caused them misfortune. The GAP project also became part of the economic pressures and expansion policy, as paradoxical as it may seem. GAP reservoirs have, in fact, helped to change the demographic picture of the Kurdish region (demographic engineering). From a military point of view, it was expedient for the Turkish side to send the Kurds from the villages to the big cities, thus gathering the Kurds scattered in different places in one place. In this context, the following statement by General Osman Pamukoglu is noteworthy: 'Where there is sea there are pirates. In this province [Hakkari] are 674 villages and hamlets. These settlements form the spider's web in which the PKK feeds itself. (. . .) [Why don't we concentrate all [villagers] in two or three main settlements'] (*Jongerden 2007: 43*).

In the following subchapters we will see the causal link between the launch of the GAP project and the start of the PKK armed struggle. We will also see how much the emergence of the GAP worried Syria, and how Syria tried to counteract Turkey's hydro projects through PKK.

7.3 PKK Between Turkey and Syria

Syria had a number of outstanding disputes with Turkey that made it willing to tolerate, if not encourage militant groups. Since Turkey and Syria emerged as new states after the collapse of the Ottoman Empire following WWI, a border dispute dominated their agenda: both Syria and Turkey claimed sovereignty over Iskandarun province (what Turkey calls Hatay), which came under Turkish control in 1938 *(Hinnebusch and Tür 2013: 27)*.

While under the Ottomans the geo-political and geo-economic structure of the Levant was fully functional, the natural and historic dynamics between the coastal and interior cities was completely broken under the Sikes-Picot agreement; thus, Aleppo was cut off from its natural port of Alexandretta, the Orontes valley from Tripoli, and Damascus from Haifa and Beirut.

France, in an attempt to win Turkey to its side against a rising Germany, facilitated the annexation of the Alexandretta governorate, with its mixed Turkish and Arab population, to Turkey; with the Turkish acquisition of Alexandretta, Aleppo was deprived of its water supply by the Turkish diversion of the river 'Qouaiq' *(Ibid: 97)*.

At the end of the 1940s a Turkish attempt to offer concessions in Hatay to Syria, for instance through the free use of the Iskandarun port, was turned down as this could have been interpreted as recognition of Turkish sovereignty over Hatay *(Ibid: 116)*.

The unification of Hatay with Turkey underlined Syrian feelings of victimization over what were perceived as 'Western imperial designs' in the region. Syria viewed Hatay as 'stolen territory, grasped by force by Turkey' *(Ibid: 18)*.

The region was mentioned occasionally as one of the Syrian territories to be regained; it was also portrayed as Syrian in a wide variety of contexts, such as news and weather reports. In an annual ritual, the Syrian government renewed its claim to Alexandretta on the anniversary of its loss of the province *(Pipes 1990: 140)*.

Hatay has remained part of Syrian maps since the early 1950s and by June 2012, the vast majority of official Syrian maps continued to include the area *(Hinnebusch and Tür 2013: 121)*. Damascus wanted the return of at least Alexandretta; ideally, it sought Cilicia and the whole region south of the Taurus and Anti-Taurus Mountains *(Ibid: 60)*.

Assad also was concerned about Turkey's ongoing large GAP dam's project, designed to harness the waters of the Tigris and Euphrates for domestic agricultural and electrical purposes. Because the two rivers originated in Turkey—the Tigris delineates part of the border with Syria before flowing into Iraq, while the

Euphrates flows across Syria and then into Iraq—the dams project would give Ankara a great deal of control over the flow of water to the more arid Syria *(Marcus 2007: 60)*.

According to international experts, a full implementation of the GAP will ultimately withdraw a maximum of 70% of the Euphrates natural flow, about 40–50% of its observed flow, and 50% of the Tigris River. The future consequences for mid-stream Syria are potentially highly problematic in light of the country's dependence on external water sources (80%) and the centrality of the Euphrates Basin for the overall water supply (65% of resources).

Return flows from upstream reservoirs are, usually, evaluated at a rate of 25–35%. A volume of 25% of the dammed water is, therefore, lost forever for downstream countries, and an additional 40% is lost in evaporation. It is also estimated that the Ataturk Dam reservoir can lose up to 1.4 BCM per year through evaporation.

Even before the construction of the GAP, upstream projects on the Euphrates and Tigris had had a significant impact, as the Qouaiq and Afrin rivers were completely dried up in Syria in the 1940s and 1970s. Consequently, the city of Aleppo has, since then, reverted to the waters of the Euphrates for its consumption needs.

A recent study has also found that insufficient efforts were made by Turkey since the 1990s to limit the negative impacts of a project such as the Ataturk dam on the ecology of the river downstream. The first GAP Master Plan of 1989 did not include the drainage of return flows from irrigation, which induces risks of water flood and water logging for downstream riparians. It is estimated that waters reaching Syria from Turkey would ultimately carry 40% of waters polluted, with return flows to the river from irrigation carrying herbicides and pesticides *(Hinnebusch and Tür 2013: 135)*. Nevertheless, in Syrian eyes, the water issue was never just about water rights. It was always perceived as a manifestation of Turkish dominance as well as an attempt to obstruct Syria's assumption of full independence and self-sufficiency *(Ibid: 98)*.

Finally, Syria believed that Turkey gave shelter to members of the Muslim Brothers, the militant opposition force that had launched an all-out attack on the Syrian government just around the time Ocalan and other renegades began to cross into Syria *(Marcus 2007: 60)*. By the end of the 1970s, increased state repression (in Syria) had forced most of the leadership of the Muslim Brotherhood to seek exile in Jordan and, to a lesser extent, in Iraq, Saudi Arabia and Turkey. Several thousand members of the Muslim Brotherhood had (also) been forced to flee the repression they suffered in Syria *(Lefevre 2013: 115, 165)*.

International and regional configurations are important for conflicts and the parties involved. A context like the Cold War, in particular, was a determinant for conflict perpetuation between Turkey and Syria and was a constraint on transformation efforts. Cold War politics had attached the two countries to opposing camps and they viewed each other through the hostile prism of bipolarity. Owing to Turkey's membership in NATO, Syria perceived it to be looking for ways to reinforce not only its own interests but also those of the Western Bloc at the expense of Arab interests. In this sense, Turkey was perceived as a Western 'tool', a 'Trojan horse' through which Western imperialism infiltrated the Middle East and a 'colonial power' in the region. Similarly, Turkey perceived Syria's Arab nationalism and instability as an opening for Soviet influence in the region. Thus, the Syrian-Turkish border functioned as a NATO-USSR border during this period. As a result, there was no way to normalize relations within this context *(Hinnebusch and Tür 2013: 15–16)*. From a realist perspective, in the bi-polar Cold War, Turkey and Syria were on opposite sides; hence their relations were naturally hostile *(Ibid: 7)*.

But Damascus had few options when it came to pressuring Turkey, which was nearly five times the size of Syria in terms of both land mass and population. Turkey was a long-standing member of NATO and a prized U.S. ally. Turkey's border with the far-western flank of the Soviet Union ensured that in Cold War terms, at least, it could not be abandoned by the West. Assad understood that militarily, at least, he had little chance of standing against Turkey. His best chance for affecting Turkish policies was to find a group whose actions matched Syria's interests.

Looking for proxies to use in its various regional conflicts was nothing new for Damascus. In fact, Syria had long relied on foreign militant groups to promote its political and military objectives. The Palestinian organizations that Syria supported, for example, were useful because their attacks against Israel furthered Assad's desire to weaken the Jewish state. They also helped secure Assad's foothold in Lebanon and could be used against other Arab states if necessary. All this could be accomplished without Syria having to get directly involved and face the risk of direct retaliation.

Likewise, Syria was engaged in a bitter rivalry with Iraq for leadership of the region. The Iraqi Kurds, dispirited by the collapse of their fight against Baghdad in 1975, proved to be willing partners for the Syrians. Iraqi Kurdish leader Jalal Talabani initially took refuge in Syria and Talabani announced his new PUK organization (Patriotic Union of Kurdistan) in a statement issued in Damascus. Likewise, the Kurdistan Socialist Party, which broke away from Talabani's PUK in 1979, also kept an office in Syria, as did the Iraqi Communist Party, which was allied with the Kurds. Syria's generosity toward Kurdish groups from Turkey and Iraq was not indicative of how it treated its own Kurds *(Marcus 2007: 60–61)*.

Thus, there were several issues between Turkey and Syria, namely territory (Hatay), water (GAP) and security (PKK). Initially water issues were dealt with in meetings of official technical delegations, but from the 1980s to the late 1990s, trans-boundary water issues moved into the realm of high politics and negotiations by political leaders. For both parties, water was not only an economic commodity, but also a tool for development and a component of power accumulation, that is, of identity and sovereignty.

The PKK was a political card in Syria's hand to be played against Turkey over the water issue and the question of sovereignty over Hatay. Syria took advantage of Turkey's Achilles' heel, the Kurdish problem, to get the upper hand and found a position of strength through 'a proxy war' that forced Turkey to sit at the negotiation table and discuss water *(Hinnebusch and Tür 2013: 18)*.

For the Syrian government the PKK provided a "terror card" in return for Turkey's "water card" and provided a bargaining chip of a possible decision to stop the water of the Euphrates River *(Bilgin and Sarihan 2013: 103)*.

Geo-economic confrontation in the Turkish-Syrian-Iraqi triangle over water, along with the eternal geopolitical rivalry, pushed these countries to use the Kurdish factor as one of their trump cards. At the same time, since the 1980s water has become "a strategic weapon in an old dispute between neighbors over the Kurdish issue." Syria's support for the PKK was largely due to its "water interests". As you know, the construction of the Ataturk Dam was planned by Ankara since the end of the 70s. Apparently, it was no coincidence that in mid-1979, the chairman of the PKK, Abdullah Ocalan, was provided with "shelter" in the Damascus-controlled Lebanese Bekaa Valley, which is the center of concentration of various extremist groups in the region.

The militant PKK, which is gaining popularity in Turkish Kurdistan, waging an "anti-colonial" war against "Kemalism", was viewed by Syria as an obstacle to the implementation of Turkish hydro projects in Kurdistan. Some of the delay in the start of construction of this largest dam on the Euphrates can be explained, along with other reasons (for example, financial and technical) and instability in Turkish Kurdistan. Apparently, it is no coincidence that the armed struggle between the PKK and Turkey began in August 1984, i.e. only a few months after the start of the construction of the Ataturk Dam (November 1983).

It is interesting that the escalation of the conflict in Turkish Kurdistan, according to scientists from the Istanbul Foundation for the Study of the Middle East and the Balkans (in the work "Separatist Terror: The Threat to the Post-Cold War, PKK in Turkey", June 1994), coincided with the implementation of the Turkey's hydro projects. This was the case, for example, with the completion of the Birecik dam on the Euphrates *(Mosaki 2005: 125)*.

Consequently, relations between the PKK and Syria became closer in 1980 as a result of the September 12 military coup in Turkey and the subsequent crack-down on all leftist and Kurdish nationalist groups. Military repression impelled Ocalan and some of his PKK cadres to seek refuge in Syria. Because of its grievances over Hatay, the water question, and probably because of some intelligence cooperation between Turkey and Israel, Syria decided to shelter and support to PKK.' The outbreak of the war between Iran and Iraq on September 22, just ten days after the military coup in Turkey, gave further cause to Syria to aid the PKK in establishing itself as a credible challenge to the Turkish state.

That eight-year war and the power vacuum that it created in northern Iraq allowed the PKK to mount a serious challenge to the Turkish government. Headquartered in Syria and at times in Lebanon, and with bases in both countries as well as in northern Iraq and Iran, by the end of the Iran-Iraq War in 1988, the PKK had become a formidable guerrilla organization that was beginning to preoccupy Ankara's domestic and foreign policies. Damascus' support for the PKK stuck in Ankara's craw, but, short or military action, there was little that could be done. Military action on the part of Turks had its risks: It could disrupt relations with its Arab neighbors and might not be successful in destroying the PKK camps or in finding Ocalan. There was also the possibility that Syria would retaliate, perhaps in the sensitive province of Hatay.

The situation had become serious enough that even before the end of the Iraq-Iran War, Turkey and Syria thought it in their interests to sign a security protocol. In 1987 Prime Minister Turgut Ozal himself went to Damascus to conduct the negotiations.' The 1987 protocol, however, resulted only in a temporary assuaging of differences. The Syrians would not even admit that Ocalan was in the country; to cover their denial, they sent him temporarily to the Beqaa Valley in Lebanon. Soon after the protocol was signed, Syria allowed Ocalan to meet with Soviet officials in Damascus.' Syria continued to aid PKK activities right up to the Gulf War in 1991, and Turkey continued to restrict the downflow of the Euphrates *(Olson 1997: 168–193)*.

Despite Turkey's reluctance to admit a linkage between Syrian support for Kurdish separatism and the water issue, they were linked in the first diplomatic attempt to solve the issue led by Turgut Ozal, the 1987 protocols. This was a deviation from the official policy of Turkish authorities, which had heretofore kept these issues separate, even as Syria sought to link them. Linkage emerged because both security and economic protocols were signed during a single visit and the content of the security protocol was kept secret. Water conflicts elsewhere are linked with other issues, but a linkage with terrorism, as in this case, is rare. For Turkey, the linkage strategically backfired and became an obstacle to conflict transformation as Assad turned the linkage back against Turkey *(Hinnebusch and Tür 2013: 18).*

Syria's support for the PKK has become a convenient excuse for Turkey to justify its "water strategy" and to demonstrate its "water weapon". So, since the late 1980s, the Turkish government has repeatedly accused Syria of violating the Protocol to the Agreement on Security and Economic Cooperation, signed on July 17, 1987 by the Prime Minister of Syria Abd al-Rauf al-Qasem and Turkish Prime Minister Turgut Ozal during the visit of the Turkish leader to Damascus. This Protocol provided for the fight against "terrorist groups" using the territory of one of these countries against another.

Ankara threatened Damascus with reducing (or even stopping) the flow of the Euphrates River into Syria if the Syrian authorities did not stop providing assistance to the PKK. Prime Minister Turgut Ozal, speaking at a seminar organized by the Vilayet organization of the Fatherland Party in Istanbul, said: "We have no intention of doing harm to anyone. If we hold back the water (of the Euphrates River) for two and a half years, then it will not flow down, but we will lead everyone to prudence. "In October 1989, Turgut Ozal, during a visit to Urfa, hinted that Turkey could use the waters of the Euphrates to force an end to support for the PKK. According to him, "of course, water will be supplied (to Syria) as long as Syria adheres to certain conditions. However, we doubt that she adheres to these conditions." Turgut Ozal also stated that Turkey "one day" would block the Euphrates and thereby force Syria to stop supporting "Kurdish separatists", although he later stated that Turkey doesn't view the waters of the Euphrates as a means of threatening Syria.

It is noteworthy that, being the President of Turkey, Turgut Ozal spoke about the inevitability of "water wars". And, for example, Tansu Chiller in 1996, when she was vice-premier, speaking at the Foundation for Strategic Research and the Future of Peace, declared: "Water replaces oil … and the water issue is becoming the most important strategic problem that threatens peace on a global scale." In general, the cliche "XXI century will be an era of conflicts over water resources" is very popular among the Turkish intellectual and political elite.

At the same time, the Turks didn't hide the fact that water is a powerful geopolitical and geo-economic tool (weapon) in the confrontation with their southern neighbors. It was often said in Ankara: "If Arabs own oil, then we own water." At the same time, the Turks are convinced of the much greater importance of water compared to oil. "They (the Arabs) have oil, we have water. So let them drink their oil! " and "changing the direction of the Euphrates, on which Syria relies heavily, to the Ceyhan River in Western Turkey, will bring Syria to its knees."

And statements like: "It would be extremely attractive to use water as a weapon, but we did not resort to this, and the Syrians should know this,"—permanently emphasized the possibility of using "water weapons" and were in fact a direct threat. Although the Turkish authorities often "invited" Syria and Iraq to join the GAP. Apparently, Damascus decided that in general, the Southeast Anatolia Project that took place does not leave Syria any special opportunities to put pressure on Turkey *(Mosaki 2005: 126–127).*

The thrust of Turkey's response to the new post-Cold War situation was to pursue a more activist role in the Middle East. Turkey was perceived by regional actors as newly involved, even though initially this was almost completely based on security concerns regarding the region. Syria at first found itself in a strategically disadvantageous position. The disintegration of the Soviet Union and the end of bipolarity meant not only the end of Soviet aid to Syria, but also the disappearance of its room for maneuver, leaving Syria without protection. In addition, the Soviet collapse strengthened the US position in the region and the potential threat from it. Hafez al-Assad had defined the collapse of the Soviet Union as its most significant event since Syria's independence.

The initial regional repercussion of the changes in the international context was the Gulf Crisis (1990–1991). This crisis paved the way for a more active policy for Turkey and Syria in the region. Ankara and Damascus were allied temporarily in the US-led coalition against Iraq. Both countries benefitted from the alliance, although this did nothing to resolve their differences over the PKK and water issues. In fact, Turkey and Syria could not easily break out of their old framings and continued to engage in power politics against each other *(Hinnebusch and Tür 2013: 16).*

But the Gulf War provided the environment for the first significant security protocol between the two capitals. In April 1992, top Turkish officials headed by Foreign Minister Hikmet Cetin, interior Minister Ismet Sezgin and Gendarmerie Commander Esref Bitlis (subsequently killed in a suspicious helicopter crash) made their way south to negotiate with President Hafez al-Assad, Foreign Minister Faruk Sharaa and top Syrian military officials. The negotiations resulted in what Sezgin characterized as "the most important protocol ever signed with Syria." The Turks held a four-hour meeting with President Assad. The negotiations took place even as Turkish Prime Minister Suleyman Demirel threatened that Turkey might bomb PKK bases in the Beqaa.

The security agreement of April 1992 is worthy of detailed examination: 1) both countries would cooperate against terrorism, "including its international form," and prevent terrorists from crossing from one country to the other; 2) neither country would give permission to any organization outlawed by the other to organize, train or make propaganda, and any captured member of an outlawed organization would be returned; 3) both would exchange information regarding outlawed organizations; 4) both would undertake measures to prevent infiltration and smuggling; 5) both would take measures to prevent "unnecessary" armed incidents on their borders. In order to ensure this cooperation, security officials would meet every three months. The final article of the agreement was the most important: "The Turks stated their objections in detail regarding PKK terrorist activities, and the Syrians declared the PKK an outlawed organization in Syria and that any members of the PKK apprehended would be delivered to the respective judicial [Syrian] authorities." Upon the signing of the agreement, Turkish Defense Minister Nevzat Ayaz said that if Syria abided by the agreement there would be "no need to bomb the Beqaa."

The April 1992 security agreement defused the tension between the two countries (Syria closed the Helwe camp) but was short-lived. After a brief respite, PKK activities emanating from Syria resumed with attacks on targets in Turkey itself. Damascus could not give up the Kurdish card, and Ankara continued to play the water card. The Turks emphasized they would not pursue earnest negotiations on the water question until Syria assured them that they would no longer support PKK activities or shelter Abdullah Ocalan.

On November 19–20, 1993 Major General Adnan Badr al-Hasan, Syria's chief of security at the Ministry of Interior, stated that Syria would not be a thoroughfare for "those who are against Turkey's interest." A few days later Nasir Kaddur, Syrian minister of state for security, said in a television interview referring to the security protocol that Syria had "begun to ban the PKK on President Hafez al-Assad's orders." Kaddur added that PKK leader Abdullah Ocalan and other "terrorists" would not be allowed to use Syrian territory or pass through Syria for operations against Turkey. The security chief noted that some PKK members had already been arrested. He further implied that henceforth Ocalan would be unwelcome in Syria. This was the first time that a high-ranking Syrian official had done so and marked a significant foreign policy departure for Syria, which had supported the PKK since it gave sanctuary to Ocalan in 1979.

On August 23, Syria participated in a foreign-minister-level summit conference with Iran and Turkey in which the Kurdish question figured prominently (the planned election in 1995 in northern Iraq). The summit made it clear there is a direct connection between the Kurdish question and the distribution of the Euphrates' water. The Turks emphasized they would not pursue earnest negotiations on the water question until Syria assured them that they would no longer support PKK activities or shelter Abdullah Ocalan. Until agreement was reached, Ankara stressed that it would be difficult to move forward on other problems such as the distribution of the Orontes River, which flows through Syria before entering Turkey's Hatay province. The Turks want an agreement that will prohibit the Syrians from severely restricting the Orontes's flow before it enters Hatay.

In late 1994 and early 1995 relations between Turkey and Syria took a brief upswing. On December 5, Yalim Erez, president of Turkey's Chamber of Commerce and Commodities Market and a close adviser of Prime Minister Tansu Ciller, led a 100-person delegation to Damascus to engage in trade discussions. Syrian Foreign Minister Muhammad Imadi made it clear that Syria was interested in improving bade relations especially if Syria's $300-million trade deficit with Turkey could be reduced, and he suggested that one way to reduce the trade deficit would be for Turkey to import phosphates from Syria rather than from Tunisia. In early February 1995, Prime Minister Ciller announced that Turkey was ready to sign a "water protocol" with Syria guaranteeing a flow of at least 500 MCM per second if Damascus would abandon its "protection of PKK terrorists."

By mid-summer, however, reports that the PKK was attempting to establish an organizational structure in Hatay, once again soured what seemed to be improving relations. The story of the PKK presence in Hatay first broke in the Turkish press on September 17, 1995. Hurriyet reported on that date that Abdullah Ocalan proclaimed he "would turn Hatay into Botan." Botan refers to the area south of Lake Van, extending into areas in northern Iraq in which bloody battles have occurred during the past decade between the PKK and the Turkish armed forces. Hatay too, said Ocalan, "must be turned into a bloody lake." According to Hurriyet, the PKK first attempted to infiltrate the Adana, Mersin and Hatay regions in the early 1990s but were successful in winning over only a few recruits in the hinterlands of Adana and Mersin. By the early 1990s these cities were already swelled with Kurds fleeing the scorched-earth policies of the Turkish armed forces in the southeast. But the PKK had tough sledding in Hatay because of the tight security blanket thrown over the entire region by Turkish security. In spite of setbacks, the PKK persisted in trying to establish itself in the region, as Hatay shares a border with Syria where the PKK have sanctuary. The PKK operatives tried to ensconce themselves along the road from Lataqiya in Syria to Samandag, a village in the Amanus mountains in Hatay. This is a road used heavily by smugglers and drug traffickers which the PKK hoped to exploit to their advantage.

The Hurriyet account emphasized that the PKK hoped to exploit the religious and ethnic diversity of Hatay. One of the first operations of the PKK was to attack the Sunni-Turkomen villages. When the Turkish government then armed the Turkomen, the PKK countered with propaganda that the state was arming Sunnis against Alevi-Arab, Turk and Kurd.

When, again according to Hurriyet, the PKK found themselves unable to advantageously exploit the religious and ethnic differences, they attempted to ingratiate themselves with the local population by purchasing food provisions at prices substantially higher than the market price. All transactions were carried out in German marks. Prices spiked: one egg sold for two DM (65,000 Turkish lira); a 50-kilo sack of flour sold for 1,000 DM (33 million lira). By their largess, the PKK hoped to establish support and receive protection from the indigenous population. In addition to exploiting the different religious and ethnic groups in Hatay, the PKK, alleged Hurriyet, also tried to take advantage of the traditionally strong leftist sentiments in Hatay by proclaiming themselves a Marxist organization. They had abandoned this strategy in the southeast to portray themselves as a moderate leftist-Islamist organization to take advantage of the Islamist upsurge of the last decade.

It indicates the PKK's intention to expand its guerrilla war from the southeast to the shores of the Mediterranean with hundreds of thousands of Kurdish refugees fleeing from ethnic cleansing. An increase in guerrilla warfare in Hatay would suggest that the PKK was bold enough or felt sufficiently compelled, whether from perceived weakness or strength, to take its war against Ankara out of the predominately Kurdish southeast region. The choice of Hatay is as significant as it is sensitive. The attempt of the PKK to enlist the minority Alevi/Alawite, Arab, and economically marginalized population against the dominant Sunni and Turkish population is bound to create more friction between the two capitals. Reports in summer 1995 of the PKK's attempts to move into Hatay further iced relations between the two countries.

It is easy to understand Turkish suspicions that Damascus is behind the PKK's attempts to establish bases in Hatay. The PKK's movement into that province was bound to drive relations between the two countries to another nadir. It would further confirm Ankara's position that Damascus supports the PKK and the Kurdish nationalist movement as instruments to weaken politically, militarily and diplomatically its big northern neighbor *(Olson 1997: 168–193)*.

When the PKK increased its Hatay operations, this situation was discussed in Turkey's National Security Council; the governor of Hatay presented a report in which he asserted that Syria treated Hatay as though it were its own, and that Damascus had instigated PKK activities against Turkmens in Hatay. He charged that Syria was encouraging ethnic Arabs to buy land, and that this was evidence of a long-range Syrian strategic plan to regain the region. In response, Turkey dispatched a note verbale to the Syrian embassy in Ankara on January 23, 1996.

This note reiterated the previous demands of Turkey and referred to Article 51 of the UN Charter, which underscores 'the inherent right of individual or collective self-defense if an armed attack occurs against a member of the UN'. Assad did not even respond to the note verbale *(Hinnebusch and Tür 2013: 20).*

At the end of 1995, Syria's sheltering of Ocalan and support for the PKK—especially the move into Hatay—in addition to the water problem remained the principal reasons for the sour state of relations between the two countries. The differences over the water issue that flared near the end of December, occupied the limelight in early 1996. The six GCC countries—Saudi Arabia, Bahrain, Kuwait, Oman, Qatar, the United Arab Emirates—and Egypt meeting in Damascus issued the Damascus Declaration, which demanded a "just agreement" for distributing the Euphrates waters. The declaration strongly criticized Ankara's intention to build another dam, this one at Birecik on the Turkish-Syrian border, as part of the GAP project and complained that the water coming from Turkey was heavily polluted." Ankara denied the charges and called for three-way talks with Syria and Iraq to attempt to resolve the quarrel. Deniz Baykal, Turkey's foreign minister stated bluntly that if Syria did not abandon its policy of serving as the headquarters of a terrorist organization, it could not expect any increase in the downflow of the Euphrates. Leading editorials were quick to point out that the annual flow of the Orontes River was estimated to be 1.2 BCM, of which only 120 MCM reached Turkey at its border with Syria in Hatay and that farmers had only that amount to use for irrigation along the river's 88-km path before it emptied into the Mediterranean. This meant, said the editorialists, only 10% of the Orontes's water was available for use by Turkey, and this amount was expected to fall to 25 MCM, or less than 2%, when Syria completed the building of two dams (Zayzun and Qastun) on the river. Furthermore, editorials claimed that Turkey used only 25 BCM of Euphrates and Tigris water for itself, allowing 50 BCM to downflow to Syria and Iraq. The Turks alleged further that the water loss from the Tabqa dam was four times greater than from the Ataturk dam, which was four times larger.

At the end of January, Ankara demanded that Syria extradite Abdullah Ocalan. While Turkey had previously made clear its unhappiness with Damascus' sheltering of the PKK leader, this marked the first time that it publicly announced its demand. Ertugrul Ozkok, the leading editorialist for the daily Hurriyet, known to be close to government, military and intelligence officials, claimed that the demand was made as it was the only alternative to cutting relations with the Assad regime. Ozkok added that another reason for the demarches was the progress of the peace talks between Syria and Israel. Ankara stated bluntly that if Ocalan was not extradited to Turkey, it would do everything in its power (apparently in league with Washington) to ensure that Syria would not be removed from the list of "countries sponsoring terrorism." If the Ocalan problem was not solved, it would seek to undermine the talks between Syria and Israel and any US-Syria rapprochement resulting from the talks.

According to Ozkok, if Damascus responded that the PKK leader was not in Syria, Ankara would provide evidence that he was; if Damascus said it would not deliver him, then Ankara would attempt to use its influence to sabotage the peace talks. Facing such alternatives, Damascus did nothing.

On February 21, a week after Ozkok's editorial, Mehmet Ali Birand, a respected journalist, reported that Syrian officials suspected that even if they handed Ocalan over, Turkey would not increase the downflow of the Euphrates, at least not to the rate Syria says it needs for irrigation and hydroelectric purposes. Thus, the two countries were at an impasse. Each believed that the state and its government would be weakened if it gave up its strongest cards without iron-clad agreements to protect its real concerns: water, and the increasingly close relations between Turkey and Israel in the case of Damascus and the desire to destroy the PKK on the part of Ankara.

The impasse between the two capitals regarding the PKK's and Ocalan's presence in Syria seems to have been a major factor in Ankara's announcement on February 24 that it had signed a "Military Education and Cooperation Agreement" with Israel. The agreement was signed in Jerusalem by Cevik Bir, the second ranking official of the general staff of the Turkish armed forces and a former commander of the U.N. forces in Somalia.

Early discussions of the content and import of the military agreement emphasized that it is Turkey's policy to achieve "balance' in its relations between Israel and the Arab countries. Leading editorialists in the Turkish press claimed that the Arab summit in Damascus in December 1995 and Arab criticism of Turkey's water policies played a role in Turkey's signing of the agreement. Ankara was chagrined that its Gulf War allies would proffer such biting criticism, especially Saudi Arabia and Egypt. Some commentators interpreted the Damascus summit as the beginning of a change of policy pursued since the Gulf War on the part of some Arab states.

There was also comment that the agreement was in "retaliation" for the military agreement between Syria and Greece that had been signed in 1995, an agreement that purportedly allowed Greek aircraft the use of Syrian airbases in case of conflict with Turkey. Subsequent reports that Israeli military personnel would help train Turkish military and intelligence units along the border with

Syria, Iraq and Iran fueled speculation that one of the main aims of the agreement was to increase Turkish effectiveness against the PKK camps in these three countries.

In late December 1996, Cemil Bayik, ARGK commander and right-hand man of Abdullah Ocalan, in an interview with well-known journalist Sheri Laizer charged that the PKK is one of the main targets of the Israel-Turkey military agreements. He charged that Israel "is supplying weaponry and high-tech security supplies for the border." (Bayik was apparently referring to the Turkey-Iraq border). Israel's aid, said the ARGK commander, includes "the laying of land mines, rolled barbed wire and trip wires that illuminate the border." Israel may also have had advisers in Ishikveren, a village close to the border on the Turkish side, where mine-laying operations took place. Bayik also claimed that Israeli officers played a planning role and provided technological advice during Turkey's March 1995 incursion into northern Iraq.

There were obviously many geo-strategic and geopolitical reasons for Turkey and Israel to sign such a military pact, not least of which was the fact that it was supported by the United States and Europe. These two thereby ensured their control over &e resources of the Gulf and Israel's dominance over the Levant. The agreement also contributes to U.S. efforts to contain the Iranian challenge in the Gulf and disturb Iranian ties with Syria and with Hizbollah in south Lebanon.

One of the major objectives of Turkey in increasing its military cooperation with Israel was obviously to put more pressure on Syria to stop supporting the PKK and to stop sheltering Abdullah Ocalan. The agreement illustrates Ankara's goal of destroying the PKK and its leaders at any cost. Since the end of the Gulf War, Ankara's war against the Kurds, estimated to be costing $6 to $8 billion a year, was limiting Turkish foreign policies in the Balkans, Central Asia and the Middle East, as well as its diplomacy with Russia and the European Union." The military agreement with Israel seemed to be another attempt by Ankara to stop the hemorrhage.

Another reason for Israel to join Turkey in a closer geostrategic posture is its long-term interest in obtaining further access to its water resources. The headwaters of the Euphrates and Tigris rivers are both in heavily populated Kurdish areas of Turkey. Ironically, too, other sources of water for Israel and its Palestinian and Arab partners, the Seyhan and Ceyhan rivers, flow through the Cilician plain, which, though outside Turkish Kurdistan, became more heavily populated with Kurds in the 1980s and 1990s, a result of the ethnic cleansing carried out by the Turkish government in efforts to destroy the PKK resistance. Adana, the largest city of the region, with a population of some 2 million, through which the Seyhan runs, may now have a population that is nearly half Kurdish. This is a region through which run two oil pipelines emanating from Iraqi Kurdistan and terminating at Yumurtalik on the Mediterranean Sea. The two oil pipelines and the four rivers symbolize the confluence of two of the world's most prized commodities: oil for the West and Japan and potential water for Israel and its new Arab partners.

The increased strength, growth and success of the Kurdish nationalist movement in Turkey, especially the PKK, presents obstacles to Israel and some of its Arab partners to gaining access to this water. This may be why Israel decided to support, more publicly than before, Turkey's war against the PKK. Israel may see the agreement as a stone that could kill two birds: Assad and Ocalan. By tightening the pincers on Assad, Ankara and Tel Aviv hope to compel him to make Ocalan leave Syria. Ocalan's flight from Syria or his death would weaken the PKK and the dominant role it plays in the Kurdish nationalist movement in Turkey, northern Iraq and Syria. If Israel could aid Turkey in achieving this goal, Ankara would undoubtedly be most obliging with its water when conditions are favorable for a downward flow. The fact that even Erbakan's Islamist-led government has agreed to continue Turkey's military and security agreements with Israel is strong evidence of this policy.

President Suleyman Demirel stated that Turkey had submitted testimony to the December 1996 Damascus summit summit that Syria was "a state that gives support to terrorism" and that under no circumstances would Turkey enter negotiations with Syria on the 'basis of "more water for no terrorism." Furthermore, Turkey would not give concessions on water to facilitate negotiations between Israel and Syria." In response, Syrian Foreign Minister Faruk Sharaa refused to categorize the PKK as a terrorist organization, but rather called it an "outlawed" organization."

Prime Minister Mesut Yilmaz underscored this tension during a visit to Hatay to celebrate the anniversary of the creation of the province in 1939. After accusing Syria of supporting "bandits" who wanted to fragment Turkey, Yilmaz said there was no way, given the situation, that Turkey would increase the downflow of the Euphrates. He stated, "We Turks are a patient people, but when our patience runs out, our response is harsh *(Olson 1997: 168–193).*

Foreign Minister Deniz Baykal reflected prevailing Turkish opinion when he said: 'Some circles may claim that they need additional water to wash the blood of terrorism from their hands' *(Hinnebusch and Tür 2013: 19).*

Arguably the most important change shaping foreign and security policy during the 1990s was the increased role of the Turkish military. Particularly since the mid-1990s, the military institution assumed a prominent role in foreign policy, especially on the PKK issue, and was instrumental in applying pressure on the government to stand firm on Syria. The increase in the military's active role was a result of its disappointment at the perceived failure of the Foreign Ministry to launch an effective international campaign against Syria. In addition, President Demirel had moved to cement his position at the forefront of this issue, sending an overt warning to Damascus in his opening speech to the National Assembly on October 1, 1998 that Turkey's patience was running out. Prime Minister Mesut Yilmaz requested parliamentary consent for war and received approval from all political parties for a declaration calling on Syria to cut its support for the PKK or be ready to bear the consequences. This tough stance won support from the military, media and the public at large, and was backed up by the deployment of land and air forces along the border.

The result was that high-ranking Turkish military and civilian officials issued a strong verbal warning to the effect that Turkey was running out of patience with Syria's support for the PKK. Chief of the General Staff, Huseyin Kivrikoglu, reported that Turkey was engaged in an "undeclared war" with Syria. Never before had Ankara's threats been made so insistently, repeatedly and explicitly over such a short period of time. As a result, the Turkish leadership's unprecedented language combined with a military build-up and exercises near the border led Syria to believe Turkish threats were credible *(Hinnebusch and Tür 2013: 23–24).*

A turning point in Turkish-Syrian relations came in 1998 in an unexpected fashion. Having failed to convince the Syrians that they should stop supporting a terrorist movement, Turkey decided that it might consider military action. The commander of the Turkish Third Army responsible for the defense of the Southern border issued an ultimatum that unless Syria stopped hosting the leadership of the PKK within two days, military action would follow. Earlier, the Syrians had denied that they were doing anything of the sort even after Turkish authorities had provided them with the address and the telephone numbers of the PKK headquarters in Damascus. Recognizing that the two countries were on the verge of war, the Hafez al-Assad Government felt obliged to close down the PKK headquarters in Damascus and sent its leader away. Since that time, relations have improved including questions concerning water. The improvement process was initiated by a meeting of the officials of the two governments in Adana on October 20, 1998 and has continued smoothly since that time *(Kibaroglu, Aysegul, Scheumann, Waltina, Kramer, Annika 2011: 185–191).*

According to the accord, Syria would no longer permit PKK activities, both countries would cooperate to combat terrorism, and most importantly, Turkey acquired the right to establish a monitoring system to enhance the effectiveness of security measures. According to Turkish President Suleyman Demirel this was

Turkey's greatest diplomatic success in 25 years. From the Syrian perspective, Turkey gave nothing in return for Syrian concessions. There was no discussion on the water issue, nor did Turkey signal any willingness to engage with the Hatay issue. The crisis ended because of the Syrian government's capitulation. Since in the short-term, Syria gained nothing from the Adana agreement, it was not balanced *(Hinnebusch and Tür 2013: 14).*

Looking at power relations in terms of material capabilities, Turkey appeared at least three times more powerful than Syria during the 1990s, according to the Composite Index of National Capabilities. After the mid-1990s, however, the military balance began to favor Turkey more dramatically than ever. Its economy had been growing steadily and Ankara was earmarking some of that increasing prosperity toward arms procurement. By contrast, Syria, hurt by the demise of the Soviet Union, from which it used to receive advanced weaponry, did little to upgrade its inventory in the 1990s. Turkish self-assurance also increased *(Ibid: 17).*

A hurting stalemate is seen in conflict resolution theory as a pre-condition to resolve conflicts. However, while a stalemate existed in that neither Turkey nor Syria was prevailing or achieving its goals, the 'hurt' was asymmetric, disproportionately suffered by Turkey. For Turkey, relations with Syria became unsustainable in the 1990s as it experienced rising physical and political costs. In physical terms, the death toll due to PKK activities was increasing. There had been about 30,000 casualties by the end of the 1990s. The economy was also worsening because of the allocation of resources to the fight. Military expenditures alone cost $6–9 billion annually. These costs led Turkey to a stalemate of desperation, with no foreseeable successful end in sight, despite great sacrifices. Political costs of the conflict can be identified at both the domestic and international levels. At the domestic level, Turkish statehood was being tested through the PKK struggle. At the international level, Turkey was concerned with the PKK's alleged growing political strength in Europe *(Ibid: 19).*

In contrast with Turkey, for Syria, the status quo was bearable. Although Assad considered Syria to be at the mercy of Turkey's control of the Euphrates waters, Syria suffered no injuries comparable to Turkey's. Through the PKK, Syria was gradually gaining at Turkey's expense, and was thus more comfortable with the status quo. As such, Turkey would have to act to make the hurt more symmetrical if there was to be a resolution satisfactory to its interests. Coercive diplomacy would be needed to bring the situation to ripeness.

Assad's lack of motivation to continue to protect the PKK can be interpreted as the most significant determinant of Syria's decision to back down in the crisis. He arguably intended to leave the country to his heir, Bashar, in as stable a condition as possible, and was prepared to sacrifice his strategic instrument, the PKK, to avoid an armed clash with Turkey.

Negotiations between Turkey and Syria in 1998 began in a tense atmosphere, as the Turkish side approached the process from a position of power. Turkey successfully forced the de-linkage of the PKK and water issues which had prevented it from previously achieving a satisfactory resolution. Yet some have argued that Turkish decision-makers were careful not to make insurmountable demands, instead focusing on clear, reasonable and limited proposals that were acceptable to Syria. Ankara asked Damascus to halt its support for the PKK and stop hosting its leader, as well as to accept the establishment of a monitoring mechanism to ensure that the terms of agreement were being implemented. Despite other issues that had strained bilateral relations, Turkey limited its demands to the PKK issue in hopes of creating goodwill between the two sides, and took care to avoid humiliating the Syrian side. Turkey was also sensitive to the need not to deliberately accuse the Syrian leadership of support for terrorism. Moreover, throughout the crisis, Ankara accompanied its threats with inducements, underscoring its determination to develop relations with Damascus in the event of its compliance. From the beginning of the crisis, in order to provoke a positive response, Turkish leaders reminded Syria that as soon as it stopped supporting the PKK, Turkey was prepared to open a new chapter of improved ties. Assad was willing to accept these demands because the PKK was a mere bargaining card rather than a vital interest *(Ibid: 25–26).*

Syria seems to finally realize that Europe and the United States do not want the destabilization or weakening of Turkey as a result of Syrian support for the PKK. When Syria, other Arab states, the Palestinians and Israel finalize their peace negotiations, Syria may well have a role to play in the regional water-sharing schemes that now abound. Any pipeline carrying water from the upper reaches of the Euphrates and the Ceyhan and Seyhan rivers are located in south-central Turkey would have to traverse Syrian territory. Syria will want to extract as much diplomatic, political and economic leverage as possible from this potentiality *(Olson 1997: 168–193).*

Typically, the crises of 1990, 1993 and 1996 were activated by one of two factors—either a significant reduction of water from the Turkish side, or a refusal to reconvene the negotiations—and then followed by an intensification of Syria's support of the Kurds. At the time of the filling of the Ataturk reservoir in January 1990, the impact on Syria became burdensome, and the Turkish Minister of Foreign Affairs agreed to again institute the 500 MCM minimum quota upon the signing of the 1992 Security Protocol with Syria in which both countries committed to fight terrorism (Syrian Arab Republic 2 August 1992). Yet, in 1993, the flows were again significantly reduced, and this trend continued and culminated with the launch of the Birecik Dam on the Euphrates, as well as the opening of the Sanliurfa canals in 1994–1995; in 1996, Turkey accused Syria of supporting the PKK, and refused to further engage in water negotiations *(Hinnebusch and Tür 2013: 140).*

Having resolved the PKK issue, Turkey had no other pressing problem with Syria. The dispute over water distribution was transformed into a mere technical matter and Damascus was willing to suppress its concerns over the Turkish-Israeli military agreement. The border dispute was also consigned to benign neglect. The key bones of contention had hence been removed and the way for cooperation was paved *(Ibid: 29).*

Nevertheless, only during periods of heightened Syrian-Turkish tension did Syria ever come close to what resembles demands for return of Hatay. This was the case during UAR period (1958–1961) when Syria and Egypt merged into one in the height of Syrian-Turkish Cold War tensions. The National Union Party, the only political party allowed to function in the UAR, in July 1960 adopted a resolution demanding the return of the area. Apart from these periods of heightened tension, Syria did not pay much attention to Hatay.

A reading of the speeches and interviews given by Hafez al-Assad further shows that Hatay was a non-topic during his reign. The area was not mentioned even once, not even when the president was asked about Syrian-Turkish relations in interviews on the eve of the 1998 crisis. During the late 1980s and 1990s there were occasional claims of Hatay being Syrian territory, although none of them stemmed directly from the Syrian government *(Ibid: 115–116).*

Like his father before him, Bashar al-Assad had not, by June 2012, brought up Hatay in any of his speeches *(Ibid: 120).* As mentioned earlier, Hatay has remained part of Syrian maps since the early 1950s and by June 2012, the vast majority of official Syrian maps continued to include the area. With regard to the Golan Heights, occupied by Israel in 1967, Syria has never ceased to actively demand its return and condemn the Israeli 1981 annexation *(Ibid: 121).*

Thus, Turkish-Syrian relations are a classic example of the fact that water problems usually arise between neighboring countries that do not have mutual trust and have historical problems. As a result, both countries found themselves in a asymmetrical hurting stalemate, as they thought that if each of them made a concession in its field (for example, Turkey in the water issue and Syria in the PKK issue), it would be worse for them, and a new problem would appear. For instance, Syria will start raising the issue of Alexandretta and Turkey the issue of distributing the waters of the Orontes River.

The above shows that though there were a number of problems between Syria and Turkey, but Syria decided to support the PKK primarily because of the Turkish-initiated hydroelectric projects in the Euphrates Basin.

Over two decades, Turkey made many attempts to persuade the Syrian government to stop giving sanctuary to the PKK and its leader. The situation was resolved only at the end of the 20th century (with the expulsion of Ocalan from Syria). Regional realignments and developments (third-party actors, non-State actors) played a big role in the solution. Yes, Syria was forced to deport Ocalan, but in our opinion, it cannot be described as a complete victory of the Turkish side. The next sub-chapters of Chapter 5 will be related to this topic, in which we will emphasize Hafez Assad's crucial role in strengthening the PKK and describe the extent of economic damage caused to Turkey by Hafez Assad through the PKK.

7.4 The Role of Hafez Al-Assad

Despite Syria's centrality, its Pan-Syrian claims lay mostly dormant for fifty years, from the French conquest in 1920 to the coup by Hafez al-Assad in 1970. During the first half of that period, French mandatory rule hindered Damascus from the serious pursuit of Greater Syria, while internal instability blocked it during the second half. Only in the mid-1970s did a Greater Syria with its capital in Damascus once again become a realistic goal *(Pipes 1990: 115)*.

Hafez al-Assad became ruler of Syria at the age of forty, in 1970, and turned the most unstable country of the Middle East into a police state (twenty-one changes of government occurred in the twenty-four years between 1946 and 1970 (including three in one year and a regime which lasted only several days)) *(Ibid: 152)*. Then it reopened the way to pursue the long-dormant goal of a united Syria *(Ibid: 100)*.

On the one hand, Assad came to power in 1970 and imposed, for the first time since independence in 1946, a strong, durable, and stable government on Syria. On the other hand, neighboring states turned inward. Lebanon experienced a complete break-down of order; Egypt signed a peace treaty with Israel and dropped out of the inter-Arab arena; Iraq became wholly consumed by war with Iran; and the oil-exporting countries lost power as their revenues declined. Internal conflicts plagued the PLO. As Assad's rivals became preoccupied with other matters, the field opened to Syrian aggrandizement. Political developments made Pan-Syrianism an operational ideology *(Ibid: 149)*.

The government of Hafez al-Assad adopted Pan-Syrian ideas and made them Syrian state policy. Circumstantial evidence strongly indicates that the Syrian government has since 1974 made Greater Syria the centerpiece of its foreign policy. Pan-Syrianism—the intention to piece together a Greater Syrian nation. The Syrian rulers remembered that until 1920, "Syria" referred to a region much larger than the Syrian Arab Republic of today, a region that stretched from the borders of Anatolia to those of Egypt, from the edge of Iraq to the Mediterranean Sea. This larger land, known since 1920 as Greater Syria, was what they dream of reclaiming. They profounded unwillingness to accept the actual size and shape of the country they administer *(Ibid: 3–5)*.

Historically, the name Syria refers to a region far larger than the one presently contained by the state called Syria. At minimum, that Syria includes an irregular rectangle bounded by the Mediterranean Sea in the west, the Taurus and Anti-Taurus Mountains in the north, and the Syrian, Arabian, and Sinai deserts in the east and south. In terms of today's political units, historic Syria comprises all of four states—Syria, Jordan, Israel, and Lebanon—as well as the West Bank, the Gaza Strip, and substantial portions of southeastern Turkey *(Ibid: 14)*.

Personally, Assad was drawn to the Greater Syria goal. By making Greater Syria a centerpiece of his policy, he achieved more to make it a reality than any other ruler of the twentieth century *(Ibid: V)*, any leader since Faysal in 1920 *(Ibid: 148)*. Assad also occasionally reminded of the great Umayyad state [when Damascus ruled a vast empire from India to Spain] *(Ibid: 132–133)*.

It is also to underline that Hafez al-Assad had been in power for more than a quarter of a century, longer than any of his predecessors in modern Syria and indeed longer than any of his Damascus-based Arab predecessors as ruler of Syria since Mu'awiyah Ibn Abi Sufyan, the famous founder, in 661, of the Syrian-based Umayyad dynasty of caliphs *(van Dam 1996: Xii)*. Hafez al-Assad also on numerous publicly performed prayers in, mostly Sunni, mosques including the famous Umayyad Mosque in Damascus *(Ibid: 142)*.

Returning to the issue of supporting the PKK in Assad, we would like to note that we agree with Murat Yetkin's assertions that the Kurdish question existed before the creation of the PKK, and the PKK is an undesirable child of the Kurdish question in Turkey *(Yetkin 2004: 19)*. We also agree with the assertion that events in other parts of the Middle East, specifically the Iran-Iraq and the Gulf wars, provided the PKK with significant political and military room to maneuver *(Barkey and Fuller 1998: 21)*.

On the other hand, we think that without Hafez Assad's support, PKK would not have achieved such success, it would not even have turned into a guerrilla organization and the world today would hardly have heard about the PKK and its leader Abdullah Ocalan. It would undoubtedly have been the usual Kurdish structure that would have gone down in history without any serious success.

There were at least 12 Kurdish separatist groups in Turkey with Marxist-Lenmist sympathies which were active in the 1970s. The PKK would become the most radical and influential *(Kirisci and Winrow 1997: 110).*

To substantiate this, we have conditionally divided Assad's support for the PKK into several categories.

7.4.1 Physical Rescue of Ocalan and Kurdish Militants (PKK)

The origins of the PKK may be traced to a meeting in 1977 in Diyarbekir organized by Abdullah Ocalan, who would become the PKK leader. At this meeting he and his immediate supporters adopted a document titled 'The Path of the Kurdish Revolution'. This depicted the Kurdish-populated areas of Turkey as a colony and argued that the Kurdish feudalists and bourgeoisie had chosen to collaborate with the Turkish ruling classes to exploit the Kurdish peasantry and working class. According to the document, a radical revolution was required to establish an independent, Marxist-Leninist Kurdistan where the peasantry and proletariat could enjoy true independence. This document subsequently became the programme of the PKK after its establishment in November 1978. The PKK's early activities were limited to small-scale armed operations and to the recruitment of young sympathizers in a small area around Siverek, the hometown of Ocalan.

Van Bruinessen has pointed out that by the end of the 1970s the activities of Kurdish nationalist groups were 'changing the self-perception of a considerable section of the Kurds. People who had long called themselves Turks started re-defining themselves as Kurds.' This development, together with the economic chaos, political instability and violence that characterized the late 1970s in Turkey, paved the way for the military intervention in September 1980. The 1980 military intervention in Turkey interrupted the activities of the PKK, forcing its leadership to flee abroad *(Ibid: 110).*

After the military coup of September 12, 1980, around 1790 PKK supporters were also arrested and imprisoned. However, Ocalan, who is the head of the organization, and the staff, including senior executives, managed to escape by leaving the country before the coup *(Akbas 2018: 13).*

While the chaotic situation in Turkey that preceded the 1980 coup allowed the PKK and many other groups to take root, the 1980 coup marked a turning point and the beginning of difficult times for subversive social movements. The military junta that took control of Turkey in 1980 invoked martial law throughout the country, and most of the predominantly Kurdish provinces in 1987 were placed under "emergency rule" for the next decade. The new military government in Ankara lashed out at all suspected subversives, including the young PKK: "By 1981, more than 2,000 alleged PKK members were in prison, while 447 were put on mass trial and accused of forming 'armed gangs' to 'annex' southeastern Turkey." Despite its small size in the late 1970s, the PKK received the heaviest of the blows directed at Kurdish separatist organizations, having the largest number of militants arrested *(Romano 2006: 78–79)*.

After the military coup most radical organizations of Turkey were scrambling to get reestablished, the bulk of their cadre in prison, their surviving leadership unsure of what to do next. The promises of liberation of both Turkish and Kurdish leftists had ended in disaster, with military rule and repression much worse than any of them had ever experienced. Dev-Yol, which before 1980 was the largest militant leftist group in Turkey, had been decimated by the coup. Most of its members were in prison, others had died in detention or were killed trying to flee. "Everyone was in shock," Metin Kahraman, a musician sympathetic to the left, said 25 years later. "I was crushed, because the revolution was going to happen soon. When 12 September happened, maybe for one, two years, in isolated places there was some resistance. But it was clear these wouldn't accomplish anything. Before everything else, exhaustion developed."

Ocalan was not surprised at the swift collapse of so many once-popular groups. In his mind, at least, this merely confirmed his leadership capabilities. As he explained a few years later, he saw his decision to flee Turkey in the summer of 1979 (Ocalan fleed across the border into Syria) as a fortuitous one, allowing him to save not just himself, but his organization, and giving him a head start when it came to competing with the Turkish revolutionary movement after the 1980 coup in Turkey. "The others could only get out two years after me, after they had already lost their organization," he later said. "Because I got out before Sept. 12, I could both save hundreds of my comrades and get them trained." *(Marcus 2007: 62)*.

In the summer of 1980, just a few months before the military coup, Ocalan sent word to the militants that they should try to get out of Turkey and join him in Syria *(Ibid: 49)*. Ocalan had always seen himself as leading the Kurdish national movement in Turkey and after that he was based in Damascus, he had time to survey what remained of the competition *(Ibid: 61–62)*. Like those who fled after the coup, Ocalan arrived on foot, crossing the lightly guarded (Turkey-Syria) border with the help of a local smuggler. His immediate goal was to save himself; his long-term plan was to arrange for PKK fighters to get training from the Palestinian militant groups in Syria and Lebanon. The Palestinians were well known for assisting foreign revolutionaries, including some Turkish leftists for brief periods in the early 1970s. But Ocalan had few, if any, contacts in Syria, and he failed to secure an introduction to the Palestinian factions that kept political bureaus in the Syrian capital *(Ibid: 54).*

In our opinion, in the late 1970s (before the 1980 coup), Ocalan was in a hopeless situation, as evidenced by at least two important factors. a) Why did he decide to flee exactly to Syria? b) Why did he decide to stay in Syria after that?

The question of whether or not to remain in Syria, an authoritarian-ruled country that repressed its own Kurds, frequently was discussed. "We debated whether we should allow ourselves to be under Syrian control," said a former member named Kamuran, who lived in France. "Because apart from the Turkish military regime, Turkey was a much better state than Syria. Syria was a dictatorship, or worse, a tyranny."

Some groups looked for alternatives to Syria, either because they did not like the idea of relying on Damascus or, more commonly, because they wanted to base their forces in Kurdistan itself, be it the Turkish or Iraqi part. But regardless of whether or not they wanted to work out of Syria, almost every group kept representatives in the capital and the top people came there for meetings. "There was a contradiction [in relying on Syria], but there were a lot of contradictions in the Middle East," noted former PKK militant Ibrahim Aydin.

Syria's support for Kurdish groups was, at least initially, more tacit than overt. In practice this meant that Damascus did not block the flow of illegal refugees from Turkey, did not make trouble for Kurdish militants setting up house in Syria, and did not impede traffic back and forth to Lebanon. It was not, however, that Syria was uninterested in the new arrivals. For starters, Syria had its own domestic Kurdish population to worry about and wanted to ensure that Syrian Kurds were not encouraged to stand against the state. The PKK was well aware of the limits, despite its official rhetoric that saw an independent Kurdistan stretching over part of Syria. "It was always clear we wouldn't take any action that was against Syria," said former militant Selahattin Celik. "There was no decision. We just knew that we couldn't do anything proper... that's it." *(Ibid: 58–59).* "If Syria wanted to, could it stop you?" asked Turkish journalist Mehmet Ali Birand in 1988, in what was the first Turkish interview with the PKK leader. "Certainly," replied Ocalan. "With a special order it could stop us." *(Ibid: 100).*

Syria's generosity toward Kurdish groups from Turkey and Iraq was not indicative of how it treated its own Kurds. Damascus had always been afraid that

Syrian Kurds might demand independence or otherwise threaten the regime's stability. In 1950, the Constitution was adopted, which proclaimed that Syria is an Arab republic, and its people are part of the Arab nation. There was no place for the Kurds as a non-Arab ethnic group in the new constitution and ideology. They were pushed out of social, economic and political life. In the next Constitution of 1973, the primacy of Arabism was preserved *(Mazur 2019: 34).*

In 1963, the Baath party came to power in Syria, which finally proclaimed the ideology of socialist secular Arabism. Baathism in Syria became a variant of pan-Arab nationalism, for which the idea of a "united Arab nation" became central, which automatically excluded the Kurds from the social and political space of Syria. Thus, all political, social and national groups that did not share Arab nationalism became illegal *(Ibid: 37).*

In the 1960s, some 120,000 Syrian Kurds were stripped of their citizenship, forcing them to live in a sort of grey zone where they could not own property, were banned from certain professions, could not own cars, and could not get passports to leave the country. Syria also banned Kurdish political parties and put limits, similar to its neighbor Turkey, on Kurdish-language publications and education. Syria's Kurdish minority chafed under these restrictions, but they had few options under the brutal, authoritarian system that Assad led *(Marcus 2007: 59–62).*

Syrian restrictions exist on the use and practice of the Kurdish language, reflecting the practices also found in Turkey, Iraq and Iran at various points during recent history. The policy of suppressing Kurdish language and culture is intended to forcibly assimilate the Kurds into the majority culture of the respective country; within Turkey, the Kurds are described as Turkish; within Syria, the aim is to assimilate the Kurds to the Arab culture and identity *(Yildiz 2005: 116–117).*

Many Kurds (in Syria) face further difficulties in obtaining employment because they have often been blacklisted for illegal political activities, even though in many cases they have not been involved in politics. Once blacklisted, an individual is barred from all public sector employment. Because the accusation that an individual is a member of a Kurdish political party can affect their employment opportunities, political party membership is often used as a tool against Kurds.

The Kurdish areas of Syria are some of the most economically deprived areas of Syria, despite comprising some of the country's most economically productive regions. Cotton, wheat, olives, tobacco, fruits, vegetables and other products all grow easily in the rich agricultural land and the majority of oil fields and water resources are also found in these areas. The consequences of Syria's Arabization policy—the removal of Syrian nationality, the land reforms and the resettlement of Arabs into Kurdish areas—have significantly impacted on the Kurds' economic well-being. This treatment has encouraged economic migration from the Kurdish areas, preventing Kurds from gaining a stronghold in the economy of these areas *(Ibid: 102–103)*.

All this proves that in 1979–1980, Ocalan had no choice but to flee to Syria, which greatly oppressed his own Kurds, and to rely on the support of Hafez Assad.

7.4.2 Establishment of Ocalan's Headquarters in Damascus

After settling in Damascus, Ocalan established his headquarters here, where he held a lot of meetings with Kurdish and foreign figures, from where he began to coordinate the actions of the Kurds in the region.

Ocalan had been out of Turkey for just over a year, and during this period he had worked hard to secure his position in the tumultuous political landscape. In Damascus Ocalan had arranged for PKK militants to stay at different apartments throughout the city. Some were the apartments of Syrian Kurds in the Palestinian or Kurdish quarters of Damascus, others apparently had been rented by Ocalan or else by his new Palestinian contacts.

After a short time in Damascus, Ocalan made his way to Beirut. Lebanon had just come out of a year-long civil war and much of the country was divided between Palestinian and Christian militias. Syrian troops, who moved into Lebanon in 1976 to force an end to the fighting, directly controlled the Bekaa Valley in Lebanon's eastern region and exerted effective control over much of the rest of the country. Ocalan found a place to stay in the Lebanese capital and made contact with Kurds living there.

A large part of the Kurdish community in Lebanon originally came from Turkey—they had immigrated decades earlier to escape the failed Kurdish uprisings and the poverty—and there always were new arrivals looking for work in the construction industry. "There were Turkish and Kurdish families there," Ocalan explained. "I used the name Ali... and in this way six months, maybe a year, passed."

In late 1979 or early 1980, Ocalan succeeded in getting a meeting in Beirut with Nayif Hawatmah's Syrian-backed DFLP. This meeting, probably arranged by Kurds that Ocalan met in Beirut, led to a second, more serious meeting in Damascus with Abu Laila (Qais Abdul-Karim), a member of the Palestinian group's political leadership. Abu Laila had known quite a few leftist revolutionaries from Turkey—many came seeking some sort of assistance, he explained—and what they said about Ocalan was not very flattering.

The Democratic Front initially agreed to take in a small number of PKK militants and train them in the basics of guerrilla warfare. The offer was not unusual. At various times, the DFLP trained Nicaraguan Sandinistas, Iranian leftists, Greek Communists, and even the odd Saudi. "We accept the Marxist-Leninist groups because we are Marxist-Leninist," explained Mamdoh Nofal, a former military commander of the Democratic Front, which was one of the largest Palestinian groups inside the umbrella PLO organization. "We are revolutionaries and we support the revolutionary movement."

The DFLP likely also had more concrete reasons for helping. Giving shelter to other leftist revolutionaries allowed the DFLP to promote the image of an important, international revolutionary movement, one to be reckoned with both by its allies and other members of the umbrella Palestine Liberation Organization. And it helped them pad their numbers at a time of rising tension with Israel. Although the DFLP did not plan to involve the Kurds in the fight against Israel—for one thing, Nofal noted, the PKK militants were too inexperienced—it was understood that the Kurds would defend the base if attacked by Israel. But PKK militants made clear they did not want to mix battles. "They had their own interests and we didn't interfere," said Nofal *(Marcus 2007: 54–55)*.

Ocalan was thus able to establish contacts by staying in Damascus and making regional visits, which helped turn the PKK into an organized force. PKK congresses were convened in Damascus to discuss further actions and tactics (for example, PKK's 2nd Congress in August 1982). Ocalan has also been sending instructions to Kurdish militants from Damascus after PKK launches armed struggle. For instance, on October 1984 Ocalan prepared about six hours of taped speeches for PKK militants in the mountains, which contained Ocalan's instructions for what he wanted the militants to accomplish the next year *(Ibid: 82)*.

7.4.3 Organizing Military Training of Kurdish Militants in the Bekaa Valley

A handful of PKK militants crossed into Syria for training in the first half of 1980; after the military coup militants arrived in large numbers. They were dispersed among a number of DFLP camps in Lebanon, including the Helwe camp, which was on the edge of the Syrian-controlled Bekaa Valley, not far from the Lebanese village al-Hilwah.

When PKK militants started training at Helwe in 1980, the DFLP-run camp could hold perhaps 100 people. Between 1980 and 1982, about 300 PKK militants arrived for training and The DFLP camps could no longer hold all the arrivals. The main building was used for political training and discussions and three or four smaller ones included sleeping quarters, a kitchen, and toilet facilities. Military training discussions were held in the big hall, but the surrounding hills were the actual training grounds, a scaled-down version of the Kurdish region where the PKK planned to fight. Palestinians and Kurds usually did their military training together but separated for political classes. "The [military] courses depended on them," said Nofal, a former military commander of the Democratic Front, which was one of the largest Palestinian groups inside the umbrella PLO organization. "Some courses were only training in explosives, which needs only 10 days or two weeks to learn. Some courses took two months, for example, for staff officers they took courses in military, topography, explosives, artillery and guerrilla fighting."

The Palestinians were experienced fighters and they trained the PKK in the mainstays of guerrilla war. "In general, we had no experience as guerrilla fighters and the Palestinians did, and their instruction was useful and seemed correct," recalled the former PKK militant best known as Sari Baran.

Nor did the Palestinian trainers ignore the other ways that groups could wage battle, such as with propaganda and with a motivated and organized civilian population. In what turned out to be popular tools for the PKK, the Palestinians educated them on the usefulness of a "civil militia" to collect information about troop movements and arrange food and shelter and setting up general committees, such as for women and students, in order to expand control and support.

Ocalan, in the meantime, successfully established similar training arrangements with other Palestinian organizations. This allowed the PKK to spread its people among the different Palestinian factions, including Yasir Arafat's Fatah, George Habash's Popular Front for the Liberation of Palestine, Samir Ghosheh's Palestinian Popular Struggle Front, and the Lebanese Communist Party. The Kurdish militants were useful. They helped build fortifications and, in case of an Israeli attack, they could be pushed to the frontline to defend.

"These people turned out to be really serious, real fighters, real soldiers," said Abu Laila (Qais Abdul-Karim), a member of the Palestinian group's political leadership. "It was clear he [Ocalan] really had some popular base in Kurdistan and that his men were much more disciplined and united than the other groups. We thought that this group [the PKK] was the most serious group in Turkish Kurdistan. This is why we kept them [in the camps]."

PKK militants viewed the situation with certain rationality. "We all wore the uniform of whatever place we were staying in, but we had agreements that the PKK would not get involved in fights among Palestinian groups or between the Palestinians and Lebanon," explained Celik. Not only did splitting up their people relieve the burden on any one Palestinian group, but it also allowed the PKK to hedge its bets, just in case Syria turned on Hawatmah or Arafat suddenly was thrown out of Lebanon.

Palestinian groups that offered to train Kurdish militants also paid attention to Syria's interests. Syria was an important backer of the Palestinians in their fight against Israel, and it exerted de facto control over much of Lebanon. Syria's views had to be considered by all Palestinian groups operating between Lebanon and Syria, but especially for those that based their political headquarters in the Syrian capital. "Without Syria's approval, no Palestinian organization would have helped Turkish or Kurdish organizations," noted Mesut Akyol, a pseudonym for a Turkish leftist who traveled in and out of Syria in this period. "Syria's approval was a condition."

One reason for Syria's feigned disinterest was that the government wanted to pretend these militants, fugitives from Turkish justice, were not there. The identity cards the Kurdish and Turkish opposition groups received—from Palestinian groups, Iraqi Kurdish and other opposition groups, the Syrian Communist Party, and, sometimes, Syrian mukhabarat—allowed Damascus to deny their presence and to deflect, at least officially, Ankara's wrath.

"We all took Arab names," recounted Kamuran, whose identity card, provided by the Syrian intelligence services, identified him as an Iraqi Kurd. "Syria said we had to take these identity cards so that when Turkey asked for us to be sent back, the Syrians could say that we weren't in the country."

"What did we gain by fleeing to Syria?" asked Celik, pausing for a moment. "In reality, we were finished as an organization after 1980. We had no strength in Europe, in Turkey we were in prison. But in Syria we could gather ourselves together. The minute we got money we used it to send people to Europe [to work in the Kurdish community there]. From the Palestinians we learned things. We learned about making demonstrations for martyrs, about ceremonies. We did a lot of reading on a people's war, we also had armed training. They gave us clothing, cigarettes. We owe the Palestinians something." *(Ibid: 56–58).*

For us, it is obvious that without the support of Hafez Assad, the PKK representatives couldn't receive military training in the Bekaa Valley, thus becoming a guerrilla organized force. This is also evidenced by the book by Daniel Pipes, which states: "The Syrian government has even forced Pan-Syrian ideology on stalwarts of Lebanese separatism, the Lebanese Forces. Any important meeting of Lebanese politicians took place in Damascus or involved Syrian officials. The Syrian foreign minister sat in on the Geneva conference of Lebanese leaders in late 1983. Most importantly, Assad's opposition to the May 1983 accord between Lebanon and Israel led to abrogation of that accord within a year.

Assad had achieved the long-sought Syrian role as Lebanon's kingmaker, benefactor, and discipliner. All sides acknowledged Syrian power in Lebanon. An Israeli source observed that "nothing happens in the Bekaa Valley without Syrian approval." Similarly, "You don't light a cigarette here without Syrian permission" was said to be a common saying in that valley. A Lebanese politician told The Washington Post in mid-1984: "Make no mistake about it, the real government of Lebanon sits in Damascus these days, not in Beirut." Antun Lahd, commander of the Army of Southern Lebanon, a militia sponsored by Israel, held that "all big and small decisions, whether crucial or mundane, are made in Damascus and then communicated to the Lebanese authorities." Yasir 'Arafat mused that no one "can move in western Beirut without the knowledge and permission of the Syrian authorities." According to c Adnan Sa'd ad-Din, a leader of the Syrian Muslim Brethren, "there are no borders between Lebanon and Syria." So great was Syrian strength that Damascus induced Lebanese leaders to make public declarations on its behalf *(Pipes 1990: 123–124)*.

7.4.4 Ensuring Visits of Kurdish Militants to Europe

After the 1980 military coup, escaping a probable arrest, or even torture or death, many Kurdish activists—as well as Turkish leftists—immigrated to Germany and other European countries as political asylum seekers, and often, as illegal immigrants. The arrival of a large, politically conscious and activist Kurdish refugee community quickened German—and Europe-wide—Kurdish mobilization. Due to having Syrian passports, PKK militants were able to travel to Europe to carry out various activities (public, media, other types of support, fundraising, (according to the Turkish authorities) even racketeering against wealthy Kurdish businessmen, etc.) *(Bilgin and Sarihan 2013: 187)*.

The PKK always had a handful of members in Europe, but in mid-1981, five senior militants were sent there to expand operations. Europe was then home to some two million so-called guestworkers from Turkey, more than half of whom lived in Germany, and as such was seen by militant groups as a good place to try and win new supporters and financial donations. Europe also was an attractive place for activists forced into exile, and tens of thousands came after the takeover in Turkey.

"Leftists would swear at Europe, calling it imperialist, but when it came time to take refuge somewhere, everyone preferred Europe," said Mesut Akyol, one of the founders of Dev-Yol, who himself chose to apply for asylum in Germany when he fled Turkey via Syria in 1977. "Because they knew that the democracy there would protect them. The second factor was the presence of so many [Turkish] workers."

It was remarkably easy for people without valid passports, some on the run from the Turkish authorities, to travel. One popular method was to get the passport of a friend or relative, change the picture, apply for a visa in Damascus and get on a plane. "With money, you could do everything in Syria," remarked former PKK militant Ibrahim Aydin, who himself flew to Germany from Syria in this period.

The PKK's initial organizational work took place in Germany, gradually spreading to other countries, starting with Holland, Sweden, and France. The centers for PKK activity were cultural clubs that doubled as cafes, reading rooms, debating centers, and social welfare offices *(Marcus 2007: 65–67).*

The 1960s also witnessed Europe—especially Germany—becoming one of the key actors in Turkey's Kurdish question. In 1961, Germany and Turkey signed an immigrant worker agreement, enabling Germany to accept large numbers of foreign workers in order to compensate for the workforce deficit caused by World War II. The main beneficiaries of this agreement were the Kurds, who constituted an overwhelming majority of the immigrant workers who came from Turkey. Apart from a new job and higher pay, the benefits offered by German law for recognized immigrants and especially for political asylum seekers rendered Germany an ideal destination of the Kurdish political exodus from Turkey. Although the OPEC crisis in 1973 had forced Germany to restrict foreign labor recruitment and close its recruitment bureaus in Turkey, Kurdish immigration increased over the years, mostly through illegal channels. By the mid-1970s, labor from Turkey constituted almost 30% of Germany's foreign workforce *(Bilgin and Sarihan 2013: 186).*

The plight of the political prisoners in Turkey and the military repression fueled the agenda of the militant groups actived in Europe. The fact that the Turkish military regime shut down civic organizations, trade unions, and political parties, fired state workers suspected of leftist sympathies, closed down newspapers, and wrote a new constitution that limited more than it allowed, only seemed to underscore leftist claims that Turkey was a fascist state that would not change without revolution. The mass arrests of opposition figures, the military trials, the reports of torture and deaths in custody, the state executions and extrajudicial executions, the torture and humiliation of Kurdish prisoners forced to chant Turkish nationalist slogans and recite Ataturk's speeches, provided rallying points for demonstrations and recruitment.

Like the other groups active in Europe, the PKK used these to promote its own political agenda. But the group gained extra respect and support because its imprisoned militants led—the PKK always said— the resistance inside Diyarbekir Military Prison, the most brutal jail in Turkey at the time. In truth, other members of other Kurdish groups also tried to stand up to the ill-treatment, but the PKK, whose militants were the majority in the prison, arguably was the most vocal and best-organized Kurdish group to do so.

"This gained a lot of sympathy [for the PKK] here and in Turkey," recounted Selman Arslan, a PKK activist in Europe, who opened the Frankfurt Workers and Culture Association in 1981. The PKK also was helped by the focus of its message. Its supporters in Europe continued to stress that the goal was armed struggle to liberate Kurdistan. Other Kurdish groups either said it was not the right time for revolution or else were engaged in internal debates on the issue *(Marcus 2007: 65–67)*.

Another important source of revenue is the large Kurdish population living in Western Europe. Numbering as many as 500,000, Kurds in Europe have contributed generously to the PKK. These funds are used not only to support the organization's activities in Europe but also to purchase arms. In addition to financing, the PKK also recruits would-be guerrillas among the Kurds in Europe and uses its diaspora population as a political trump card of sorts.

The PKK has also put its financing to important use in the establishment of a PKK-dominated Kurdish-language TV station that operates by satellite transmission out of the U.K. The broadcasts are widely available to Kurds in Europe, Turkey, and even in northern Iraq by satellite. The station, called "Med-TV," provides daily news and commentary on the Kurdish world in both Kurdish and Turkish.

Med-TV is an important source of alternative news and information about the PKK and things Kurdish. But most important, it fills a large cultural vacuum: This is the first time Kurds in Turkey have ever had television programming dedicated to aspects of their own culture. As a result, the programming commands a wide viewership *(Barkey and Fuller 1998: 30–33)*.

The PKK's annual revenue from its European wing is estimated at between $50 million and $100 million. About a fifth of the PKK's revenue is raised in semi-legal ways, through a vast web of approximately 400 front-organisations, half of which are in Germany, with the remainder in Austria, Belgium, Britain, Greece, France, the Netherlands, Sweden and Switzerland. The PKK also has an enormous propaganda-recruitment network in Europe, covering everything from publishing houses to newspapers such as Yeni Ozgur Politika in Germany, to radio stations and satellite television channels, notably Roj TV (successor to the British-licensed Med TV) in Denmark and Firat News Agency in the Netherlands *(Orton 2017: 22)*.

Syria has also played an important role in realizing financial flows from Europe. The PKK had relations with many workers, was collecting large sums of money from these workers, and some of this money flowed to Damascus *(Ersever 1993: 85)*.

Turkey restarted its European accession process following the military coup administration. The collapse of the Soviet Union and the shift in the bipolar world system brought new challenges for Turkey. Although human rights abuses and the Kurdish problem were well-known facts concerning Turkish democracy, through much of the Cold War, Europe and the United States kept silent over such violations pointing to the strategic importance of Turkey. However, Turkey's "Western" credentials that were taken for granted during the Cold War started to come under increasing scrutiny after the collapse of the Soviet Union, as the Soviet Union was no longer a threat and Turkey's role as covering NATO's southern flank was no longer relevant.

In political terms, more conservative European political parties—especially in Germany and Greece—established strong ties with the European Kurds and most human rights organizations, adopting their rhetoric in order to exclude Turkey from full membership in the European Union. The leftist libertarian parties, on the other hand, were even more willing to make alliances with the European Kurds, given the socialist rhetoric of the Kurdish activists, initiating much of the European Parliament debates on the Kurds in Turkey. Thus, by the late 1980s, the European Kurds could already voice their concerns against Turkey through the European Parliament, rendering the Kurdish conundrum as a litmus test for Turkey's fulfillment of the European Union accession criteria. In many cases, the European Parliament could affect Council or Commission decisions, considerably affecting Turkey's relations with the EU institutions, rendering the EP one of the three most important legislatures exerting influence over Turkey's Kurdish question *(Bilgin and Sarihan 2013: 187)*.

According to Ahmet Davutoglu, the fight against the PKK has left a negative mark on Turkey's EU membership process. On November 8, 2012, Davutoglu announced in Brussels that "Turkey missed the train to the EU in the 1990s, and today the EU misses the train to Turkey. The Balkans underwent changes in the 1990s, while Turkey gave priority to its security because of the terrorist threat

(PKK). "As a result, the reforms in Turkey were postponed, and Turkey missed the EU train" *(Haberler: 08.11.2012).*

7.4.5 Syria as a Transit Country for Arms and Militants

Syria has played an important role in establishing a PKK base in northern Iraq and moving Kurdish militants there.

According to Turkish authors, PKK militants were able to supply weapons through Syria, including from Europe. For example, weapons and explosives purchased from Serbia, by means of Admiral Andonis Naksakis, retired from Greek intelligence EIP, were transported to (Southern) Cyprus via Greece, and from there to PKK camps via Syria's Latakia port, by showing scrap iron. The person who established this traffic together with Naksakis was Fethi Ugur, the Greek responsible of the PKK *(Yetkin 2004: 53).*

Besides, in the Lebanon Helwe camp, the personnel brought from Europe were subjected to military and political training, those who completed the training would undergo intensive ideological training at homes in Syria, and those who completed their training here would be sent to Northern Iraq and be subjected to survival tests in mountain conditions. Thus, Europe provided ample staff resources, ample money, convenient propaganda opportunities and press activities *(Ersever Ankara: 84).*

The fall of the Iranian Shah's regime in 1979 and Iraq's invasion of Iran in 1980 gave the Iraqi Kurdish parties an old card to play: once again, they were useful to the larger regional powers. KDP forged close ties with the Iranian Islamic regime, which needed assistance to put down a rebellion by Iranian Kurds hoping to wrest autonomy from the new government. On the other side, Talabani's PUK become an ally of the Iranian Kurdish KDP, with which it shared a leftist outlook, helping Iranian Kurdish rebels in their attack on the city Mahabad. And simultaneously, the two Iraqi Kurdish groups fought with each other.

Ocalan had little interest in the intra-Kurdish clashes in Iraq, but he was interested in setting his people up in northern Iraq. A few PKK militants had gone to Iran right before the start of the Iran-Iraq war, where they settled into KDP camps near the Turkish border. Such small-scale mixing was not uncommon and Iraqi Kurdish fighters— perhaps because for so long they were the most powerful and most active—frequently hosted people from Turkish Kurdish groups. But the PKK was looking for more than just a temporary resting spot. It needed free passage through northern Iraq in order to stage attacks inside Turkey—and withdraw, if necessary—and it needed bases, however crude. The Israeli invasion of Lebanon in the summer of 1982 had made the situation in the Bekaa unstable. And Syria, while a good place for taking refuge, was not appropriate for launching attacks. The terrain between Turkey and Syria was too flat, and anyway, Damascus did not want PKK militants fighting from its territory. That would be too much of a provocation to Turkey.

Ocalan's realization that he needed access to northern Iraq—specifically, that part controlled by Barzani's KDP—in order to reach Turkey forced him to reconsider his previously derogatory stance toward the Barzani family. Ocalan's vicious criticisms of Mulla Mustafa Barzani had been rendered moot by the KDP chieftain's death and, in any case, Ocalan was usually careful to put practicalities ahead of ideologies. Sometime in 1982, Ocalan reached a deal with Massoud Barzani to allow the PKK to use the border territory controlled by Barzani's fighters. Under the agreement, which was formalized and made public a year later, the Iraqi Kurdish group gave Ocalan's militants space to build camps in northern Iraq and agreed not to stop them from crossing into Turkey from KDP-controlled land.

"Ocalan developed good relations with Barzani at the end of 1981 or during 1982... and the conclusion of these talks was that the PKK received permission to settle in northern Iraq," said Akyol, who frequently met with Ocalan in their capacity as leading members of the FKBD-C alliance. "After one of the talks, Ocalan himself told me that from the PKK perspective, this was a historical turning point.

The agreement was crucial to the PKK's plan to launch war inside Turkey and as important, if not more so, than its ties with Syria. Without the agreement, the PKK would have faced the impossible task of trying to launch and run a guerrilla war from inside hostile Turkish territory. What Barzani realized from the deal was more amorphous. In the years since Mulla Mustafa Barzani retreated into exile, the KDP had lost support. It was no longer the sole Iraqi Kurdish party and its willingness to attack Iranian Kurdish forces at the behest of Tehran had hurt its image. The KDP had also lost its former allies in the Turkish Kurdish national movement, if only because most of these groups no longer were active, and it faced armed threats from the PUK. The agreement with Ocalan reaffirmed—in however a limited way—the pan-Kurdish appeal of the KDP.

"For us, it is always a source of pride that in regions that we have liberated with the cost of our blood, we have opened the area as a fortress for every Kurdish fighter," Barzani told an interviewer years later. "We signed the alliance with the PKK with this logic and for these reasons."

The PKK did not waste any time in taking advantage of the new agreement. It built its main camp in Lolan, a clutch of valleys and mountains on the edge of the area known as the ucgen, or triangle, the stretch of territory that straddles the Iranian, Turkish, and Iraqi borders. Lolan always had been an important base for KDP fighters, and its proximity to the Turkish border made it perfect for the PKK. PKK militants who had been staying with various Iraqi Kurdish groups were called to the new, central camp or dispersed in smaller, mountain outposts along the Turkish border. Some flew from Damascus to Tehran and then crossed the border on foot into Iraq; others walked across the sharp intersection of the Syrian-Turkish-Iraqi border, cutting briefly into Turkey before entering Iraq, and continued on foot from there. Thus, when Kurdish rebels could not cross the Syrian border into Turkey, they took a plane to Tehran or else crossed the Syrian-Iraqi border *(Marcus 2007: 68–71).*

Meanwhile, the PKK had placed a group of its men in Iran and Northern Iraq. Those in Iran were settled in the city of Urmia, which is adjacent to Northern Iraq and Turkey, with the knowledge of the Iranian intelligence agency. From there, they could enter and exit both Turkey and Northern Iraq. The Syrian Government had provided their passage to Iran by sending them by plane, in agreement with Iran *(Ersever 1993: 73).*

A magic hand brought the PKK and the Barzani KDP together at the end of 1982. After this agreement, Massoud Barzani came to his senses and began to be respected by leftist circles. He was invited to Syria. Because Hafez Assad administration was looking for a pawn to fight against Saddam on behalf of Syria on Iraqi soil. Iraq was serving as a rearguard for the Muslim Brotherhood in the events that exploded in the Syrian city of Hama in early 1982. Syria blamed the Iraqi state for the uprising of the Muslim Brotherhood that took place in Hama in 1982 and accused Saddam of harboring the militants of the Muslim Brotherhood.

For this reason, Syria wanted to punish Iraq and to activate Celal Talabani and Massoud Barzani together. While Barzani was in Damascus, a KDP office was opened immediately and KDP notables began pouring weapons and money into Northern Iraq. On the other hand, Iran, which was at war with Iraq at the time, embraced the struggle that the KDP started against Saddam. He allowed Barzani to set up camps in Iran and leave freely *(Ibid: 79–80, 92).*

7.4.6 Direct Penetration of Kurdish Militants and Arms From Syria to Turkey

Regular troops replaced the gendarmerie the Syrian border because of the latter's inefficiency and suspected corruption (after the start of the PKK armed struggle). It was well-known that local authorities routinely turned a blind eye to massive smuggling, and benefited from it. It was now becoming increasingly clear that smuggling and PKK activity were tightly entwined. Sheep might be herded out of Turkey, and weapons brought on back on the return journey *(McDowall 2007: 428).*

Iran, Iraq, and Syria were experienced in using their neighbors' Kurds as proxies in battles with their own Kurdish groups and in their disputes with each other. Now, a Turkish Kurdish group had emerged that appeared strong enough to be of use. Syria was the first to take advantage of this, while Iraq initially failed and Iran's relations only started to develop at the end of the 1980s.

Although Damascus did warn the PKK not to cross from Syria into Turkey, it is unclear how long this stayed in effect *(Marcus 2007: 99).* The previous subchapter already mentioned the great activities of the PKK in Hatay, which is geographically quite far from Northern Iraq. This may indicate that in the mid-1990s, Kurdish militants began crossing the Turkish border from Syria into Hatay. We also do not rule out that in the 1980s, many Kurds from Syria could infiltrate Turkey directly to carry out various operations. For example, Syrian intelligence services could send Kurdish militants across the border for reconnaissance, sabotage and other purposes.

7.4.7 Allowing Recruitment and Fundraising Among the Syrian Kurds

Hafez al-Assad also weaponised the PKK for his domestic policy, allowing the PKK to disseminate its ideology and recruit freely among Syrian Kurds. Ocalan denied "the existence of Kurdistan in Syria and the existence of a Kurdish problem in Syria," contending that "most Syrian Kurds are immigrants" from Turkey, and the PKK's path was to "return them to their original homeland". This matched the imperatives of Syria's Arabizing government, which had stripped more than 100,000 Kurds of citizenship, claiming they were "alien infiltrators" from Turkey. The Assad regime was content for the PKK to channel the discontents Syria's marginalized Kurdish population away from demands for national rights or prosperity within Syria, and redirect their energies against Turkey. As other Kurdish groups were not allowed to operate, Assad enabled the PKK to co-opt much of the political space among Syria's Kurds. As a result, the PKK recruited very widely in Syria *(Orton 2017: 18).*

Damascus was wary of its own Kurdish minority and it continued to make clear to the PKK that it could not agitate on behalf of Syrian Kurds. However, Damascus began encouraging the PKK to recruit members from among the Syrian

Kurdish population, hoping this would redirect local Kurdish attention away from fighting for change inside Syria. The PKK already was fairly well known among Syrian Kurds. In his first few years in Syria, Ocalan gave speeches to Syrian Kurds, and PKK militants often traveled around the Syrian Kurdish villages to make propaganda and collect money.

Syrian Kurds, especially university students, were excited by the PKK and its promise of an independent Kurdish state, even if it was going to be a Turkish Kurdish state. Syrian Kurdish political parties barely were active—between the in-fighting and the state pressure, they had little chance to put together a viable program—while the PKK actually was fighting.

Syrian Kurds generally saw no contradiction in their supporting a Turkish Kurdish party. They often had relatives on the Turkish side, and the brisk smuggling trade between helped maintain family ties and encouraged political links.

"Turkish Kurdistan was the biggest part and it was always in our imagination," said Kamiran Hajo, a Kurdish activist from Syria who initially was interested in the PKK. "We thought that we had to support Turkish Kurdistan because we failed [to make a state] in Iraqi Kurdistan."

"We students were convinced that this time, something would happen," said Hasan, a former PKK European representative. When Hasan joined in 1985, there were just a few Syrian Kurds inside the PKK. Within a year the number had increased to about 45 and the year after that it tripled to about 130. And this number reflected only the active members trained at Helwe. In the Syrian Kurdish villages along the border, there were many more willing to help out with food, money, and shelter.

Besides, the PKK's program envisioned a greater Kurdistan that would unite Kurds from Turkey, Iraq, Iran and Syria. The group's focus was on liberating the Kurdish region inside Turkey's borders, but after that was done the other Kurdish regions were expected to wage their own war with the guidance of the new Turkish Kurdish state *(Ibid: 100–101)*.

7.4.8 Conclusion

These 7 points show that without the support of Hafez Assad, the PKK would not survive after the 1980 military coup, gather strength, become a powerful guerrilla organization, expand its geographical activities, and become a serious headache for the Turkish state. At the same time, we do not claim that Hafez Assad created the PKK.

Although Hafez Assad managed to achieve his goal only partially by using the "more water for less terrorism" formula (we mean the protocol signed by T. Ozal in 1987), nevertheless Hafez Assad was able to cause considerable economic damage to Turkey. In our opinion, in the 20th century, Turkey suffered much more economic losses in the fight against the PKK than it was able to gain economic benefits from large-scale water projects in the Euphrates, as well as in the Tigris basin (this trend continued in the 21st century).

We are going to compare these two factors in the next sub-chapter. We consider such a comparison appropriate, as we believe that Turkey's water projects (GAP) played a key role in Hafez Assad's decision to support the PKK against Turkey, despite the fact that, as mentioned earlier, there were other factors for supporting to the PKK. In the previous sub-chapter we have already shown the close interrelationship between the PKK and the GAP.

7.5 The Fight Against PKK and Hydro Projects: Financial Comparison

In this sub-chapter we want to compare Turkey's achievements and losses from the hydroelectric projects implemented in the Euphrates-Tigris basin. In this context, it is necessary to emphasize two important factors.

1. It has already been mentioned that in the 20th century, Turkey mainly focused on large-scale hydroelectric projects in the Euphrates River Basin, while in the Tigris River Basin it did not implement large-scale projects.
2. In the 20th century, implementing large hydro projects in the Euphrates Basin, Turkey focused on the implementation of energy projects, i.e. to build HEPPs and receive electricity. Meanwhile, only a small part of the irrigation projects had been implemented, which means that Turkey has not been able to irrigate significant lands, receive a large volume of agricultural products, thus providing additional serious income for itself.

Thus, in the 20th century, Turkey mainly earned revenues from its energy projects on the Euphrates. As of the end of 2001, the volume of total production of electricity within the framework of GAP amounted to almost 184 billion kWh, the overwhelming majority of which fell to the Euphrates HEPPs (Table 7.1). The electricity generated during the entire period of the GAP was equivalent to $11 billion, which is more than a third of the total cost of the Project *(Mosaki 2005: 67)*.

Table 7.1 Electricity produced by HEPPs

Euphrates		
Karakaya	106.8	billion kWh
Ataturk	74.5	billion kWh
Birecik	1.6	billion kWh
Karkamish	0.6	billion kWh
Overall	**183.5**	billion kWh
Tigris		
Kralkizi	0.3	billion kWh
Dicle (Tigris)	0.1	billion kWh
Overall	**0.4**	billion kWh

In October 2018, the Anadolu news agency reported that Turkey had earned $27 billion in 25 years from the electricity generated by the three major HEPPs on the Euphrates (Keban, Karakaya, Ataturk). The energy produced by them has reached almost 30 billion megawatt hours in 25 years, which corresponds to approximately $27 billion. $27 billion also includes the Keban HEPP index, which is not part of the GAP *(Anadolu 25.10.2018)*.

It means that generally this index ($27 billion) should be reduced, because Keban HEPP (1330 MW) is more powerful than Birecik and Karkamish HEPPs together (852 MW). Moreover, Keban HEPP is slightly lower than Ataturk and Karakaya HEPPs in terms of annual electricity production (Table 7.2).

Table 7.2 Annual electricity production of 3 main HEPPs of the Euphrates

Dams	Electricity	**2018**	**2019**
Keban	million kWh	3445	7015
Karakaya	million kWh	4113	7600
Ataturk	million kWh	3491	8175
Overall	million kWh	**11.049**	**22.790**

As the Keban HEPP was built earlier than Karakaya and Ataturk HEPPs, it is the "historical" leader in terms of electricity produced in the 20th and 21st centuries (Table 7.3).

Table 7.3 20th and 21st century electricity production of 3 main HEPPs on the Euphrates

HEPP	Start of production	Production deadline	Billion kWh
Keban	1974	February 2020	267
Karakaya	1987	February 2020	217
Ataturk	1992	February 2020	184
Overall	1974	2020	**668**

Table 7.4 shows that in 2019 energy production in Turkey's 3 largest dams increased by 106 percent. The energy production in these dams, which was 11 billion 49 million kilowatt-hours in 2018, increased by 106 percent and reached 22 billion 790 million kilowatt-hours in 2019. Keban Dam made a great contribution to the country's economy with its energy production of 267 billion kilowatt-hours in 46 years. Ataturk Dam, which was completed in 1992 and started to produce electricity, has produced approximately 184 billion kilowatt-hours of electricity since its establishment. And Karakaya, which was put into service in 1987, has produced 219 billion kilowatt-hours of electricity to date. Thus, Turkey's 3 largest dams have produced approximately 670 billion kilowatt-hours of energy so far *(Anadolu 18.02.2020)*.

Table 7.4 2018 and 2019 electricity production of 3 main HEPPs on the Euphrates

HEPP	2018 Billion kWh	2019 Billion kWh	Overall Billion kWh
Keban	3445	7015	**10,460**
Karakaya	4113	7600	**11,713**
Ataturk	3491	8175	**11,666**
Overall	**11,049**	**22,790**	**33,839**

These are the benefits that Turkey has received from the energy component of the GAP. Let us now present Turkey's financial losses in the fight against the PKK. In this regard, Turkish officials and experts have given various numbers, as in the case of Turkish military losses (Table 7.5).

Table 7.5 Financial estimates for the struggle against PKK

Term	Name	Position	Billion $
2007	Koksal Toptan	Speaker of Parliament	250
2008	Cemil Cicek	Deputy Prime Minister	300
2011	Faruk Celik	Minister of Labor and Social Security	400
2011	Taner Yildiz	Minister of Energy and Natural Resources	300
2011	Binali Yildirim	Transport Minister	1000 (300 direct)
2013	Recep Tayyip Erdogan	Prime Minister	400
2013	Zafer Caglayan	Economy Minister	300–400
2016	Ufuk Tutan	Turkish expert	1200
2016	Mehmet Simsek	Deputy Prime Minister for Economy	350–1000
2018	Numan Kurtulmus	Minister of Culture and Tourism	1500
2019	Numan Kurtulmus	AKP Deputy Chairman	2000
2021	Mete Yarar	Turkish expert	500
2021	Devlet Bahceli	Turkish politician	1207
2021	İzzet Akyol	Turkish researcher and writer	3000

Besides, we would like to quote a number of statements made by Turkish officials on this topic.

In 2007, Turkish Deputy Prime Minister Cemil Cicek announced: "About $300 billion has been spent in the fight against the PKK since 1984. If that money was invested in the country's economy, Turkey would be the 7th most economically developed country in the world (G-8) today".

In 2013 Prime Minister Erdogan stated: "If there had been no terror scourge, today's Turkey would not have exist: there would be a very different Turkey". In 2019 AKP Deputy Chairman Numan Kurtulmus said, "The cost of PKK terror to Turkey is $2 trillion. This means the destruction of 25 years of Turkey."

In 2011 Transport Minister Binali Yildirim stated that it could be built with the money spent on the struggle against terrorism 15 thousand schools with 25 classrooms, 9 thousand full-fledged training and research hospitals, 200 Bosphorus bridges, 120 Ataturk Dam and 450 thousand kilometers of divided roads.

In July 2008, Turkish Deputy Prime Minister and Government Spokesman Cemil Cicek stated that the PKK had caused $300 billion in damage to the country in 25 years. He reported that the cost of GAP is $32 billion. Turkey would have completed the GAP 10 times".

In this context, we want to emphasize that as of 1997, $12.5 billion had been spent on the GAP, which was 39% of the planned funds. As of April 1998, these data were, respectively, $13 billion (41%), and at the end of 1999—just over $14 billion (44%). By the beginning of 2002, a little more than $15 billion had been spent within the framework of the GAP, which was 48.1%.

As Salih Yildirim, the Turkish State Minister for GAP Affairs stated in 1997, the continuation of funding for the Southeast Anatolia Project in the current volume may extend this process for 72 years (!). Realizing that it will not be possible to complete the GAP by 2006, on June 4, 1998, the Turkish Council of Ministers decided to extend the completion date of the project until 2010. According to Salih Yildirim, as of April 1998, "the cost of ensuring security in the eastern and southeastern regions reached $84 billion, which is "4.5 times the amount required to complete the GAP." *(Mosaki 2005: 54).*

Moreover, it turns out that as of 1998, Turkey spent only $13 billion on the implementation of the GAP project, while in the fight against the PKK—$84 billion (if we base our calculations on the smallest of the above figures for the fight against PKK).

Thus, these are the telling facts presented by Turkish officials and experts, which reflect the economic side of the fight against the PKK.

According to Berat Guncicek, the PKK's intense use of "political and military" violence had three important economic objectives. First; to disrupt the economic balances by causing an increase in military mobility, paralyze the country's finances, such as material consumption, increase the number of flights, and ammunition consumption. Second; to disrupt the economic and social structure by reducing the income sources of the state. Third; to make the state incapable of doing business as a result of military expenditures and declining revenues. Thus, a suitable ground will be prepared for the organization by causing economic, political and social crises in Turkey *(Guncicek 2015: 43).*

We don't consider it expedient to detail how the armed struggle against the PKK has affected certain branches of the Turkish financial sector, as the issue is multi-layered and subject to separate research (sectors such as infrastructures, tourism, transportation, trade, insurance, agriculture and livestock, financial markets, investment, development and employment).

We also don't want to talk about destroyed schools, health centers, post offices, transformers, roads, bridges, banks, cash machines, security forces buildings, vehicles, business centers and vehicles belonging to citizens, railways, petrol and gas pipelines, about delaying the construction of HEPPs in Turkey.

However, we would like to quote some data from the report on the financial consequences of the PKK terror in Turkey compiled by the AKP. "Between 1986 and 2012, the total defense and security expenditures amounted to 162 billion liras. If there were no terrorism, defense expenditures were 50% less" *(Ibid: 65–66)*.

A total of 263 billion 800 million TL direct investment came to Turkey in 28 years. If there were no terrorism, 10% more (26 billion 300 million TL) foreign direct investment would be come to Turkey every year between 1986 and 2012. It has also been determined that if 20% more foreign direct investors came every year, 52 billion 600 million TL additional foreign direct investment would have been obtained" *(Ibid: 117)*.

According to the research, "Between 1986 and 2012, Turkey earned a total of 600 billion TL in tourism revenue. It is evaluated that in the absence of terrorism, tourism revenues will increase by 10% every year and an additional income of 60 billion 300 million TL will be obtained". In case of an increase of 20%, it is evaluated that 120 billion 600 million TL additional income can be obtained *(Ibid: 82)*.

The activities of the PKK also contributed to the spread of smuggling. According to the 2011 report of the Agriculturalists Association of Turkey, illegal food and agricultural products inflow reach a value of $10 billion, almost approaching the amount of official imports *(Ibid: 95–97)* (Table 7.6).

Table 7.6 Illegal food and agricultural products in Turkey

Products	Country	Quantity/worth	Damage/tax evasion,
Cigarettes	North Irak	25.000 tons	$ 2,5 billion
Tea	Iran, Syria	60.000 tons	$ 75 million
Sugar	Iran, Irak	500.000 tons	$ 750 million
Livestock (mostly small cattle) the annual value of illegal meat	Iran, Irak, Syria	Around 500.000	$ 750 million $ 5 billion
Alcoholic drinks		100.000 bottle	$ 200 million
Fruit	Iran		$ 500 million
Canned goods, meat, commodity products etc.	Middle East		$ 1 billion

Since 1984, the Turkish state spent 10 billion dollars annually in the armed struggle against the PKK. In addition, this struggle led to the fact that the World Bank—the world's largest and multilateral development institution, refrained from financing the infrastructure of the GAP zone *(Yildiz & Duzgoren 2001: 34)*.

This means that financially, Turkey's fight against the PKK has cost several times more than the benefits that Turkey has received from carrying out hydro projects in the Euphrates-Tigris River basin. In other words, Hafez Assad managed to inflict much more financial damage on Turkey through the PKK than Turkey was able to benefit from the implementation of hydropower projects. At the same time, Syria has not suffered too much from Turkey's water projects in the Euphrates Basin. It is true that Syria has suffered some, but it has many reasons besides Turkey's water projects (hot weather in Syria and high rates of evaporation, demands of Turkey, Syria and Iraq from the Euphrates, which exceed the annual flow of the Euphrates, etc.).

7.6 Concluding Summary of Chapter 5

In the first sub-chapter of the 5th chapter, we describe the difficult situation of the Kurds after the establishment of the Republic of Turkey, various pressures on the Kurds, violating their rights, etc. We emphasize that such a policy has created a significant basis for the emergence of the PKK and the start of an armed struggle. Moreover, the bloodiest military coup that took place in Turkey on September 12, 1980 contributed to the start of the armed struggle of the PKK, after which the Kurds were severely persecuted. In response, the PKK started an armed struggle inside Turkey, which was somewhat unexpected for the Turkish authorities. That struggle quickly developed so much, gained so many supporters, that the Turkish authorities were forced to make changes in the GAP project. The initial success of PKK led to convert of the GAP Master Plan, developed in 1989, into an integrated development project (in 1989 GAP Regional Development Administration was established). Despite this, the PKK's armed struggle continued and gained even more momentum in the early 1990s.

In the second sub-chapter, we describe the migration of Kurds from Kurdish-populated provinces and show that the Turkish authorities did not intentionally make large investments and create jobs in those provinces, thus creating conditions for the migration of Kurds to the west and emptying the Kurdish-populated region. We emphasize that, as paradoxical as it may seem at first glance, the GAP project, among other goals, also served the purpose of emptying the eastern and southeastern regions of Turkey from Kurds. This is especially related to the flooding of Kurdish villages by building major reservoirs, which also harmed the PKK militants, who were deprived of the opportunity to find shelter and recruit supporters in these villages. In addition, the reservoirs were built on the communication routes of the PKK militants and made their movement difficult. The construction of major reservoirs was also aimed at making it impossible for those displaced from the villages to return. Going forward, we should note that this policy was also preserved in the 21st century.

In the third sub-chapter, we note that the PKK is turning into a factor between Turkey and Syria, that mainly in response to Turkey's construction of large reservoirs in the Euphrates basin, Syria decided to support the PKK and through it try to, if not cancel, at least delay the construction of the reservoirs. In Syria, they hoped that by turning the east and southeast of Turkey into a war zone, they would scare off potential investors in the context of building these reservoirs, which created problems for Turkey with limited financial opportunities. Besides, the Syrian authorities, using the PKK as a trump card against Turkey's water projects, hoped to force Turkey to release more water through the Euphrates, which they partially succeeded in 1987, when Turkey agreed to release 500 m3/second of water through the Euphrates. This is known as the "less terrorism for more water" formula.

In the fourth sub-chapter, we present the role of Hafez Assad in several points, not in the creation of the PKK, but in maintaining and strengthening its existence. We emphasize that if it were not for Hafez Assad's multilateral support to the PKK, today the world would hardly have heard about the PKK and its founder and leader Abdullah Ocalan. We present the internal and external political motives of Hafez Assad to take such steps. We also emphasize that Hafez Assad was just using the PKK, that in fact he oppressed the Syrian Kurds no less and even more severely than the Turkish authorities. And when supporting the PKK became too dangerous for Hafez Assad, the latter immediately abandoned it and expelled Ocalan from Syria, hoping to get additional water from the Euphrates River that way.

In the fifth sub-chapter, we make a simple financial comparison between the financial benefits Turkey has received from the major hydroelectric dams built by Turkey in the Euphrates basin over the decades, and the financial costs incurred by Turkey in the fight against the PKK in that region (and beyond). The comparison shows that in nearly 40 years, Turkey has suffered much greater financial losses in the armed struggle against the PKK than it has received financial benefits from the major hydroelectric dams it has built in the Euphrates-Tigris basin. For the sake of justice, it should be noted that the start of the PKK's armed struggle, and Hafez Assad's support for its preparation and progress, were not solely due to Turkey's water projects in the Euphrates basin (it is known that the Tigris does not enter Syria, and that Turkey in the 20th century mainly focused on had crossed the Euphrates). And yet, they played a key role in Assad's rescue of the PKK, then strengthening it and directing it to Turkey, and without that support, as already mentioned, the PKK would not even be able to survive. In any case, the water projects implemented by Turkey in the Euphrates basin have provided an opportunity to obtain a large volume of electricity, which has been used for the purposes of Turkey's survival and development. We also emphasize that Turkey, in addition to financial losses in the fight against the PKK, also suffered losses of a different nature (for example, the delay in the process of joining the EU).

GAP in the 21th Century—Justice and Development Party

8

8.1 GAP Plans during rule of JDP

8.1.1 GAP Regional Development Plan (2002–2010)

With the Master Plan dated 1989 and revision introduced in 2002, the GAP was transformed into an integrated regional development project on the basis of multi-sector sustainable human development encompassing investments in agriculture, industry, transportation, education, health and rural and urban infrastructure building. Integrated projects are multi-purpose projects prepared for the overall development of a region. GAP is not just an agriculture and energy project: it is a structural transformation project that will carry out cultural and social transformation in the region. During the preparation of the Plan, were determined three main objectives.

- Developing development infrastructures and protecting the environment,
- Developing human resources,
- Reducing intra-regional development disparities.

Regional Development Plan has been prepared for these purposes. Along with the regional development plan, the completion date of the GAP was determined as 2010 by shifting 5 years. It is stated that an additional $ 13 billion is required to complete the GAP (as of the end of 2006, $ 19 billion had been spent on GAP). According to the Master Plan in 1989, it turns out that the project, which should be completed in 2005, will not reach 2010. In June 1998, Prime Minister M. Yilmaz announced that GAP will be completed by 2010. According to him, 40% of GAP was completed at that time and the decision of NSC (the National

H. Gabrielyan, *Turkey's Water Policy as Part of the Political Strategy*, Politik, Wirtschaft und Gesellschaft im Spannungsverhältnis der Regionen Südosteuropa und Mittlerer Osten, https://doi.org/10.1007/978-3-658-44070-1_8

Security Council) is necessary for the full completion of the project. In 1998, Demirel said, that Turkey will do the GAP program for 10 years. The completion of the GAP by 2010 at the latest is decided by the Council of Ministers on 04.06.1998 with the number 98/11231. However, neither the NSC's decision nor Demirel's will was enough to finish the GAP. In 2007, the 60th Government of the Republic decided to have the large part of the GAP completed within 5 years, but it didn't happen. Officials say that only 54% of the entire project has been completed (only 14 of the 22 dams planned for irrigation, and only 8 of the 19 planned HEPPs have been completed). The aim of GAP is stated to contribute $ 4.3 billion annually to the Turkey's economy, including $ 2.1 billion of irrigation and $ 2.2 billion of energy, to employ approximately 3.8 million people and a 209% increase in per capita income.

Hydropower

74% of HEPP projects and about 15% of irrigation projects have been completed. Of the installed capacity of the 7476 MW hydroelectric power plant within the scope of GAP, 5513 MW have been materialized and 18.3 billion kWh have been generated in 2007. From the commissioning of GAP's 8 HEPPs until the end of 2006, 274.3 billion kWh of electricity was produced. The contribution of the produced energy to the national economy has been determined as $16.5 billion (1 kWh = 6 cent). In 2006 44.2 billion kWh of hydroelectric energy was produced in Turkey, GAP (7 HEPPs) had a share of 48.5% with 21 billion kWh. Yet Turkey in 2006, a total of 175.7 billion kWh of energy generation (thermal—131.4 billion kWh, wind—0.13 billion kWh) in GAP, the share was 12.2%. Table 8.1 presents the production indicators of 7 GAP HEPPs‘ taking account that Urfa HEPP started to generate electricity in 2010 *(USİAD GAP Raporu 2008: 27–29).*

Table 8.1 Electricity generation of 7 GAP HEPPs

Dam & HEPP	Transition Year	Electricity Generation (Billion kwh)
Karakaya	1987	143,1
Ataturk	1993	111,2
Kralkizi	1998	1,0
Karkamish	1999	2,6
Dicle	1999	1,1

(continued)

Table 8.1 (continued)

Dam & HEPP	Transition Year	Electricity Generation (Billion kwh)
Birecik	2000	13,1
Batman	2003	1,5
Total	**274,3**	

Irrigation

Only 270,000 ha of the area planned to be irrigated 1.8 million ha have reached the water and additional irrigation facilities for 100.000 ha of land are under construction. It seemed that priority was given to hydropower in GAP and therefore irrigation projects left behind. But it is not exactly accurate descriptions. The land planned to be irrigated with existing dams is 853,000 hectares, which corresponds to half of the entire irrigated area in the GAP. The cost of the energy generation system in dams built for both energy production and irrigation is about four or one fifth of the total investment value of the dam. Therefore, installing power plant systems in these dams does not prevent or displace the construction of irrigation systems.

On the other hand, you cannot have the luxury of not generating energy from a dam where you complete the power plant. However, the delay of the irrigation system in dams for energy and irrigation naturally highlights the other construction purpose of the dam, namely the energy production. The fact that the percentage of completion of irrigation systems in GAP is low is independent from the high energy realization. There is no need for any preparation other than substations and transmission lines for the distribution and utility of energy production. However, especially in the GAP region, for an efficient and rational irrigation so many socio-cultural parameters come into play and preparation is required from land consolidation to farmer education.

It is known that an irrigation project consists of storage (dam) where water is accumulates, then transmissions to the main channel and transports to the irrigated area delivering to the parcels in the irrigation area. It is clear that storage units, i.e. dams, must be constructed first and then the construction of main canal and network. The most suitable method for the completion of the dam and irrigation system in coordination is to tender the dam and irrigation together and to prepare the necessary infrastructure within the construction period. Insufficiency of appropriation arises as the most important reason for the failure to complete the irrigation system. The appropriation for irrigation projects carried out by DSI was 10–15% of the demand. A study was carried out by the DSI General Directorate in 1998 on the completion of the GAP by 2010, in which the need for funds covering the 12-year period between 1999 and 2010 was determined. This allowance program could not be implemented due to the restriction of investments, the earthquake disaster in 1999, and the lack of financial resources due to economic crises in recent years.

According to the basic strategy in the GAP, the region should become "agricultural export base". GAP region, which shares the energy sector's benefits with the whole of Turkey, will be able to get almost all of the agricultural sector benefits. As of 2007, 270,261 ha of the 1,821,046 ha irrigation area in the GAP region were brought under irrigation, while construction continues in the 111,483 ha area. This means that only 15% of all envisaged irrigation investments could be realized so far. Thus, as of the beginning of 2007, the irrigated lands in the Euphrates basin amounted to 231,773 ha. It was equivalent to 19.4% of the Euphrates basin irrigate areas (1.191.391 ha). Irrigation works of 59,198 ha (4.9%) were underway in the Euphrates basin. The area already irrigated in the Tigris Basin has reached 38,488 ha (6.1%), the irrigation of 52,285 ha (8.2%) was underway. Thus, 270,261 ha (14.8%) have already been irrigated, and 111,483 (6.1%) ha were under way.

From 2002 GAP Regional Development Plan period to 2007, the total area opened to irrigation in the GAP region was 55,261 ha (from 215,000 ha to 270,261 ha). This corresponds to an increase of approximately 3% in the total irrigation area of 1.8 million ha. It is observed that an average of 13–14 thousand hectares of additional fields have been put into operation in the GAP for the last ten years (before 2007). If the field, which is put into operation every year, remains at this level, the completion of GAP agricultural sector projects will take approximately 100 years *(Ibid: 55–65)*.

Why GAP Slows Down?

The main reasons for the loss of initial speed and excitement in the GAP can be listed as the decrease in the budget allocated to the project and the political interest in the project after the economic crises experienced during this period (between 1991 and 2001, Turkey experienced 3 financial crises). The reason for this decrease in interest is that it focuses on other priorities due to the economic and political difficulties experienced at that time and the problems brought about it. The problems arising from the periodic priorities were effective in not getting results from the search for new finance model for GAP. The slowdown in the integrated progression of the GAP was largely due to the reduced interest and political support for GAP at the political level *(Ibid: 97)*.

In November 2002, conservative political party—the Justice and Development Party (Turkish: Adalet ve Kalkınma Partisi, AKP) came to power in Turkey which is still in power 20 years later. It has been accepted by the existing Political Government that the GAP has been progressing very slowly for a long time, and therefore lost its vitality, and statements were made in November 2007 that JDP initiated the "Revival of the GAP". At the time Minister of State and Deputy Prime Minister Nazım Ekren stated that 60% of the project was completed, and work will be done for regional and sectoral incentives to start in 2008 *(Ibid: 112).*

8.1.2 GAP Action Plans (2008–2012 & 2014–2018)

The GAP (first) Action Plan was launched in 2008 to complete the large part of projects related to economic and social development in the region. With the implementation of the Action Plan important outcomes were observed and significant changes took place in South-Eastern Anatolia. The acceleration step prioritized basic infrastructure investments including those related to irrigation in the first place.

The major objectives of the GAP include improving the level of income and life quality of people living in the region by utilizing regional resources; reducing and eventually eliminating development gaps between the region and other regions of the country; and contributing to national targets of economic development and social stability by improving rural productivity and opportunities of employment. In the GAP Action Plan (2008–2012) there are four development axes and 73 major actions under these axes. There are over 300 individual projects and activities under major actions. Four strategic axes are:

- Economic Development,
- Social Development,
- Infrastructure Building, and
- Institutional Capacity Building.

The GAP irrigation program was revised so as to complete those components with already available water resources; projects with ongoing main canal constructions or whose designs were largely completed and others where gravity irrigation would take place as well as first stage pumped irrigation projects. The GAP ultimately envisages irrigation on 1,820,000 ha of land it is now planned to complete the irrigation infrastructure of 1,060,000 ha of this land until 2012. The plan also envisages the completion of irrigation networks related to these projects through bilateral cooperation and public–private partnerships. As far as irrigation investments under the GAP are concerned, priority was given to water reservoirs (dams). Thus far 15 dams were completed and a water holding capacity sufficient for irrigating 1 million ha of land was created.

The first stage in the GAP was the construction of dams as water reservoirs. This was followed by the construction of main canals to carry water from these reservoirs to irrigation areas and irrigation networks reaching to farms. The GAP Action Plan took steps at this second stage and main canals reaching 934.7 km in total were completed; 701.3 km part of this total was completed in the period 2008–2013. The rate of physical realization in GAP energy projects is 74% now, but upon the completion of Ilisu Dam and HEPP this rate will go beyond 90% and reach 93% upon the completion of Cizre Project.

The GAP (second) Action Plan (2014–2018) has five development axes and 115 major actions under these axes. There are 494 individual projects and activities under major actions. Five strategic axes are:

- Achieving Economic Development
- Ensuring Social Development
- Increasing Livability in Cities
- Infrastructure Development
- Development of Institutional Capacity

The (second) GAP Action Plan was developed, under the coordination of the Ministry of Development and GAP Administration, by soliciting the opinions and suggestions of relevant public organizations as well as local requests collected at province and region level by development agencies. The primary objectives of the GAP-AP (2014–2018) include the completion of investments launched during the first AP; full utilization of the potential created by investments so as to accelerate economic, social and cultural development; enhancement of the competitive power of the region and carrying the project further ahead. The Action Plan includes human-focused, innovative and sustainable projects and programs that are intended to reduce income disparities, gives priority to disadvantaged groups and areas and to provide habitable spaces. On the basis of trained and qualified human resources, projects and programs in the Action Plan are geared to accelerating regional development, creating employment, protecting natural resources, the environment and cultural properties, upholding technological advances and completing projects in irrigation, transportation and industrial infrastructure.

Urbanization and urban centers recently becoming the focus of growth, increasing dominance of urban economies and urban way of life and importance of urban centers in terms of information-based, competitive and specialized economic and financial services, R&D and innovative capacity are all factors to take into account in any development plan. Considering these developments, the GAP-AP (2014–2018) gives place to a new axis as "Improving Habit-ability in Urban Centers" that comprises actions targeting settlements with high life quality.

Table 8.2 shows the irrigation area of the GAP (according to DSI).

Table 8.2 GAP Irrigations

GAP Irrigations	**Area (ha)**	**(%)**
Pumping Irrigation	255,000	
Gravity Irrigation	295,000	
Total in Operation	550,000	51,51
Under Construction	205,000	18,68
Bidding Phase	8000	0,75
Remaining	297,000	29,02
Total	**1,060,000**	**100**

According to the GAP's official website total area opened to irrigation is 558,507—53% of second GAP AP (Table 8.3). It means that 285,535 ha opened to irrigation in 2008–2018 (146,999 ha opened to irrigation in 2014–2018). In 2007, the irrigated area scope of GAP was 272,972 ha. Canals length of GAP is 1,501.1 km. In 2008–2018, 1267 km of canals were built, 566.4 km of which in 2014–2018. As of 2007, there were 233.4 km of canals in the GAP region.

Table 8.3 In 2002–2018 total area opened to irrigation

	Irrigated Area (ha)	**Main Canal (km)**
2002	198,854	
2007	272,972	233.4
2012	377,672	843.5
2014	424,710	971
2015	474,528	1032.6
2016	502,154	1496.6
2017	547,333	1475.6
2018	558,507	1501.1

(Ministry of Industry and Technology of Turkey: 4–50).

8.2 Water Projects in the Euphrates-Tigris Basin in Turkey

8.2.1 Euphrates River

Hydropower

During the JDP's rule, water projects in the Euphrates Basin continued to be implemented. Since it was impossible to build a new large reservoir on the Euphrates River (before the JDP—in the 20th century five reservoirs were built on the Euphrates), the JDP focused on the two branches that make up the Euphrates, Karasu and Murat, and their tributaries.

Table 8.4 shows the dams built, under construction and planned on the Murad River and their parameters.

Table 8.4 Murat River dams

HEPP	Installed Power MW	Annual Average Production GWh	Completion date	Province
Alpaslan 1	160	488	2012	Mush
Alpaslan 2	280	862,28	2020	Mush
Yukari Kalekoy	627	1504,71	2018	Bingol
Ashagi Kalekoy	500	1193,17	2020	Bingol
Gozeler	141	362,76	?	Bingol
Beyhan 1	582	1294,35	2015	Elazig
Beyhan 2	326,7	747,10	?	Elazig
Palu	144,5	334,12	?	Elazig
Total	**2761,2**	**6786,49**		

Table 8.5 shows the dams built, under construction and planned on the Karasu River and their parameters.

Table 8.5 Karasu River dams

HEPP	Installed Power MW	Annual Average Production GWh	Completion date	Province
Eric	283	813,6	?	Erzincan
Bagistas 1	141	478	2015	Erzincan
Kemah	198	565,4	?	Erzincan
Sasna	85	?		Erzincan
Ayranli	17	?		Sivas
Total	**724**	**1857**	–	

Irrigation

Ataturk Reservoir remains the main source of irrigation in the Euphrates Basin in the 21st century. Moreover the role of the Ataturk Reservoir has increased due to the implementation of new irrigation projects. We would like to introduce just two of these projects.

Mardin—Ceylanpinar Main Canal

In 2021, Mardin-Ceylanpinar Canal completed, which was to provide welfare to Sanliurfa and Mardin provinces. With the works carried out by the General Directorate of DSI, the Mardin Plain will meet the water of the Euphrates. The storage facility, which is under construction after the end of the canal, and the network work on the main canal continue rapidly *(En Son Haber: 15.06.2021).* The Mardin-Ceylanpinar irrigation channel project is set to irrigate over 2 million decares of agricultural land and contribute immensely to the region's economy. "*We are irrigating 2,167,930 decares of land along the 221-km canal. As part of this irrigation, 433,500 people will be employed,*" the DSİ's regional head, Oguz Kasap, told state-run Anadolu Agency, adding the project would raise some 500 million Turkish Liras annually. *"The entire plain will have access to water by the end of 2019 with the Second GAP Action Plan,"* Kasap added, to emphasize the project would not only benefit Mardin and neighboring Sanliurfa province but the entire region. JDP Mardin deputy Ceyda Bolunmez Chankiri also praised the project, defining the canal as "Turkey's biggest river". Mardin-Ceylanpinar Plains Irrigation area is increased from 328.000 ha to 388.000 ha by adding the 60.000 ha area which is planned to be irrigated by groundwater. The investigation of the problems of Harran Main Drainage Channel was also within the scope of this work *(Hurriyet Daily News: 11.07.2016).*

According to DSI General Manager Murat Acu, 221-km canal will be Turkey's largest artificial river and the capacity of it is 200 cubic meters/second, which is equal to the flow of Kizilirmak Rivers in March *(Mardin Life: 16.03.2018).* According to Sadrettin Karahocagil, Head of GAP Regional Development Administration at least 90 cubic meters of water pass per second in the main canals. "Especially in the main irrigation canal of Mardin, it has a current of 360 cubic meters of water per second. Considering that the normal flow of the Kizilirmak River is 180 cubic meters of water per second, it turns out that there is a very serious water flow in the main irrigation canals. At GAP, we are currently planning to construct main canals of approximately 2,500 km in length",—he said *(Haber Türk: 26.06.2019).*

The Suruc Water Tunnel (in Turkish: Suruç Tüneli), which opened on March 9, 2014, is a water supply tunnel located in Suruc district of Sanliurfa Province. The purpose of the tunnel is to provide irrigation for the Suruc Valley from Ataturk Dam. The construction cost about $ 2 billion. With its inner diameter of 7 m and its length of 17.185 km Suruc Tunnel is the country's longest tunnel and is the fifth biggest irrigation tunnel in the world. Thanks to the water pumped from Ataturk Dam, 94.814 hectares gross area is able to be irrigated. With the commissioning of the Suruc Tunnel, 90 m3 of water per second flows from Ataturk Dam to Suruc Plain, in other words, a river flows. The Suruc Tunnel aims to provide employment to approximately 190 thousand people and an annual income increase of 316 million TL in the national economy *(Anadolu: 09.03.2014).*

8.2.2 Tigris River

Hydropower

The Ilisu Dam Project

In 1954, the Turkish government began feasibility studies for a hydroelectric dam on the Tigris river, in the village of Ilisu in Southeastern Anatolia—in the culturally rich Upper Mesopotamia, i.e. the cradle of civilization—with the understanding that if the dam were to be built, most of the historic town of Hasankeyf would become submerged. In 1978, Hasankeyf became a class I protected archaeological site under Turkish law. That designation implied a prohibition of all new construction at the site, which had to be preserved in its original state. However, when in 1982 the Turkish government announced it would pursue the goal of revitalization of the poor southeastern part of the country in the framework of the GAP, Ilisu was listed as one of the 22 dams to be constructed as part of the ambitious initiative.

In 1998, archaeological excavations at Hasankeyf began. In the same year, the Turkish government signed an agreement with the Swiss companies Sulzer Hydro and ABB Switzerland, as a result of which the first consortium involved in the hydroelectricity project at Ilisu was born. This agreement was later terminated due to noncompliance with the project conditions on the Turkish side. In 2001, the Council of Europe's Committee on Culture, Science and Education prepared an information report which highlighted the importance of compliance with the conditions relating to the protection of cultural heritage in the execution of this project. The authors of the report observed that unlike the ancient town of Zeugma on the Euphrates, where Birecik dam buried precious Greco-Roman mosaics and a countless number of unstudied archaeological sites underneath its reservoir waters in 2000, Hasankeyf's treasures could still be saved if "the contract is [...] given to contractors who will [not] ignore these [project] conditions and [...] respect conservation of the cultural heritage".

The First Consortium

Since Turkey could not count on the World Bank's funding due to its downstream neighbors Iraq and Syria's protests against the project, it had to turn to look elsewhere for funding. Early attempts to finance the project failed due to lack of interest on the part of investors. A second attempt to attract funding led to the formation of the first consortium (1998–2002), which included the British company Balfour Beatty as consortium leader, the Italian Impregilo, Swedish Skanska, Turkish Nural, Kiska, and Tekfen, and the Union Bank of Switzerland (UBS). In 1998, the European companies applied for loan guarantees from the ECAs of their respective States to cover the financial risk. This met with intensified local, regional, and international protests in view of the expected catastrophic impacts of the dam. In the same year, the London-based "European Ilisu campaign" was founded as a result of concerted efforts of a number of European NGOs, including the Swiss Berne Declaration, the Austrian ECA-Watch, German World Economy, Ecology and Development (WEED, later to become the Gegen Stromung, or Counter Current network) and support from a number of international civil society and activist groups. As a result of growing pressure over the expected impact of the dam from NGOs, the public, and some politicians, in January 1999 the European ECAs requested that Turkey meet four conditions before the credit guarantees for the Ilisu project could be granted:

1. Develop a resettlement program based on internationally accepted standards and with independent monitoring;
2. Make provisions for upstream water treatment plants to maintain water quality;
3. Consult with Syria and Iraq and ensure adequate downstream flows at all times; and.
4. Produce a detailed plan to rescue and preserve as much of Hasankeyf's archaeological heritage as possible.

In the meantime, in November 2000 the World Commission on Dams (WCD) published its ground-breaking report, commissioned to develop "internationally acceptable criteria, guidelines and standards, where appropriate, for the planning, design, appraisal, construction, operation, monitoring and decommissioning of dams". The report sounded a stark warning about the social, cultural, and ecological cost of dams, and highlighted the importance of participatory decision-making according to the "rights and risks" approach, whereby all stakeholders whose rights are affected by the development, and all those who face a risk imposed on them involuntarily, ought to be included in the relevant procedures. In the framework of the Ilisu project, NGOs took on the role of educating the public and putting pressure on decision-makers to comply with the findings of the WCD as well as other international and Turkish standards. The NGOs also drew attention to, inter alia, the contradiction between the governments refusing to fund the project through the World Bank, but willing to support it privately through their ECAs, without following the Bank's sustainability safeguards. Protests in the ECA States also made it clear that the taxpayers did not want their governments to support a project with such catastrophic impacts.

Not long afterwards, the NGOs exposed Turkey's failure to meet the requested social, environmental, and cultural impact conditions. No appropriate mitigation measures had been implemented, and basic documents were missing. In the face of growing international opposition to the project as being in violation of international (and Turkish) standards, the main contractor, British engineering company Balfour Beatty, decided it was "not in the best interests of its stakeholders to pursue the project further", as meeting the conditions would not be possible without "substantial extra work and expense and considerable further delay", and together with the Italian civil engineering company Impregilo withdrew from the project at the end of 2001. After the Swiss UBS pulled out of the project amid further concerns, the consortium fell apart in 2002. Nevertheless, Turkey expressed its intention to continue with the project as soon as new financing was found.

The Second Consortium

In 2005, a second consortium composed of German, Swiss, Austrian, and Turkish companies was formed. The European members of the consortium again applied for export credit guarantees from their respective national ECAs, and for export loans from European banks: German DekaBank, Austrian Bank Austria Creditanstalt, Italian UniCredit, and French Société Générale, as well as two Turkish banks, Akbank and Garantibank. Due to pressure from members of the German, Swiss, and Austrian governments, as well as from the exporting companies to approve the export risk guarantees, the ECAs decided to take on the project. The ECAs own active involvement in the United Nations Environment Programme's follow-up process to the WCD, and the common fear that if Europe refused to help Turkey would turn to China, which would build the dam without any concern for environmental, cultural, and social standards, may also have been a factor in their decision.

However, having learned their lesson from the first consortium and due to pressure by NGOs, the ECAs requested from the outset that Turkey fulfill a set of project conditions relating to the social, environmental, and cultural impacts of the project, modeled after the World Bank standards, and submit to a strict periodic monitoring procedure, with three subcommittees separately examining issues of resettlement, cultural heritage, and the environment. The credit guarantees would thus be granted only if Turkey agreed to and enforced standards on dam construction relating to its impact on the affected people (including downstream riparian States), cultural heritage, and the environment. The ECAs also resolved to take their decisions jointly. Typically, ECAs come much later into a project (when it is time to insure the exporters' deliveries of goods or services overseas), and so their role is usually limited to requesting that exporters demand compliance with international best practices. What was therefore remarkable about the role of ECAs in the Ilisu case is that by requesting the project conditions at an early stage of their involvement, they were able to shape the process and its outcome in line with some of the best practices and the concerns over the human, cultural, and ecological costs of the project as voiced by the NGOs and the public.

In return for "in principle" credit guarantees, in an agreement with the ECAs signed in October 2006 ("the 2006 Agreement") the Turkish government committed to fulfilling 160 conditions, or Terms of Reference (ToR), to bridge the gap between the standards applicable in Turkey and those used by the World Bank in such situations to mitigate the negative impacts of the project. Thirteen of these conditions were related to cultural heritage. The implementation of the ToR was to take place according to two deadlines: 27 conditions were to be met within 18 months from signing the agreement (by March 2008), and the remaining 133 before the construction was commenced. This incremental approach was criticized as contrary to World Bank policies, which recommend compliance before the final financial commitment is made. Upon signing the 2006 Agreement, there had been no proper resettlement plan and no appropriate environmental impact assessment (EIA) for Ilisu (the EIA prepared in 2005 by the National Water Administration pursuant to Turkish Environmental Law from 1983 fell short of World Bank's standards), and no cultural heritage impact assessment whatsoever, in spite of such a requirement under international law. In case of Turkey's default on any of the social, cultural, and environmental conditions, the 2006 Agreement stipulated that both the ECAs and the European banks, which granted export loans, would withdraw from the project.

Terms of Reference on the protection of cultural heritage and the expert review by NGOs In light of the ToR related to cultural heritage, Turkey was required to, inter alia:

- provide baseline data on the archaeological finds in the affected area;
- submit a comprehensive Cultural Heritage Action Plan for all archaeological surveys and excavations, including a time schedule, responsible personnel, budgets, etc.;
- submit a list of involved institutions and their responsibilities, and coordinate their work;
- submit a plan for the investigation and excavation of mounds;
- ensure the availability of experts to supervise the archaeological works and to deal with chance finds;
- ensure that 50% of the workers were persons affected by the project;
- provide the legal basis for the relocation of monuments;
- carry out ethnographic studies by conducting interviews with the population to collect the history of the villages and the stories of the people;
- develop a concept for the Cultural Park;
- provide monitoring reports on the surveys and excavations, the rebuilding of monuments in the Cultural Park, and the Park's construction and operation.

Although a step in the right direction, these predominantly technical requirements did not exhaustively address the challenges of protecting the cultural heritage of Hasankeyf. An expert review launched by the Berne Declaration, ECA-Watch Austria, WEED, and other NGOs after the 2006 Agreement was concluded identified a series of shortcomings in the ToR, and the cultural heritage provisions were no exception. Among the shortcomings identified by the NGOs were: lack of any clear indicators as to how cultural heritage was to be safeguarded, leaving a lot to the discretion of the Turkish authorities (for example, the decision about which monuments were to be salvaged before the flooding); lack of a requirement to undertake mitigation measures for the monuments at risk of submersion, and to consult with the relevant NGOs and the affected groups. This latter point was particularly important, as according to a survey conducted at Hasankeyf in 2012 by the environmental organization Doga Dernegi, the majority of the town's population is against the dam and the government's plans toward the site's cultural heritage and resettlement; 67.8% of respondents stated they did not want to leave Hasankeyf. However, the locals have generally been excluded from any relevant decision-making processes. Furthermore, alleged security considerations allowed the government to limit access to the site and crack down on protests against the dam project, especially after the proclamation of the state of emergency following the 2016 coup. The review by NGOs also noted that the ToR ignored the importance of Hasankeyf's particular setting for its cultural value, failed to entertain the option of in situ preservation as per current international and Turkish law, and did not consider the matter of feasibility of the relocation of monuments *(Drazewska: 2018)*.

So, the second Ilisu consortium, which was formed of Turkish, German, Swiss, and Austrian companies in March 2005, began the construction works in August 2006. But it was interrupted two years later following a successful campaign launched by environmental groups and international organizations. The consortium was dissolved in 2009. This led to the cancellation of international funding support from European governments and several private firms. Determined to see the project through, Turkey sought other lenders, both domestically and abroad. Construction work resumed in 2010.

According to the Turkish authorities the project aims to meet the country's rising energy demand, create jobs and stimulate economic growth in Turkey's impoverished south-east. The proposed Ilisu Dam on the Tigris River thus is one of the world's most controversial hydropower projects. The project itself and the policies of the consortium were heavily criticized by several environmental and human rights groups. Critics of the project claim that the region's cultural heritage will suffer irreparable damage with the flooding of the ancient city of Hasankeyf and neighboring areas and the involuntary resettlement of tens of thousands of people, while at the same time causing further environmental damage to the Mesopotamian Marshlands. It will displace up to 70,000 people (mostly Kurds), drown the 10,000 year-old city of Hasankeyf, and destroy valuable biodiversity. Iraq's government has also expressed concerns that Turkey will use the Ilisu Dam to control the flow of the Tigris to the detriment of the downstream countries.

Thus, the controversial Ilisu Dam Project has raised concerns among a wide range of stakeholders including the main Tigris riparians, local residents who will be displaced, export credit agencies and international nongovernmental organizations. While the dam's design was finalized in 1982, social, historical, environmental and financial concerns have stalled its implementation for decades. As one of a total of 22 dam projects in GAP, the Ilisu Dam is located near the Kurdish village of Ilisu, about 65 km from the Syrian-Turkish border. It will be the largest HEPP on the Tigris within a framework of GAP with a hydropower capacity of 1200 MW, producing an expected 3800 GWh/yr. With a planned height of 135 m, the dam will have a 10.4 BCM reservoir. The Ilisu Project includes plans to build the smaller Cizre Dam for irrigation purposes and additional hydropower production.

Turkey started on May 19, 2020 the first turbine at the Ilisu Dam on the Tigris River in southeastern Mardin province. One of the largest irrigations and energy projects in Turkey, Ilisu Dam will have a total of six turbines when complete. Ilisu, a project carried out within the framework of GAP to boost development in the region. "*Turkey's fourth-largest dam, Ilisu Dam, will contribute TL 2.8 billion ($412 million) to the Turkish economy annually, contribute to the development of the southeast, and it is expected to generate 4.1 billion kilowatt-hours of electricity per year*," President of Turkey Recep Tayyip Erdogan said. "*By discharging the water collected here to the Cizre Dam, which we will soon build, we will both generate 1.1 billion kilowatt/hour energy and irrigate 765,000 decares of land*," he added *(Daily Sabah: 19.05.2020).*

In November, 2021 Erdogan inaugurated Ilisu Dam in the country's southeastern province Mardin. Addressing the opening ceremony, he said the project has been completed despite obstacles, including financing issues and terror attacks. He said it is the largest dam on the Tigris River, and the fourth largest Turkish hydroelectric plant. 'This dam is the second-largest dam in the country after Turkey's Ataturk Dam and the largest in the world in terms of filling volume among the 'concrete faced rockfill dam' types,' he said. Saying the project cost 20 billion Turkish liras ($2 billion), he argued that its contributions to the Turkish economy will be around 3 billion Turkish liras ($309 million) annually *(Anadolu: 06.11.2021).*

Silvan Dam is an embankment concrete-face rock-fill currently under construction on the Batman River in the district of Silvan, Diyarbekir Province in southeastern Turkey. It is part of GAP and located upstream of the Batman Dam. Construction began on 26 July 2011 and is expected to be complete in 2023. It is designed to irrigate an area of 245,000 ha (610,000 acres). The power station will have an installed capacity of 160 MW. The dam, which was built for energy and irrigation purposes, will acquire the title of the second largest irrigation investment after Ataturk Dam, within the scope of GAP, with a reservoir volume of 7.3 BCM. Height of 175.50 m and reached 8 million 743 thousand cubic meters of fill volume with Turkey's and Europe's highest dam in front of the filling capacity will be 8.4 million cubic meters of concrete faced dam levels.

According to data compiled from DSI data, Silvan, Pamukchay, Ambar, Kuruchay, Bashlar, Kibris, Karacalar and Bulaklidere dams are being constructed within the scope of Silvan Project, where 8 dams and 23 irrigation facilities are targeted. The Silvan Dam was delayed for 2 years due to PKK attacks, is of great importance in achieving irrigation targets in the region.

Turkey Chambers of Agriculture Union (TZOB) Board Member and Diyarbekir Chamber of Agriculture Provincial Coordination President Mehmet Cevat evidence, Silvan Project will irrigate about 2 million 350 thousand hectares. Pointing out that the water in the dam will be transferred to the plains through the Silvan and Babakaya tunnels, Delil said, "There will be a 4–5 times increase in agricultural production and hence the income of the producer in the lands where will reach water. This will increase the welfare of the local people and will decrease the migration from the village to the city. Thanks to the produce of harvest twice a year, the agricultural industry will also develop rapidly in Diyarbekir. This project will create 300,000 jobs" *(News1: 04.05.2020).*

The Cizre Dam is a proposed dam on the Tigris River north of Cizre, Turkey. The Cizre Dam is to be built downstream of the Ilisu Dam. The Cizre Dam is also one of the planned dams of GAP. The purpose of the Cizre Dam is irrigation, hydro-power and to control the tail waters of the Ilisu Dam. A tender for the Cizre Dam was unsuccessfully issued in May 2008 but another issue on 15 May 2014 left Zorlu Energy as the winning bidder. The Cizre Dam will have a hydro-power capacity of 240 MW and will provide irrigation for 121,000 ha.

8.3 Rivers for Cooperative Endeavors

In the first decade of the 2000s, transboundary water policies evolved from hostile to cooperative. Political will expressed at the highest decision-making levels was most decisive in building these cooperative frameworks. However, water bureaucracies also had a role in that change.

Shortly after signing of the Turkish-Syrian Ceyhan Security Agreement in October 1998, Syria requested the resumption of the JTC meetings to enable the water issue to be considered. The Ceyhan Agreement (Adana Accords) marked the beginning of a new era based on more cooperative initiatives of interest to both sides. One of the first initiatives was the 2001 Joint Communiqué between the Southeastern Anatolia Project Regional Development Administration (GAP RDA) under the Turkish prime minister and the General Organisation for Land Development (GOLD) under the Syrian Ministry of Irrigation. The GAP RDA-GOLD cooperation was based on the common understanding of the sustainable utilization of the region's land and water resources through joint rural development and environmental protection projects, joint training programs, exchanges of experts and technology, and study missions.

Syrian and Turkish delegations visited each other's development project sites. During these contacts, the two sides had opportunities to exchange their experiences of positive and negative impacts of water and land resource development projects going back several decades. Once again, the water issue was relegated to the technical level, as in the 1960s, and left to intergovernmental networks composed of technocrats. However, unlike the technical negotiations in the 1960s, the GAP-GOLD dialogue covered such disparate issues as urban and rural water quality management and rural development (participatory irrigation management and agricultural research). Even though the dialogue between these two leading institutions has not resulted in concrete project implementation or regular exchange programs, it has served as a semiformal consultation mechanism and paved the way for initiatives taken by other government departments and agencies in 2008 and 2009.

8.3.1 High-Level Strategic Cooperation Councils and Water

In 2008, the Turkish government embarked on a number of cooperative foreign policy initiatives involving its southern neighbors, Syria and Iraq in particular. The political reasons behind these initiatives can be analyzed at contextual, regional, bilateral, and domestic levels. However, the political will expressed and sealed at the highest level in Turkey for broader cooperation with its southern neighbors was also reflected in official statements and cooperative transboundary water development and management initiatives in the Euphrates, Tigris, and Orontes river systems.

In this context, Turkey and Iraq signed a Joint Political Declaration on the Establishment of the High-Level Strategic Cooperation Council (HSCC) on 10 July 2008. The first ministerial meeting of the HSCC, a forum for joint meetings of the Iraqi and Turkish cabinets, was held in Istanbul on 17–18 September 2009. The Turkish foreign minister was accompanied by seven executive members of the cabinet, including the ministers of trade, energy, transport, agriculture, and the environment (water) while the Iraqi minister was accompanied by nine executive cabinet members, the counterparts of the Turkish ministers, and their deputy ministers.

According to the strategic partnership agreement between Turkey and Iraq, the HSCC was to meet at least once a year, with the prime ministers of the two countries chairing the meetings. Ministerial meetings, on the other hand, would be held at least three times a year and technical delegations would come together four times a year. Decisions made by the HSCC would be implemented within the framework of an action plan. Barham Salih, Iraq's former deputy prime minister, called the agreement "the starting point of the Middle East common market" and likened the improving relations between Iraq and Turkey to the relationship between France and Germany in the 1950s.

On the other front, the first Turkish-Syrian HSCC meeting took place in Damascus on 22–23 December 2009. These cooperative initiatives taken at the highest political level made it possible to resolve prolonged disputes between Turkey and Syria. Thus, under the chairmanship of two ministers, Syria's minister of irrigation and Turkey's minister of the environment and forestry, a commission composed of technocrats and diplomats from the two countries met in Ankara on 8 December 2009 to prepare the framework and contents of the series of protocols, Memorandums of Understanding (MoUs), on the modalities of development, management, and use of the waters of the Euphrates, the Tigris, and the Orontes rivers.

That period of rapprochement showed that, led by politicians at the highest level, the riparians preferred functional cooperation and a benefit sharing approach. One productive approach to the development of transboundary waters was to take a regional view of the benefits to be derived from the basin. The Euphrates-Tigris case supports the observation that, when negotiations focused solely on water sharing, upstream and downstream differences were exacerbated, giving greater prominence to water gains and losses. This has regularly required the riparians to see water as more than just a commodity to be divided—a zero-sum, rights-based view—and to develop a positive-sum, integrative approach that ensures the equitable allocation not of the water but of the benefits derived from it. Adding development opportunities in other sectors may enlarge the area of possible agreement and make implementation more manageable. Multiresource linkages may offer more opportunities for the generation of creative solutions, allowing for greater economic efficiency through a "basket of benefits."

Broadening the scope of the cooperation agenda to take in sectors of socioeconomic development, including water, and simultaneously fostering a situation of regional interdependence were in fact the main aims underlying the establishment of both the Turkish-Syrian and Turkish–Iraqi HSCCs, which were set up to address more than the water predicament in the region. However, the comprehensive and strategic nature of the HSCCs resulted in an innovative approach to transboundary water issues in that the water and diplomatic bureaucracies were empowered to draft and sign a series of protocols addressing problems associated with water development, management, and use. In fact, the Turkish and Syrian authorities managed to convene the second meetings of their HSCC at ministerial and prime ministerial levels in October and December 2010, respectively. In addition to issuing a joint statement on bilateral and regional cooperation, they evaluated the progress made in implementing the agreements between the two countries signed in 2009. The second meeting of the Turkey-Iraq HSCC was postponed, however, due to the delay in the formation of the Iraqi government in 2010.

8.3.2 New Water Protocols and New Perspectives on Transboundary Water Issues

The Water Protocol Between Turkey and Iraq

At the Turkey-Iraq HSCC meeting, forty-eight MoUs were signed by the two countries on 15 October 2009, one of them concerning water. Even though the river is not referred to by name in the title, the text of this MoU explicitly states that it concerns the waters of the Euphrates and the Tigris rivers. In line with the envisaged functional approach, the MoU was signed by Iraq's Ministry of Water Resources and Turkey's Ministry of the Environment and Forestry (MoEF), the government departments responsible for all technical matters relating in particular to water development and management and the protection of water resources. The MoU identified particular issues requiring urgent transboundary cooperation, including assessment of water resources, which are tending to diminish because of increases in water use and climate change; assessment and calibration of existing hydrological measuring stations; modernization of existing irrigation systems; prevention of water losses from domestic water supply systems and provision of safe water; construction of water supply and water treatment facilities in Iraq, with the participation of Turkish companies; development of mechanisms to solve problems arising during the dry period; and joint investigation, planning, and projects for flood protection.

The modalities of cooperation are also described in the MoU. The parties agree to transfer knowledge, experience, and technology on water management practices by developing cooperative projects and conducting research and development activities. It is interesting to note that, rather than arguing over only their respective water shares, as happened at past JTC meetings, the Iraqi and Turkish authorities focused on common issues in transboundary water management and use. Those issues are directly related to water development, use, and management practices at national level, which actually have direct impacts on transboundary water policies and practices. The protocol also specifically addresses emerging regional (and global) issues such as the effects of climate change on regional water resources, which had been neglected for decades. Another distinct characteristic of the MoU is that it envisages involving such nongovernmental entities as academic institutions, private firms, and nongovernmental organizations in the activities that it covers.

The Orontes: From a Bone of Contention to a Medium of Cooperation
At the first meeting of their HSCC held in Damascus on 23–24 December 2009, Turkey and Syria signed fifty protocols, four of which concerned regional waters (i.e., those of the Euphrates, Tigris, and Orontes). In this context, the parties agreed to build a joint dam where the Orontes River crosses the Turkish-Syrian border. They agreed to share the cost of the dam, which is to produce energy for both sides and irrigate 20,000 ha of agricultural land in Turkey and 10,000 ha in Syria. The foundation stones were laid in February 2011, with the Turkish and Syrian prime ministers in attendance, just before the unrest broke out in Syria in the spring of 2011.

The signing of an official protocol on the waters of the Orontes was a breakthrough in Turkish-Syrian hydropolitics and also in wider political relations. For decades, Syria did not recognize the Turkish-Syrian political border where the Orontes crosses it, claiming territorial rights to the Turkish province of Hatay (historically, Alexandretta). The signing of the protocol implied the recognition of the border. Also for decades, Turkey called for regulation of the waters of the Orontes River, which often fluctuated, causing severe flooding or drought in downstream Turkish towns and villages. However, Syria never agreed to build water development structures on the border, arguing that the Orontes is a national river. In this respect, the Protocol of December 2009 marks a major change in Syria's attitude. In fact, it marks the beginning of flourishing cooperation between otherwise hostile riparian states after their agreement to build joint dams on their joint borders.

Syria's Emerging Need for Water from the Tigris
Turkey and Syria signed a protocol on the Tigris under which Turkey agreed that Syria could withdraw an annual 1.25 km3 of water, provided that the flow of water is within the average. The withdrawals are based on monthly flows and are to be made at appropriate times and places. This protocol is further evidence of a change in the positions of the water and diplomatic bureaucracies, particularly in Syria. When the hydropolitical tensions were at their peak in the 1980s, Syria had never agreed to discuss the waters of the Tigris, considering it to be insignificant because of its geographical location in the basin: the Tigris forms the boundary between Turkey and Syria and between Syria and Iraq for about 40 km. At that time, Syria focused almost exclusively on the Euphrates, prioritizing the completion of the Euphrates Valley Project. As Syrian technocrats eventually encountered technical and social difficulties in reclaiming land in the Euphrates Valley, their attention turned to northeastern Syria where it was possible to expand the amount of irrigated land.

8.3.3 Issues of Common Concern: Protocols on Water Efficiency, Drought Management, and Quality Remediation

The other two protocols signed by Turkey and Syria cover issues that have only recently come to the agenda of transboundary water negotiations among the technocrats and diplomats concerned. In this respect, it is interesting to note that this was the first official agreement concluded by the two countries on the protection of the environment, water quality management, water efficiency, drought management, and flood protection with a view toward addressing the adverse effects of climate change. Unlike the bilateral protocol concluded in 1987 on sharing the waters of the Euphrates, these protocols focused on how the riparian states were to use, manage, protect, and develop the diminishing water resources of the Euphrates and the Tigris rivers. An analysis of the wording of these two protocols reveals that the water bureaucracies had a chance to open up the countries' black boxes. On the basis of the political will expressed at the highest level of the HSCC, water technocrats have together concentrated on the urgent problems of the acute shortage and deteriorating quality of water resources. Gone are the days when the two countries adopted reserved and rigid positions on their water shares and rights: now they openly discuss new and efficient methods and procedures for managing the supply of and demand for water for agricultural, industrial, and domestic purposes. The protocols cover a range of issues. These include various forms of supply management such as cloud seeding (artificial rain) to increase precipitation, the installation of early flood warning systems and flood protection measures, and agricultural practices with drought-resistant crops. They also include various forms of demand management such as sharing of knowledge and experience about modern irrigation techniques; prevention of water losses in domestic water supply; organization of training programs relating to the operation of dams and the efficient utilization of water resources; sharing of knowledge and technology pertaining to wastewater storage and the reuse of treated wastewater in agriculture and industry; and cooperation on the development of land use techniques to increase the amount of soil and water saved. The general approach and the content of the protocols reveal too that Turkey's firsthand experience with the European Union's water policy and approach to water management has been broadly translated into the principles envisioned in the protocols.

8.3.4 The Ministers' Network and the JTC Revitalized

On 22 March 2007, at the opening of an international conference in Antalya, Turkey, the Turkish minister of the environment and forestry invited the Syrian minister of irrigation and the Iraqi minister of water resources to join him in discussing how to set up a cooperative framework to deal with regional water issues. These ministers decided that the periodic meetings of the JTC, which had been held between 1982 and 1992 before being completely abandoned, should be resumed. Thus, a series of JTC meetings have been held since, the first in Damascus, Syria, on 7–11 May 2007, which was followed by a tripartite ministerial meeting in Damascus, on 10–11 January 2008, at which it was agreed that training programs on irrigation water management and efficient utilization of water resources would be conducted. At the second JTC meeting held in Istanbul on 23–24 February 2009, officials decided that the next ministerial meeting would be held in Baghdad, opportunities for developing joint projects would be seized, and a JTC bylaw stating its mission and responsibilities would be adopted.

On 3 September 2009, both a tripartite ministerial meeting and the third meeting of the JTC took place in Ankara. The three sides decided to cooperate in initiating water training programs and in monitoring and exchanging information on climate change and drought conditions in the three countries. They also agreed to erect new water flow gauging stations and to modernize the existing ones. After talks between the Iraqi foreign minister and the Turkish environment minister, Turkey further agreed to provide 550 m3/sec of water from the Euphrates River during the dry season in the autumn of 2009. In March 2008, the Turkish, Iraqi, and Syrian ministers agreed to establish a joint water institute in Turkey, with each riparian appointing fifteen water engineers to conduct studies on water use efficiency and improved water management in the region. The institute was to map water resources in the region and draw up a report on measures that the respective countries should take to ensure effective management of those resources. The engineers from the three countries have been meeting to exchange information and know-how. The first training activity in this context concerned modern irrigation practices in the region and the second focused on dam construction and safety. The group has also developed an interest in studying climate change and its impacts on regional waters. The training institute in Istanbul hosted the third training program for experts in that field.

The ministers' initiative in reconvening the JTC has facilitated the drafting of a series of MoUs, putting an official seal on cooperation. Moreover, their network has also led to a series of training programs that have helped water bureaucracies in particular to achieve a certain level of common understanding and discourse. Furthermore, the ministerial network has proved to be capable of flexibility and spontaneity in addressing acute water shortages in the region by making swift decisions to adjust flows to meet the needs of downstream riparians.

8.3.5 The Euphrates-Tigris Initiative for Cooperation: A Network of Academics and Professionals

Another significant development in the region is the Euphrates-Tigris Initiative for Cooperation (ETIC), which was established in May 2005 by a group of scholars and professionals from the three main riparian countries. The overall goal of the initiative is to promote cooperation among the three riparians with a view toward achieving technical, social, and economic development in the Euphrates-Tigris region. ETIC's composition and role are remarkably consistent with the epistemic community's theory and role in institutional bargaining. An epistemic community is defined as a "network of professionals with recognised expertise and competence in a particular domain and an authoritative claim to policy-relevant knowledge within that domain or issue-area."

ETIC's origins can be traced back to early meetings of scientists from Iraq, Syria, and Turkey as well as the United States in 2004. This group of dedicated scholars has been meeting with flexible agendas. At the first stage of these gatherings, the participants shared information on national water policies and raised the significance of water issues in the context of the three riparian countries' socioeconomic development targets. The members of the group were quick to develop a common understanding of existing conditions, pressing problems, and needs in the region, which led them to decide to turn their expertise and experience to account in ETIC.

ETIC is a track-two effort, meaning that it is voluntary, nonofficial, nonbinding, not for profit, and nongovernmental. It is not affiliated with any government, but seeks to contribute positively to efforts, official and unofficial, that will enhance the dialogue, understanding, and collaboration among the riparians of the Euphrates-Tigris system. As a multiriparian initiative, ETIC has been unique in that it looks beyond water rights per se to themes related to environmental protection, development and gender equality, water management, governance, and grassroots participation in a holistic, multistakeholder framework.

ETIC's members contend that awareness of socioeconomic development is essential to an understanding of the real dynamics of the region. ETIC's ultimate objective is defined by the founders as being a situation in which the "quality of life for people in all communities, including rural and urban areas, is improved, and harmony among countries and with nature in the Euphrates-Tigris region is achieved," so that cooperation on technical, social, and economic development in the Euphrates-Tigris region may be promoted. In line with its vision and overall goal, ETIC prepares and implements joint training and capacity-building programs as well as undertaking research projects aimed at responding to the common needs and concerns of the people in the region. In conducting these activities, ETIC has built partnerships with international organizations, nongovernmental organizations, and universities.

Thus, a partial institutionalization of water cooperation had already begun before it was abruptly halted in late 2011 as overarching bilateral political relations worsened. When it has a chance to resume, transboundary water cooperation should start from a variety of perspectives and issues, which may again provide opportunities for regional cooperation. In such a context, the array of perspectives and issues should include, among other things, joint initiatives for the collection of reliable data on surface and groundwater resources. In fact, water technocrats drafting the recent protocols have already emphasized this aspect by referring to the issue of the assessment of water resources and the calibration of existing hydrological measurement stations in the bilateral protocols. On the basis of such objective and consistent knowledge of the river system, joint projects could be conducted in such water-related development fields as energy, agriculture, the environment, and health. ETIC might engage a variety of stakeholders such as academics, professionals, and representatives of civil society organizations and business circles as well as the competent authorities of international agencies in the implementation of small-scale, but sustainable cooperative projects relating to various aspects of common concern: water quantity and quality management, health, agricultural development, energy production, infrastructure development, and environmental protection *(Kibaroglu: 2013).*

Thus, Turkey also started shifting its discourse over water from focusing on sovereignty to the advocacy of benefit-sharing. The water issue was somewhat de-securitized and addressed as a technical issue (the meetings of JTC—which were regularly held from 1982 to 1992—were also resumed in 2007; meetings took place in Syria (May 2007), Istanbul (February 2009), and Baghdad (September 2009)) *(Hinnebusch & Tür 2013: 141).*

8.4 Water as Turkey's Leverage Against Neighboring Countries

In the 21st century, in addition to water cooperation with Syria and Iraq, Turkey began to use water as leverage against these countries. This is especially relevant in the second decade of the 21st century, when Turkey largely replaced the policy of "zero problems with its neighbors" with a "neo-Ottoman" policy (aimed at increasing Turkish influence in the territory of the former Ottoman Empire). On the one hand, this was related to the significant rise of Turkey in the 21st century, and on the other hand, the significant decline experienced by Iraq and Syria, due to the American invasion of Iraq and its consequences and the start of the civil war in Syria. As a result, the role of Turkey in becoming a hydro-hegemon in all its aspects was emphasized (they were mentioned in the first chapter), while in the 20th century Hafez Assad's Syria and Saddam Hussein's Iraq were almost equivalent countries to Turkey and even militarily superior to it (compared to Turkey, Syria had more tanks, and Iraq had the most powerful army in the entire Arab world).

In the 21st century, there are many testimonies that the authorities of Syria and Iraq accused Turkey of depriving their countries of water. There are many publications on the Internet in which Turkey is accused of using water as a weapon and the consequences of its influence on neighboring countries are presented—"Turkey proxies weaponizing water in north Syria with river dams", "Water Drop in Euphrates River Increases Tensions Between Syrian Kurds, Turkey", "Euphrates River is weaponized by Turkey against Syria, Iraq", "Turkey is reportedly depriving hundreds of thousands of people of water", "Iraq asks Turkey to release more water along Tigris, Euphrates", "The Impact of Hydro-Politics on the Relations of Turkey, Iraq, and Syria". We are not going to present that whole string of accusations. Our goal is to show how Turkey uses water as a lever against Syria and Iraq, and what kind of concessions Turkey was able to extract from those countries in various fields. In this context, we emphasized 4 "water episodes", which are related to the policy of the Turkish authorities towards Syria and Iraq (Iran), as well as towards the Kurds of Syria and Iraq.

8.4.1 The Case of Syria—Friendship Dam

After the Ocalan crisis was de-escalated with his expulsion in 1999, political rapprochement between Turkey and Syria began in the 2000s. This significant shift in relations lasted until the Syrian War in 2011. Cooperation on water initially started with lower ranking water bureaucracies followed by cooperation at higher political levels. Revitalisation of the Joint Technical Committee and establishment of the High-Level Strategic Cooperation Council (HLSCC) were important steps to galvanise cooperation on water and non-water issues. In the context of political rapprochement, four memorandum of understanding (MoU) out of thirty envisioned interstate cooperation regarding water issues. Those MoUs include construction of a joint dam on the Orontes River and construction of pumping stations that would enable Syria to extract water from the Tigris River, enhancing cooperation on effective water utilisation to combat drought and enhancing cooperation to improve water quality. The agreement between Turkey and Syria on the Orontes River is of vital importance for three reasons.

First, just like symbolism is often made by the ruling elites to portray dams as symbols of national progress, the joint dam is regarded by the Turkish and Syrian elites as a symbol of the political rapprochement. Thus, the dam was named as the "Friendship Dam" to emphasize this symbolism.

Second, while other cooperative frameworks realised during the rapprochement set out limited cooperation with respect to water, the Friendship Dam aimed to resolve the Orontes dispute effectively. According to the MoU, each party will take the required water for their irrigation needs from the dam reservoir and they will notify their monthly extractions from the dam at the beginning of every year (MoU on Friendship Dam 2011, Article 10). Furthermore, the parties also agreed upon establishment of a joint commission that will operate the dam and determine each party's water needs for irrigation. Therefore, the Friendship Dam project also served as a robust tool in the resolution of the long-standing water conflict between Syria and Turkey in the Orontes River.

Third, Syria has never officially declared that it gave up its territorial claims over the Alexandretta province. Syria's policy during the political rapprochement with Turkey was not to put the issue on the political agenda in bilateral relations.

According to this view, the issue is "put off for coming generations". Therefore, the agreement on the construction of the Friendship Dam was considered as a major policy shift in Syria's policy on the Alexandretta issue as well as in regard to the Orontes dispute.

That major changes in the political context and power dynamics led to this shift. Global and regional dynamics pushed Syria and Turkey to seek friendly relations due to the following reasons. First, as the USA pressure on Syria intensified after the invasion of Iraq, the Syrian leadership sought for diversifying alliances to shield against the USA. In this context, Turkey was regarded as one of the key regional actors to achieve this aim. Second, one of the important political consequences of the invasion of Iraq is the territorial integrity of Iraq. Both Turkey and Syria had shared interests concerning the future of Iraq. Third, Syria also had to choose either to cooperate with Turkey or to continue to support the PKK. The political context pushed the Syrian government to choose the former. Therefore, the PKK was no longer a form of leverage. Turkey's doctrinal shift towards the Middle East affairs has strengthened its economic and political ties with Middle Eastern countries. Cooperation with Syria became more important for Turkey, since Syria was seen as the opening gate to the Middle East. Political rapprochement also resulted in improving economic ties between Turkey and Syria, and Turkey became a major trading partner with Syria. Finally, by the 2000s, almost all the major dams were already completed particularly on the mainstream Euphrates as part of the GAP plan. This enormous storage capacity and water control enabled Turkey a significant leverage in hydropolitics on the Euphrates and Tigris Basin.

However, a decade-long political rapprochement ended after the beginning of the Syrian War. As the first demonstrations started across Syria only 1 month after the inauguration of the Friendship Dam, the relations between the two countries have gradually worsened. Notably, after the Turkish jet was shot down by Syria (in the summer of 2012), relations were permanently suspended. As relations have continued to deteriorate since 2011, the discourse that portrays the Alexandretta province as a "stolen territory" returned to the Syrian political agenda. The decision-making platforms such as the HLSCC that enabled such cooperation on different issue were also suspended. Bilateral deals including the construction of the Friendship Dam were suspended. Therefore, the construction works also halted *(Conker and Hussein: 2019).*

In general, we agree with all the arguments presented by Conker and Hussein, but we want to emphasize the moment that Turkey achieved significant concessions from Syria by using the water factor as well. It has already been mentioned in the previous chapters that in the 20th century, Syria refused to accept the loss of Alexandretta, to recognize it as part of Turkey, and in that context to discuss water issues related to the Orontes River with Turkey, stressing that "that river is completely in its territory and therefore has nothing to discuss with Turkey." However, during Bashar Assad's rule, Syria not only started negotiating with Turkey over the Orontes River, but also signed an agreement with it on the construction of the Friendship Dam, and thus de facto recognized Turkey's territorial integrity (regardless of the fact that later this issue returned to Syria's political agenda). In our opinion, Turkey achieved such a result also due to the use of the water card (not denying the arguments made by Conker and Hussein).

In the early 2000s within the frame of a free trade area planned along the Syrian-Turkish border, an agreement was made to open four border trade centres in Turkey, one of them in Cilvegozu in Hatay. The fact that Syria agreed that a centre be established in Hatay is an additional indirect recognition of Turkish sovereignty over the area. During Syrian Prime Minister Naji al-Otri's visit to Turkey in July 2004, Turkish Foreign Trade Minister Kurshad Tuzmen stated that the troubles between Turkey and Syria regarding the border had been overcome (although he did not mention Hatay by name). The signing of an official protocol on the waters of the Orontes was a real breakthrough in Turkish-Syrian hydropolitical and even broader political relations. It manifested a drastic change in the Syrian attitude *(Hinnebusch & Tur 2013: 119, 155)*.

All this shows that although by opening the border checkpoint in Hatay, Syria indirectly recognized Turkey's sovereignty over that area, from Turkey's point of view, it was further strengthened by the water protocols signed in December 2009. Syria was already forced to recognize Hatay as Turkish territory also in the context of water issues. We want to divide the water factor into 3 components: Euphrates, Tigris and Orontes, as on 23 and 24 December 2009, the two riparians signed fifty protocols, of which four addressed water cooperation on the Euphrates, Tigris and the Orontes. In our opinion, Syria hoped that in the context of water issues by improving relations with Turkey and recognizing its territorial integrity the following situation will result.

- Syria will receive more water through the Euphrates River and perhaps will sign a new water agreement with Turkey on the waters of the Euphrates. In the fall of 2009, Turkey agreed to a minimal flow of 550 m3/second on the Euphrates (it had barely reached 450 m3/s between 2000 and 2001).
- By jointly building a reservoir with 110 MCM on the Orontes River, it will be able to irrigate the border areas. Of that total, 40 MCM will be used to prevent flooding and the rest for energy production and irrigation.

- Turkey will not object to certain use of Tigris waters by Syria. For the first time since the start of trilateral negotiations in 1982, Syria agreed, in January 2008, to discuss and sign a MoU with Turkey and Iraq on the Tigris waters. In the 1980s, Syria had never agreed to discuss the waters of the Tigris, perceiving this river less significant than the Euphrates Basin. However, as Syrian technocrats faced technical and social difficulties in reclaiming land in the Euphrates Valley, their attention turned towards northeast Syria where there is potential to expand irrigated land. The agreement stipulates that Syria can extract up to 1.25 BCM per year from the Tigris River, when the flow of water was within the average. The water withdrawals are arranged according to monthly flows, and pumping will be done when the time and place allows.
- Syria hoped to improve the quality of water entering Syria from Turkey and solve a number of other similar problems. In this respect, it is interesting to note that within a framework of an official agreement the parties have dealt, for the first time, with the protection of the environment, management of water resources quality, and scrutinized the issues of water efficiency, drought management and flood protection in tackling the negative impacts of climate change. As opposed to the bilateral agreement concluded in 1987 on sharing the waters of the Euphrates, those protocols focused on how the riparian states use, manage, protect and develop the diminishing water resources of the Euphrates and Tigris rivers. The issues covered in the protocols are diverse, ranging from various ways of supply management, such as cloud seeding (artificial rain) to increase precipitation, installation of early flood warning systems and flood protection measures, agricultural practices with drought resistant crops; to various means of demand management, such as sharing of knowledge and experience on modern irrigation techniques, prevention of water loss in domestic water supply; the operation of dams and efficient utilization of water resources; sharing knowledge and technology pertaining to waste water storage and the reuse of treated waste water in agriculture and industry; and cooperation on the development of land use techniques to increase the saving of soil water.

Perhaps it is not superfluous to describe the situation in the water sector in Syria in the 2000s, how it suffered from droughts and in that context asked Turkey for more water from the Euphrates River. Droughts are recurring climatic events, which often hit Syria, bringing significant water shortages, economic losses and adverse social consequences. In the last 10 years, increasing population has added to the growing demand for water and other natural resources in Syria. The latest drought (2007–2009) affected more than 1 million people, with severe impacts felt in Al-Hasakah, Ar-Raqqah, Aleppo or Halab, and Dier ez-Zor Governerates, socio-economic instability, health problems, food insecurity and migration have further exacerbated the effects of drought. The study of the drought frequency of Syria in 10 years (2000–2010) illustrates the following results:

- An area of about 1.54 million ha (that represent 8.33% of the total area of Syria) was a subject to drought for less than 2 years out of 10 years,
- An area of about 6.67 million ha (that represent 36.05% of the total area of Syria) was a subject to drought for 2–4 years out of 10 years,
- An area of about 7.56 million ha (that represent 40.88% of the total area of Syria) was a subject to drought for 4–6 years out of 10 years.
- An area of about 2.5 million ha (that represent 13.49% of the total area of Syria) was a subject to drought for 6–8 years out of 10 years, and.
- An area of about 0.23 million ha (that represent 1.25% of the total area of Syria) was a subject to drought for more than 8 years out of 10 years *(UN ISDR 2011: 22).*

In the summer of 2009, the UN published the Syria Drought Response Plan (SDRP), in which we read: "Syria receives water from three sources—rivers, underground water, and rainfall (all rivers that cross through Syria are trans-boundary and flow from neighboring countries). In recent years, pressure on water resources has increased due to water scarcity caused by environmental changes, increased use of water in agricultural production, and increased urbanization (90% of the total water in the country is consumed by the agriculture sector). During the current planting season 2008/2009, rainfall levels were better than last seasons, but still much below the annual average. The balance between used and renewable sources in underground water is presently negative and at a critical stage as a result of over exploitation. There has been a 40% reduction of the groundwater in some sub-basins during the last two years due to drought and over exploitation. Water storage capacity in the steppe is now only about 17% of the total capacity. For the population of the semi-arid steppe in eastern Syria, availability of water is of prime importance. In many areas water shortage has reached critical levels. The recurrent drought during the past three to four years has resulted in increasing the depth of the water level in wells from 90–100 m to 120–150 m in the best cases. As a result, wells have either dried up or require much more time and costs to pump out water.

In addition to water scarcity, its quality has also deteriorated. Well water has been increasingly contaminated with salts and nitrite, rendering it useless for human consumption. As a result, wells have been left neglected and gone out of use. In Ar Raqqah and Hasakah governorates, respectively, 47% and 7% of wells have gone out of service during the past four years. Inhabitants of many villages depend on water trucking by the government or through private contractors (at a charge). In many cases, however, the quality of water trucked privately is below acceptable standards.

Shortages of potable water and the great distances to the nearest available source are forcing many families to revert to unsafe water from wells or ponds for their daily use. In some areas, for example in Rural Damascus, herders reported that they had to travel 30–40 kms to find water for their herds, and had to travel even farther to obtain good quality potable water for their own use. As a result, Hasakah and Dayr Az-Zawr governorates saw an increase in water-related diseases by 25%, whilst in Ar-Raqqah governorate the prevalence of these diseases increased almost six-fold. The drought-affected governorates of eastern Syria face dramatic water shortage: more wells and some rivers may dry up in the next years. The third consecutive year of drought is affecting subsistence communities that have a limited adaptive capacity. The drought has also seriously affected the viability of some livelihoods unless effective measures are taken to protect and diversify them through adaptation. In a context where global climatic change suggests drought in Syria may become more frequent, variable and intense, it is critical that initiatives to increase the resilience of populations at the local level are made now.

One of the most visible impacts of the drought on drought-affected fields in the Raqqah governorate two groups in particular are particular affected: • Farmers, as most of them had already lost their entire 2008 harvests; • Herders as they cannot find feeds for their animals in drought-affected rangelands, and have to buy feeds from markets due to lack of resources. In a few cases, herders still have three to ten sheep surviving out of flocks of over 100.

According to the UNICEF MICS malnutrition in Syria gradually decreased in the 1990s, but the most recent survey conducted in 2007 indicated an increase in all three malnutrition indicators. This was driven mainly by the effects of the drought on north-eastern Syria, visible already at the time of the 2007 survey. Consecutive years of drought have deteriorated the health of the general population, particularly vulnerable groups such as children and women of child-bearing age. Malnutrition is the main health problem resulting from the continued drought. Poor nutrition in turn is expected to weaken children's immunity, hence increasing their susceptibility to communicable diseases, and may lead to increased morbidity and mortality. A recent study conducted by the Ministry of Health (MoH), Damascus University and UNICEF in 2008 showed that 50% of deaths among children under five year of age in Syria occur in the north-eastern governorates" *(UN 2009: 10–11)*.

This UN report shows how the reduction of water quantity and deterioration of water quality in Syria is an important problem for that Arab country and how many sectors it affects. Furthermore, there are claims that a three-year drought in Syria in the late 2000s was the reason for the civil war that broke out in Syria in 2011.

In the view of many Western policymakers and commentators, the Syrian civil war was caused, in part, by anthropogenic climate change. Former US President Barack Obama claimed that climate change-related drought 'helped fuel the early unrest in Syria, which descended into civil war' (Obama, 2015); former Secretary of State John Kerry argued that 'it's not a coincidence that immediately prior to the civil war in Syria, the country experienced its worst drought on record' (Kerry, 2015); erstwhile Democratic presidential candidates Martin O'Malley and Bernie Sanders have claimed similarly (Democracy Now!, 2015; Schulman, 2015); and in the UK, Prince Charles has maintained that 'there is very good evidence indeed that one of the major reasons for this horror in Syria was a drought that lasted for five or six years' (Mills, 2015). International organisations (e.g. the World Bank: Verme et al., 2016: p. 33), leading NGOs (e.g. Friends of the Earth: Bennett, 2015), official governmental and intergovernmental reports (e.g. Adelphi et al., 2015; King et al., 2015), defense think tanks (e.g. CNA Military Advisory Board, 2014: pp. 13e14), academics (e.g. Cole, 2015; Malm, 2016), activists (e.g. Brand, 2015) and commentators of various political persuasions (e.g. Box & Klein, 2015; Friedman, 2012, 2013)—all have argued similarly.

Three separate studies provide the underpinning evidence for the Syria-climate conflict thesis: (1) a two page briefing document by Francesco Femia and Caitlin Werrell of the Center for Climate and Security in Washington DC (Femia & Werrell, 2012) which, despite its brevity, was the primary reference point for proponents of the thesis up until 2015 (see e.g. Friedman, 2012; Quinn & Roche, 2014); this briefing has subsequently been extended and published in peer-reviewed form (Werrell et al., 2015); (2) a peer-reviewed article by Peter Gleick, one of the foremost scholars of water is- sues worldwide (Gleick, 2014); and (3) a further peer-reviewed article by Colin Kelley and colleagues, mostly earth scientists at the universities of California and Columbia (Kelley et al., 2015).

All three studies, and most other discussions of the subject, in essence advance a three-step argument about the role of anthropogenic climate change in the Syrian civil war: firstly, that anthropogenic emissions were, or may have been, their contributory to the severe late 2000s drought experienced in Syria; second, that this drought led to large-scale internal migration; and third, that these internal migrants were an important contributory factor in the 2011 unrest which spiralled into Syria's civil war. However, a number of experts deny these claims *(Selby and others: 2017).*

Since this topic is beyond the scope of our study, we want to emphasize again that the droughts of the 2000s caused quite a lot of damage to Syria and could significantly force the local authorities to make concessions to Turkey including its territorial integrity in the hope of receiving additional water (in the 2000s, Syria repeatedly asked Turkey to supply more water through the Euphrates).

8.4.2 The Case of Iraq—Ilisu Dam

Turkey had planned to start the process of filling the Ilisu Dam in March 2018, but in January 2018, it became known that, upon the request of Iraqi Prime Minister Hayder Al-Abadi, that process postponed to June (75% of the annual flow of the Tigris River occurs from February to June). In the post shared in Turkish and Arabic from the social media account of the Embassy of Turkey in Baghdad, it was said: "The filling of the Ilisu Dam was planned to start at the end of March 2018. Taking into account the water needs of the brotherly country Iraq, it was postponed to June 2018, upon the requests of Iraqi Prime Minister H. Abadi and Iraqi Minister of Water Resources Hasan Cenabi. In this way, Iraq will have the opportunity to store the amount of water it will need in the summer" *(DHA: 23.01.2018).*

Almost a month and a half after meeting this Iraqi request (on March 11) Turkey launched a ground military operation in northern Iraq. The operation Tigris Shield extended to the Hakurk and Kani Rash areas in the depth of 25–30 km. In addition to F-16 s, attack UAVs also provided support to ground forces in the operation. UAVs and spy satellites also provide technical intelligence support *(Unlu: 10.06.2018).*

It should be noted that Turkey's Tigris Shield military operation in northern Iraq, which lasted for more than a year, started when Turkey's "Olive Branch" operation in Afrin in northern Syria was in its final stages (it ended on March 24). It was obvious that Erdogan, who is going to early elections on June 24, 2018, wanted to create a favorable environment for himself inside Turkey before that, by carrying out trans-border operations in the territories of neighboring countries, to raise his own ranking inside Turkey and especially among nationalists, to get their votes and thus win presidential (also parliamentary) elections. Erdogan needed to win these elections at all costs, because he successfully held a referendum on constitutional reforms in April 2017, as a result of which the next president of

Turkey would receive unprecedented broad powers (the post of prime minister was abolished).

When in 2014 Erdogan became the first president of Turkey directly elected by the people (before that the president of Turkey was elected by the parliament), he did not have broad powers, such powers were held by the country's prime minister (Ahmet Davutoglu). And Erdogan immediately announced that he is an exceptional president as the first popularly elected president of Turkey, and therefore cannot have representative functions. That is why Erdogan needed to win the presidential elections scheduled for November 3, 2019 necessarily (the 17th anniversary of JDP coming to power in Turkey) and for that he went for early elections, calling them in April—just two months before June 24th. Erdogan thus wanted to take the Turkish opposition by surprise, so that it could not organize and seriously oppose. In addition, Erdogan thereby achieved the point that the local government elections scheduled for March 31, 2019 did not precede the presidential and parliamentary elections, but followed them. Erdogan's party, JDP, usually collects fewer votes in local government elections than in parliamentary elections, which is why Erdogan did not want the local government elections to precede the presidential and parliamentary elections, so as not to create a negative background before these two elections (Erdogan's calculation came out right: in the 2019 elections JDP lost Istanbul and Ankara).

On June 24, 2018, Erdogan took advantage of two more important circumstances when calling for presidential and parliamentary elections. a) He managed to partially correct the economic situation of Turkey, stabilize the lira exchange rate, etc. b) To raise his authority and attract the nationalist electorate to his side with Olive Branch and Tigris Shield military operations. As a result, Erdogan won more than 50 percent of the vote (52.59%) in that election, which gave him the chance to win the first round of the presidential election (which was very important for him, because in the second round the opposition/neutral electorate could unite against Erdogan) and receive unprecedented broad powers. In fact, the Olive Branch and Tigris Shield military operations carried out by Turkey in northern Syria and Iraq in 2018 played a certain role in increasing Erdogan's popularity and winning the presidential elections of the same year. The Turkish press emphasizes that this is a fairly common practice during the period of Erdogan's rule, when the authorities carry out cross-border military operations before the elections or during difficult economic periods *(Gurkan: 12.08.2022)*. Table 8.6 illustrates the Turkish authorities' cross-border military operations before elections or during difficult economic periods.

Table 8.6 Cross-border military operations before the elections or during difficult economic periods

1	Operation Shah Euphrates in Syria, 22.02.2015	General Election in Turkey, 07.06.2015
2	Trench operations against PKK in Turkey, 08.08.2015–09.03.2016	General Election in Turkey, 01.11.2015
3	Operation Euphrates Shield in Syria, 24.08.2016–29.03.2017	Constitutional referendum in Turkey, 16.04.2017
4	Operation Olive Branch in Syria, 20.01.2018–24.03.2018	Presidential and General Elections in Turkey, 24.06.2018 Local elections in Turkey, 31.03.2019
5	Operation Tigris Shield in Iraq, 11.03.2018–28.05.2019	
6	Operation Claw (Pence) in Iraq, 28.05.2019	Istanbul repeat mayoral elections, 23.06.2019
7	Operation Peace Spring in Syria, 09–18.10.2019 Operation Spring Shield in Syria, 27.02.2020–05.03.2020	Problems of pandemic, economic downturn, refugees

The fact that Erdogan used the Tigris Shield military operation for electoral purposes was also announced by the Iraqi side at that time. Saad al-Hadithi, spokesman for the prime minister's office, said Turkey's statements about launching military operations in Iraq are politically motivated as Erdogan is trying to impress voters before the June 24 elections. "Turkey wants the Turkish citizens to vote in favor of the Turkish president in the elections," Hadithi told Al-Monitor *(Abu Zeed: 21.06.2018).*

Thus, the operation "Tigris Shield", which is the most significant launched by Turkey in Iraq for more than a decade, somewhat helped Erdogan to win the upcoming presidential elections. It is known that before that, Iraq opposed Turkey's ground military operation in its territory, but in our opinion, Turkey, in fact, received such a permission in exchange for delaying the process of filling the Ilisu reservoir. The given decision regarding Ilisu was announced on January 23, two days after Turkish Foreign Minister Mevlut Chavushoglu's visit to Iraq.

On the issue of the Ilisu reservoir diplomatic traffic between the two countries has increased in parallel with Turkey's completion of the construction of the dam. Iraqi Minister of Water Resources Hasan al-Cenabi has been to Turkey four times. Veysel Eroglu, Minister of Forestry and Water Affairs of Turkey, also went to Baghdad. Erdogan told Abadi, who visited Ankara in October 2017 that they will start to fill the dam as of March. This issue was decided at the meeting of the ministers from both sides on 25–26 December 2017. However, Cenabi, who came to Ankara in January, demanded the postponement of the process. A few days later, Prime Minister Binali Yildirim called Abadi and informed him that the process was postponed to 1 June *(Taştekin: 2018)*.

Turkey started to hold water for the Ilisu dam for the first time in early June 2018. Iraqi Prime Minister Haider Al-Abadi said the issue was "political". Pointing to the elections to be held on June 24 in Turkey, Abadi said that the Turkish government made such a decision to win the votes of the farmers. Turkey's Ambassador to Baghdad, Fatih Yildiz, denied Abadi's allegations. Iraqi Water Resources Minister Hassan al-Senabi announced at a press conference on June 7 that the country's water reserves could drop to 30 billion cubic meters by the end of 2018, adding that this is the lowest level since 1931 *(Saadoun: 12.06.2018)*.

After that it became known in June 2018 the Iraq will again ask Turkey to delay filling the Ilisu reservoir with water. Acting President Hammam Hammoudi stated that the issue is urgent and that they will send a delegation to Turkey to reach an agreement *(EuroNews: 04.06.2018)*. As a result of negotiations Turkey announced that it postpones the filling first until June 7 and then until July 1 in order to give Iraq a little more time to solve the water crisis. Though the Ilisu Dam was brought to the stage of filling in 2018, it did not begin to hold water, since the works to protect and save the historical and cultural assets remaining in the dam lake area continued, as well as because of Iraqi complaints. This process was started only on July 19, 2019 *(MidyatHaber: 04.11.2021)* and Turkey started to use the first turbine of Ilisu Dam on May 19, 2020.

We think that the construction of the Ilisu, as well as the Silvan and Cizre reservoirs in the near future will open up new opportunities for Turkey to play the water card in relations with Iraq. Turkey can also demand oil and gas from Iraq (water for oil/gas) as well as economic benefits etc. in exchange for releasing more water to Iraq. The probability of this is also increasing because, according to the forecasts, the situation in the water sector in Iraq will worsen, also due to the fact that Iran has joined Turkey and Syria in depriving Iraq of water. In this context we consider necessary to present also the water relations between Turkey and Iran, considering that they are interconnected with the Turkey-Iraq water relations and that Iran considers itself a victim of Turkey's water policy.

8.4.3 Case of Iran and the Kurds of Iraq

Unlike the Kurds of Syria, the Kurds of Iraq were in a better position in water matters until recent years, due to the fact that the Tigris River and its tributaries were for a long time out of the attention of Turkey and Iran (also Syria). However, the given situation has changed significantly recently: both Turkey and Iran constructed/constructs reservoirs in the Tigris basin, which put official Baghdad in a difficult position. In the context of the Tigris basin, the interests of Turkey and Iran intersect indirectly in the territory of Iraq (Iran is a significant downstream country in the Euphrates-Tigris basin). The Iran factor plays a certain role in Turkey's water relations with Iraq. In recent years, Iran has accused Turkey of building the Ilisu dam and other dams in the Tigris river basin in general, stressing that as a result, the swamps on the Iran-Iraq border dry up, and the sandstorms of the region sometimes reach to Tehran, making it difficult to breathe.

Tehran claims that Turkey's Ilisu Dam on the Tigris poses environmental risks not only to Iraq but also to Iran. Iranian officials have held Turkey responsible also for dust storms as a result of drought, which they blame on reduced water flows in the Tigris and Euphrates. The Ilisu Dam is argued to cause dust storms and make the threat of drought in Iraq and Hoor al-Azim wetland in Iran more serious. Turkey retorted that the Iranian claims are "far from scientific," noting that Africa and the Middle East are the actual origins of dust and sand storms, which have increased due to drought, land degradation, deforestation and desertification as a result of climate change. And on the issue of transboundary waters, Turkey is open to any "rational and scientific cooperation" with Iran. Turkish officials blame Iran's water shortages on its mismanagement of water resources and see Tehran's accusations as a diversion to quell the growing water grievances of its populace.

Baghdad and the Kurdistan Regional Government (KRG), which borders Iran, in turn accuse Iran of diverting tributaries of the Tigris at the expense of Iraq. Iran has sought to revive its dying Lake Urmia by transferring water from the Little Zab, while diverting also the waters of the Sirwan River. On the Iraqi side, the water level has dropped by 80% in the Little Zab and by 85% in the Sirwan. In 2020, KRG authorities reported that the flow of Little Zab, which feeds the Dukan dam and on which 100,000 people depend for water, was completely cut. In 2019, Tehran announced a plan to build another 109 dams in two years, aiming to transfer water to drought-hit cities. Tehran argues that its water activities are legitimate given that both rivers originate in Iran *(Tastekin: 2022)*.

According to the researches, Iran is building dams to direct a part of the water to the center, and this represents one of the reasons behind the water scarcity in

Iraq. Iran is one of the countries that recently built most dams in the world (the number of Iran's dams grew to 647 in 2018 from 316 in 2012). Hassan al-Janabi, former Iraqi Minister of Water Resources, said in a statement that Iran has small but numerous dams which together functions as a single large dam. The Iraqi Ministry of Water Resources stated that "the increase in the salinity of Shatt al-Arab is caused by Iran's water drainage, and caused the death of millions of fishes and serious environmental degradation". In southern Iraq bordering Iran, the Mesopotamian Marshes are shrinking despite restoration efforts. This wetland area was once the largest ecosystem in western Eurasia. The drainage of the marshes along with dam structures causes severe salinization in rivers, including the Karun. Iran extracts water from this river and discharges harmful water through it into the Shatt al-Arab, a process that further increases salinity. Iraq defines Iran's activities on transboundary waters as a violation of international codes. Lastly, the Iraqi Ministry of Water Resources declared that it is going to fill a complaint in the International Court of Justice against Iran as a last-ditch since they could not solve the water crisis between them and Iran *(Delibas: 2021 & Keynoush: 2021)*.

In January 2023, Mohsen Musavi Khansari, Secretary General of Iran's National Large Reservoir Committee, announced that in recent years, due to Turkey's water policy, climatic changes have been recorded in Iran's West Azerbaijan (*Atrpatan*) and East Azerbaijan (*Atrpatan*) provinces, where the air temperature has risen by 4 degrees. By implementing the GAP project in the Euphrates-Tigris basin and the DAP project in the Aras basin (a total of 50 dams, 35 in Eastern Anatolia and 15 in Southeastern Anatolia, have been built in the region), Erdogan seeks to take 100 percent control over the waters flowing to Iran, Iraq and Azerbaijan. Since Turkey does not have oil, Erdogan can offer the 'water-for oil' project *(Eghtesadmihan: 12.12.2022)*.

In January 2023 advisor to Iran's Minister of Energy, Mohammad Ali Farhanakia regarding the diplomacy of Iran and Turkey in the water sphere, stated that Iran is not directly affected by the decrease of the flow of Tigris and Euphrates in Syria and Iraq, but it may affect us on the flow of Shatt al Arab *(Mehr News: 12.12.2022)*. In our opinion, the objective and subjective positions of all players in the Euphrates-Tigris basin may lead to the Shatt al Arab will become unnavigable in the future, and it will affect Iran's only navigable river, the Qarun, which joins the Shatt al Arab in Iraqi territory.

We believe that Iran complains to Turkey about the Tigris basin because it is quite late in the matter of reservoir construction, it has fallen behind Turkey (the Ataturk Reservoir alone stores more water than all of Iran's reservoirs combined). Almost at the same time as Turkey, Iran has built a lot of reservoirs in the Tigris basin, causing a doubly difficult situation in Iraq. It has already been noted that the Tigris is of greater importance to Iraq than the Euphrates, and that if Turkey concentrated on the Euphrates in the 20th century, Iraq did not suffer so much because it had the Tigris River, the basin of which it exploited almost alone (Syria did not use the border river Tigris, Turkey used very little Tigris water, Iran did too). Meanwhile, in the 21st century, both Turkey and Iran started building large reservoirs in the Tigris basin almost at the same time (the issue of certain use of Tigris waters also appeared in Syria), which significantly complicated the situation in Iraq. As a result, when Iran finally joins the process of dewatering Iraq along with Turkey and Syria for objective/subjective reasons, the situation in Iraq becomes much more difficult. And the experts do not rule out that the scarcity of water may cause a serious conflict between Iran and Iraq in the near future. In addition, this policy of Turkey and Iran forced Iraqi Kurds to store more water in the autonomous territory, which in turn will complicate the situation in the rest of Iraq. In fact, before reaching Baghdad, the waters of the Euphrates and Tigris and their tributaries are significantly used and will be used within the framework of the 3 + 1 format: Turkey, Syria, Iran and the Kurdish autonomy of Northern Iraq.

In 2020 to address the problem, the KRG took unilateral action through an aggressive dam-construction project in the north. While the Kurdistan Region, located in the country's north, historically enjoyed ample water resources, they are under increasing stress due to droughts, internal mismanagement that causes unnecessary waste, upstream water infrastructure, and reduced rain and snowfall. The Tigris and Euphrates' once-abundant flows have fallen 30% since the 1980s, with the Iraqi government predicting a further decline of up to 50% before 2030. Since 2014, to compensate for these losses and secure its own water resources, the Kurdistan Regional Government, the official ruling body of the region, has proposed building 245 dams over an undefined time period. These would be in addition to 17 existing dams and would leave no river in the territory undammed.

The KRG says that these new dams are essential to generate power and provide water for irrigation, fisheries, and tourism, even if they hinder water supply to other parts of Iraq. This is also despite the fact that the region has ample water resources of its own, although they are poorly managed. A proposed dam-building spree in the autonomous Kurdistan Region in northern Iraq threatens several major tributaries of the Tigris River, which, along with the Euphrates, feeds the Mesopotamian Marshes.

Once the largest wetland in the Middle East, Mesopotamian Marshes wending waterways and thick towering reeds historically stretched across 20,000 km2, supporting rich biodiversity and the unique Marsh Arab culture. In the early

1990s they shrunk to 7% of their historical extent after being drained by Saddam Hussein, to flush out the Shiite rebels hiding in them. Their partial restoration post-2003 is widely heralded as a success. But now, the shortage of water will be reflected in the amount of water allocated to the marshes, and it will affect water quality and biodiversity of the marshes, an UNESCO World Heritage site *(Walker, 10.08.2020)*.

8.4.4 The Case of the Kurds of Syria

For tactical and strategic reasons, water frequently plays a significant role in violent conflicts and wars. Sensitive components of the water infrastructure, such as treatment plants, piping systems, pumping stations or reservoirs can become targets for military violence and be destroyed. However, the use of water as a weapon—in the sense of military tool—is much more complex and primarily serves to put pressure on the population and the opponents' political leadership. Drastic interventions in water and electricity supplies are meant to break resistance and gain the support of the population by force, or else drive it out. The aim can also be to destroy agriculture and food production, and render whole areas uninhabitable. The strategic dimension of water in conflict situations is most evident with rivers because control over the resources in the upper reaches makes it possible to gain influence over, or inflict targeted damage on, larger and more distant areas, without necessarily directly attacking, occupying or controlling them militarily. There are essentially three ways of using water resources as a weapon: by making sure that too little water is available, or too much, or water of insufficient quality.

Too little water: Targeted water and electricity shortages can be created in certain areas, or existing supply problems exacerbated, if pipes and cables are cut, or if water supplies are kept back, withdrawn or diverted at a dam. Whoever has control over a dam can cause downright droughts over large swathes of land downstream.

Too much water: Whoever has control over water can also flood areas—either upstream of a dam, by damming and diverting the water, or downstream, by releasing large volumes of water at once.

Insufficient quality: Finally, water can be used as a weapon by soiling or poisoning water resources. This practice can relatively easily be "exported" to other regions since an attack of this kind causes great damage with comparatively simple means *(von Lossow 2016)*.

In the 21st century, Turkey repeatedly uses the waters of the Euphrates and Tigris against the Kurds of Syria and Iraq. In the case of the Syrian Kurds, it became evident in 2011, since the start of the civil war in Syria. In the last more than 10 years, there are many publications in the international press that Turkey is depriving Syrian Kurds of water. In early December 2020, Turkey and allied Syrian opposition factions led by the Free Syrian Army (FSA) cut off the water to the Alouk water station in the countryside of Ras al-Ain. This is the 17th time Turkey has deprived locals of water since taking control of Ras al-Ain and Tell Abyad in October 2019 during Operation Peace Spring against Kurdish fighters. The Alouk water station is the only source of potable water supplying the city of Hasakah and its countryside where about 1.2 million civilians reside, including thousands of displaced persons from various Syrian areas living in camps. The Alouk station also supplies the Mabrouka power station, which provides potable water to Tel Tamr and its countryside *(Ahmed: 2020).*

According to the International Committee of the Red Cross, when Turkey-backed Syrian National Army (SNA) cutting off the water supply from the Alouk water station, water shortage disrupts people's daily lives and undermines their abilities to follow basic hygiene precautions to prevent COVID-19 infections. "Amid a global pandemic that is burdening even sophisticated ruling regimes and infrastructures, the Turkish authorities have cut off the water supply for one of the most vulnerable areas in Syria. The Turkish authorities have to make every effort to resume water supply for those communities immediately," Michael Page, deputy director in the Middle East and North Africa division at Human Rights Watch tells Daraj. Human Rights Watch also documented terrible human conditions in those refugee camps, including clogged toilets, sewage water flowing into the torn tents, and displaced people drinking from washing tanks with worms inside of them. These conditions are likely to exacerbate after the water supply was cut off, and residents are more susceptible to be infected with the Coronavirus *(Al-Ahmad: 2020).*

As early as last March, 2021 UNICEF's representative in Syria, Fran Equiza, warned of the consequences of leaving 1 million people without water and relying on temporary solutions, particularly in times of a pandemic. "The interruption of water supply during the current efforts to curb the spread of the coronavirus disease puts children and families at unacceptable risk. Hand-washing with soap is critical in the fight against COVID-19," he said. Temporary responses organized by local authorities and human rights organizations, such as tankers carrying water to surrounding villages, are no real substitute. The water is more expensive, of a lower quality and is not suitable for drinking. Syria claims that Turkey is behind the water outages, and accuses Turkey of having a major interest in destabilizing the region with the (mainly Kurdish-Syrian) population of around 1 million in cities such as Al-Hasakah, more than 45 villages and many official and unofficial refugee camps. Officially, Turkey doesn't take any responsibility for the repeated outages and claims they are due to technical issues *(Holleis: 2021)*.

In the summer of 2020, it was reported that Syrian farmers who rely on the Euphrates fear a severe blow to their livelihood as its water level declines. The water loss is caused in part by Turkey, the upstream state, decreasing the river's flow through its extensive dam system. Water from the river is the backbone to many parts of life in the Qara Qawzaq area near Kobani, northern Syria. The water pumps farmers use to irrigate their land run on electricity. According to locals, electricity supply has dropped to 10 h a day, when it used to be 18. Kurdish officials in northeast Syria supposed to receive 500 cubic meters of water [per second], but this has decreased to 160 cubic meters *(Rudaw: 06.07.2020)*.

Children in Northern and Eastern Syrian cities, which have electricity and water problems due to Turkey's decrease in the flow of the Euphrates, are sick because there is no drinking water. After Turkey reduced the flow of water in the Euphrates, the water shortage in Northern and Eastern Syria has been going on for months. The people, who have electricity and drinking water problems, are facing a serious humanitarian crisis with temperatures above seasonal normals. In the region where animals die of thirst, children are also at risk of epidemics. Stating that they could not use coolers due to power cuts at temperatures reaching 40 degrees Celsius, a resident of Tal Tamir Omer Abdullah said that the girl who could not stand the temperatures fell ill. Speaking to ANHA, O. Abdullah said, "Children's body temperatures rise when there is no electricity. When the electricity comes on, the children try to cool off from the air conditioner and fan. This causes our children to get sick," he said. The Turkish state's reduction of the Euphrates water brought the drinking water problem along with the electricity problem. Stating that they treat 70 children a day, Dilo Mihemed, an employee of Legerin Hospital, said, "People have to drink dirty water because the water is cut off. "Children get intestinal infections because of dirty water," he said. In the Al-Hasakah Canton of Northern and Eastern Syria, where summer temperatures are above normal, the air temperature reached a record level and thermometers showed 50 degrees on June 29. Power shortages consequently mean having no air conditioning amid temperatures reaching as high as 52C (125 F) and having to make an impossible choice between using water for hygiene or drinking it *(Yeni Yasam: 26.07.2020)*.

As the Turkish government continues to block the flow of Syria's water share in the Euphrates river for a second consecutive year, giving Syria only 200 cubic metres or less of water in some days and months, the Raqqa Agriculture Authority has called on farmers to resort to a new agricultural plan, which is to cultivate 25% of the land area of yellow maize. Blocking of the flow of Syria's water share in the Euphrates River, which is the major source of water for drinking, irrigation and generating electricity, has also caused the degradation of livestock and agriculture on the banks of the Euphrates River. The Syrian Observatory for Human Rights (SOHR) renewed their warning of an environmental catastrophe threatening food security in the Cizire region and humanitarian crises which pose a threat to nearly two million and a half people in different areas in Raqqa, Hesakah, Deir ez-Zor and Kobani. The Turkish water seizure and subsequent drought of Euphrates River water in Deir Ezzor and other areas in north and east Syria have led to water pollution and the spread of rubbish on large spaces of the river. The decreased level of Euphrates River water threatens the summer crops which are irrigated with the river's water in north-east Syria region, particularly in Deir ez-Zor. The official responsible for water affairs in Deir ez-Zor told SOHR that problems have been detected in water stations and other problems which have affected farmlands and livestock. The official also pointed out that the drought has badly impacted crops, especially summer crops such as vegetables and cotton, as they need water at this time of the season in order to ripen. On the other hand, a 54-year-old farmer known as Taha Al-Ahmed from Deir Ezzor countryside told SOHR, that this season, wheat did not grow as they could not provide it with the needed amounts of water in the wake of the current crisis *(ANF News: 20.06.2022).*

In May 2022 Hemud El Hemadin, one of the Tishrin Dam officials, spoke to ANHA and said that they could supply electricity only for 6 h per day due to the lack of water, only between 16.00 and 22.00. He added that they could provide electricity to the region for up to 8 h before. "The Turkish state has been dropping the water of the Euphrates River since January 27, 2021. Only 200 cubic meters of water per second is allowed to flow downstream, which is supposed to be 500 cubic meters of water per second. A few years ago, the flow rate in the Euphrates reached a thousand cubic meters per second in the spring season. Dams need 300 cubic meters of water per second to operate properly. Furthermore, a turbine needs 105 megawatts of electricity to operate. However, the amount has dropped to 200 or 125 cubic meters per second," El-Hemadin noted. The Turkish state, which pursued the same policies last year, has caused the water of the Euphrates to dry up almost completely. The water drop in the Euphrates increases the risks for northern and eastern Syria: jeopardizing agriculture, electricity, drinking water, fisheries and industry, food and water security *(ANF News: 11.05.2022).*

All this shows how the Kurds in the north-east of Syria suffer from a lack of water, one of the main reasons for which is decreasing the flow of the Euphrates by Turkey (the reasons also include global warming and the resulting frequent droughts, the unwise use of water in Syria, which Turkey blames to Syria, etc.). However, there is another area of Turkey's use of water against the Syrian Kurds, which is related to security. On the night of 2 July, 2014 ISIS gangs attacked the Kurds of Syria with 10 tanks heavy weaponry. Clashes between ISIS and the People's Defense Units (YPG) have been concentrated around the village of Zor Mixar 45 kms to the west of Kobani town. The Zor Mixar hill is the highest point in the area and is 2 kms from Jarablus, that's why control of the hill means control of the town and surrounding area. According to local sources, ISIS has captured Kurdish villages for the first time since the Syrian war began in 2011. There were reports that the number of villages under the control of ISIS around Kobani is 7–8 *(Kasapoglu: 2014)*.

This attack of ISIS on Syrian Kurds was unexpected for many, because in the ideology of ISIS, importance is given not to the ethnic, but to the religious factor. And the Sunni ISIS, along with the fight against Bashar Assad's Alawite regime, started targeting the Syrian Kurds, who are Sunni. In any case, it was not too surprising, given the dozens if not hundreds, of reports on the Internet about close cooperation between Turkey and ISIS. As a result, it appeared that ISIS started to deal with the solution of the "Kurdish question" in Syria, which was in the interests of Turkey.

At the beginning of July 2014, the Turkish press, citing the British press, wrote that Turkey cut the Euphrates, and the villages were left without water. The Guardian claimed that Turkey started "water wars" reducing the water of the Euphrates. Because of that the Assad Lake, which is the largest dam on the Euphrates in Syria and meets the water needs of Aleppo, has dried up. The 85-km-long Assad Lake held more than 14.2 billion cubic meters of water until recently. The independent Raqqa Media Center (RCM) stated that only three of the eight turbines of HEPP supplying electricity to the Syrian city of Raqqa, which is controlled by ISIS. According to RCM, "Turkey does not allow the water of the Euphrates to flow into Syria for political reasons." The RCM claimed that the reducing of the flow of Euphrates has begun in May and Turkey completely cut off the water flow in mid-June, as a result of which, the amount of water held in Lake Assad has dropped to 1.6 billion cubic meters and the water level decreased by 6 meters[1] *(Milliyet: 04.07.2014)*.

[1] There is also an opinion that the reason for the sharp drop in the water level in Lake Asad is the significant exploitation of its hydroelectric power plant by ISIS, which has operated all

It is possible that Turkey completely cut off the flow of the Euphrates during that period in order to enable ISIS to launch an armed attack from Jarablus (west bank of Euphrates) towards Kobani (east bank of Euphrates), so that ISIS could overcome a mighty water barrier like the Euphrates without hindrance (the same trick was used by ISIS in Iraq for the same purpose). It is noteworthy that north of Jarablus, beyond the border, in the Turkish part, there is the city of Karkamish with the reservoir of the same name and the (Kurdish) Human Rights Association (İnsan Hakları Derneği, IHD in Turkish acronym) reported that Karkamis Camp become the training center of ISIS, which uses Turkey as a logistics base (*Halkın Sesi: 26.07.2014*).

IHD drew attention to the fact that ISIS started the attack on the Syrian Kurds with the calculation that they would enter Kobani on July 19. "On July 19, 2012, the Kurds and other peoples acting together with the Kurds carried out a revolution of historical importance in Syria's Rojava Region (de facto autonomous region in northeastern Syria). During the Syrian civil war, they created their own self-government and announced it to the world. On the 2nd anniversary of the Rojava Revolution, those who tried to strangle this revolution did not stay idle and engaged the jihadist organizations. The attacks of jihadist organizations such as ISIS, Al-Qaeda, Al Nusra, especially against Rojava, are actually attacks aimed at disrupting the Rojava Revolution and the self-government of the peoples. It is now known that jihadist organizations use Turkey as a logistics base and carry out various attacks. This latest assault on the Rojava revolution appears to be the most dangerous of a series of attacks over the last 2 years,"—stated in the reports of İHD branches *(IHD: 08.10.2014)*.

This seems plausible to us, considering that the Prime Minister and then President of Turkey, Recep Tayyip Erdogan is a big fan of symbolic strikes (ISIS was supposed to enter Kobani on July 19—The Rojava revolution of 19 July 2012 also started in Kobani). It is noteworthy that in 2019, the process of filling the Ilisu reservoir with water in Turkey started on July 19. We also consider the historical role of Kobani. In July 1979 Abdullah Ocalan went from Suruc to Kobani and stayed there for 40 days (the town of Kobani is only 10 to 15 kms from the district centre of Suruc in Sanliurfa province). The contacts he made there enabled him to access the Middle East, but his relationship with Kobani did not end. He got to know almost all the families there through reciprocal visits. Thousands of women and men who joined the PKK from Kobani died in different regions of Kurdistan. The first guerrilla from Rojava to die in the ranks of the PKK was

turbines of the hydroelectric power plant 24 h a day in order to obtain electricity *(Chudacoff: 2014)*.

from Kobani. For all these reasons Kobani is now a town of historic significance for the Kurds.

To the east of Tel Abyad, which is already under ISIS control, there is Ras al-Ayn and then the Cizire (Jazira) canton. Maintaining contacts between the cantons of Kobani and Cizire is very difficult. The aim of ISIS was to seize Kobani and thus completely sever contact between Cizire in the east of Rojava from Afrin in the west. They wanted to occupy Kobani to achieve military and political superiority over the Kurds and connect Jarablus and Tel Abyad.

This plan is the one Turkey has been trying to implement in the Ras al-Ayn area since 2012. They wanted to capture Ras al-Ayn and occupy Cizire. If this had happened there would now be a bloodbath in Rojava and the cantons would be a mere dream. But circumstances were different then and things did not work out as they had planned. The aim of ISIS and the forces directing them is to carry out a pincer movement on Rojava with the 'motivation' they have gained in Iraq, to throttle the revolution, or, at the very least, prevent its consolidation *(Kurdistan Question: 14.07.2014)*.

8.5 Turkey's "Water Weapon" Against the PKK

In the previous chapter, we described the fact that large reservoirs in Turkey had a security function in addition to their four main purposes. These reservoirs built in the Euphrates and also the Tigris basin led to the flooding of many Kurdish villages, thus depriving PKK militants of the opportunity to find shelter and supporters, leaving their communication channels under water and thus complicating their movement within Turkey. Besides, it contributed emigration from Kurdish areas and thus partially emptying the given region. This tendency to use the water factor against the Kurds in Turkey continued in the 21st century and even became more multilateral. The security factor was the most striking and we have singled out 3–4 episodes in this context.

8.5.1 Security Reservoirs (Hakkari and Sirnak Provinces)

In September 2013 Ercan Ayboga, a member of Initiative to Keep Hasankeyf Alive, published an article with the title 'With 'Security Dams', History, Nature, Life and Balance Disappear', in which mentioned: "In addition to 50 dams built for energy and irrigation in the region so far, nearly 30 dams and hundreds of HEPPs that that are under construction and are planned to be built in recent years, have more of a security than energy function. Since the dams under construction and planned to be built in Bingol, Sirnak, Hakkari, Batman, Mardin, Diyarbekir and Dersim provinces will directly affect the historical sites in the region, residential areas, endemic plant species and living ecosystems, these projects frequently face the reaction of the public. In addition, the villages that were burned and emptied in the 1990s and restored in the 2000s will now be emptied due to the lake areas created by the dams in question: the dams may cause the migration of more than one hundred thousand people.

While these projects often bring great social and ecological harm to local people and only limited benefits in some cases, they provide economic and political profits to the government and the companies involved in the projects. In the name of 'development' defined by the state and for the progress of the 'nation', local communities and peoples are forced to migrate, leave their lands and accept the low compensation price foreseen. The Republic of Turkey due to serious lack of democracy with the 1500 dams has directly displaced at least 400 thousand people and deprived the living resources of many more (although the 2011 Annual Report of DSI mentions 355 thousand displaced people). The second group includes peasants and people living in areas adjacent to stream beds that have been dried by HEPPs, those whose agricultural lands have been partially taken away. It is expected that due to 2000 dam and HEPP planned, half to one million more people will be directly affected.

Until the mid-2000s, the Republic of Turkey did not establish any pre-project dialogue with the people affected by dams and did not include them in the decision process. However, after the start of the dam construction project, he was paying compensation for the structures and lands that had title deeds, which was generally insufficient. The state could also use its armed forces directly in some cases in case of popular reaction. The state many times did not even inform the people who should be migrate during the filling the dam with water, and people had to flee without even getting their belongings. In short, the state was acting in a very repressive way. In the conflicted areas, that is, in most of the Kurdish provinces, this pressure was very extreme.

A 1997 legislative amendment required an Environmental Impact Assessment (EIA) process and the resulting report; but only for projects decided after 1993. Although the EIA law has many shortcomings (the affected people cannot express their opinions and influence the project before the final decision is taken) and it does not meet international standards, this relatively positive law is not implemented seriously even with its shortcomings. The EIA process is often implemented by outright violation of laws, non-enforcement of court orders, cheating, threats, and the purchase of institutions, NGOs and people. In short, EIA provides little improvement, therefore it is only for show and to save the image. State officials do not listen to all these broad and long-term objections, do not consider the objections sincerely and persistently try to implement the projects. Except for a few exceptions, no dam project has been canceled with a decision taken by the government as a result of criticism.

Reasons for Dam Construction Within the Scope of Energy, Agriculture and Development Models Implemented by Turkey

Within the scope of the Energy, Agriculture and Development models implemented by Turkey, the reasons for the construction of dams are explained by different segments from different perspectives and with different emphases. While every reason for dam construction is not wrong on its own, often a single reason is not enough for most dams to be built.

a) The main reason for insisting on dam construction is antiecological and antisocial **energy, agriculture and development** model. These policies were taken from the energy, agriculture and development policies implemented in Western industrial states until the 1960s. Until the 1960s, in the core of the policies implemented by Western states prevailed following approaches: state centralism (that is, the lack of a voice of local governments), lack of participation (authoritarian and sacred state influence still common), trying to solve problems with big investment projects (easy way), unlimited exploitation of natural elements and waters, ignoring the social values of nature and waters based on balanced life for thousands of years, etc.. Though some positive changes made in Western countries since the 1970s (participation principle, nature/ecosystem restoration and natural conservation areas redevelopment concepts, protection of water quality improvement, protection of plant and animal species in danger of extinction, etc.), such changes did not take place in Turkey. Underdeveloped states such as Turkey were tougher during the implementation of these policies than western industrialized countries.
b) There are other strong reasons for the construction of dams in Turkey. Chief among these are the **anti-democratic features** of the political system. When the system is anti-democratic, large segments of the society and those directly affected are not included in the decision-making process of investment projects such as dams. Politicians and bureaucrats make the decision on their own and they expect society will adapt to it. That segment finds it wrong even for the society to express its views on energy and agriculture. Even though some positive legal reforms have been made in the last ten years (such as the enactment of the EIA law), this feature of the political system has

not changed and has not gone beyond image regulation. For example, within the scope of anti-democratic features, the state's armed forces in many places sometimes use great force against those who protest the dams.

c) Another strong reason is that the phenomenon of **corruption** is widespread and deep-rooted in the political and bureaucratic system. It was 'very normal' and systematic that companies aiming to make investments pay high bribes to politicians and bureaucrats who decide on the projects. With the effect of this bribery, politicians defend the criticized investment projects more and definitely want to implement them. The absence of democratic, transparent and social control mechanisms causes this bribery system to continue.

d) Of course, we must also take into account the accumulation of **capital** in the world today, which has emerged as a result of the neo-liberal policies and have become widespread since the 1980s. It has become imposing on the basis of the investment, infrastructure and energy projects that have increased in the last 15–20 years in the world. Although this capital accumulation has only recently developed in Turkey, the international level of accumulation is more decisive. Foreign capital has been very effective in the rapid growth of the economy in the last ten years. Another important investment area chosen by this international capital is dams (especially HEPPs). The fact that energy dams generally pay for themselves in 7–12 years and energy consumption increases every year—although not at the rate stated by the government—makes investment in this area attractive. Normally, while governments in most states determined where and which dams will be built, which was the case in Turkey, as a result of a privatization process that started in 2004, companies got opportunity to apply for licenses for dams with HEPPs in rivers on their own initiative. When companies use it heavily, the above-mentioned 2000 planned dam projects in Turkey emerge.

e) Building dams on rivers flowing outside the borders of the state also has additional strategic "benefits" according to the "**state logic".** With large dams built on rivers such as the Tigris, Euphrates, Aras, and Chorokh, the Turkish state has the opportunity to store and control the water flowing and used in downstream countries. While the Turkish government has not overtly threatened downstream states affected by dams on 'international' rivers in recent years, such dams that have been built are critical. Because the Turkish state does not establish a dialogue with the downstream states while making the decision to build these dams, so there is no question of sharing the use of water. Only when the dams are at the construction stage, they provide some information to the downstream states and decide unilaterally how much water to leave on average. In the light of this approach, the Republic of Turkey does not sign any international conventions that form a framework for sharing about 'international' rivers. Chief among these is the 1997 UN (United Nations) convention on transboundary waterways that are not navigable. Apart from the Republic of Turkey, a few more anti-democratic states such as China do not act in accordance with the laws concerning international rivers. Undoubtedly, Syria and Iraq are among the states that are negatively affected by Turkey's international water policy. With the dams built on the Euphrates and Tigris, the right of access to water (for drinking and irrigation purposes) for millions of people living in these two states is restricted or completely taken away.

f) **The view of water hegemony** is also effective in the insistence of the Republic of Turkey on dam construction. We mean the use of dams as a means of state domination over communities. This system of control and exploitation does not want local features and uniqueness. It wants the developed dominant and capitalist culture of life and consumption to be adopted by the whole society. In particular, nation-states aim to standardize local cultures through developing technical-scientific possibilities. With the dam lake (or the drying up of the rivers), the people living in that area are forcibly deported to other places. Immigrants live predominantly in cities, were detached from production and were generally poorer. This break with production works for the dominant powers because these people leave a self-sustaining economy and start to lead a consumption-based life. While these people used to produce most of their own needs, now they have to buy everything. While the purchasing power of these segments is not high in the first place (this may increase in a generation or two), companies benefit by selling their products to these people.

Thus, wider sections of society are fully included in the capitalist mechanism of exploitation. Again, since these displaced people are generally unemployed, they put pressure on the already insufficient employment area, causing the value of labor to decrease further. Along with this exploitation, the state control over these people is also increasing. Where previously they regulated their own lives in remote rural areas, now the state and its organizations can better control people. Another dimension related to this migration is the dissolution of the immigrants into the dominant culture and urban culture. The person who accepts the dominant culture accepts everything given by the system and does not question much. This makes exploitation and control easier. However, in the river beds and valleys, people have developed a rich and unique culture in direct contact with nature. This unique culture is an important cultural heritage that expresses a deep experience based on centuries and millennia. Local culture in areas in close contact with a stream is more unique than in other areas. The forms of production based on rivers are more advanced and again, water is a very rich source of inspiration for literature. Local riparian cultures of different peoples (ethnicity) and beliefs and are different from the uniform culture defended by the nation-state. The state that tries to create a nation is rigid and authoritarian, while solidarity and tolerance are prominent in local cultures. This is also true for Anatolia and Mesopotamia. The uniform culture that the state of the Republic of Turkey wants to develop means the rejection of local cultures and thus the past of the society.

g) With the HEPPs built with dams, it becomes easier to **exploit the mines** in certain mountainous regions. Considering that there is a great need for electrical energy in mining, HEPPs are easily accessible electricity sources in regions where there are many 'mines' targeted for exploitation. This dimension is more common in the Black Sea. Those who criticize and resist dams in these regions also criticize projects that otherwise have no benefit for society. Considering that the demand for mines is increasing in the world, we can say that HEPPs are a very profitable business for mining companies.
h) While the above-mentioned reasons for building dams are valid in many countries of the world, in a few conflict states such as the Republic of Turkey, **military/security** or fighting against riots can also be a reason for building dams. When a part of the population for one or several reasons attempts an armed revolt against the state on an ethnic, religious and/or class basis, the state may entail the establishment of a purposeful dam to suppress or limit the revolt, where geography and hydrology allow. Dams with this purpose can be built on the border with their lakes or in more inland areas. Unfortunately, such a development has emerged in the Republic of Turkey in recent years.

Introduction to 'Security Dams'

The first construction activities of eleven safety dams, which were decided by DSI in 2007, started at the end of 2008 (the term 'security dam' is based on the sentence on page 142 of the 2007 activity report of DSI). For the first time the Turkish state wants to build the dams on the Iraqi border in order to ensure its own "security". Various Turkish media outlets, which are closer to the state and government policies, have stated that these dams can prevent PKK guerrilla's infiltration from the border and thus make an important contribution to the fight against terrorism.[2]

---

[2] Look at the following news: a) Radical: Threatened period in the fight against PKK, 11.07.2009; b) Internet News: TAF to PKK 'damaged blockade', 08.05.2011; c) Milliyet:

It was the first time that military purposes of these dams ('security dams') were officially included in Turkey. According to the information obtained from the NGOs that conduct international research on dams, this term has no analogues in the world: no dam has been officially established for military purposes. When the worldwide and widely criticized dams are considered, it is seen that does not exist the dams, which were officially built for security/political reasons. Many dams built in many conflict regions of the world have undoubtedly been built for political and/or military purposes, but there is no government that officially announces/names this. Thus, the eleven 'security' dams are the first of their kind in the international arena and Turkey introduced a new term such as 'security dam' to the international literature—unfortunately.

In the last 20 to 30 years, dams, especially dams within the scope of the GAP, have been frequently criticized for their hidden/indirect that is, not accepted by the state, political objectives as well as negative socio-cultural-ecological effects. The criticism here is that the state does not build the dams only for economic reasons that the dams are actually or additionally to political aims. These criticisms were expressed especially by those living in the region where the dams were built and opposing to the state. The following points regarding controversial dams in the Kurdish provinces are the subject of criticism: a) Further emigration of Kurds, whose at least two million people faced forced migration in the 90 s, and continued evacuation of mountainous-rural areas, b) The fragmentation of the geography where the Kurds live and better control of the population movement, c) The assimilation policy on the Kurds covers more segments with migration to the cities due to dams, d) Facilitating the conditions of long-standing state struggle against PKK guerrillas in favor of the Turkish Armed Forces with dam lakes, e) Desiring to gain a stronger position in the Middle East by using water as a weapon against Iraq and Syria and selling water as a commercial commodity in the Middle East in the coming decades.

Technical Specifications of Projects

Eleven security dams are concentrated in three regions in order to make it difficult for PKK guerrillas to cross the 380 km long Turkey-Iraq border. The first and largest is the region where there are seven dams lined up on the Robozik river in Sirnak's Uludere district. If all dams were built here, the 50-km border line would be better controlled by dam lakes. It is expected that both of Cukurca and

Two of those dams planned against the PKK are complete…, 26.11.2011; d) Radical: 103.5 million was spent on PKK dams, 11.03.2012; e) Milliyet: These dams are for the PKK, 12.03.2012.

Semdinli districts in Hakkari province will have two security dams each. The examination in detail of these three regions shows that it does not mean that the entire border region will be affected and/or that all the valleys on the border will be filled with dam lakes. The ability to build a dam in a parallel place close to the border or on a long line depends on the geographical features and the direction and amount of water flow of existing rivers and streams. All of the security dams are built in the form of fill dams and their body heights vary between 35 and 80 m. The average flow rates of the rivers in which they are established vary between 15 and 80 cubic meters per second. With these features, dams do not fall into the category of technically too complicated, so they can be built by Turkish and local companies without any problems and international companies are not needed.

Table 8.7 shows the security dams built in Hakkari and Sirnak provinces bordering Iraq.

Table 8.7 Security dams of Hakkari and Sirnak provinces

Number	Dam name	Province/District	Height of dam [m]	Name of the stream
1	Silopi	Sirnak/Uludere	79,5	Hezil
2	Sirnak	Sirnak/Uludere	56,8	Ortasu (Robozik)
3	Uludere	Sirnak/Uludere	55,5	Ortasu (Robozik)
4	Balli	Sirnak/Uludere	49	Ortasu (Robozik)
5	Kavsaktepe	Sirnak/Uludere	66	Ortasu (Robozik)
6	Musatepe	Sirnak/Uludere	34,5	Ortasu (Robozik)
7	Cetintepe	Sirnak/Uludere	60,5	Ortasu (Robozik)
8	Cocuktepe	Hakkari/Cukurca	45,5	Guzeldere
9	Golgeliyamac	Hakkari/Cukurca	42	Guzeldere
10	Beyyurdu	Hakkari/Semdinli & Yuksekova	48	Bembo
11	Aslandag	Hakkari/Semdinli & Yuksekova	60	Bembo

Sirnak Province

At the end of August 2012, DSI announced to the public that the construction of the first three dams (Sirnak, Silopi and Uludere dams) in the above table was completely completed and the other projects (4–7) are under construction. The total cost of the dams in Sirnak is 207 Million TL. In fact, all 7 projects were planned to be completed in 2011, but there is a delay of at least two years due to geographical and technical difficulties and the ongoing armed conflict between the Turkish Armed Forces and PKK guerrillas. As a result of the armed conflicts that intensified in the summer of 2012, the construction works of 4 dams, which were under construction, came to a standstill. The construction of these four dams was accelerated again in March 2013, as the PKK declared a ceasefire, the clashes stopped, and the PKK withdrew its guerrillas to the Iraqi territories. The Turkish state, taking advantage of the political environment, aims to complete these projects very quickly in 2013.

Hakkari Province

The construction of the four dams in Hakkari started three years ago, but the construction was constantly stopped due to armed conflicts between the Turkish Armed Forces and the PKK. In July 2012, the activities of these four dams were completely stopped due to the intensifying clashes between the PKK and the Turkish Armed Forces throughout the province. The total cost of the dams in Hakkari is 105 Million TL. According to the news in August 2012, while the Beyyurdu dam was completed as 98%, there is no definite information about the physical realization rate of the other dams in Hakkari. As a result of the military attacks of the PKK in July 2013, the construction of the dams not only stopped, but also the construction vehicles were burned and the construction site was severely damaged. It is expected that the projects under construction will inundate 45 km of the highway (not the main highway between the two provinces) between the provincial centers of Sirnak and Hakkari. It is stated that since these projects will become the target of the PKK, towers consisting of concrete and positions resistant to all kinds of attacks will be built on the dominant hills near the dams. In addition, there will be 24-h surveillance, in case of the detection of moving points an intervention will be performed.

Problems in the Tender Process

Security dams were included in DSI's 2007 report and construction tenders were given to companies in the same year, but the public became aware of these projects in 2008. Normally, dams and hydroelectric power plants are specified in DSI's concepts, plans and reports years ago. But until 2007, no information was found about these eleven 'security dams'. The result is that the projects were developed hastily. According to DSI standards and rules, at least 2 years are required for hydraulic and meteorological research. It is necessary to measure the precipitation and water flow in at least one year, and to obtain more reliable information, it is necessary to study for 2 or 3 years. Normally such measurements are taken decades before making a water structure. The said surveys have not been carried out at all in medium and small-scale rivers in Sirnak and Hakkari. The long-term risk here is that in the event of heavy rainfall and flooding during the construction phase, the construction site or the dam body will collapse due to inadequate security of the dam area. With such destruction, a large wave flooding the valley in the downstream areas could result in the death of people and animals. A further and perhaps even greater danger is the complete or partial collapse of a constructed and water-filled dam due to excessive flooding. As a result, the water wave that may occur in the downstream regions can cause terrible destruction for people, plants and animals. If the eleven security dams in question are broken in this way, the disaster may make itself felt as far as Iraqi Kurdistan.

Another striking point is that most of the dam projects were tendered to regional companies. İnelsan is headquartered in Hakkari and Yuzenler is headquartered in Van. This is most likely intended to ensure that public criticism of the projects is kept at a low level, because it is said to the public that these are regional companies and that the people of the region will earn money from here (the economic situation in both provinces is very bad). The aim of the Turkish state is to 'ensure the security of the border' or, more directly, to limit the passageways and sheltering opportunities of the PKK, which has been in an armed uprising against the state since the 1980s. The purpose of electricity generation added to the projects at the last moment does not change this situation. In addition to the military purposes of these dams, economic objectives such as collecting water to irrigate the lands and supplying water to the cities were also added. These additional targets aim to cover more dam projects.

Social and Ecological Impacts of Dams

It is not clear from the official documents and plans how many settlements will be flooded due to the eleven dam projects in question. It is estimated that the number of those who will be directly affected will be relatively small, because on the one hand, the dam lakes will be several kilometers (usually between 5 and 10 km) long, and on the other hand, most of the villages in these two provinces were destroyed by the Turkish army in the intense war environment of the 1990s systematically destroyed and burned. Even giving an estimate is not easy: it may be expressed in hundreds, perhaps in thousands. During the serious decrease in armed conflicts in the region in 2000s there has been a partial return to these villages of the villagers' by own means. Even this, the return of people has been more limited due to the fact that the state pressure has never decreased seriously in these two provinces and the armed conflicts have increased especially in the last five years. It is undisputed that the compensations that will be received by the owners of the land who will migrate will be insufficient. Based on other examples of displacement and compensation, this can be easily stated. Turkey's resettlement and expropriation laws provide for low compensation amounts and do not guarantee the maintenance of the standard of living. The social, cultural, psychological and economic problems of people who will migrate to cities such as Hakkari, Van and Diyarbekir will be more or less the same as people who have migrated due to other infrastructure projects. Most of these people can live with a small amount of money for a period (estimated 2 to 3 years) in these cities however due to the lack of professional qualifications they can find jobs such as labor at most. The problems that women will face are more extensive and deeper. In rural areas, the probability of them falling from a producer position to a consumer position is very high. Again, the risk of social shrinkage is great. The risks that children will face (crime, alcohol or drug abuse, non-compliance with school education, etc.) are not investigated by any government institutions. On the other hand, these migrations will accelerate the unhealthy growth of cities.

With the migration, the original cultural features in the valleys will continue to disappear. Let's not forget that in addition to the loss of the rich culture of the region with urbanization, the cultural accumulation in the river basins may be more diverse. Legends, myths, poems and songs that have a close connection with water are disappearing with the immigrants. One of the negative cultural effects is the destruction of churches or church ruins under water in many of the villages in the valleys. No research has been carried out on plants and animals in order to determine what will be lost ecologically due to dams. This region has a very rich natural diversity, since until today it has suffered little from the destruction of nature, with the exception of war. No major dams have been operating in these two provinces to date, only it has a small-scale flood protection, erosion and sediment control facilities. Again, the settlements are not very large (not exceeding 100 thousand, but growing rapidly) and there is no medium to large scale industry. In addition, agriculture is limited to the valleys (except in the Southwest region of Sirnak) and industrial agriculture is almost non-existent.

The negative ecological effects created by the dams can be briefly listed as follows: as a result of the dams, the connection is broken in terms of species in the rivers and the ecosystem is divided into two. Flowing water is artificially turned into stagnant water in the reservoir area. The resulting dam lake leaves many areas under water, making these areas uninhabitable for terrestrial animals and plants. The properties of the water (temperature, oxygen content, nutrient content, etc.) are changing in the lake and downstream regions. In dam lakes whose flow has been stopped by a dam and whose water quality has decreased, the number of fish, small animal and plant species has decreased significantly and only a few species can benefit from this (sometimes no species can benefit). The animals in that valley can no longer benefit from the degraded water. Local and regional climate changes are also emerging with new artificial lakes and are starting to affect ecosystems in the much wider region (like less snowfall). If we consider that the three rivers in question have flowed freely until now, all the negative ecological effects of these dams emerge in their entirety. Dams not only inundate the valleys, but also cause numerous adverse effects in downstream areas. Low quality, colder and sandless/sedimentless running water seriously affects the downstream stream bed (erosion, deprivation of floods, etc.) and living life",—noted Ayboga *(Ayboga 2013).*

8.5.2 Ilisu and Silvan Dams

It has already been mentioned that in the 20th century, the Euphrates River was the focus of Turkey's attention in the matter of reservoir construction, but in the 21st century, Turkey's attention was focused on the Tigris as well. And Turkey started building its largest reservoir on the Tigris, the Ilisu Reservoir, which also has security significance, for which it was attacked by the PKK during its construction. The PKK militants repeatedly hit the construction site of the Ilisu reservoir with grenade launchers, kidnapped the builders, set fire to the construction equipment, and set mines on the roads leading to the construction site. At the same time, Kurdish non-governmental organizations and politicians were holding many protest actions aimed at preventing the construction of the Ilisu reservoir, which was supposed to flood the 12,000-year-old Hasankeyf settlement. And although the Kurdish side managed to significantly delay the construction of the Ilisu reservoir and thereby cause serious financial damage to Turkey (this hydroelectric junction will bring about 400 million dollars to the Turkish economy annually, that is, more $ 1 million per day), still, the Turkish authorities managed to complete the construction of the Ilisu reservoir and to open it in November 2021 (the first turbine of Ilisu HEPP was commissioned on May 19,

2020[3]). Thus, it can be stated that the PKK won the battle regarding the Ilisu Reservoir, but lost the war. In our opinion, the multiple attacks of the PKK during the construction of the Ilisu reservoir were caused by several circumstances at once.

Logistic connection—The Ilisu reservoir with an area of more than 300 km2 and a volume of almost 10 BCM will flood PKK's communication routes. Ilisu Reservoir would raise the level of the Tigris arm/tributary Botan River, the latter would become navigable and the river crossing would be complicated. Botan Gorge's role was very important for PKK, it was the "nest" of the PKK during the initial phase of the armed struggle and afterwards. In the "Botan Gorge region" (Kato, Judi and Gabar mountain peaks) PKK established its first military camp in Turkey and from where its attacks began (Botan River is also called Eastern Tigris). The mountain zone of Botan has borders both Iraq and Iran, which makes it easier for the PKK militants to escape. The following words belong to Kurdish leader Abdullah Ocalan: "If there were 3 more Katos in the region, we would have won the war" *(Alptekin 2019: 35–40).*

Back in 2012 Turkish experts Soner Cagaptay and Altai Otun wrote: "The PKK heavily exploits the mountainous terrain of the border zone to move its fighters from camps in Iraq to Turkey. These canyons stretch for tens of miles and are hundreds of feet deep. From a military point of view, it is practically impossible to control these canyons in the necessary way, and they have turned into a kind of land bridge between Iraq and Turkey, which PKK militants have been using for decades. It will not be an exaggeration if these canyons are called "PKK highways" (highway). A PKK member in Iraqi territory can enter one of these canyons and walk literally hundreds of miles to enter the depths of Turkey undetected. Now the Ilisu reservoir should leave those canyons under water. The Ilisu reservoir can go down in history as the first "hydro-victory" against terrorism *(Cagaptay & Otun 2012).*

Thus, the Ilisu reservoir will leave PKK's communication channels under water. We think that it will probably become the second "front" of Turkey's "water defense" against the PKK. The first "front" will be the 11 "security reservoirs" of the provinces bordering Iraq, and the second "front", the Ilisu reservoir, which is located in the "Van-Mardin-Diyarbekir" triangle, and should significantly prevent the further advance of Kurdish militias to other provinces which

---

[3] The launch date was not chosen by chance: on May 19, Turkey celebrates Ataturk's commemoration, youth and sports day (on May 19, 1919, Mustafa Kemal arrived in Samsun, which is considered the start of the Kemal movement). Moreover, the first turbine test was carried out on April 23, the 100th anniversary of the founding of the Grand National Assembly of Turkey (GNA).

has already infiltrated Sirnak and Hakkari from Northern Iraq. It is known that the provinces of Van, Mardin and Diyarbekir are in the center of attention of the Turkish authorities. Before 2014 and 2019 the local elections, Erdogan set a goal for his party to win in Diyarbekir, Van and Mardin at any cost, but he failed in both cases. The entry of Kurdish militants from Northern Iraq to Hakkari and Sirnak, which are not socio-economically developed regions, is perhaps not so problematic for the Turkish authorities. It is perhaps more problematic for them that the Kurdish militants penetrate from Hakkari and Sirnak into the provinces of Van, Diyarbekir and Mardin.

Secret Bunkers—The Ilisu Reservoir also floods the mountain caves of the PKK, the hideouts in which its militants used to hide themselves or hide their weapons and ammunition (many large and small mounds will be flooded). And it is no coincidence that in 2020 the ancient settlement of Hasankeyf, which has more than 5,000 caves, also appeared under water (according to the Kurdish side, 12 thousand years of memory will be erased due the 50-year dam). The PKK militants made great use these caves both to take shelter and to store weapons, ammunition, food and other necessary items. Now a part of the caves is under water, and the other part can be reached only by boats. In addition, under the pretext of getting rid of "falling dangerous stones", the Turkish side blows up many caves in Hasankeyf with dynamite and destroys them with the help of construction equipment. It is obvious that all this is done so that the PKK cannot use those caves. And it should not be surprising that the Turkish side was not stopped by the perennial protests of environmentalists and Kurds aimed at preserving Hasankeyf. By the way, Hasankeyf also had great touristic significance, but the Turkish authorities found a way to compensate for it, stressing that yachts will be launched in the reservoir, recreation areas will be created around the reservoir, fish farming and waters sports will develop, etc.

Settlements—About 200 settlements were emptied and 60—70,000 people were evacuated due to the Ilisu reservoir. The fact that hundreds, if not thousands, of settlements in the southeast of Turkey have been emptied due to the construction of large reservoirs is not new, and the Ilisu reservoir is no exception in that regard. In addition to solving certain demographic (and also cultural) problems, this process also has a security implication. It is taken into account that leaving settlements under water deprives the PKK of the opportunity to find shelter and supporters there. Therefore, this process also has a negative tone for the activities of the PKK, whose members would be deprived of spending the night in these villages, receiving shelter, recruiting supporters from their residents, receiving information, and other opportunities.

Military checkpoints—The appearance of a strategic object like the Ilisu Reservoir in the region means an increase in the Turkish military presence. New military guard posts and checkpoints are being created around the newly constructed reservoir, which will also serve as a serious obstacle for the activities of the PKK. By increasing the military presence, the Turkish authorities also increase the number of their supporters in the upcoming elections in the Kurdish region (the military and their families usually vote for the ruling Justice and Development Party and its allied National Movement Party).

Silvan Reservoir
Perhaps the same thing can be said about the Silvan Reservoir being built in the Tigris Basin, which has the distinction of being the largest irrigation dam after Ataturk Dam. 7.3 BCM of water can be stored in the Silvan Dam, which is the highest concrete-lined dam in Turkey and Europe with its height of 175.5 meters. The Silvan Dam Project is aimed to contribute 1.2 billion liras to the country's economy annually. This reservoir was constantly targeted by the PKK during its construction. End of July 2022 former Minister of Agriculture and AK Party Diyarbekir Deputy Mehdi Eker said that 52 attacks were carried out to prevent the construction of the Silvan Dam, which will add great wealth to the region *(Sabah: 29.07.2022)*. In January 2021, the Turkish pro-government press wrote that after the foundations were laid 9 years ago most of the construction of the dam has been completed despite the fact that and the PKK organised approximately 25 terrorist attacks with bombs, guns and mines *(Sabah: 23.01.2021)*. The Silvan reservoir and the Silvan project in a broader sense will also have security functions similar to the Ilisu reservoir, which is why it has been targeted by PKK militants.

8.5.3 Blockade of Dersim with Reservoirs

As a result of many controversial dams and HEPPs planned and built in the late 90 s in Dersim (Tunjeli), a region populated by Kurds, the use of dams as weapons against Kurds and other ethnic communities in the Republic of Turkey began to come up. The dam and HEPP projects built in Dersim were supposed to force the Kurds to migrate from their own culture and assimilate them, and thus completely eliminate the rebellious character of the region, rather than the socio-economic purpose of the dams (Dersim province has the most frequent clashes with PKK along with Hakkari and Sirnak provinces). The dams built since the 1980s within the framework of the GAP Project were also partly discussed critically within this framework *(Ayboga 2013)*.

14 dams and Hydroelectric Power Plants are planned to be built in the Munzur Valley, which is located on an area of 42 thousand hectares between Dersim and Ovacik and was declared a "National Park" in 1971. Munzur Valley National Park is an area with unique endemic species in terms of plant and animal diversity, and it is an important area with its natural features and beauties. There are 1,518 plant species, 43 of which are unique to Munzur and 228 are endemic. In Munzur National Park, there are also animal species unique to the valley such as hook-horned goat, mountain goat named bezuvar, gall partridge, red-spotted trout. Under the dam's waters, the holy places of the people with predominantly Alevi Kurdish identity will also be under water. Dersim Nature activists frequently state that if dams are built, all their holy places will be destroyed. The geography of Dersim will be divided into 2–3 with the construction of the dams. East and West Dersim will be separated from each other: East and West Dersim will be divided into several parts by means of dams. Dams will necessitate migration. It is estimated that a population of at least 5 thousand people, including about 100 villages, will be displaced in Dersim due to these dams. Dozens of villages that were completely evacuated after the 1990s will also be flooded. Returns to the village will also become impossible. Dersim Environmental Initiative activists stated that the dams cause great harm to nature and humanity, that the dams disrupt the ecosystem of the region, destroy the existing living things, that because of climate changes and dams the oak forest, which used to grow by 60 cm per year, is now growing by 10 cm per year *(KSAM: 08.08.2012)*. For instance, Kigi HEPP works on Peri River in Bingol turned into a massacre of nature and history. While the stones of the historical Kigi Castle were used in the construction of the dam, the rocky ground on which the castle was built was detonated with dynamite *(Ayboga: 17.06.2010)*.

In the summer of 2015, 'Tigris Haber' wrote that Dersim is under dam blockade! "In Dersim, where all kinds of massacres, oppression and forced migration have been practiced due to "dehumanization" policies since the Ottoman period, the city is surrounded on four sides by reservoirs and power plants, as a continuation of that policy. In this region, where 27 dams and HEPP projects, most of which are for security purposes, are still on the agenda, Dersim is almost besieged from all four sides with 7 dams operating in the Peri, Munzur, Pulumur and Mercan valleys that mark its borders with Bingol and Erzincan. While almost the entire border of Dersim-Elazig was separated by the Keban Dam, the Pembelik, Seyrantepe and Tatar dams established in the Peri Valley, which form the border line between Dersim's Nazimiye and Elazig's Karakocan districts and

Bingol. Again, Dinar, Mercan, Cemisgezek and Uzuncayir dams were built in the Munzur, Pulumur and Mercan Valleys, which form the provincial borders of Dersim-Bingol and Dersim-Erzincan" *(Tigris Haber: 09.07.2015)*.

We argue that the example of the Dersim reservoirs shows that Turkey is showing diversity in the water fight against the PKK (Kurds). It shows that the Turkish authorities have decided to use another tactic of water struggle here: to completely surround the province by building dams on the Munzur and its tributaries and thus turn Tunjeli into an "island". This policy of Turkey's suppression of its Kurds reminds us of the former Iraqi leader Saddam Hussein's policy of suppressing the swamp Arabs through the water factor. We are talking about the The Glory River (Glory Canal or Prosperity Canal, Third River) built in Iraq in the early 1990s, which led to the destruction of a large part of the Mesopotamian swamps, the habitat of the "Marsh Arabs", and their deportation. There is no doubt that the Third River could bring great benefits to agriculture, but they served greatly to dewater the marshes. Iraq denies that the canal was completed to drain the marsh *(Stepanova 2016: 564–565)*.

8.5.4 Mardin-Ceylanpinar Irrigation Main Canal

In March 2017, the pro-government newspaper Yeni Akit published an article titled "Here is the project that will end the PKK: Mardin-Ceylanpinar Main Irrigation Canal", stating that, the Mardin-Ceylanpinar Irrigation Main Canal with a length of 221 km has been made completely ready, while the construction of the storage station, which was started in the Derik District of Mardin, continues (the water in Ataturk Dam is divided into two canals, Mardin and Sanliurfa). Visiting the storage station built 55 km from Mardin, AK Party Mardin Deputy Ceyda Bolunmez Cankiri said that the people of the region and farmers are looking forward to the implementation of the project, which will irrigate 2 million 167 thousand 930 decares of agricultural land. Cankiri stated that the project, which will provide employment for 400 thousand people and an annual income of 500 million lira, will be completed this year and fertile lands will get water. Reminding that the works for the Mardin-Ceylanpinar Irrigation Main Canal started in 1997 and were completed in the current period, Cankiri from the AK Party explained that 200 cubic meters of water will come per second in terms of volume, which is higher than the annual average flow of the rivers in Turkey. Expressing that electricity consumption will decrease with the transition to modern irrigation, the problem of unemployment will disappear and the level of welfare in the region will increase with the increase in agricultural production,

Cankiri said this project will eradicate terrorism. "Turkey's largest river, so to speak, will be brought to the region. Our people and farmers are looking forward to the days when this project, which is of vital importance for our region, will be completed immediately and the fertile Mardin plain will meet the water of the Euphrates. Ancient Mesopotamia and the Mardin Plain await the rushing water of the Euphrates impatiently. We believe that with the project, significant progress will be made in revival and construction practices and in solving the problem of terrorism. Hopefully, we will all work together to bring these fertile lands back to their good old days",—said he *(Yeni Akit: 15.03.2017).*

Although Cankiri suggests that this canal will bring prosperity to the local people and it will help solve the issue of terrorism, we also argue that the Mardin-Ceylanpinar canal and other irrigation canals of region can also have a security function, because they will hinder the movement of PKK militants. These irrigation canals stretch for tens and even hundreds of kilometers and in that sense will serve as a serious obstacle for PKK. PKK militants can cross them only in limited places—bridges, which control is much easier for the Turkish authorities. Thus, the Mardin-Ceylanpinar Canal will contribute to ending the activities of the PKK, but not only by providing prosperity to the local residents, as Cankiri claims, but also by impeding the movement of PKK militants. In addition, we do not rule out that canals can also have the function of further dividing the Kurdish region as is the case with major reservoirs.

8.6 Concluding Summary of Chapter 6

Chapter 6 presents the GAP plans and the GAP implementation process during the administration of JDP, which came to power in Turkey at the beginning of the 21st century. Since Turkey had built 5 reservoirs on the Euphrates in the 20th century, JDP has focused on the tributaries of the Euphrates in the 21st century, as well as building major reservoirs on the Tigris and its tributaries. Although the deadlines for the implementation of the GAP project has been announced several times, it has not yet been completed for various reasons.

In our opinion, one of the reasons is that Erdogan is more focused on the implementation of mega-projects in Istanbul and in the west of Turkey in general. In addition, the gradual implementation of the GAP gave Erdogan the opportunity to use it for electoral reasons: to implement any component of the GAP before each local government or parliamentary and presidential election. For example, the opening of the Suruc tunnel took place just before the 2014 local government elections. This means that the Turkish authorities implement the GAP components not only to punish the local Kurds, but also to woo them, especially before various elections.

If in the 20th century Turkey in the GAP region was more focused on producing electricity, then in the 21st century, while maintaining this trend, the emphasis was placed on the construction of canals, which will enable irrigation of large areas. This, in turn, will make it possible to ensure Turkey's food security on the one hand, and to export a large batch of agricultural products on the other hand. In this context, Turkey's priority target is the rich Arab countries of the Middle East, which have a problem with water and therefore with agricultural products.

The development of technology in the 21st century, the rise of Turkey in various fields gave it the opportunity to first develop reservoir construction in the Tigris basin (Ilisu & Silvan dams), which, as mentioned earlier, is technologically more complex compared to the Euphrates basin. And secondly, the strengthening of Turkey and the decline of Iraq and Syria at the same time created conditions for the Turkish side to focus more on irrigation, which creates significant problems with downstream countries. Strengthened Turkey may not worry too much about opposition from weaker neighbors (by building major reservoirs on the Euphrates in the 20th century, Turkey did not exclude the option of flooding Syrian tanks with water from those reservoirs in case of an attack by Syria, thus assigning security functions to the dams of Euphrates).

And although the JDP began to significantly cooperate with Syria and Iraq on water issues in the first years of its administration, in our opinion, this was due to the fact that at that time Erdogan's positions were quite weak both inside the country and abroad. It was also manifested in the fact that Turkey pursued a policy of "zero problems with its neighbors" in the foreign political field, which should regulate Turkey's relations with neighboring countries, including in the economic sphere, increase Turkey's foreign political maneuverability, and enable Turkey to mediate between regional and extra-regional countries and forces, to increase Turkey's demand in the region and beyond its borders.

Meanwhile, just prior to JDP rule in the 1990s, Turkey was quite weak economically and had significant problems with neighboring/regional countries and was even facing the threat of a 2.5 war (according to Turkish "2.5 War" strategy Turkey should be able to wage 2 wars at the same time, say against Greece in the northwest of the country, against Syria in the southeast, and parallely wage a half war inside the country against the PKK).

In the late 2000s and early 2010s, successfully implementing the "zero problem with neighbors" policy, as well as taking advantage of the opportunities provided by the "Arab Spring", JDP made a transition to a harder foreign (and also domestic) policy, neo-Ottomanism. It was meant to increase Turkey's influence in the domain that was previously part of the Ottoman Empire. Turkey's neo-Ottoman policy was also reflected in the hydro policy, as Turkey began to use the water factor to a large extent to achieve its goals. It was particularly related to Syria and Iraq, which are in a weakened state and are downstream countries. And Turkey managed to extract various concessions from those countries using the water card, which will continue in the future. While acknowledging that the water situation in Syria has also worsened due to climate changes, and Turkey is increasingly in need of water and electricity, we believe that Turkey nevertheless uses Euphrates water in a number of cases as leverage against the Syrian authorities and as punitive measure against Syrian Kurds.

In the previous chapter, we mentioned that Turkey used the water factor to a great extent against its Kurds as well. In our opinion, in the 21st century, this policy became more multilateral, and in particular it was reflected in the security and electoral plans. Water also played a major role in limiting the PKK's activities in Turkey. Keeping the functions, it received in the 20th century, in the 21st century Turkey's water policy against its own Kurds thus acquired new shades and began to be applied anew against them.

The reflection of these cases of Turkey's use of the water factor against its neighbors Syria and Iraq, and to some extent also Iran, the Kurds of those countries, as well as its own Kurds, comes to confirm our thesis that Turkey is a unique country in this regard in the whole world, that any other the country is not able to use (does not use) water in such a multi-purpose and multi-sector way due to its own geographical and historical features (China's hydro policy has significant similarities with Turkey's hydro policy).

Conclusion 9

This chapter will conclude the study by summarising the key empirical findings in relation to the research aims and questions and discussing the value and contribution thereof. It will also review the limitations of the study and propose opportunities for future research.

Water is extremely important in people's lives, it is used in a wide variety of areas, from daily life (household), agriculture (the main area of consumption of fresh water) to industry, electricity generation, etc.. It is known that neither people, nor animals, nor plants can survive without water. In the 21st century, water is becoming the most strategic resource in the world, surpassing oil in that sense. If oil has an alternative, water has no alternative. On the other hand, as mentioned earlier, water also has negative aspects, such as the spread of infectious diseases, floods, etc.

It seems that there are enough water resources on the planet Earth. However, in reality, the vast majority of water resources are found in seas and oceans, are salt water and not fresh water. In addition, the vast majority of fresh water are located in glaciers and also underground. This complicates the life of our planet even more.

Annual reports of the United Nations on water topics regularly state that the consumption of water in the world is increasing, that the rate of growth of water consumption is much higher than the growth of the population of the planet. This is facilitated not only by the growth of the world population, but also by global warming and the significant reduction of underground water. As a result of all that, the issue of water immigrants in the world will be more and more aggravated. This concerns millions of people whose areas run out of water and they are forced to leave their places of residence.

H. Gabrielyan, *Turkey's Water Policy as Part of the Political Strategy*, Politik, Wirtschaft und Gesellschaft im Spannungsverhältnis der Regionen Südosteuropa und Mittlerer Osten, https://doi.org/10.1007/978-3-658-44070-1_9

It is expected that in the coming decades, the water problem will worsen on a global scale and especially in water-scarce regions, the "water status" of a number of countries will change. For example, Turkey, which today is not considered a poor country in terms of water resources, may become such a country in the next decade. Moreover, not only the volume of water, but also the issue of water quality is becoming more and more problematic. The role of the latter is not emphasized in many cases, but in fact it can be more important, because when the upstream country releases a sufficient volume of water to the midstream or downstream country, but it is unsuitable for use, then in this case the important thing is the quality of the water and not the volume.

And finally, in the case of a number of countries (for example, Turkey), the problem is not only the scarcity of water resources, but their location, in other words, their "incorrect", uneven distribution within the country. This means that if the given country has enough water resources, it does not at all guarantee that a number of its regions do not experience a lack of water.

Considering all this, it should not be surprising that the 20th century saw a great development of hydropolitics/hydrodiplomacy, which aims to consider water as an object of cooperation and conflict. International water law (1997 UN Convention) was developed, the principles of which, on the one hand, are a huge progress in solving water conflicts, but on the other hand, it has a number of shortcomings (in reality, it may be impossible to develop such "water rules" that all parties will be happy with). A number of water terms appeared, such as transboundary rivers, international water flow, malign and benign hydro-hegemonic country, organization of river basin countries, hydropolitical interdependence gained special importance, under which one can understand the mutual connection of internal and external politics with hydropolicy.

It turned out that just being an upstream country and thus controlling most of the river's flow does not necessarily mean that it must be a hydro-hegemon. The hydro-hegemon can also be the country of the middle stream (Syria in the case of the Orontes River), as well as the country of the down stream (Egypt in the case of the Nile). For this, the given country, as mentioned earlier, is required to be strong in 4 main factors: geographical power, material power, bargaining power, ideational power. Hydro-hegemons can be malign (laggards) or benign (pushers).

We argue that in the case of some countries (for example, Turkey), being a bad or good hydro-hegemonic country can only be temporary, depending on who is leading that country at the moment. If authoritarianism is established in the country instead of democracy or semi-democracy, then the probability that that country will become an evil hydro-hegemonic country increases. In the future, if democracy is established in the given country, it can again become a good hydro-hegemonic country. Being a bad or good hydro-hegemon also depends on the plans and ambitions of the leadership of the given country, because there is a fear that in order to achieve all that, it may resort to the help of the water factor, to use water as a lever against its neighbors.

The above affects the position of the country's leadership: to be guided by defensive or offensive realism in the water sector, to insist on absolute or limited territorial sovereignty in water relations with neighboring countries, to demonstrate liberalism and constructivism or not? Realism and liberalism, as well as constructivism, thus precede and follow each other in Turkey's hydro policy. In this context we can say the same about offensive and defensive realism, which are also precede and follow each other. And it will probably continue in the future, depending on who will be the authorities of Turkey, as well as Syria and Iraq, and what will be the situation of those riparian countries.

Although The Pacific Institute presented 3 stages in the Water Conflict Chronology (Trigger, Weapon, Casualty), we have changed the content of those 3 stages, but not the name. We tend to think that by building reservoirs and thus gaining water leverage, hydrohegemon can point the gun at a neighboring country (trigger), even "shoot" at it cuting off a significant part of the water flow (weapon), and thus make it a victim (casualty).

We also assert that the reservoir may have more functions than stated in official Turkish sources. According to them, a dam may have 4 functions: drinking water supply, irrigation water supply, electricity supply and flood prevention. We believe that reservoirs have much wider functions, including internal political, security, military aspects, and we are trying to prove it by the example of Turkey. That is why we consider the construction of reservoirs by Turkey in the Euphrates-Tigris basin not only from financial-economic and moral-legal aspects, but also from political-military aspects.

Water and waterways have played an important role not only in the Republic of Turkey, but also in the Ottoman Empire, which controlled the belt from the Danube to the Euphrates and Tigris, as well as the Nile Delta, and basically had no water problems with neighboring countries (there was a small problem with Persia regarding the Shatt al-Arab river). Apart from domestic-agricultural spheres in the empire, the importance of water and waterways was also expressed in the military context. It specifically refers to solving the water problem during the Ottoman army's raids in desert and semi-desert zones, as well as using the Euphrates and Tigris for military purposes as partially navigable waterways. It is due to the Euphrates and Tigris that the Ottoman Empire was able to keep Mesopotamia under its control (the area of present-day Iraq) for a long time and conversely, not controlling the water-scarce areas of the central Arabian Peninsula (where there are no major rivers).

In 1923 after its establishment, the Republic of Turkey had many economic and other problems and started paying attention to water resources already in the next decade. In this matter, he was first inspired by the USA and the USSR, which implement major water projects, and then also by its neighbors, and especially by the downstream country Iraq, which was the first of the riparian countries to start building reservoirs in the Euphrates-Tigris basin. The role of the individual is also very important in implementing water projects in Turkey. Suleiman Demirel, who was an engineer by profession and had personally seen the Hoover Dam built on the Colorado River in the US, was well aware of the importance of building reservoirs and hydropower plants on the Euphrates for Turkey which has limited oil, gas and coal reserves. Later, becoming the prime minister of Turkey several times and once the president, Demirel got the opportunity to implement his water projects and go down in history as the architect of GAP. According to him, rivers can be a source of both prosperity and misfortune, and each country must decide which way to go. Due to his efforts, Turkey chose the first path (prosperity), building large reservoirs on the Euphrates River in the 20th century.

In the 20th century, Turkey's target was to build large reservoirs in the Euphrates basin itself, because the Euphrates in Turkey is longer than the Tigris and is more abundant (in Iraq, the Tigris becomes more abundant mainly due to the tributaries coming from Iran). In addition, the Tigris basin was considered mountainous, difficult to access and technically more difficult. As a result, Turkey in the 20th century was content with building only a few reservoirs of limited volume in the Tigris basin.

The first reservoir built by Turkey on the Euphrates is the Keban reservoir (completed in the mid-1970 s), and Syria simultaneously completed the construction of the Tabqa Reservoir on the Euphrates, resulting in water disagreements between the riparian countries, particularly Iraq and Syria. The situation in Iraq was complicated by the fact that Turkey and Syria started simultaneously reducing the flow of the Euphrates to Iraq, which was an unusual phenomenon for the latter. However, both Turkey and Syria were not going to limit themselves to building the Keban and Tabqa reservoirs, and Iraq's situation will become more and more difficult and water disputes would turn into water conflicts (Iraq also built reservoirs on the Euphrates, and in this context, Turkey and Syria built reservoirs on the Euphrates building cannot be considered an extraordinary step).

Despite the fact that Syria and Iraq were Arab countries and, in the case of the Euphrates, were also downstream countries (although Syria can be called a middle-stream country), they could not put aside their differences, unite their efforts against the upstream country Turkey, which had begun to store some of the river's water in its territory. It specifically refers to Turkey's implementation of the GAP project, which planed to build 22 reservoirs and 19 hydropower plants in the Euphrates-Tigris basin, which would affect both Syria and Iraq. This can be considered Turkey's success, taking into account that in the 1970–80 s, Hafez Assad's Syria and Saddam Hussein's Iraq were almost equal countries to Turkey, which we can't say for "Erdogan's Turkey" and the same Syria and Iraq in the 2010–2020 s.

It is obvious that the growth of Turkey's economy and population, the level of urbanization, the demand for electricity, the general failure to find large oil reserves in Turkey, the crises in the world oil markets and a number of other factors pushed Turkey to build large reservoirs on its most abundant river, the Euphrates. Moreover, the production of agricultural products was not in Turkey's priority plan, which is why in the 20th century the energy part of the GAP was implemented by more than 80 percent, while the irrigation part (construction of canals and aqueducts) did not even reach 20 percent.

There are perhaps three main explanations for this, one of which is that unlike building hydroelectric power plants and laying power lines and thus getting electricity, the situation in the irrigation sector is much more complicated, because the state, in addition to building canals, should work with farmers, teach them the rules of agriculture, etc.. The second important reason is that irrigation (agriculture) causes the main problems with neighboring countries, that irrigation accounts for the largest expenditure of fresh water, that irrigation causes the most concern with downstream countries. As a third factor, it can be noted that Turkey did not want to raise the standard of living of the people living in the Kurdish provinces, which could have happened by giving a big boost to agriculture in those provinces.

And although in the 20th century, Turkey did not send water from the Euphrates reservoirs for irrigation in a large volume, nor did it dehydrate the countries downstream significantly, it still had water conflicts with them. The fact that the downstream countries did not want to depend on Turkey, which could use water as leverage against them, also played a role in this. Downstream countries realized that even the reservoirs built by Turkey on the Euphrates for the purpose of generating electricity pose a serious threat, because Turkey would thus have the opportunity (potential) to turn the "energy reservoir" into an "irrigation reservoir" at any time. They also realized that if the growth rate of the economy and population in Turkey is maintained/strengthened, the demand for water in Turkey will increase.

However, in the case of the Euphrates, Turkey's opportunities were not unlimited, because if Turkey uses the water of the Euphrates for irrigation purposes, it will negatively affect the work of the largest Ataturk Reservoir hydropower plant, it will produce less electricity. Thus, we see a interdependence, a cause-and-effect relationship of energy and irrigation needs for Turkey.

And despite all this, in the 20th century, water conflicts were registered between riparian countries, two of which are memorable. One of them referred to the construction and filling of the Ataturk Reservoir, which is considered the largest reservoir in Turkey and Europe, and the second one referred to the construction and filling of the Birecik Reservoir located further down. The example of Turkey, Syria and Iraq shows that water conflicts usually arise between countries that lack an atmosphere of trust and that also have other problems, both historical and current.

As a historical issue, it should be especially noted that Iraq and Syria were under the control of the Ottoman Empire for 300–400 years, and it brings back bad memories for them. Nowadays, the issues of Aleppo, Kirkuk and Mosul are raised from time to time in Turkey, which passed to Syria and Iraq after the collapse of the Ottoman Empire. Turks, for their part, remember The Great Arab Revolt that appeared during the First World War, and consider it a betrayal, a blow from behind.

In turn, the Arabs consider Turkey a traitor for being the first in the Muslim world to recognize Israel, and later (in the 1990 s) for developing military-military-industrial ties with Israel. Turkey's capture of Alexandretta in the 1930 s also evoked bad memories in Syria. There were also problematic relations between the three countries due to the Cold War, due to which the parties found themselves at opposite poles (for example, Turkey became a member of NATO in 1952, and Syria came under the auspices of the USSR). In such an atmosphere, it is natural that the parties strongly do not trust each other in water matters, including the data of river flows.

In the 20th century by building 5 reservoirs, 3 of them large, on the Euphrates River, Turkey was able to control 100% of its flow to Syria. And it is natural that this provoked the discontent of Syria, put Syria in serious dependence on Turkey, considering the importance of the Euphrates for Syria. In response, Turkey claims that Syria has done the same with regard to the Orontes River, building reservoirs on it and thus reducing the flow of the river to Turkey. In any case, for both Syria and especially Turkey, the Euphrates has a much greater importance than the Orontes, and therefore we see asymmetric mutual dependence between Turkey and Syria.

The Orontes and Euphrates examples show that both Syria and Turkey are playing a double game, demanding each other to release more water from these rivers when they are in lower/midstream country status. However, when they are in superior positions (in the case of Turkey on the Euphrates and Syria on the Orontes), they do not want to release too much water to the neighboring country and insist on their rights to the water resources of those rivers. As for the water relations between Turkey and Iraq, there is only Iraq's dependence on Turkey.

The example of the Orontes is also interesting in the sense that Syria, being a country in the middle course of this river, has become a hydro-hegemon, primarily due to the fact that most of this river flows through its territory. The second reason is that the upstream country was the weaker Lebanon, which was obliged by Syria for a long time not to use large volumes of Orontes water. In the case of Turkey, Syria refused to start negotiations regarding the waters of the Orontes River, claiming that it is not transboundary, because the Alexandretta (Hatay province in the Turkish version) belongs to it.

Simultaneously, Syria, being a midstream country in the case of the Euphrates, has not been able to achieve such success, because the Euphrates flow begins in Turkey, Turkey controls a significant part of the length of the river, and in terms of power and influence, Turkey cannot be compared to Lebanon. These examples of the Orontes and Euphrates prove that only being an upstream (midstream) country is not enough to become a hydro-hegemon, that for this the given country must be strong in the above 4 points (geographical power, material power, bargaining power, ideational power), as well as in the 8 components mentioned by Hans Morgenthau (geography, natural resources, industrial capacity, military preparedness, population, national character, national morale, the quality of diplomacy).

The history of water conflicts between Turkey, Syria, and Iraq in the Euphrates-Tigris and Orontes basins shows that water has served as a trigger, but not the root of the conflict here. The roots of the conflicts between the three countries, as already mentioned, come from the depths of centuries and have become more acute in the 20th century. It is because of multiple problems, the atmosphere of mistrust that Turkey could not implement The Peace Water Pipeline project, which provided for the purchase of "Turkish water" by the Arabs and the water dependence of the Arab countries on Turkey.

When in the 20th century, Turkey controlled 100% of the flow of the Euphrates, Syria could perceive it as a trigger. In other words, it became Turkey's weapon in the direction of Syria, with its finger on the trigger. And Syria realized that if not today, then tomorrow Turkey could fire that weapon (in other words, start large-scale irrigation works and thus significantly dehydrate itself), and it would appear as the victim, because it has no alternative to the Euphrates (as much as the Orontes River is considered an important water resource for Syria, it cannot replace the Euphrates for the reasons of not being so abundant and flowing through different geographical zones).

And despite such a vulnerable position, in the 20th century, Syria managed to force Turkey to sit down at the negotiating table and agree to release more water through the Euphrates River (1987 protocol). This became possible thanks to the support of the Syrian President Hafez Assad to the PKK. Although Hafez Assad did not establish the PKK (it was founded by the Kurdish leader Abdullah Ocalan), he saved Ocalan and a number of PKK leaders from arrest, gave them shelter in Syria, contributed to the strengthening of the PKK in various ways, helped to the moving to Northern Iraq and to start an armed struggle in the territory of Turkey in 1984. The PKK's armed success in the early years was also due to decades of persecution of the local Kurds by the Turkish authorities, violation of their rights, and assimilation policy towards them. In other words, in 1980 after the generals came to power in Turkey and a great wave of violence against the Kurds arose, Hafez Assad, while saving the PKK from defeat, may have realized that a favorable environment was created in Turkey for the success of the PKK's armed struggle and he will be able to influence on the Turkey's leadership through it.

Due to the successes of the PKK, in the late 1980 s, Turkey was also forced to change the nature of the GAP from a purely water project to a general regional development project to prevent the PKK from joining the ranks of local residents. The initial successes of the PKK (not only military, but also the fact that a large number of Kurds began to join its ranks) were shocking for the Turkish authorities, as is evidenced by Turgut Ozal's visit to Syria in 1987 and the signing of a water protocol by which Turkey committed to release 500 m3/s of water through the Euphrates River.

This means that Hafez Assad managed to apply "more water for less terror" tactic to Turkey, despite Turkish President Suleiman Demirel rejecting such a formula. And if Turkey played the water card against Syria, Syria was able to play the PKK card against Turkey. The fact that there is a connection between these two factors is also evident from the fact that the PKK intensified its armed struggle in the early 1990 s, when Turkey began to fill the Ataturk Reservoir, much to Syria's displeasure.

Our financial comparison shows that Turkey has spent (lost) much more money in the fight against the PKK than it has benefited from the reservoirs built on the Euphrates and, in particular, from the electricity produced by their HEPPs. Of course, we do not argue that the PKK fought only to solve Hafez Assad's water and other problems, but we emphisize that without Hafez Assad's support, the PKK established in 1978 would not have be able to survive the 1980 military coup, to become powerful, start an armed struggle on the territory of Turkey and achieve success.

The financial comparison of the costs incurred by Turkey in the armed struggle against the PKK and the benefits received by Turkey from the Euphrates hydro nodes is current and true in the sense that in both cases the statements of the Turkish authorities served as a basis for us (about the losses suffered in the fight against the PKK) and the statistics presented by them (about the electricity produced by the Euphrates HEPPs). It is the Turkish authorities who have regrettably stated many times that if Turkey had not spent so much money (from several hundred billion dollars to several trillion dollars, taking into account the indirect costs as well) in the fight against the PKK, then Turkey would be a completely different country, it would have a completely different economy, other infrastructures, etc..

This example of Turkey and Syria shows that if an upstream country begins to dehydrate a middle or downstream country, it can receive a much stronger and unexpected blow from it. In other words, the hunter can become the hunted. This blow by Hafez Assad to Turkey through the PKK was also effective because in the 20th century, Turkey greatly oppressed its Kurds, including by playing the water card. It is particularly related to emptying Kurdish villages by building large reservoirs (leaving those villages under water), organizing a large migration from the Kurdish provinces to the west and thus trying to assimilate the Kurds. With this, an attempt was also made to promote the migration of Kurds from the villages to the regional centers of their provinces, which would facilitate their control.

As a result, Kurdish peasants were transformed from producers to consumers, facing great problems in leading urban life, which especially affected women. Thus, the Turkish authorities were able to divide the Kurdish region with the help of reservoirs, fragment it and make it easier to manage. Reservoirs also left unwanted historical and cultural monuments under water of other nations. The reservoirs of the Euphrates, as well as the Tigris basin also solved security problems. For example, hundreds of villages were flooded, and PKK militants were deprived of finding shelter and food in them at night, getting information from local residents, replenishing their ranks from local residents, etc..

This Kurdish policy of Turkey continued and even expanded in the 21st century under the AKP administration. A new type of reservoir appeared, a new term—"security reservoirs", whose primary number one purpose was not to generate electricity or irrigate land, but to provide security. Those "security reservoirs" were built in the border zone with Iraq and were aimed at submerging the mountain canyons, the paths through which the Kurdish militants penetrated from Northern Iraq to Turkey and vice versa. In addition to the routes (highways) of the Kurdish militants, mountain hideouts (bunkers) and caves, in which the Kurdish militants were hiding, as well as their weapons, clothing, etc., also appeared under water.

In the 21st century, Ilisu, Silvan, and a number of other reservoirs built on the Tigris and in its basin in Turkey have similar functions. All of them, apart from the importance of energy and irrigation, leaving significant areas under water, thus hindering the movement of PKK militants. Perhaps the irrigation canals also have such functions, especially the 221 km long Mardin-Ceylanpinar canal, which is also called the artificial river of Turkey, which is longer than the Suez Canal and 3 times longer than the Panama Canal. In our opinion, such irrigation canals also create significant complications for the movement of PKK militants and are aimed at ensuring Turkey's hydro-victory against the PKK. Besides, they also divide Kurdish region by parts like major dams.

We argue that the small "security reservoirs" built on the border with Iraq can be considered the first line of "water defence", meanwhile the Ilisu reservoir, which is located in the "Mardin-Van-Diyarbekir" triangular region—quite important zone from the point of view of the Turkish authorities, as the second line. Perhaps it was because of the PKK factor that Turkey did not stop at anything and left the 12,000-year-old Hasankeyf settlement under water with the construction of the Ilisu reservoir, which caused a lot of noise, including at the international level. It is known that there are 4,000–5,000 caves in Hasankeyf, which, according to the Turkish authorities, were largely used by PKK militants. The Ilisu Reservoir left a significant part of these caves under water, as well as some of the caves were blown up with dynamite by the authorities, citing safety reasons (due to the risk of hanging and collapsing rocks). As a result, the unexploded and unsubmerged caves can only be approached by boat.

As for the PKK's struggle against the construction of the reservoir, in the 20th century the PKK did not stand out. Simply, his armed struggle in the Kurdish region drove away foreign investors, who considered it risky to build a reservoir in the Euphrates basin under such conditions, to make large investments. And it was a sensitive blow for Turkey, which was not so strong financially and technologically.

Unlike in the 20th century, in the 21st century, the PKK militants decided to actively prevent the construction of the above-mentioned reservoirs, and especially the Ilisu and Silvan reservoirs. They repeatedly attacked the construction zones of the reservoirs with grenade launchers, kidnapped the employees, set fire to the construction equipment, and set mines on the roads leading to the reservoirs. PKK militants, however, were able to delay, but not prevent, the construction of reservoirs with such measures. However, even it should be recorded in the PKK asset. For example, the construction of the Ilisu Reservoir lingers a long time (years), and this is a huge sum of money for the Turkish economy (the Ilisu Reservoir provides the Turkish economy with more than 1 million dollars per day).

Perhaps also based on the experience of the 20th century, in the 21st century the PKK realized that it is necessary to prevent the construction of reservoirs at the stage of construction, not to allow it to be completed, because if they were built, the PKK could not blow up the given reservoirs. There were 2–3 serious obstacles for that. The first of them is that in the event of an explosion, the surrounding Kurdish villages would suffer seriously, there would be hundreds, if not thousands of victims, great destruction, which was not part of the PKK's plans.

The second factor was that the PKK realized that after the completion of the construction and commissioning, the large reservoirs would receive the status of objects of strategic importance, and military checkpoints would be located near them, which would also complicate the life of the PKK militants. And finally, the third important point is related to the fact that the dam is a rather thick and strong concrete structure, and it is not so easy to blow it up.

In fact, guided by these considerations, the PKK in the 21st century sought to prevent the construction of major reservoirs in the Euphrates-Tigris basin, but it only managed to delay the process. In other words, the PKK only managed to win the battle, but lost the war. After construction of reservoirs the PKK believes that one day the Kurds will gain independence, and the large reservoirs built by Turkey will be part of the Kurdish state, and the Kurds will become a serious player in the water context.

In the 21st century, Turkey is also implementing another tactic of water struggle against the Kurds. The province of Dersim (Tunjeli), which in terms of the frequency of military conflicts is perhaps second only to the provinces of Hakkari and Sirnak bordering Iraq, was surrounded by new reservoirs built on the Mndzur, Peri and other rivers and turned into an "island". The Keban Reservoir, built on the Euphrates about 50 years ago, also contributes to this, which turned the large land border of Dersim and Elazigh provinces into a water border. By surrounding Dersim with reservoirs, the Turkish authorities are trying to make it difficult for PKK militants to enter this province.

In the 21st century, not only the Kurds of Turkey, but also the Kurds of Iraq and especially Syria suffered from Turkey's water policy. The Kurds of Iraq are in a better situation in the water context compared to the Kurds of Syria.

However, recently, their situation has also worsened due to Turkey's construction of reservoirs in the Tigris basin and Iran's construction of reservoirs on the Tigris' tributaries. These steps of Turkey and Iran complicate the situation of the Kurdish autonomy of Northern Iraq, forcing it to build new reservoirs in its territory and thus store more water. And this, in turn, complicates the situation throughout Iraq (official Baghdad).

In the 20th century Iraq was mostly affected only by the water projects of Turkey and Syria on the Euphrates (Euphrates basin) and was able to fix the situation to a large extent due to the Tigris, which is a river with more water in its territory than the Euphrates (Iraq had built an aqueduct from the Tigris to the Euphrates to make up for the Euphrates' lack of flow, thereby unwittingly supporting Turkey's thesis that the Euphrates and the Tigris are one, unified water system).

However, in the 21st century the picture is different. The Tigris River and its tributaries have been targeted by Turkey and Iran, as well as the Kurdish autonomy of Northern Iraq (in the 21st century, even Syria wants to use the waters of the Tigris). This makes Iraq extremely vulnerable and dependent. In essence, Iraq will be forced to work with Turkey on the "oil/gas for water" formula.

On the other hand, it is not necessary to overestimate the possibilities of Turkey dewatering the Tigris. The Silvan Reservoir, which will be the second largest irrigation reservoir in Turkey (after Ataturk Reservoir), is being built in the area north of the Ilisu Reservoir. This means that if Turkey sends too much water for irrigation, it may negatively affect the efficiency of the Ilisu HEPP. This situation is similar to the situation created around the Ataturk Reservoir, when Turkey is forced to make a certain choice in matters of giving priority to producing electricity or irrigating the lands.

Iraq is greatly angered by the construction of reservoirs in the Tigris basin by both Turkey and Iran, and there is an impression that Iraq is more critical of Iran than of Turkey. Iran, in turn, accuses Turkey of building the Ilisu reservoir and contributing to dry up the swamps on the Iran-Iraq border, as a result of which sandstorms occur in Iran's territory, reaching as far as Tehran and making it difficult to breathe.

However, in reality, Iran is doing the same thing in the Tigris basin, reducing the water flow to Iraq by building reservoirs. In our opinion, Iran is just late in entering the "water game" and joined the process of dewatering Iraq after Turkey and Syria (Iran considers that Turkey successfully took advantage of the 1980–1988 Iran-Iraq war to build the Ataturk Reservoir). And perhaps it is for this reason that the "water relations" between Iraq and Iran have become quite strained in recent years, that it is Iran's actions that anger the official Baghdad the most (for decades, it has become common for Iraq that Turkey and Syria reduce the flow of transboundary rivers).

The example of the Ilisu reservoir shows that although Turkey is not dewatering the territory of Iran, a water dispute/conflict has arisen between the parties. Historical and current factors play their role here as well. Iran and Turkey (their predecessors, Safavid Persia and the Ottoman Empire) have been fighting each other for leadership in the region and the Islamic world for half a millennium with certain interruptions. It continues even today. In Iran, perhaps, they fear that Turkey will succeed in increasing its influence in Iraq by using the water factor, where Iran has strong positions.

In addition, perhaps Turkey is trying to use the water card to drive a wedge between Iran and Iraq, to pit them against each other. Iran also considers that Turkey has targeted the oil-rich neighboring countries, Iran, Iraq and Azerbaijan, and accordingly, by dewatering the Tigris and Araks, Turkey is trying to have a great influence on these oil-rich countries and receive oil from them by using the water card.

In any case, the dewatering of the Euphrates and Tigris by Turkey and Iran and other actors will negatively affect the flow of the Shatt al-Arab river, and if it becomes unnavigable, it will be a sensitive blow for Iran, whose only navigable river, the Karun, joins the Shatt al-Arab in the territory of Iraq, and Iran will be deprived of the opportunity to transport goods through this waterway.

Regarding the Euphrates, in the 21st century, Turkey focused on its tributaries, on building reservoirs in its basin, some of which are also large reservoirs (it was not possible to build a new reservoir on the Euphrates). In the 21st century, Turkey's water policy (reducing the flow of the river) in the Euphrates basin significantly affects not only Syria, which is experiencing severe droughts, but also the Syrian Kurds. Turkey has been repeatedly accused of using the Euphrates as a water weapon against both the Syrian authorities and the Syrian Kurds, which has created serious and diverse problems during the COVID-19, severe droughts, the Syrian civil war, and especially the military attacks of ISIS in Syria.

If in the 20th century, Turkey mainly focused on building reservoirs on the Euphrates and partly also on the Tigris, mainly to get electricity, then in the 21st century, Turkey continued large-scale water projects in the Euphrates basin, started to implement large-scale water projects on the Tigris and in its basin. All this will give Turkey the opportunity to control not only the flow of the Euphrates but also the Tigris 100 percent in its territory.

Moreover, Turkey is already carrying out great works in the direction of not only the energy but also the irrigation purpose of the reservoirs, is building canals, aqueducts, water tunnels with a total length of hundreds of kilometers to irrigate large areas. Turkey considers that the Arab countries of the Middle East, which have little water resources, but are quite rich, can become a good consumption market for Turkish agricultural products, and have planned to significantly expand the export of Turkish agricultural products. These large irrigation plans show that in the 21st century, Turkey is not afraid of using water for agricultural purposes, which is known to be the main area of fresh water consumption.

Turkey is also not afraid to use the water lever against the neighboring countries and their Kurds in order to extract political (domestic political, foreign political), security, economic concessions and benefits. And although 3 state actors (Syria, Iraq and also Iran) and 3 non-state actors (Kurds of Turkey, Syria and Iraq) suffer from Turkey's water policy in the Euphrates-Tigris basin, this is not the main indicator of the effectiveness of that policy. For us, it is the various sphere of concessions and benefits that makes Turkey a unique country in the field of hydropolitics in the world. We do not see that any other hydro-hegemon country is able (has the opportunity) to use the water factor in the 21st century to obtain such diverse and important concessions from neighboring countries (Turkey's hydropolitics has certain similarities with China's hydropolitics).

However, what makes Turkey a unique water country is not only its hydropolitics, but also a number of factors, such as the peculiarities of Turkey and the region, and first of all, geographical and historical aspects (its geographical location—upstream-hegemon country): existence of the Kurdish question within the country, characteristics of the surrounding geographical zone (region), in particular (currently) weaker neighbors-downstream countries, the existence of a Kurdish population in them.

The fact that Turkey is able to take bold steps in the field of hydropolitics in the 21st century, and in particular to build new reservoirs and canals, to send a significant part of the water to irrigation and to dewater the downstream countries (as well as their Kurds) in a larger volume, is possible thanks to 2 parallel processes. In the 21st century, Turkey experienced a significant rise in economic, military, geopolitical and other aspects, while Iraq and Syria have weakened significantly, primarily due to their internal problems. As a result, Turkey got great advantage over them regarding the above-mentioned 4 factors forming the hydro-hegemonic situation and most of the 8 power components mentioned by Morgenthau. And that immediately found its reflection in Turkey's hydropolitics, turning it into a unique water country in the world.

There are two main factors for such an opinion: 1) Quantitative: Turkey's hydro policy in the Euphrates-Tigris basin affects 3 states and 3 non-state actors. The first group includes Syria, Iraq and also Iran, and the second group includes the Kurds of Turkey, Syria and Iraq. 2) Qualitative: This is the most important factor and is primarily related to what kind of concessions Turkey has received/ receives from those neighboring countries, using water as a lever, and how diverse the scope of those concessions are. The same should be said about Turkey's use of water against the above-mentioned non-state actors and thereby solving problematic issues.

* * *

This study aimed to investigate the evolution of Turkey's hydropolicy, its changes, the reasons for those changes, to describe how Turkey's hydro policy in the Euphrates-Tigris basin impacts (determines) its foreign and domestic policies. The results indicate that the reasons why Turkey started building reservoirs in the Euphrates-Tigris basin (and also in the areas near them) are different. In this context, we consider it necessary to distinguish four factors in a broad sense, among which we bring the economic factor to the fore: economic factor, foreign political factor, domestic political factor, security-military factor. This study shows that hydropolitics is interdependent with foreign policy on the one hand and domestic policy on the other.

Future researchers can try to further develop and substantiate this version of Turkey being a unique country in the water sector, to further develop not only the existence of interdependence between hydro policy and foreign policy, but also the interdependence between hydro policy and domestic policy. That's why in many cases, water can be used/is used not only against the neighboring, riparian countries, but also against the ethnic and/or religious minority within the country itself. This is more interesting in the Euphrates-Tigris basin, where not only Turkey has acted in this way, but also Iraq, suppressing the Shia (Marsh) Arabs through water.

We argue, that in the hydropolicy, the importance of non-state actors will probably increase in the future, as theoretically one day they can turn into a state actor and subject as well: initially, they can achieve autonomy and then also independence (Iraqi Kurds and to some extent also Syrian Kurds already have autonomy).

Our study is also an example of the fact that if a country (Turkey) has an internal problem, even not a very active problem at the moment (PKK), then it should think several times before implementing large water projects. It must calculate how the downstream country will suffer as a result, what countermeasures it will implement and what damage it will cause to the upstream country. Future researchers can take this precedent into account and try to find similar examples in the case of other hydro-hegemon countries.

The study is limited to the coverage of Turkey's water policy in the Euphrates-Tigris and Orontes basins, it does not include issues related to other transboundary basins (Araks, Kur, Chorokh, Maritsa) of Turkey and partially presents the hydro policy of Syria and Iraq in the Euphrates-Tigris and Orontes basins.

The potential weaknesses of the study may be distance learning, time and budget restrictions for the author, not knowing Arabic (Syria and Iraq are Arab countries), which caused some problems for reading books and collecting data in that language, not knowing the disputes over other transboundary rivers as thoroughly as the disputes over the Euphrates, Tigris and Orontes rivers, as well as not being a water expert (hydrologist). During writing the study, we tried to be as objective as possible, objectively present and analyze Turkey's water policy (in the case of the author, being Armenian has not created obstacles).

Reference List/Bibliography

Abu-Zeid, K. (July 2001), International Water Law from Helsinki Rules to the United Nations Convention on the Law of the Non-Navigational Uses of International Watercourses, Water Resources Impact, Volume 3, November 4.

Abu Zeed, A. (21.06.2018), Turkey tries to legitimize incursion in northern Iraq, Al-Monitor.

Ağıralioğlu, N. (2014), Ataturk dam and its effects on Turkey (in Turkish—Atatürk barajı ve Türkiye'ye etkileri), İstanbul.

Ahmed, A. (30.12.2020), Authorities in northeast Syria seek alternatives due to Turkish disruption of water supplies, Al-Monitor.

Akbaş, S. (2018), Terror-economy relationship: The case of Turkey (in Turkish—Terör-ekonomi ilişkisi: Türkiye örneği), Gaziantep.

Alan, E. (2016), Terror—PKK & 40 Years of Betrayal (in Turkish—Terör—PKK & 40 Yıllık İhanet), Ankara.

Al-Ahmad, A. (23.08.2020), "Al-Hasakah Needs Water", Will Turkey Bear the Responsibility for Their Thirst?, DARAJ.

Allan, J. A., Mallat C. (ed) (1995), Water in the Middle East: Legal, Political and commercial implications, London-New York.

Alptekin, H. (2019 October), Analysis of PKK Terrorism (in Turkish—PKK Terörünün Analizi), SETA, Istanbul.

Altinbilek, D. (March 2004), Development and Management of the Euphrates–Tigris Basin, Water Resources Development, Vol. 20, No. 1, 15–33.

Anadolu (09.03.2014), Turkey's longest irrigation tunnel opened (in Turkish—Türkiye'nin en uzun sulama tüneli açıldı).

Anadolu (25.10.2018), 27 billion dollars energy income from the Euphrates River (in Turkish—'Fırat Nehri'nden 27 milyar dolar enerji geliri).

Anadolu (17.02.2020), Energy production in Turkey's 3 largest dams increased by 106 percent (in Turkish—'Türkiye'nin 3 büyük barajında enerji üretimi yüzde 106 arttı).

Anadolu (06.11.2021), President Erdogan inaugurates huge Ilisu Dam in southeastern Turkey.

ANF News (11.05.2022), Reduction of Euphrates water decreases electricity production in North-East Syria.

ANF News (20.06.2022), Turkey continues to seize Syria's share of Euphrates water.

H. Gabrielyan, *Turkey's Water Policy as Part of the Political Strategy*, Politik, Wirtschaft und Gesellschaft im Spannungsverhältnis der Regionen Südosteuropa und Mittlerer Osten, https://doi.org/10.1007/978-3-658-44070-1

Ayboga, E. (September 2013), Security Dams in the Context of Turkey's Dam and HEPP Policies (in Turkish—Türkiye'nin Baraj ve HES Politikaları Bağlamında Güvenlik Barajları), Su Hakkı.

Baldwin, D.A. (1993), Neoliberalism, neorealism, and world politics, New York.

Ballabio, R., Comair F.G., Scalet, M., Scoullos, M. (eds.) (2015), Science diplomacy and transboundary water management, The Orontes River case, Verona.

Barkey, H.J., Fuller, G.E. (1998), Turkey's Kurdish Question, New York.

Bash, H. (September 2016), Traditional River Transportation on Tigris and Euphrates Rivers and Its Usage in the Iraq Front in World War I (in Turkish—Dicle-Fırat'ta Geleneksel Nehir Taşımacılığı ve I. Dünya Savaşı'nda Irak Cephesinde Kullanımı).

Bilen, Ö. (2003), Environmental Imperialism and the Example of the Ilisu Dam, (in Turkish—Çevre Emperyalizmi ve Ilısu Barajı Örneği), Ankara.

Bilgen, A. (August 2019), The Southeastern Anatolia Project (GAP) in Turkey: An alternative perspective on the major rationales of GAP, Journal of Balkan and Near Eastern Studies 21(5):532–552.

Bilgin, F., Sarıhan, A. (eds) (2013), Understanding Turkey's Kurdish Question, Lanham.

Biswas, A.K. (ed) (1994), International Waters of the Middle East: From Euphrates-Tigris to Nile, Oxford.

Britannica, Neorealism.

Bull, H. (1995), The Anarchical Society: A Study of Order in World Politics, Second Edition, London.

Çağaptay S., Otun A. (14.05.2012), Flooding Out Terror? Turkey's Ilisu Dam Project, The Washington Institute.

Center for strategic research (SAM) (June-August, 1996), Water Issues between Turkey, Syria and Iraq, Ankara.

Chalabi, H., Majzoub, T. (1995), "Turkey, the Waters of the Euphrates and Public International Law," in J. Allan, Ch. Mallat eds., Water in the Middle East: Legal, Political and Commercial Implications, London.

Chudacoff, D. (07.07.2014), 'Water war' threatens Syria lifeline, Al Jazeera.

Clegg, S.R., Haugaard, M. (eds.) (2009), The SAGE Handbook of Power, Los Angeles.

Conker, A., Hussein, H. (13.12.2019), Hydropolitics and issue: linkage along the Orontes River Basin: an analysis of the Lebanon–Syria and Syria–Turkey hydropolitical relations.

Daily Sabah (05.06.2019), Water level at Turkey's Ataturk Dam hits 7-year high after rainfall above average.

Daily Sabah (19.05.2020), Turkey starts operating 1st turbine at huge Ilısu Dam.

David Bice and Timothy Bralower, Distribution of Water on the Earth's Surface.

Delibaş, A. (17.11.2021), Iran's Reactions to the Inauguration of the Ilisu Dam, IRAM Center, as well as **Keynoush, B. (18.03.2021)** Water scarcity could lead to the next major conflict between Iran and Iraq, MEI.

Deniz Haber Ajansı (11.05.2011), Euphrates River may be a trade and tourism route (in Turkish—Fırat Nehri ticaret ve turizm hattı olabilir).

DHA (23.01.2018), Iraq demanded, Turkey postponed the impoundment of the Ilisu Dam for 3 months (in Turkish—Irak istedi, Türkiye Ilısu Barajı'nda su tutma işlemini 3 ay erteledi).

DIIS (Danish Institute for International Studies) (2004), What Happened to the Iraqi Marsh Arabs and their Land?, Copenhagen.

Dolatyar, M., T.S. Gray (2000), Water Politics in the Middle East, London.

Drazewska, B. (2018), Hasankeyf, the Ilisu Dam, and the Existence of "Common European Standards" on Cultural Heritage Protection, SAACLR, Number 2, (4).

DSİ (General Directorate of State Hydraulic Works), Hydraulic works 1954–2018.

Dursun, A. (2006), Holy Lands and Unshared Waters Euphrates—Tigris (in Turkish—Kutsal Topraklar ve Paylaşılamayan Sular Fırat—Dicle), Istanbul.

Earle, A., Jägerskog A., Öjendal J. (eds.) (2010), Transboundary Water Management: Principles and Practice, London-New York, 2010.

Eghtesad Mihan (12.12.2022), Erdogan is implementing a water project against Iranian oil / Iran, the main loser in the construction of the Turkish dam on the Araks (in Persian—اردوغان به دنبال پروژه آب در برابر نفت ایران/ ایران، بازنده اصلی سدسازی ترکیه بر روی ارس).).

Ekinci İ. (2007), Ottoman-British rivalry in the Euphrates and Tigris: Hamidiye ferry administration (in Turkish—Fırat ve Dicle'de Osmanlı-İngiliz rekabeti: Hamidiye vapur idaresi), Ankara.

Elhance, A. (1999), Hydropolitics in the Third World: Conflict and Cooperation in International River Basins, Washington.

En Son Haber (15.06.2021), Mardin-Ceylanpınar Main Canal completed (in Turkish—Mardin-Ceylanpınar Ana Kanalı tamamlandı).

Entessar, N. (1992), Kurdish Ethnonationalism, Boulder.

Erdem, M. (March-May 2003), The Tigris-Euphrates rivers controversy and the role of international law, Center for strategic research (SAM), Ankara.

Ersever A.C. (1993), Kurds, PKK and A. Ocalan (in Turkish—Kürtler, PKK ve A. Öcalan), Ankara.

EuroNews (04.06.2018), Iraq wants the impoundment at the Ilisu Dam to be delayed again (in Turkish—Irak Ilısu Barajı'ndaki su tutma işleminin tekrar ertelenmesini istiyor).

Falode, A. (2009), The Theoretical Foundation of Realism, Nigerian Journal of International Affairs, Vol. 35, No. 2.

Günçiçek, B. (2015), Economic Effects of Terrorism (in Turkish—Terörün Ekonomik Etkileri), Diyarbekir.

Gundes, S. (2006), Project Finance and Hydropower Projects: a case study of Birecik dam and hydroelectric power plant project in Turkey (Conference paper), Conference: Joint 2006 CIB, Construction in the XXI Century: Local and global challenges, Rome.

Gürkan, D. (12.08.2022), Devrim Will the cross-border operation lead to winning the election? (in Turkish—Sınır ötesi operasyon seçim kazandırır mı?), Muhalif.

Haberler (08.11.2012), 'EU Shouldn't Miss Turkey's Train' A. Davutoğlu (in Turkish—'AB, Türkiye Trenini Kaçırmasın' A. Davutoğlu).

Haber Türk (26.06.2019), Irrigation channels give life to the fertile lands of the GAP (in Turkish—Sulama kanalları GAP'ın verimli arazilerine hayat veriyor),

Halkın Sesi (26.07.2014), 'Karkamis Camp is the training center of ISIS' (in Turkish—'Karkamış Kampı IŞİD'in eğitim merkezi').

Hall, I., Waltz, K. (24.06.2013), The Man Who Saved Realism, E-International Relations.

Harutyunyan, K. (2005), Water politics in the Middle East (in Armenian—Ջրային քաղաքականությունը Մերձավոր Արևելքում), Yerevan.

Haugaard, M., Lentner, H. (eds.) (2006), Hegemony and Power: Consensus and Coercion in Contemporary Politics, Lanham.

Heper, M. (2007), The State and Kurds in Turkey: The Question of Assimilation, New York.

Hinnebusch, R., Tür, Ö. (eds) (2013), Turkey-Syria Relations: Between Enmity and Amity by Farnham.

Holleis, J. (24.01.2021), Syria: Is water being weaponized?, DW.

Human Rights Watch (January 2003), The Iraqi Government Assault on the Marsh Arabs, Briefing Paper.

Hurriyet Daily News (11.07.2016), New irrigation canal to bring water to Turkey's Mardin.

Husain, F. H. (2021), Rivers of the Sultan: The Tigris and Euphrates in the Ottoman Empire, Oxford.

IHD (08.10.2014), We condemn the attacks on the Rojava revolution and the Kobane canton (in Turkish—Rojava devrimine ve Kobanê kantonuna yapılan saldırıları kınıyoruz).

Jawad, L. A. (ed.) (2021), Tigris and Euphrates Rivers: Their Environment from Headwaters to Mouth (Aquatic Ecology Series, 11).

Jongerden, J. (2007), The Settlement Issue in Turkey and the Kurds An Analysis of Spatial Policies, Modernity and War, Boston.

Kangarani, H. M. (2005), Euphrates and Tigris watershed Economic, social and institutional aspects of forest in an integrated watershed management, FOWECA/WP/1, Rome.

Kasapoğlu, Ç. (14.07.2014), Rojava: Why is ISIS targeting Kobani? (in Turkish—Rojava: IŞİD neden Kobani'yi hedef alıyor?), BBC Türkçe.

Keohane, R., Nye J. (2012), Power & Interdependence (4th Edition), Boston.

Kibaroglu, A. (April 2013), Evolution of Transboundary Politics in the Euphrates-Tigris River System: New Perspectives and Political Challenges, Article in Global Governance.

Kibaroglu, A., Waltina, S., Annika, K. (eds.) (2011), Turkey's Water Policy National Frameworks and International Cooperation, Istanbul.

Kirisci, K., Winrow, G.M. (1997), The Kurdish Question and Turkey: An Example of a Trans-state Ethnic Conflict.

Kliot, N. (1994), Water Resources and Conflict in the Middle East, London.

Kodaman, T. (2007), The Euphrates-Tigris Issue and Its Effect on Turkey-Syria Relations (in Turkish—Fırat-Dicle meselesi ve Türkiye-Suriye İlişkilerine Etkisi), Ankara.

Krishna-Hensel, S.F. (ed) (2016), Hydropolitics in South American international relations: A perspective on water governance at the Prata basin—between conflict and cooperation (1960–1992), Chapter 6, London.

KSAM (08.08.2012), With 'Security Dams', History, Nature, Life and Balance Disappear (in Turkish—'Güvenlik Barajları'yla Tarih De Doğa Da Yaşam Da Denge De Yok Oluyor).

Kurdistan Question (14.07.2014), What's happening in Kobane?.

Lefevre, R. (2013), Ashes of Hama—The Muslim Brotherhood in Syria, Oxford.

Lorenz, F., Erickson E.J. (2013), Strategic Water Iraq and Security Planning in the Euphrates-Tigris Basin, Virginia.

Marcus, A. (2007), Blood and Belief: The PKK and the Kurdish Fight for Independence, New York.

Mardin Life (16.03.2018), Mardin-Ceylanpınar Irrigation Main Canal is about to be completed (in Turkish—Mardin-Ceylanpınar Sulama Ana Kanalı tamamlanmak üzere).

Mazur, O. (2019), "The Kurdish Question in the Political Conflict in Syria", Moscow.

McCaffrey, S.C. (21 May 1997), Convention on the Law of the Non-Navigational Uses of International Watercourses, New York.

McDowall, D. (2007), A Modern History of the Kurds, Third Edition, London-New York.

Mearsheimer, J. (2001), The Tragedy of Great Power Politics, New York.

Midyat Haber (04.11.2021), President Erdogan will inaugurate the Ilisu Dam on Saturday (in Turkish—Cumhurbaşkanı Erdoğan, Cumartesi günü Ilısu Barajının açılışı gerçekleştirecek).

Mehr News (12.12.2022), Iran-Afghanistan water negotiations (in Persian مذاکرات آبی ایران و افغانستان).).

Milliyet (12.08.2012), On the way to 30 years of the fight against the PKK (in Turkish—PKK ile mücadelenin 30 yılına doğru).

Milliyet (04.07.2014), Turkey cut the Euphrates and the villages were left without water (in Turkish—Türkiye Fırat'ı kesti köyler susuz kaldı).

Ministry of Industry and Technology of Turkey, Southeastern Anatolian Project.

Morgenthau, H. J. (1948), Politics Among Nations: The Struggle for Power and Peace, First Edition, Revised, New York.

Morgenthau, H. J. (1978), Politics Among Nations: The Struggle for Power and Peace, Fifth Edition, Revised, New York.

Mosaki, N. (2001), Hydrostrategical Profile of Kurdish Question (article), Middle East and Modernity—Collection of Articles (eleventh edition), Moscow (in Russian—Гидростратегические аспекты курдского вопроса. // Ближний Восток и современность. Сборник статей (выпуск одиннадцатый)).

Mosaki, N. (2005), "Kurdistan: resources and policies. Part 1", Moscow, (in Russian—"Курдистан: ресурсы и политика. Часть 1").

Mosaki, N. (2012), Migration of Kurds in Turkey (article), Muslim space along the perimeter of the borders of the Caucasus and Central Asia—Collection of Articles, Moscow (in Russian—"Миграция курдов в Турции").

News1 (04.05.2020), 97 percent of the filling work in Silvan Dam has been completed.

Olson, R. (May 1997), Turkey-Syria Relations Since the Gulf War: Kurds and Water, Middle East Policy, Volume 5, Issue 2.

Orton, K. (2017), The Forgotten Foreign Fighters: The PKK in Syria, London.

Pashakhanlou, A.H. (23.07.2009), Comparing and Contrasting Classical Realism and Neo-realism, E-International Relations.

Pipes, D. (1990), Greater Syria: The History of an Ambition, New York-Oxford.

Pohl, B. (Lead author) (2014), The rise of hydro-diplomacy. Strengthening foreign policy for transboundary waters, Berlin.

Rep. of Turkey Ministry of Foreign Affairs, Turkey's Policy on Water Issues.

Romano, D. (2006), The Kurdish Nationalist Movement: Opportunity, Mobilization and Identity, Cambridge.

Rudaw (06.07.2020), Syrian farmers fear for their livelihoods as Euphrates dries up.

Saadoun, M. (12.06.2018), Turkey postponed the Ilisu plan, Iraqis took a breather, albeit for a short time (in Turkish—Türkiye Ilısu planını erteledi, Iraklılar kısa süreli de olsa nefes aldı), Al-Monitor.

Sabah (29.07.2022), "Silvan dam was attacked 52 times" (in Turkish—"Silvan barajı 52 kez saldırıya uğradı").

Sabah (23.01.2021), Silvan Dam, which the PKK attacked 25 times, is complete! (in Turkish—PKK'nın 25 kez saldırdığı Silvan Barajı tamam!).

Sarikaya, M. (ed.) (2018), From the pen of Ataturk, Syria and Iraq (in Turkish—Atatürkün kaleminden, Suriye ve Irak), Istanbul.

Schmeier, S. (2015), Governing International Watercourses River Basin Organizations and the Sustainable Governance of Internationally Shared Rivers and Lakes, New York.
Selby, J., Dahi, O.S., Fröhlich, C., Hulme, M. (2017), Climate change and the Syrian civil war revisited.
Şen, S. (ed.) (1993), The water problem, Turkey and the Middle East (in Turkish—Su sorunu, Türkiye ve Orta Doğu), Istanbul.
Smith, S., Hadfield, A., Dunne, T. (ed.) (August 2016), Foreign Policy: Theories, Actors, Cases (3-rd ed.), 2-nd Chapter, William C. Wohlforth, Realism and foreign policy.
Stepanova, N.V. (2016), History of Iraq. The 20th century (in Russian—История Ирака. XX век), Moscow.
Su Hakkı (17.06.2010), Historical Kighi Castle being detonated with dynamite (in Turkish—Tarihî Kiğı Kalesi dinamitle patlatılıyor),
Sümer, V. (12.04.2017), Handle With Care! Tabqa Dam Tragedy (in Turkish—Dikkatle Ele Alınız! Tabka Barajı Trajedisi), Orsam, Ankara.
Taştekin, F. (28.06.2018), How does Ankara view the water crisis in Iraq? (in Turkish—Irak'taki su krizine Ankara nasıl bakıyor?), Hidropolitik Akademi.
Taştekin, F. (13.05.2022), Is a water crisis brewing between Turkey and Iran?, Al-Monitor.
T.C. GAP Bölge Kalkınma İdaresi Başkanlığı, Impounding started at Kralkızı and Dicle Dams, gap.gov.tr.
Thesiger, W. (2008), The Marsh Arabs, London.
Tigris Haber (09.07.2015), Dersim is under dam blockade! (in Turkish—Dersim baraj ablukası altında!).
Topdemir, R. (2009), Ataturk's East-Southeast Anatolia Project and GAP (in Turkish—Atatürk'ün Doğu-Güneydoğu Anadolu Projesi ve GAP), Istanbul.
Turgut, H. (2000), GAP and Demirel (in Turkish—GAP ve Demirel), Ankara.
UN (2009), Syria Drought Response Plan.
UN ISDR (2011), Drought Vulnerability in the Arab Region: case study—Drought in Syria Ten Years of Scarce of Water (2000–2010).
UN-ESCWA and BGR (2013), Inventory of Shared Water Resources in Western Asia, Beirut.
United Nations (2018), World Water Development Report 2018|UN-Water.
United Nations (2019), World Water Development Report 2019|UN-Water—Leaving No One Behind.
United Nations (1997), International Water Law Project, International Agreements, 1997 UN Convention on the Law of the Non-navigational Uses of International Watercourses. Adopted by UNGA 21 May 1997; Entered into force 17 August.
Ünlu, F. (10.06.2018), Tigris Shield to Kandil (in Turkish Kandil'e Dicle Kalkanı), Sabah.
USİAD GAP Raporu (Mart 2008), GAP'ta ne oldu! Bölgede Ekonomik, Stratejik ve Siyasal Gelişmeler, ed. Dursun Yıldız, 1. Baskı, Istanbul.
Van Dam, N. (1996), The Struggle for Power in Syria: Politics and Society Under Assad and the Baʿth Party, London.
Von Lossow, T. (2016), Water as Weapon: IS on the Euphrates and Tigris.
Walker, K. (10.08.2020), Dam building risks water stress in Iraq, DW.
Waltz, K. (1979), Theory of International Politics, London.
WWF (World Wildlife Fund), Water Scarcity, Threats.

Yamakoğlu, C. (2015), GAP and Turkey in the heat of the Middle East (in Turkish—Ortadoğu sıcağında GAP ve Türkiye), Istanbul.

Yeni Akit (15.03.2017), Here is the project that will end the PKK: Mardin-Ceylanpınar Irrigation Main Canal (in Turkish—İşte PKK'yı bitirecek proje: Mardin-Ceylanpınar Sulama Ana Kanalı).

Yeni Yaşam (26.07.2020), Turkey keeps Karbala alive: Children are getting sick from thirst (in Turkish—Türkiye Kerbela'yı yaşatıyor: Çocuklar susuzluktan hastalanıyor).

Yetkin, M. (2004), Kurdish Trap From Damascus to Imrali Ocalan (in Turkish—Kürt Kapanı Şam'dan İmralı'ya Öcalan), Istanbul.

Yıldız, D. (2009), GAP, Economic, strategic and political developments in the region, (in Turkish—GAP, Bölgede ekonomik, stratejik ve siyasal gelişmeler), İstanbul.

Yıldız, D. (September 2018), The Peace Water Pipeline and innovative hydro diplomacy. Is Turkey's "Peace Water Pipeline Project" Worthwhile to be Considered Again?, Hydropolitics Academy of Turkey.

Yıldız, D., Özbay, Ö. (2012), Water policies and law from the Ottoman period to the present (in Turkish—Osmanlı'dan Bugüne Su politikaları ve hukuku), Istanbul.

Yıldız, K. (2005), The Kurds in Syria, The Forgotten People, London.

Yıldız, K., Düzgören, K. (2001), Hasankeyf and Ilisu Dam (in Turkish—Hasankeyf ve Ilısu Barajı), Istanbul.

Yüksel İnşaat, Karkamış Dam and HEPP.

FSC
www.fsc.org
MIX
Papier aus verantwortungsvollen Quellen
Paper from responsible sources
FSC® C105338

If you have any concerns about our products,
you can contact us on
ProductSafety@springernature.com

In case Publisher is established outside the EU,
the EU authorized representative is:
Springer Nature Customer Service Center GmbH
Europaplatz 3, 69115 Heidelberg, Germany

Printed by Libri Plureos GmbH
in Hamburg, Germany